SECOND EDITION

Ordinary Americans

U.S. History Through the Eyes of Everyday People

Edited by Linda R. Monk

Close Up Publishing

CLOSE UP®
F O U N D A T I O N

Close Up Publishing

Director
George W. Dieter

Managing Editor
Charles R. Sass

*Manager of Art, Production,
and Scheduling*
Tisha L. Finniff

Copy Editor
Joseph T. Harris

Photo Researcher
Matt Payne

Cover Photo
National Archives

Close Up Foundation
Stephen A. Janger
President and Chief Executive Officer

The Close Up Foundation, a nonprofit, nonpartisan civic education organization, informs, inspires, and empowers people to exercise the rights and accept the responsibilities of citizens in a democracy. Close Up connects individuals of all ages to their communities and institutions through challenging educational programs and products. By building partnerships with the education community, the private and philanthropic sectors, and all branches and levels of government, Close Up makes civic participation a dynamic and meaningful experience.

Close Up Publishing, a branch of the Close Up Foundation, develops books, teachers' guides, video documentaries, and other materials that encourage critical thinking and interest in current issues, government, international relations, history, and economics. To find out more about Close Up's original and timely resources, call 800-765-3131.

Close Up Foundation
44 Canal Center Plaza
Alexandria, VA 22314-1592
www.closeup.org

Library of Congress Cataloging-in-Publication Data

Ordinary Americans : U.S. history through the eyes of everyday people
/ edited by Linda R. Monk; foreword by Ken Burns.—2nd ed.
     p. cm.
     ISBN 1-930810-05-9 (alk. paper)
     1. United States—History—Sources. 2. United
States—Biography. I. Monk, Linda R.
E173.076   2002
973—dc21   2002034364

06 05 04 03 02   5 4 3 2 1

The histories . . . are all written out by "big bugs," generals and renowned historians. . . . They tell of great achievements of great men, who wear the laurels of victory, have grand presents given them, high positions in civil life, . . . and when they die, long obituaries are published telling their many virtues, their distinguished victories, etc., and when they are buried, the whole country goes into mourning. . . . But in the following pages I propose to tell of the fellows who did the shooting and killing, the fortifying and ditching, the sweeping of the streets, the drilling, the standing guard. . . .

—Private Sam Watkins
First Tennessee Regiment, C.S.A.

We were just ordinary people, and we did it.

—Sheyann Webb
civil rights marcher

Foreword

American history is a loud, raucous, moving, exquisite collection of noises, that in the aggregate often combine to make the sweetest kind of music, and I have tried to listen to as much as I can in putting together the Civil War series and my other films. More than anything else, these myriad voices remind us that history is not just the story of wars and generals and presidents, but of ordinary people, like you and me, who form the real fabric of our history and society.

Woodrow Wilson felt this strongly. He wrote: "When I look back on the processes of history, when I survey the genesis of America, I see this written over every page: that the nations are renewed from the bottom, not from the top; that the genius which springs up from the ranks of unknown men is the genius which renews the youth and energy of the people. Everything I know about history, every bit of experience and observation that has contributed to my thought, has confirmed me in the conviction that the real wisdom of human life is compounded out of the experience of ordinary men."

But for most of the life of this republic, the way we have formally told our history was from the top down. This has been called the history of the state or of great men. It relies on an erroneous belief that this history trickles down and touches experiences common to us all. It rarely does. It does exhibit, or has exhibited, an understandable arrogance, and we have to rely on family memory and community recollection for the good stuff. Or at least the stuff that made all that political history meaningful.

In New Orleans a decade ago, I visited an old friend, a retired judge and fierce opponent of Huey Long's named Cecil Morgan, who had given my film about Long one of its strongest and most dramatic interviews. This time, prompted by a remark that I was considering making a film on the Civil War but hadn't gotten up the courage to do so, Cecil brought out an old book, written by his ancestor James Morris Morgan. It was called *Recollections of a Rebel Reefer,* a reference to Cecil's grandfather's service in the Confederate Navy.

Just as I was politely returning the book to Cecil, a scrap of paper fell from the pages to the floor. It was a short, yellowed, typed note from old James Morris Morgan to his great-niece. It read: "Dear Louise, When the incidents recorded in this volume seem ancient to you, try to remember that I can remember your Grandfather's grandmother Morgan and her tales of how she danced with George Washington. The past to the aged does not seem as far away as does the dim future, and the only thing that abides with us always is the love of those who are dear to us."

James Morris Morgan's letter needs no comment. His truth is plain and direct, to the heart—another important ingredient of good history. We must in our historical excavations be more like emotional archeologists than clinical scientists, exposing to modern air not just the dry facts of life before us, but the moving undercurrent of real human affections and failings. History—especially personal, ordinary Americans' kind of history, as revealed in these pages—is alive, breathing, contemporary. This is the way history should be told.

For many of us, we are brought to our history in just this fashion. With story, memory, anecdote, feeling. These emotional connections become a kind of glue that makes the most complex of past events stick in our minds and our hearts, permanently a part of who each of us is now.

But as we have grown older as a country, as we have moved around more, lost touch with place more, these personal histories have dried up for most people, and we began to forget. History became a kind of castor oil of dry dates and facts and events of little meaning, something we knew was good for us, but hardly good tasting. History became just another subject, but not the great pageant of everything that has come before this moment. This moment.

About twenty or thirty years ago we woke up, partially, to this problem and began to insist on relevance in our teaching of history and on a new social history that would focus on real people doing real and recognizable things. This would be history from the bottom up, not top down, and people would respond. They did not. Relevance became an excuse for not even teaching history. And the new social history became so bogged down in statistical demographics and micro-perceptions that history began to sound like the reading of the telephone book. A new arrogance replaced the old—equally understandable, but equally devastating to the national memory. Someone expressed the new tyranny quite well when they said a history of Illinois could be written without mentioning Abraham Lincoln. Something had to change.

I'm pleased to report that in some ways it has. We have begun to speak of a synthesis of the old and new histories, a way to combine the best of the top-down version, still inspiring even in its "great men" addiction, with the bottom-up version, so inspiring too at times, with the million heroic acts of women, minorities, labor, ordinary people.

This comprehensive and inspiring book of ordinary Americans exemplifies the sort of good history that strikes a balance between these two polarities, never allowing formal considerations to overwhelm and capsize the truth of events, nor allowing a dry recitation of fact to render its meaning unintelligible or worse—boring. In an age of changing media, these dangers and pitfalls become even more critical, require even more of our vigilance and attention if we are to survive. For it is a question of survival. Without any past, without remembering, we will deprive ourselves of the defining impressions of our being.

We tend to think, and this is part of the forgetting, that those people of the past, those Americans, were not the same as us, and thus we cut the thread of identity and responsibility that really binds us to them all the same. But they were very like us. These similarities, these connections, emerge from the stories told in this book.

Too often as a culture we have ignored the joyful noise of American history, becoming in the process blissfully ignorant of the power those past lives and stories and moments have over this moment, and indeed, our unknown future. *Ordinary Americans* celebrates the special messages the past—our common heritage—continually directs our way. Let us listen.

—Ken Burns
Walpole, New Hampshire

Preface

In American democracy, every person counts because he or she has a vote and a voice. But this is not so in most history books. Too often, history is told top down from the perspective of the elite, the political and military leaders—most often wealthy white males. Thus, generations of Americans have come to think of history as dry, uninteresting, and remote, because it is unconnected to their experience.

Recently, however, a movement has begun to tell history from the bottom up, from the viewpoint of ordinary people instead of the famous. Journalists, filmmakers, and historians have all joined in this trend, focusing most of their efforts on one particular historical period. This book scans the entire panorama of American history, so that readers can experience the progress of nationbuilding through the eyes of everyday people.

Ordinary Americans covers five centuries of American history, from 1492 to 2001, in more than 200 readings, plus scores of archival photographs. The book relates the traditional events of American history, but as an ordinary person lived them. Thus, the story of the Boston Tea Party is told, not by Samuel Adams, but by George Hewes, a cobbler. The story of the Civil War draft is told, not by General Robert E. Lee, but by Private Sam Watkins. The story of the 1965 civil rights march in Selma, Alabama, is told, not by the Reverend Martin Luther King, Jr., but by Sheyann Webb, a 9-year-old.

While most of the readings are by people who were relatively obscure, a few of the authors achieved some degree of fame—such as Fannie Lou Hamer, a sharecropper who became a national leader in the civil rights movement. Some readings are by people who were socially prominent in their time, such as plantation owner Bennet H. Barrow. Even one reading is by a cabinet officer, Gideon Welles, who describes the impact President Abraham Lincoln's death had on black people in the nation's capital. But what all the readings have in common is that they open a window into the everyday lives of Americans and show how ordinary people were making history.

Some of the selections have been edited to make them more readable, without losing their overall tone. Variances in capitalization, punctuation, and other minor issues of style have also been edited for consistency. In the vast majority of the readings, ellipses indicate that portions of the original have been omitted.

The history made by ordinary Americans is no less important than that of their more famous compatriots. In truth, there is no such thing as an "ordinary" American. There are just some people whose stories have been told and some whose have not. The goal of this book is to give voice to the many everyday people who shaped American history, but whose names are seldom remembered.

Table of Contents

ix

❦ *1865-1919*

Industrializing America *109*

Reconstruction *111*

Conquering the West *120*

A "New World," A New Nation

❦ The history of the United States begins with the peoples of Asia, Europe, and Africa. Asiatic hunters and gatherers became the first inhabitants of North America when they tracked their prey into the continent between 12,000 and 30,000 years ago. Over thousands of years, these first Americans developed diverse cultures adapted to the natural environment. ❦ Europeans, starting in the 1400s, came to North America for many reasons. They hoped to find riches, religious freedom, and adventure. The Africans who came, on the other hand, left their homes not out of choice, but in bondage. Both Europeans and Africans transplanted some of the Old World to the New World, but they reshaped their economic, political, and social structures to meet the demands of the varied landscape. In a vast area that seemed to offer freedom and opportunity for all free white men, the Europeans replaced traditional notions of hereditary monarchy and nobility with greater democracy and equality. Africans extended their family networks in America to ease the pain of slavery. ❦ Europeans survived in America with the help of native people who introduced them to new crops such as corn and squash

...Listing continued on next page

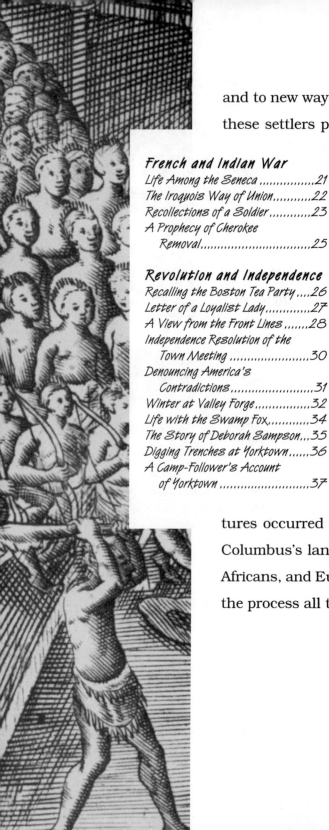

and to new ways of using the resources of the land. Many of these settlers prospered because of the labor of Africans in the tobacco and rice fields of the South and the commercial success of the slave trade for northern merchants. Yet in the late eighteenth century, the new nation's stated principles of democracy and the right to "life, liberty, and the pursuit of happiness" had not yet been extended to slaves and Native Americans. By 1783, in fact, when cartographers drew the borders of a new nation on the globe, much of the native population had been destroyed by disease and by war with European settlers. The native cultures that were not destroyed were transformed forever. ❦ A clash of cultures occurred in North America in the centuries following Columbus's landing in the "New World." Native Americans, Africans, and Europeans began creating a new nation, and in the process all three were transformed.

nted by James Reeve

"Forerunners of a New Mestizo Population"

The People Who Met Columbus

Irving Rouse and José Juan Arrom

When Columbus landed in the Bahamas on October 12, 1492, he was greeted by the Taínos. They had no written language, like all Native American cultures except the Mayans, and their culture disappeared in the mid-1500s. Fray Ramón Pané, a priest who accompanied Columbus on a later voyage, wrote a study of Taíno civilization. This study has been newly reconstructed by scholar José Juan Arrom. The article excerpted here is based on Pané's work.

When Columbus reached the Taíno heartland he found its inhabitants living in large permanent villages, each composed of family houses grouped around a plaza. They practiced an advanced form of agriculture, growing two root crops, cassava and sweet potato, in large mounds known as *conuco*. They also cultivated corn or maize (the latter term in fact derives from the Taíno language), peanuts, pineapples, cotton, tobacco, and other indigenous plants, using irrigation where necessary. Ironically, while Columbus searched vainly through the Antilles for the precious spices and medicinal plants of the East Indies, which of course were not present, these humbler vegetables and plants, many of which the conquistadors took back to Spain from Hispaniola, turned out to be among the most important of the New World's agricultural gifts to the Old. . . .

Hispaniola and the rest of the Taíno heartland were ruled by hierarchies of regional, district, and village chiefs *(caciques)*. . . . Each village was also served by priests and medicine men *(behique)* and was divided into two social classes *(nitaino* and *naboria)*, which the Spaniards equated with their own nobles and commoners. . . .

The Taínos were the first native Americans to come into contact with the Europeans, and they bore the brunt of the early phase of the conquest. Relatively few died in military confrontations, for they soon realized that their simple wooden clubs *(macana)* and wood-tipped spears or arrows were no match for the steel swords and lances, the horses and dogs trained for warfare, and the firearms of the conquistadors.

The Taínos who submitted to Spanish rule were put to work in gold mines, ranches, or households. Most were assigned to individual Spaniards in a system of forced labor called *encomienda* in which they remained under the leadership of their village chiefs and were supposed to be allowed to return to their homes periodically for rest and relaxation. In practice, however, they were often overworked and poorly fed, and many died from exhaustion and malnutrition or committed suicide by

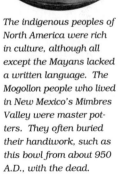

The indigenous peoples of North America were rich in culture, although all except the Mayans lacked a written language. The Mogollon people who lived in New Mexico's Mimbres Valley were master potters. They often buried their handiwork, such as this bowl from about 950 A.D., with the dead.

3

hanging themselves or drinking cassava juice. They also suffered severely from European diseases, to which they lacked immunity. In 1518 an epidemic of small-pox killed almost half the remaining population.

Assimilation also played an important role in the Taínos' disappearance.

There was such a shortage of European women in the colony that its men married Taíno women, often in the church and with the approval of authorities. These women were absorbed into the dominant Spanish society; their children were neither Indians nor Spaniards but forerunners of a new *mestizo* population.

"So Large a Market Place . . . They Had Never Beheld Before"

Spanish Conquest of the Aztecs

Bernal Díaz

After Columbus landed in North America in 1492, Spanish conquistadors spread out over the American continents. Their goal, according to Bernal Díaz del Castillo (1492-1584), was "to serve God and His Majesty, to give light to those in darkness, and to grow rich." Díaz, a footsoldier in Hernando Cortes's army, described the Spanish conquest of the Aztec Empire from 1519 to 1521 in his book, The True History of the Conquest of New Spain.*

The Aztec capital, which the Spanish called "another Venice" because of its extensive canal system, was located in the midst of a vast lake where Mexico City now stands. In his book, Díaz vividly depicted the capital and its ruler, Montezuma (or Moctezuma to the Aztecs). Writing near the end of his life, Díaz complained that, unlike the captains he served, he had "gained nothing of value to leave to [his] children and descendants but this true story, and they will presently find out what a wonderful story it is."

The Great Montezuma was about 40 years old, of good height and well proportioned, slender and spare of flesh, not very swarthy, but of the natural color and shade of an Indian. He did not wear his hair long, but so as just to cover his ears; his scanty black beard was well shaped and thin. His face was somewhat long, but cheerful, and he had good eyes and showed in his appearance and manner both tenderness and, when necessary, gravity. He was very neat and clean and bathed once every day in the afternoon. . . .

As we had already been four days in Mexico, and neither the captain nor any of us had left our lodgings except to go to the houses and gardens, Cortes said to us that it would be well to go to the great Plaza of Tlaltelolco and see the great Temple of Huichilobos [an Aztec war god]. . . .

. . . When we arrived at the great market place, called Tlaltelolco, we were astounded at the number of people and the quantity of merchandise that it contained, and at the good order and control that was maintained, for we had never seen such a thing before. Each kind of merchandise was kept by itself and had its fixed place marked out. Let us begin with the dealers in gold, silver, and precious stones, feathers, mantles, and embroidered goods. Then there were other wares consisting of Indian slaves both men and women, and I say that they bring as many of them to that great market for sale as the Portuguese bring Negroes from Guinea [West Africa]. . . .

When we arrived near the great Cue [temple] and before we had ascended a single step of it, the Great Montezuma sent down from above, where he was making his sacrifices, six priests and two chieftains to accompany our captain. On ascending the steps, which are 114 in number, they attempted to take him by the arms so as to help him to ascend (thinking that he would get tired) as they were accustomed to assist their lord Montezuma, but Cortes would not allow them to come near him. When we got to the top of the great Cue, on a small plaza which has been made on the top where there was a space like a platform with some large stones placed on it, on which they put the poor Indians for sacrifice, there was a bulky image like a dragon and other evil figures and much blood shed that very day.

When we arrived there, Montezuma came out of an oratory [small chapel] where his cursed idols were, at the summit of the great Cue, and two priests came with him, and after paying great reverence to Cortes and to all of us he said: "You must be tired . . . from ascending this our great Cue," and Cortes replied through our interpreters who were with us that he and his companions were never tired by anything. Then Montezuma took him by the hand and told him to look at this great city and all the other cities that were standing in the water, and the many towns on the land round the lake, and that if he had not seen the great market place well, that from where they were they could see it better. . . .

. . . [W]e turned to look at the great market place and the crowds of people that were in it, some buying and others selling, so that the murmur and hum of their voices and words that they used could be heard more than a league off. Some of the soldiers among us who had been in many parts of the world, in Constantinople, and all over Italy, and in Rome, said that so large a market place and so full of people, and so well regulated and arranged, they had never beheld before. . . .

There were some braziers with incense, which [the Aztecs] call copal, and in them they were burning the hearts of three Indians whom they had sacrificed that day, and they had made the sacrifice with smoke and copal. All the walls of the oratory were so splashed and encrusted with blood that they were black, the floor was the same and the whole place stank vilely. . . .

. . . Our captain said to Montezuma through our interpreter, half laughing: "Señor Montezuma, I do not understand how such a great prince and wise man as you are has not come to the conclusion, in your mind, that these idols of yours are not gods, but evil things called devils, and so that you may know it and all your priests may see it clearly, do me the favor to approve of my placing a cross here on the top of this tower, . . . and you will see by the fear in which these idols hold it that they are deceiving you."

Montezuma replied half angrily . . . and said: ". . . if I had known that you would have said such defamatory things I would not have shown you my gods. We consider them to be very good, for they give us health and rains and good seed times and seasons and as many victories as we desire, and we are obliged to worship them and make sacrifices, and I pray you not to say another word to their dishonor."

"There Came to Be Prevalent a Great Sickness"

History Through Aztec Eyes

The Florentine Codex

To Bernal Díaz, the conquest of the Aztecs was a "wonderful story." The Aztec account of the invasion is not as cheerful. During the 1550s, Friar Bernardino de Sahagún compiled his General History of the Things of New Spain, *known as the Florentine Codex, which contains a history of the conquest written by Aztecs. According to Sahagún, the book's authors were "prominent elders . . . who were present in the war" when Mexico was conquered.*

Written in the repetitive style of Aztec oratory, the Florentine Codex describes Moctezuma's first news of the Europeans, the Spanish lust for gold, and the smallpox epidemic that decimated the native population. With no immunity to European diseases, the Aztecs were defeated more by germs than by guns.

Moctezuma enjoyed no sleep, no food. No one spoke to him. Whatsoever he did, it was as if he were in torment. Ofttimes it was as if he sighed, became weak, felt weak. No longer did he enjoy what tasted good, what gave one contentment, what gladdened one.

Wherefore he said: "What will now befall us? Who indeed stands [in command]? Alas, until now, I. In great torment is my heart; as if it were washed in chili water it indeed burns, it smarts." . . .

And when he had so heard what the messengers reported, he was terrified, he was astounded. . . .

Especially did it cause him to faint away when he heard how the gun, at [the Spaniards'] command, discharged [the shot]; how it resounded as if it thundered when it went off. It indeed bereft one of strength; it shut off one's ears. And when it discharged, something like a round pebble came forth from within. Fire went showering forth; sparks went blazing forth. And its smoke smelled very foul; it had a fetid odor which verily wounded the head. And when [the shot] struck a mountain, it was as if it were destroyed, dissolved. And a tree was pulverized; it was as if it vanished; it was as if someone blew it away.

All iron was their war array. In iron they clothed themselves. With iron they

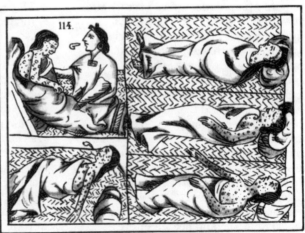

This illustration from the Florentine Codex depicts Aztecs suffering from smallpox. European diseases decimated the Native American populations, making expanded European settlement possible. Some historians have noted that America was not a virgin land, but a widowed one.

covered their heads. Iron were their swords. Iron were their crossbows. Iron were their shields. Iron were their lances.

And those which bore them upon their backs, their deer [horses], were as tall as roof terraces.

And their bodies were everywhere covered; only their faces appeared. They were very white; they had chalky faces; they had yellow hair, though the hair of some was black. Long were their beards; they also were yellow. They were yellow-bearded. [The Negroes' hair] was kinky, it was curly. . . .

And when Moctezuma so heard, he was much terrified. It was as if he fainted away. His heart saddened; his heart failed him. . . .

[Moctezuma] only awaited [the Spaniards]; he made himself resolute; he put forth great effort; he quieted, he controlled his heart; he submitted himself entirely to whatsoever he was to see, at which he was to marvel. . . .

And when [the Spaniards] were well settled, they thereupon inquired of Moctezuma as to all the city's treasure—the devices, the shields. Much did they importune him; with great zeal they sought gold. . . . And when they reached the storehouse . . . , thereupon were brought forth all the brilliant things; the quetzal feather head fan, the devices, the shields, the golden discs, the devils' necklaces, the golden nose crescents, the golden leg bands, the golden arm bands, the golden forehead bands.

Thereupon was detached the gold which was on the shields and which was on all the devices. And as all the gold was detached, at once they ignited, they set fire to, applied fire to all the various precious

"Different Nations Have Different Conceptions of Things"

Iroquois Ideas on Education

Canasatego

As first contact made clear, Native Americans and Europeans had different values on many issues. One example of this conflict happened during negotiations over the Treaty of Lancaster of 1744. In a goodwill gesture, the Virginia Colony offered to educate six Iroquois braves at its college for Native Americans in Williamsburg. Canasatego, chief of the Iroquois, refused—offering instead to take a dozen of Virginia's sons and "make men of them."

We know that you highly esteem the kind of learning taught in colleges, and that the maintenance of our young men, while with you, would be very expensive to you. We are convinced, therefore, that you mean to do us good by your proposal, and we thank you heartily. But you, who are wise, must know that different nations have different conceptions of things, and you will therefore not take it amiss if our ideas of this kind of education happen not to be the same with yours. We have had some experience of it. Several of our young people were formerly brought up at the colleges of the Northern Provinces. They were instructed in all your sciences, but, when they came back to us, they were bad runners, ignorant of every means of living in the woods, unable to bear either cold or hunger, knew neither how to build a cabin, take a deer, nor kill an enemy, spoke our language imperfectly, were therefore neither fit for hunters, warriors, nor counsellors; they were totally good for nothing. We are, however, not the less obliged by your kind offer, though we decline accepting it, and, to show our grateful sense of it, if the gentlemen of Virginia will send us a dozen of their sons, we will take care of their education, instruct them in all we know, and make men of them.

things [which remained]. They all burned. And the gold the Spaniards formed into separate bars. . . . And the Spaniards walked everywhere; they went everywhere taking to pieces the hiding places, storehouses, storage places. They took all, all that they saw which they saw to be good. . . .

. . . [T]here came to be prevalent a great sickness, a plague. It was in Tepeilhuitl that it originated, that there spread over the people a great destruction of men. Some it indeed covered [with pustules]; they were spread everywhere, on one's face, on one's head, on one's breast, etc. There was indeed perishing; many indeed died of it. No longer could they walk; they only lay in their abodes, in their beds. No longer could they move, no longer could they bestir themselves, no longer could they raise themselves, no longer could they stretch themselves out on their sides, no longer could they stretch themselves out face down, no longer could they stretch themselves out on their backs. And when they bestirred themselves, much did they cry out. There was much perishing. Like a covering, covering-like, were the pustules. Indeed many people died of them, and many just died of hunger. There was death from hunger; there was no one to take care of another; there was no one to attend to another.

"Deprived of All Chance of Returning to My Native Country"

A Slave's Account of Coming to America

Olaudah Equiano

Olaudah Equiano (1745-1801), also known as Gustavus Vassa, was born in Benin, now part of southern Nigeria. He was kidnapped into slavery at age 11 and taken to America, where he worked on a Virginia plantation, for a British naval officer, and for a Philadelphia merchant. He eventually bought his freedom, converted to Methodism, and moved to England to promote the abolition of slavery. Equiano wrote the first important slave narrative, The Interesting Narrative of the Life of Olaudah Equiano, or Gustavus Vassa, the African; by Himself, *which was published around 1790. The book was immensely popular in both America and England.*

My father, besides many slaves, had a numerous family, of which seven lived to grow up. . . . In this way I grew up till I turned the age of 11, when an end was put to my happiness in the following manner: Generally, when the grown people in the neighborhood were gone far in the fields to labor, the children assembled together in some of the neighbors' premises to play, and commonly some of us used to get up in a tree to look out for any assailant or kidnapper that might come upon us; for they sometimes took those opportunities of our parents' absence to attack and carry off as many as they could seize. . . . One day, when all our people were gone out to their works as usual, and only I and my dear sister were left to mind the house, two men and a woman got over our walls, and in a moment seized us both, and without giving us time to cry out, or make resistance, they stopped our mouths and ran off with us into the nearest wood. . . .

[Equiano describes his travels and enslavement among various African tribes.]

. . . Thus I continued to travel, sometimes by land, sometimes by water, through different countries and various nations, till, at the end of six or seven months after I had been kidnapped, I arrived at the sea coast.

The first object which saluted my eyes when I arrived on the coast, was the sea, and a slave ship, which was then riding at anchor, and waiting for its cargo. These filled me with astonishment, which

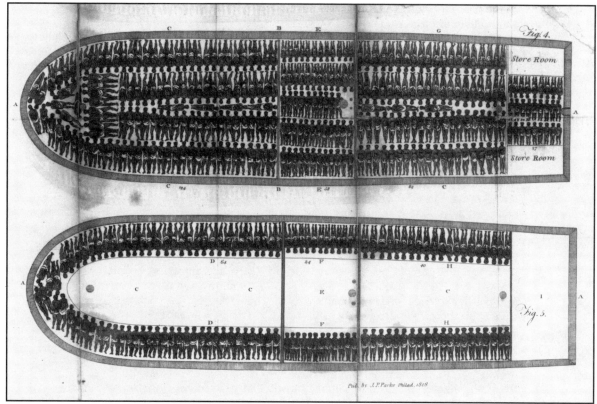

In the crowded conditions of slave ships, about 10 to 20 percent of the Africans aboard died.

was soon converted into terror, when I was carried on board. I was immediately handled and tossed up to see if I were sound, by some of the crew, and I was now persuaded that I had gotten into a world of bad spirits, and that they were going to kill me. Their complexions, too, differing so much from ours, their long hair, and the language they spoke (which was very different from any I had ever heard) united to confirm me in this belief. Indeed, such were the horrors of my views and fears at the moment, that, if ten thousand worlds had been my own, I would have freely parted with them all to have exchanged my condition with that of the meanest slave in my own country. . . .

I now saw myself deprived of all chance of returning to my native country, or even the least glimpse of hope of gaining the shore, which I now considered as friendly, and I even wished for my former slavery in preference to my present situation, which was filled with horrors of every kind, still heightened by my ignorance of what I was to undergo. I was not long suffered to indulge my grief; I was soon put down under the decks, and there I received such a salutation in my nostrils as I had never experienced in my life: so that, with the loathsomeness of the stench and crying together, I became so sick and low that I was not able to eat, nor had I the least desire to taste anything. I now wished for the last friend, death, to relieve me, but soon, to my grief, two of the white men offered me eatables, and, on my refusing to eat, one of them held me fast by the hands and laid me across, I think the windlass, and tied my feet, while the other flogged me severely. I had never experienced anything of this kind before, and although not being used to the water, I naturally feared that element the first time I saw it, yet, nevertheless, could I have got over the nettings, I would have jumped over the side, but I could not, and besides, the crew used to watch us very closely who were not chained down to the decks, lest we should leap into the water, and I have seen some of these poor African prisoners most severely cut for attempting to do so and hourly whipped for not eating. This indeed was often the case with myself. . . .

At last, when the ship we were in had got in all her cargo, they made ready with many fearful noises, and we were all put under deck, so that we could not see how they managed the vessel. . . .

At last, we came in sight of the island of Barbados, at which the whites on board gave a great shout, and made many signs of joy to us. . . . Many merchants and planters now came on board, though it was in the evening. They put us in separate parcels, and examined us attentively. They also made us jump, and pointed to the land, signifying we were to go there. We thought by this, we should be eaten by these ugly men, as they appeared to us, and, when soon after we were all put down under the deck again, there was much dread and trembling among us and nothing but bitter cries to be heard all the night from these apprehensions, insomuch that at last the white people got some old slaves from the land to pacify us. They told us we were not to be eaten, but to work, and were soon to go on land, where we should see many of our country people. This report eased us much. And sure enough, soon after we landed, there came to us Africans of all languages.

We were conducted immediately to the merchant's yard, where we were all pent up together, like so many sheep in a fold, without regard to sex or age. . . .

We were not many days in the merchant's custody before we were sold after their usual manner, which is this: On a signal given (as the beat of a drum), the buyers rush at once into the yard where the slaves are confined and make choice of that parcel they like best. The noise and clamor with which this is attended and the eagerness visible in the countenance of the buyers serve not a little to increase the apprehension of terrified Africans. . . . In this manner, without scruple, are relations and friends separated, most of them never to see each other again. I remember in the vessel in which I was brought over, in the men's apartment, there were several brothers who, in the sale, were sold in different lots, and it was very moving on this occasion to see and hear their cries at parting. O, ye nominal Christians! Might not an African ask you, "Learned you this from your God, who says unto you, 'Do unto all men as you would men should do unto you'?" Is it not enough that we are torn from our country and friends, to toil for your luxury and lust of gain? Must every tender feeling be likewise sacrificed to your avarice?

"Let People Stay in Their Own Country"

Emigrating from Germany to Pennsylvania

Gottlieb Mittelberger

Not all Europeans came to America as conquerors. Poor people, who had the most incentive to leave their native lands, had the least means to do so. Many paid for their voyages to the New World by becoming indentured servants, agreeing to work for several years in exchange for having their fares paid. This system created a thriving market for ships' captains, whose agents (known as Newlanders) often exaggerated the riches of America to attract more passengers.

10

In 1750, Gottlieb Mittelberger made the journey from his native Germany to Pennsylvania. Disillusioned by the conditions aboard ship and by the hard life in America, he returned to Germany in 1754. Mittelberger's book, Journey to Pennsylvania, *published in Germany in 1756, warned his fellow Germans not to be "seduced into the voyage" to America and instead to "stay in their own country." His experiences make an interesting comparison to those of African slaves described by Olaudah Equiano.*

This journey [from Germany, via Holland and England, to Pennsylvania] lasts from the beginning of May until the end of October, that is, a whole six months, and involves such hardships that it is really impossible for any description to do justice to them. . . .

In Rotterdam, . . . the people are packed into the big boats as closely as herring, so to speak. The bedstead of one person is hardly two feet across and six feet long, since many of the boats carry from four to six hundred passengers, not counting the immense amount of equipment, tools, provisions, barrels of fresh water, and other things that also occupy a great deal of space. . . .

When the ships have weighed anchor for the last time, usually off Cowes in Old England, then both the long sea voyage and misery begin in earnest. For from there the ships often take eight, nine, ten, or twelve weeks sailing to Philadelphia, if the wind is unfavorable. But even given the most favorable winds, the voyage takes seven weeks.

During the journey the ship is full of pitiful signs of distress—smells, fumes, horrors, vomiting, various kinds of sea sickness, fever, dysentery, headaches, heat, constipation, boils, scurvy, cancer, mouth-rot, and similar afflictions, all of them caused by the age and the highly salted state of the food, especially of the meat, as well as by the very bad and filthy water, which brings about the miserable destruction and death of many. Add to all that shortage of food, hunger, thirst, frost, heat, dampness, fear, misery, vexation, and lamentation as well as other troubles. Thus, for example, there are so many lice, especially on the sick people, that they have to be scraped off the bodies. All this misery reaches its climax when in addition to everything else one must also suffer through two to three days and nights of storm, with everyone convinced that the ship with all aboard is bound to sink. In such misery all the people on board pray and cry pitifully together. . . .

Among those who are in good health impatience sometimes grows so great and bitter that one person begins to curse the other, or himself and the day of his birth, and people sometimes come close to murdering one another. Misery and malice are readily associated, so that people begin to cheat and steal from one another. And then one always blames the other for having undertaken the voyage. Often the children cry out against their parents, husbands against wives and wives against husbands, brothers against their sisters, friends and acquaintances against one another.

But most of all they cry out against the thieves of human beings [Newlanders]! Many groan and exclaim: "Oh! If only I were back at home, even lying in my pigsty!" Or they call out: "Ah, dear God, if I only once again had a piece of good bread or a good fresh drop of water." . . .

Children between the ages of 1 and 7 seldom survive the sea voyage, and parents must often watch their offspring suffer miserably, die, and be thrown into the ocean, from want, hunger, thirst, and the like. I myself, alas, saw such a pitiful fate overtake thirty-two children on board our vessel, all of whom were finally thrown into the sea. Their parents grieve all the more, since their children do not find repose in the earth, but are devoured by the predatory fish of the ocean. . . .

When the ships finally arrive in Philadelphia after the long voyage only those are let off who can pay their sea freight or can give good security. The others, who lack the money to pay, have to remain on board until they are purchased. . . . In this whole process the sick are the worst off, for the healthy are preferred and are more readily paid for. The miserable people who are ill must often still remain at sea and in sight of the city for another two or three weeks—which in many cases means death. . . .

This is how the commerce in human beings on board ship takes place. Every day Englishmen, Dutchmen, and High Germans come from Philadelphia and other places, some of them very far away, . . . and go on board the newly arrived vessel that has brought people from Europe and offers them for sale. From among the healthy they pick out those suitable for the purposes for which they require them. Then they negotiate with them as to the length of the period for which they will go into service in order to pay off their passage, the whole amount of which they generally still owe. When an agreement has been reached, adult persons by written contract bind themselves to serve for three, four, five,

or six years, according to their health and age. The very young, between the ages of 10 and 15, have to serve until they are 21, however.

Many parents in order to pay their fares in this way and get off the ship must barter and sell their children as if they were cattle. Since the fathers and mothers often do not know where or to what masters their children are to be sent, it frequently happens that after leaving the vessel, parents and children do not see each other for years on end, or even for the rest of their lives. . . .

Our Europeans who have been purchased must work hard all the time. For new fields are constantly being laid out, and thus they learn from experience that oak tree stumps are just as hard in America as they are in Germany. . . .

. . . So let people stay in their own country and earn their keep honestly for themselves and their families. Furthermore, I want to say that those people who may let themselves be talked into something and seduced into the voyage by the thieves of human beings are the biggest fools if they really believe that in America or Pennsylvania roasted pigeons are going to fly into their mouths without their having to work for them.

"The Country Itself Is Large and Great"

Luring Settlers to the New World

The Virginia Company of London

England hoped to claim its share of New World riches—along with Spain, France, and Holland—by chartering the Virginia Company of London, a joint-stock company that financed settlement in Virginia by selling shares to private investors. In 1607, the Virginia Company established James-town, which originally was intended to be only a fortified trading post but instead became the first successful English colony in North America.

    This 1609 tract by the Virginia Company was designed to attract both investors, who would finance the company by purchasing stock, and adventurers, who would actually travel to the New World as employees of the company. Although the tract promised that Virginia was a land brim-ming with riches, in 1609 starvation was so great in Jamestown that there were even some instances of cannibalism.

The country itself is large and great assuredly, though as yet, no exact discovery can be made of all. It is also commendable and hopeful every way, the air and climate most sweet and wholesome, and very agreeable to our nature. It is inhabited with wild and sav-age people, that live and lie up and down in troupes like herds of deer in a forest. They have no law but nature; their appar-el, skins of beasts, but most go naked. The better sort have houses, but poor ones. They have no arts nor sciences, yet they live under superior command such as it is; they are generally very lov-ing and gentle, and do entertain and relieve our people with great kindness. The land yields naturally for the suste-nance of man, abundance of fish, infinite store of deer, and hares, with many fruits and roots.

    There are valleys and plains stream-ing with sweet springs; there are hills and mountains making a sensible proffer of hidden treasure, never yet searched. The land is full of minerals, plenty of woods; the soil is strong and sends out naturally fruitful vines running upon trees and shrubs. It yields also resin, turpentine, pitch, and tar; sassafras, mulberry trees, and silkworms; many skins and rich furs; many sweet woods and costly dyes; plenty of sturgeon [and] timber for shipping. But . . . if bare nature be so amiable in its naked kind, what may be hope[d] when art and nature both shall join and strive together to give best content to man and beast?

"What Can You Get by War?"

Speech to Captain John Smith

Powhatan

The Jamestown settlers, many of whom were gentlemen unaccustomed to physical labor, spent their time looking for gold instead of planting crops. They thus depended greatly for food upon local Native Americans—the thirty tribes of the Powhatan Confederacy led by Wahunsonacock, known to the English as Powhatan. The relationship between the English and the Native Americans was ambivalent, vacillating between peaceful trade and outright warfare.

Captain John Smith, the leader of Jamestown, was captured by the Powhatan Confederacy in 1608. According to Smith, Powhatan's daughter, Pocahontas, intervened to save Smith's life, although historians doubt the story. Pocahontas did marry John Rolfe, an English nobleman, in 1614, cementing an alliance with the settlers. The following statement by Powhatan to Captain Smith was recorded by two of Smith's companions in 1609 and published in 1612.

After Powhatan's death in 1618, relationships between the Virginia settlers and the Native Americans deteriorated. In 1622, the Powhatan Confederacy killed 347 English people in the worst uprising since Jamestown was founded. Within two years the Virginia Company had gone bankrupt, and King James I made Virginia a royal colony supervised by the crown.

Captain Smith, you may understand that I, having seen the death of all my people thrice and not one living of those three generations but myself, I know the difference of peace and war better than any in my country. But now I am old, and ere long must die. My brethren, namely Opichapam, Opechankanough, and Kekataugh, my two sisters, and their two daughters, are distinctly each other's successors. I wish their experiences no less than mine, and your love to them, no less than mine to you. But this brute [noise] from Nansamund that you are come to destroy my country so much frightens all my people as they dare not visit you. What will it avail you to take that perforce you may quietly have with love, or to destroy them that provide you with food? What can you get by war, when we can hide our provision and fly to the woods, whereby

According to legend, Pocahontas prevented her father, Chief Powhatan, from executing Jamestown leader Captain John Smith, as shown in a picture taken from Smith's General History of Virginia (1624).

you must famish, by wronging us your friends? And why are you thus jealous of our loves, seeing us unarmed, and both do and are willing still to feed you with that you cannot get but by our labors? Think you I am so simple not to know it is better to eat good meat, lie well, and sleep quietly with my women and children, laugh, and be merry with you, have copper, hatchets, or what I want being your friend than be forced to fly from all, to lie cold in the woods, feed upon acorns, roots, and such trash, and be so hunted by you that I can neither rest, eat, nor sleep, but my tired men must watch, and if a twig but break, every one cry, "There comes Captain Smith." Then must I fly I know not whether, and thus with miserable fear end my miserable life, leaving my pleasures to such youths as you, which, through your rash unadvisedness, may quickly as miserably end, for want of that you never know how to find? Let this therefore assure you of our loves, and every year our friendly trade shall furnish you with corn, and now also if you would come in friendly manner to see us, and not thus with your guns and swords, as to invade your foes.

"There Is Nothing to Be Gotten Here but Sickness and Death"

An Indentured Servant Writes Home

Richard Frethorne

Life for the English settlers at Jamestown was full of hardship. Disease, starvation, and attacks by Native Americans led many to wish they had never left England. The following letter was written by Richard Frethorne, an indentured servant, to his parents on March 20, 1623. Frethorne begged his parents to "redeem" him, that is, buy out the contract binding him to work for a period of several years. Frethorne was not exaggerating when he said his redemption was a matter of life or death: from 1619 to 1623 the mortality rate in Jamestown was between 75 and 80 percent.

Loving and kind father and mother . . . , this is to let you understand that I your child am in a most heavy case by reason of the nature of the country is such that it causes much sickness, as the scurvy and the bloody flux, and diverse other diseases, which make the body very poor and weak, and when we are sick there is nothing to comfort us. For since I came out of the ship, I never ate anything but peas and loblollie (that is water gruel). As for deer or venison I never saw any since I came into this land. There is indeed some fowl, but we are not allowed to go and get it, but must work hard both early and late for a mess of water gruel and a mouthful of bread and beef. A mouthful of bread, for a penny loaf must serve for four men, which is most pitiful. . . . [P]eople cry out day and night, Oh that they were in England without their limbs and would not care to lose any limb to be in England again, yea though they beg from door to door, for we live in fear of the enemy every hour. . . . We are in great danger, for our plantation is very weak, by reason of the dearth, and sickness, of our company. . . .

I have nothing to comfort me, nor there is nothing to be gotten here but sickness and death, except that one had money to lay out in some things for profit; but I have nothing at all, no not a shirt to

[handwritten margin notes: "telling about diseases & sicknesses. nothing to comfort them." / "Lots want to go ~~back~~ to England." / "all of the stuff he doesn't have." / "15"]

my back, but two rags nor no clothes, but one poor suit, nor but one pair of shoes, but one pair of stockings, but one cap . . . ; my cloak is stolen by one of my own fellows, and to his dying hour would not tell me what he did with it, but some of my fellows saw him have butter and beef out of a ship, which my cloak [no] doubt paid for. . . .

I am not half, a quarter, so strong as I was in England, and all is for want of victuals, for I do protest unto you, that I have eaten more in a day at home than [is] allowed me here for a week. You have given more than my day's allowance to a beggar at the door, and if Mr. Jackson had not relieved me, I should be in a poor case, but he like a father and she like a loving mother doth still help me. . . . They be very godly folks and love me very well and will do anything for me, and he much marvelled that you would send me a servant to the company; he said I had been better knocked on the head—and indeed so I find it now to my great grief and misery—and said that if you love me you will redeem me suddenly, for which I do entreat and beg. . . . Good father, do not forget me, but have mercy and pity my miserable case. I know if you did but see me you would weep to see me. . . . The answer of this letter will be life or death to me; therefore, good father, send as soon as you can. . . .

[handwritten margin note: telling his parents how much they did for him before.]

"So Many Christians Lying in Their Blood"

Taken Captive in King Philip's War

Mary White Rowlandson

[handwritten margin note: 2nd English colony. wars between N/A & settlers]

The next English colony after Virginia was the Plymouth Colony, founded in Massachusetts in 1620. The Massachusetts and Virginia colonies had similar experiences with the Native Americans they encountered. Both initially depended on help from local tribes to survive; both were eventually attacked in an attempt to end English incursions on tribal lands. Massasoit, the leader of the Wampanoags, forged an alliance in 1621 with the Pilgrims who founded Plymouth. But his son Metacom, known to the colonists as King Philip, led New England tribes in a war against settlers from 1675 to 1676. In proportion to population, King Philip's War inflicted the greatest casualties of any war in American history.

Mary Rowlandson lived in Lancaster, Massachusetts, then on the western frontier. When her village was attacked during King Philip's War, Rowlandson was taken captive for about three months until she was ransomed by a group of Bostonians. Her book, published in 1682, was the first of many "captivity narratives" written by colonists who had been kidnapped by Native Americans. Rowlandson saw her ordeal as a test of her Puritan faith and depicted Native Americans as barbarians and savages. But Mary Jemison, whose story is included in this chapter's section on the French and Indian War, describes the Native Americans who adopted her as kind and honorable.

On the 10th of February, 1675, came the Indians with great numbers upon Lancaster: their first coming was about sun-rising. Hearing the noise of some guns, we looked out; several houses were burning, and the smoke ascending to heaven. . . .

At length they came and beset our house, and quickly it was the dolefulest day that ever mine eyes saw. . . . Some in our house were fighting for their lives, others wallowing in blood, the house on fire over our heads, and the bloody heathen ready to knock us on the head if we stirred out. . . . Thus were we butchered by those merciless heathens, standing amazed, with the blood running down to our heels. . . . It was a solemn sight to see so many Christians lying in their blood, some here and some there, like a company of sheep torn by wolves. All of them stript naked by a company of hell-hounds, roaring, singing, ranting, and insulting, as if they would have torn our hearts out: yet the Lord by his almighty power preserved a number of us from death; for there were twenty-four of us taken alive and carried captive.

I had often before this said that if the Indians should come, I should choose rather to be killed by them, than taken alive: but when it came to the trial, my mind changed. Their glittering weapons so daunted my spirit, that I chose rather to go along with those (as I may say) ravenous bears, than that moment to end my days. . . .

On the morrow morning we must go over Connecticut River to meet with King Philip. . . . Then I went to see King Philip; he bid me come in, and sit down, and asked me whether I would smoke [a pipe] (a usual compliment nowadays, among the saints and sinners), but this no ways suited me. For though I had formerly used tobacco, yet I had left it ever since I was first taken. It seems to be a bait the devil lays to make men lose their precious time. I remember with shame, how formerly, when I had taken two or three pipes, I was presently ready for another; such a bewitching thing it is. But I thank God he has now given me power over it;

surely there are many who may be better employed, than to sit sucking a stinking tobacco-pipe.

. . . During my abode in this place, Philip [asked] me to make a shirt for his boy, which I did; for which he gave me a shilling. . . . Afterward he asked me to make a cap for his boy, for which he invited me to dinner; I went, and he gave me a pan-cake, about as big as two fingers; it was made of parched wheat, beaten and fried in bear's grease, but I thought I never tasted pleasanter meat in my life. . . .

. . . [W]e came to another Indian town, where we stayed all night. In this town there were four English children captives, and one of them my own sister's. I went to see how she did, and she was well, considering her captive condition. I would have tarried that night with her, but they that owned her would not suffer. Then I went to another wigwam, where they were boiling corn and beans, which was a lovely sight to see, but I could not get a taste thereof. Then I went into another wigwam, where there were two of the English children. The squaw was boiling horses' feet; she cut me off a little piece, and gave one of the English children a piece also. Being very hungry, I had quickly eaten up mine; but the child could not bite it, it was so tough and sinewy, but lay sucking, gnawing, and slabbering of it in the mouth and hand, then I took it of the child, and ate it myself, and savory it was to my taste. That I may say as Job 6:7, "The things that my soul refuseth to touch are as my sorrowful meat." Thus the Lord made that pleasant and refreshing, which another time would have been an abomination. Then I went home to my mistress's wigwam, and they told me I disgraced my master with begging, and if I did so any more, they would knock me on the head: I told them they had as good do that as starve me to death. . . .

[The Indians] would pick up old bones, and cut them in pieces at the joints, and if they were full of worms and maggots, they would scald them over the fire, to make the vermin come out, and then boil them, and drink up the liquor, and then beat the great ends of them in a

getting treated a little better

what she ate; what they ate.

→

when she was captured. what she does, sees & feels.

mortar, and so eat them. They would eat horses' guts and ears, and all sorts of wild birds which they could catch. Also bear, venison, beavers, tortoise, frogs, squirrels, dogs, skunks, rattlesnakes. Yea, the very bark of trees; besides all sorts of creatures and provision which they plundered from the English. I can but stand in admiration to see the wonderful power of God in providing for such a vast number of our enemies in the wilderness, where there was nothing to be seen, but from hand to mouth. . . . But now our perverse and evil carriages in the sight of the Lord have so offended him, that instead of turning his hand against them, the Lord feeds and nourishes them up to be a scourge to the whole land. . . .

I have seen the extreme vanity of this world. One hour I have been in health and wealth, wanting nothing, but the next hour in sickness, and wounds, and death, having nothing but sorrow and affliction. Before I knew what affliction meant I was ready sometimes to wish for it. . . . Affliction I wanted, and affliction I had full measure, pressed down and running over. Yet I see when God calls persons to ever so many difficulties, yet he is able to carry them through, and make them say they have been gainers thereby, and I hope I can say, in some measure, as David, "It is good for me that I have been afflicted." . . . If trouble from smaller matters begin to rise in me, I have something at hand to check myself with, and say, Why am I troubled? It was but the other day, that if I had had the world, I would have given it for my freedom, or to have been a servant to a Christian. I have learned to look beyond present and smaller troubles, and to be quieted under them, as Moses said [in] Exodus 14:13, "Stand still and see the salvation of the Lord."

nothing is ever right.

"New England, Thou Hast Destroyed Thyself"

The Salem Witchcraft Trials

Robert Calef

In the Puritan society of the New England colonies, a sin was a crime. In 1692, an outbreak of "witchcraft" in Salem Village, Massachusetts, led to the execution of twenty colonists. The episode began when young girls, known as the "afflicted," exhibited unusual behavior after playing fortune-telling games. Under intense questioning by adults, who suspected witchcraft, the girls accused certain neighbors of tormenting them. Historians speculate that the girls might have been trying to get attention from their elders, since some of their behavior would today be regarded as teenage rebellion.

Robert Calef (1648-1719) was a Boston merchant who opposed the witchcraft trials. His controversial book, More Wonders of the Invisible World, *was published in London in 1700. Calef criticized* Wonders of the Invisible World *(1693), a book describing alleged incidents of witchcraft written by Cotton Mather, a Puritan leader. Using court documents, Calef argued that innocent people had been killed by "the devils of envy, hatred, pride, cruelty, and malice."*

We are told in *Wonders of the Invisible World* that the devils were walking about our streets. . . .

If this be the true state of the afflictions of this country, it is very deplorable, and beyond all other outward calamities miserable. But if on the other side, the matter be as others do understand it, that . . . the accusations of a parcel of possessed, distracted, or lying wenches, accusing their innocent neighbors, pretending they see their spectres (i.e., devils) in their likeness afflicting of them, and that God in righteous judgment . . . may have given them over to strong delusions to believe lies, etc. And to let loose the devils of envy, hatred, pride, cruelty, and malice against each other; yet still disguised under the mask of zeal for God, and left them to the branding one another with the odious name of witch; and upon the accusation of those above mentioned, brother to accuse and prosecute brother, children their parents, pastors and teachers their immediate flock unto death; shepherds becoming wolves, wise men infatuated; people hauled to prisons, . . . while some are fleeing from that called justice, justice itself fleeing before such accusations, . . . some making their escape out of prisons, rather than by an obstinate defense of their innocence to run so apparent hazard of their lives; estates seized, families of children and others left to the mercy of the wilderness (not to mention the numbers [condemned], dead in prisons, or executed, etc.).

All which tragedies, though begun in one town, or rather by one parish, has plague-like spread more than through that country. And by its echo giving a brand of infamy to this whole country, throughout the world.

If this were the miserable case of this country in the time thereof, and that the devil had so far prevailed upon us in our sentiments and actions, as to draw us from so much as looking into the scriptures for our guidance in these pretended intricacies, leading us to a trusting in blind guides, . . . then though our case be most miserable, yet it must be said of New England, thou hast destroyed thyself, and brought this greatest of miseries upon thee. . . .

At execution, Mr. Noyes urged Sarah Good to confess, and told her she was a witch, and she knew she was a witch, to which she replied, "You are a liar; I am no more a witch than you are a wizard, and if you take away my life, God will give you blood to drink." . . .

. . . And though the confessing witches were many; yet not one of them that confessed their own guilt and abode by their confession were put to death.

Here follows what account some of those miserable creatures gave of their confession under their own hands.

We whose names are under written, inhabitants of Andover, when as that horrible and tremendous judgment beginning at Salem Village, in the year 1692, (by some) called Witchcraft, first breaking forth at Mr. Parris's house, several young persons being seemingly afflicted, did accuse several persons for afflicting them, and many there believing it so to be; we being informed that if a person were sick, that the afflicted persons could tell what or who was the cause of that sickness. Joseph Ballard of Andover (his wife being sick at the same time) he either from himself, or by the advice of others, fetched two of the persons called the afflicted persons, from Salem Village to Andover. Which was the beginning of that dreadful calamity that befell us in Andover. And the authority in Andover, believing the said accusations to be true, sent for the said persons to come together, to the meetinghouse in Andover (the afflicted persons being there). After Mr. Bernard [a local minister] had been at prayer, we were blindfolded, and our hands were laid upon the afflicted persons, they being in their fits, and falling into their fits at our coming into their presence (as they said) and some led us and laid our hands upon them, and then they said they were well, and that we were guilty of afflicting of them; whereupon we were all seized as prisoners, by a warrant from the Justice of the Peace, and forthwith carried to Salem. And by reason of that sudden surprisal, we knowing ourselves altogether innocent of that crime, we were all exceedingly astonished and amazed, and consternated and frightened even out of our reason; and our nearest and dearest relations, seeing us in that dreadful condition, and knowing our great danger, apprehending that there was no other way to save our lives, as the case was then circumstantiated, but by our confessing ourselves to be such and such persons, as the afflicted represented us to be, they out of tender love and pity persuaded us to confess what we did confess. And indeed that confession, that is said we made, was no other than what was suggested to us by some gentlemen; they telling us that we were witches, and they knew it, and we knew it, and they knew that we knew it, which made us think that it was so; and our understanding, our reason, and our faculties almost gone, we were not capable of judging our condition; as also the hard measures they used with us rendered us incapable of making our defense, but said anything and everything which they desired, and most of what we said was but in effect a consenting to what they said. Sometime after, when we were better composed, they telling of us what we had confessed, we did profess that we were innocent and ignorant of such things. And we hearing that Samuel Wardwell had renounced his confession and quickly after [was] condemned and executed, some of us were told that we were going after Wardwell.

—*MARY OSGOOD, MARY TILER, DELIV. DANE, ABIGAIL BARKER, SARAH WILSON, HANNAH TILER*

"I Was Called Dickewamis"

Life Among the Seneca

Mary Jemison

During the first half of the eighteenth century, France and England strug-gled for dominance in North America. Native American tribes engaged in extensive diplomacy with both countries, often playing them against each other to retain the balance of power. The French and Indian War (1754-1763) forced the tribes to choose whether England or France would best end white settlers' expansion into native lands.

Mary Jemison (1743-1833) was kidnapped as a girl during the war by a Shawnee and French war party. She was later adopted by the Seneca tribe, part of the Iroquois Confederacy. She married, had chil-dren, and lived the rest of her life as a Seneca woman. Unlike Mary Rowlandson, whose captivity narrative appeared earlier in this chapter, Jemison believed that Native Americans "are naturally kind, tender and peaceable towards their friends." Her story was printed in 1824.

In the afternoon we came in sight of Fort Pitt . . . where we were halted while the Indians performed some customs upon their prisoners which they deemed neces-sary. That fort was then occupied by the French and Indians, and was called Fort Du Quesne. . . .

I was now left alone in the fort, deprived of . . . everything that was near or dear to me but life. But it was not long before I was in some measure relieved by the appearance of two pleasant looking squaws of the Seneca tribe, who came and examined me attentively for a short time, and then went out. After a few minutes absence they returned with my former masters, who gave me to them to dispose of as they pleased. . . .

At night we arrived at a small Seneca Indian town, at the mouth of a small river, . . . where the two squaws to whom I belonged resided. . . .

Having made fast to the shore, the squaws left me in the canoe while they went to their wigwam or house in the town, and returned with a suit of Indian clothing, all new, and very clean and nice. My clothes, though whole and good when I was taken, were now torn in pieces, so that I was almost naked. They first un-dressed me and threw my rags into the river; then washed me clean and dressed me in the new suit they had just brought, in complete Indian style; and then led me home and seated me in the center of their wigwam.

I had been in that situation but a few minutes before all the squaws in town came in to see me. I was soon surrounded by them, and they immediately set up a most dismal howling, crying bitterly, and wringing their hands in all the agonies of grief for a deceased relative. . . .

In the course of that ceremony, from mourning they became serene—joy sparkled in their countenances, and they seemed to rejoice over me as over a long lost child. I was made welcome amongst them as a sister to the two squaws before mentioned and was called Dickewamis,

"We Are a Powerful Confederacy"

The Iroquois Way of Union

Canasatego

The Iroquois Confederacy so impressed Benjamin Franklin that he wrote: "It would be a very strange thing if Six Nations of ignorant savages should be capable of forming a scheme for such a union, and be able to execute it in such a manner as that it has subsisted ages, and appears indissoluble; and yet that a like union should be impracticable for ten or a dozen English colonies." In 1754, Franklin used the Iroquois Confederacy as a model for the Albany Plan of Union, which would have helped the English colonies unite to fight the French, but the plan failed. Canasatego, an Iroquois chief, had advocated such a union among the colonies in 1744.

We heartily recommend union and good agreement between you, our brethren. Never disagree, but preserve a strict friendship for one another, and thereby you, as well as we, will become the stronger.

Our wise fore-fathers established union and amity between the Five [later Six] Nations; this has made us formidable; this has given us great weight and authority with our neighboring nations.

We are a powerful confederacy, and by your observing the same methods our wise forefathers have taken, you will acquire fresh strength and power; therefore, whatever befalls you, never fall out one with another.

A wampum belt commemorates the creation of the Iroquois Confederacy, which united the Seneca, Cayuga, Onondaga, Oneida, and Mohawk tribes of western New York in the 1500s. In the 1700s, the Tuscaroras became the sixth member tribe.

which I arrived there in order to receive a prisoner or an enemy's scalp to supply their loss.

It is a custom of the Indians when one of their number is slain or taken prisoner in battle to give to the nearest relative . . . a prisoner if they have chanced to take one, and if not, to give him the scalp of an enemy. On the return of the Indians from conquest, . . . the mourners come forward and make their claims. If they receive a prisoner, it is at their option either to satiate their vengeance by taking his life in the most cruel manner they can conceive of, or to receive and adopt him into the family in the place of him whom they have lost. . . .

It was my happy lot to be accepted for adoption, and at the time of the ceremony I was received by the two squaws to supply the place of their brother in the family, and I was ever considered and treated by them as a real sister, the same as though I had been born of their mother. . . .

About planting time, our Indians all went up to Fort Pitt to make peace with the British and took me with them. We landed on the opposite side of the river from the fort and encamped for the night. Early the next morning the Indians took me over to the fort to see the white people that were there. It was then that my heart bounded to be liberated from the Indians and to be restored to my friends and my country. The white people were surprised to see me with the Indians, enduring the hardships of a savage life at so early an age and with so delicate a constitution as I appeared to possess. They asked me my name, where and when I was taken, and appeared very

which being interpreted signifies a pretty girl, a handsome girl, or a pleasant, good thing. That is the name by which I have ever since been called by the Indians.

I afterwards learned that the ceremony I at that time passed through was that of adoption. The two squaws had lost a brother in Washington's war sometime in the year before, and in consequence of his death went up to Fort Pitt on the day on much interested on my behalf. They were continuing their inquiries when my sisters became alarmed, believing that I should be taken from them, hurried me into their canoe and recrossed the river. . . . So great was their fear of losing me, or of my being given up in the treaty, that they never once stopped rowing till they got home. . . .

Not long after the Delawares came to live with us at Wiishto, my sisters told me that I must go and live with one of them, whose name was Sheninjee. Not daring to cross them, or disobey their commands, with a great degree of reluctance I went, and Sheninjee and I were married according to Indian custom.

Sheninjee was a noble man: large in stature, elegant in his appearance, generous in his conduct, courageous in war, a friend to peace, and a great lover of justice. He supported a degree of dignity far above his rank, and merited and received the confidence and friendship of all the tribes with whom he was acquainted. Yet, Sheninjee was an Indian. The idea of spending my days with him at first seemed perfectly irreconcilable to my feelings, but his good nature, generosity, tenderness, and friendship towards me soon gained my affection, and, strange as it may seem, I loved him! To me he was ever kind in sickness and always treated me with gentleness; in fact, he was an agreeable husband and a comfortable companion. We lived happily together until the time of our final separation. . . .

. . . Notwithstanding all that has been said against the Indians, in consequence of their cruelties to their enemies—cruelties that I have witnessed and had abundant proof of—it is a fact that they are naturally kind, tender and peaceable towards their friends, and strictly honest, and that those cruelties have been practiced only upon their enemies according to their idea of justice.

"I Must Stand Still to Be Shot At"

Recollections of a Soldier

David Perry

Colonial militias fought under British command during the French and Indian War. British officers regarded Americans as bad soldiers, because the militia system, which relied on citizen-soldiers, lacked the strict military discipline of a professional army. Colonial troops also insisted on following their own officers, which British commanders saw as treason.

David Perry, a 16-year-old cobbler's apprentice who had recently joined a Massachusetts militia company, enlisted to serve in the French and Indian War in the spring of 1758. He was amazed by the formal rules of European warfare, in which soldiers "must stand still to be shot at," rather than the customary guerrilla tactics of the frontier. Perry also was shocked by the harshness of British military discipline. Perry wrote his memoirs in 1819, in which he described the attack on Fort Ticonderoga excerpted here.

23

Major Rogers with his Rangers was the first to land. He was joined by Lord Howe and his party, and we had proceeded but a short distance into the woods before we were met by the enemy, and a brisk fire ensued. It was the first engagement I had ever seen, and the whistling of balls and roar of musquetry terrified me not a little. At length our regiment formed among the trees, behind which the men kept stepping from their ranks for shelter. Colonel Preble, who, I well remember, was a harsh man, swore he would knock the first man down who should step out of his ranks, which greatly surprised me, to think that I must stand still to be shot at. Pretty soon, however, they brought along some wounded Frenchmen; and when I came to see the blood run so freely, it put new life into me. The battle proved a sore one for us. Lord Howe and a number of other good men were killed.

The army moved on that day to within a short distance of the enemy, and encamped for the night. In the morning we had orders to move forward again, in a column three deep, in order to storm the enemy's breast-works, known in this country by the name of "the Old French Lines." Our orders were to "run to the breast-work and get in if we could." But their lines were full, and they killed our men so fast that we could not gain it. We got behind trees, logs, and stumps, and covered ourselves as we could from the enemy's fire. The ground was strewed with the dead and dying. It happened that I got behind a white-oak stump, which was so small that I had to lay on my side and stretch myself; the balls [were] striking the ground within a hand's breadth of me every moment, and I could hear the men screaming and see them dying all around me. I lay there some time. A man could not stand erect without being hit, any more than he could stand out in a shower without having drops of rain fall upon him, for the balls come by handsfull. It was a clear day—a little air stirring. Once in a while the enemy would cease firing a minute or two, to have the smoke clear away, so that they might take better aim. In one of these intervals I sprang from my perilous situation and gained a stand which I thought would be more secure, behind a large pine log, where several of my comrades had already taken shelter but the balls came here as thick as ever. One of the men raised his head a little above the log, and a ball struck him in the center of the forehead, and tore up his scalp clear back to the crown. He darted back, and the blood ran merrily, and rubbing his face, said it was a bad blow, and no one was disposed to deny it, for he looked bad enough. We lay there till near sunset and, not receiving orders from any officer, the men crept off, leaving all the dead and most of the wounded. . . .

There is one thing I would here notice, which shows a specimen of British cruelty without a parallel, I could hope, in the history of that nation. Three men, for some trifling offense which I do not recollect, were tied up to be whipped. One of them was to receive 800 lashes, the others 500 apiece. By the time they had received 300 lashes, the flesh appeared to be entirely whipped from their shoulders, and they hung as mute and motionless as though they had been long since deprived of life. But this was not enough. The doctor stood by with a vial of sharp stuff, which he would ever and anon apply to their noses, and finding, by the pain it gave them, that some signs of life remained, he would tell them, "damn you, you can bear it yet," and then the whipping would commence again. It was the most cruel punishment I ever saw inflicted, or had ever conceived of before—by far worse than death. I felt at the time as though I could have taken summary vengeance on those who were the authors of it, on the spot, had it been in my power to do it.

"Compelled to Seek Refuge in Some Distant Wilderness"

A Prophecy of Cherokee Removal

Dragging Canoe

The French and Indian War brought the differing interests of the American colonists and the British to the forefront, paving the way for the Revolutionary War. American settlers continually pushed the frontier westward, encroaching on tribes that had been allied with the British during the French and Indian War. In the Proclamation of 1763, the British agreed to limit settlement beyond the Appalachian Mountains to alleviate friction between colonists and Native Americans.

But the proclamation did little to stop westward expansion, as the colonists increasingly sought independence from Britain. In March 1775, aging Cherokee chiefs sold much of modern Kentucky and Tennessee, almost half of their land, to keep peace. But Tsiyu Gansini, known as Dragging Canoe, opposed the treaty. His prophetic speech anticipated the complete removal of the Cherokees in 1838 from their eastern homeland to Oklahoma, which is included in Chapter Two.

We had hoped that the white men would not be willing to travel beyond the mountains. Now that hope is gone. They have passed the mountains, and have settled upon Cherokee land. They wish to have that usurpation sanctioned by treaty. When that is gained, the same encroaching spirit will lead them upon other land of the Cherokees. New cessions will be asked. Finally the whole country, which the Cherokees and their fathers have so long occupied, will be demanded, and the remnant of Ani-Yun-wiya, "The Real People," once so great and formidable, will be compelled to seek refuge in some distant wilderness. There they will be permitted to stay only a short while, until they again behold the advancing banners of the same greedy host. Not being able to point out any further retreat for the miserable Cherokees, the extinction of the whole race will be proclaimed. Should we not therefore run all risks and incur all consequences, rather than submit to further laceration of our country? Such treaties may be all right for men who are too old to hunt or fight. As for me, I have my young warriors about me. We will have our lands. *A-waninski,* I have spoken.

"A General Huzza for Griffin's Wharf"

Recalling the Boston Tea Party

George Hewes

After the French and Indian War, Britain decided that the American colonies should help pay for their defense. Parliament passed the Stamp Act of 1765, which levied the first direct tax on the colonies. Riots broke out against the law, which the colonists decried as "taxation without representation." In Boston, a hotbed of dissent, colonists were also required under the Quartering Act to feed and house British troops. Intense conflicts between soldiers and civilians led to the Boston Massacre on March 5, 1770, in which British troops killed several colonists.

Even their teapots expressed colonists' opposition to the Stamp Act.

Parliament passed the Tea Act in May 1773, giving the financially troubled British East India Company a monopoly in the American colonies. In protest, Philadelphia and New York refused tea ships permission to dock, but in Boston Thomas Hutchinson, the royal governor of Massachusetts, insisted that tea be unloaded. When negotiations with Hutchinson failed, a group of colonists dressed as Mohawks dumped the tea into Boston harbor. George Hewes, a poor cobbler, participated in the Boston Tea Party on December 17, 1773.

The tea destroyed was contained in three ships lying near each other at what was called at that time Griffin's wharf and were surrounded by armed ships of war, the commanders of which had publicly declared that if the rebels, as they were pleased to style the Bostonians, should not withdraw their opposition to the landing of the tea before a certain day, the 17th day of December 1773, they should on that day force it on shore, under the cover of their cannon's mouth. On the day preceding the seventeenth, there was a meeting of the citizens of Suffolk convened at one of the churches in Boston for the purpose of consulting on what measures might be considered expedient to prevent the landing of the tea, or secure the people from the collection of the duty. At that meeting a committee was appointed to wait on Governor Hutchinson and request him to inform them whether he would take any measures to satisfy the people. . . . When the committee returned and informed the meeting of the absence of the governor, there was a confused murmur among the members, and the meeting was immediately dissolved, many of them crying out, "Let every man do his duty and be true to his country," and there was a general huzza for Griffin's wharf.

It was now evening, and I immediately dressed myself in the costume of an Indian, equipped with a small hatchet, which I and my associates denominated the tomahawk, with which, and a club, after having painted my face and hands with coal dust in the shop of a blacksmith, I repaired to Griffin's wharf, where the ships lay that contained the tea. When I first appeared in the street after being thus disguised, I fell in with many who were dressed, equipped, and painted as I was, and who fell in with me and marched in order to the place of our destination.

When we arrived at the wharf, there were three of our number who assumed an authority to direct our operations, to which we readily submitted. They divided us into three parties, for the purpose of boarding the three ships.... We were immediately ordered by the respective commanders to board all the ships at the same time, which we promptly obeyed. The commander of the division to which I belonged, as soon as we were on board the ship, appointed me boatswain and ordered me to go to the captain and demand of him the keys to the hatches and a dozen candles. I made the demand accordingly, and the captain promptly replied and delivered the articles, but requested me at the same time to do no damage to the ship or rigging. We then were ordered by our commander to open the hatches and take out all the chests of tea and throw them overboard, and we immediately proceeded to execute his orders, first cutting and splitting the chests with our tomahawks so as thoroughly to expose them to the effects of the water.

In about three hours from the time we went on board, we had thus broken and thrown overboard every tea chest to

---

"Curse All Traitors!"

Letter of a Loyalist Lady

Anne Hulton

Not all Americans supported revolution. A virtual civil war broke out between rebels and loyalists. In a letter to a friend on January 31, 1774, written in Boston not long after the Tea Party, Anne Hulton describes how many loyalists were treated.

I suppose you will have heard long before this arrives of the fate of the tea.... After the destruction of the tea, ... the violent fury of the people ... subsided a little. One would have thought before that all the malice that earth and hell could raise were pointed against the governor....

But the most shocking cruelty was exercised a few nights ago, upon a poor old man, a tidesman, one Malcolm. He is reckoned [crazy], a quarrel was picked with him, [and] he was afterward taken and tarred and feathered. There's no law that knows a punishment for the greatest crimes beyond what this is of cruel torture.... He was stript stark naked, one of the severest cold nights this winter, his body covered all over with tar, then with feathers, his arm dislocated in tearing off his clothes. He was dragged in a cart with thousands attending, some beating him with clubs and knocking him out of the cart, then in again. They gave him several severe whippings, at different parts of the town. This spectacle of horror and cruelty was exhibited for about five hours.

The unhappy wretch they say behaved with the greatest intrepidity and fortitude all the while. Before he was taken, [he] defended himself a long time against numbers, and afterwards when under torture they demanded of him to curse his masters, the King, Governor, etc., which they could not make him do, but he still cried, "Curse all traitors!" They brought him to the gallows and put a rope about his neck, saying they would hang him. He said he wished they would, but that they could not, for God was above the Devil. The doctors say it is impossible this poor creature can live. They say his flesh comes off his back in steaks....

These few instances amongst many serve to show the abject state of government and the licentiousness and barbarism of the times. There's no magistrate that dare or will act to suppress the outrages. No person is secure.

---

be found in the ship, while those in the other ships were disposing of the tea in the same way, at the same time. We were surrounded by British armed ships, but no attempt was made to resist us.

We then quietly retired to our several places of residence, without having any conversation with each other, or taking any

measures to discover who were our associates. . . . There appeared to be an understanding that each individual should volunteer his services, keep his own secret, and risk the consequence for himself. No disorder took place during that transaction, and it was observed at that time that the stillest night ensued that Boston had enjoyed for many months.

During the time we were throwing the tea overboard, there were several attempts made by some of the citizens of Boston and its vicinity to carry off small quantities of it for their family use. To effect that object, they would watch their opportunity to snatch up a handful from the deck, where it became plentifully scattered, and put it into their pockets. One Captain O'Connor, whom I well knew, came on board for that purpose, and when he supposed he was not noticed, filled his pockets, and also the lining of his coat. But I had detected him and gave information to the captain of what he was doing. We were ordered to take him into custody, and just as he was stepping from the vessel, I seized him by the skirt of his coat, and in attempting to pull him back, I tore it off, but, springing forward, by a rapid effort he made his escape. He had, however, to run a gauntlet through the crowd upon the wharf, each one, as he passed, giving him a kick or a stroke.

Another attempt was made to save a little tea from the ruins of the cargo by a tall, aged man who wore a large cocked hat and white wig, which was fashionable at that time. He had [secretly] slipped a little into his pocket, but being detected, they seized him and, taking his hat and wig from his head, threw them, together with the tea, of which they had emptied his pockets, into the water. In consideration of his advanced age, he was permitted to escape with now and then a slight kick.

The next morning, after we had cleared the ships of the tea, it was discovered that very considerable quantities of it were floating upon the surface of the water, and to prevent the possibility of any of its being saved for use, a number of small boats were manned by sailors and citizens, who rowed them into those parts of the harbor wherever the tea was visible, and by beating it with oars and paddles so thoroughly drenched it as to render its entire destruction inevitable.

"March Immediately to Bunker Hill"

A View from the Front Lines

Captain John Chester

In retaliation for the Boston Tea Party, the British Parliament passed the Coercive, or Intolerable, Acts in 1774. These acts halted Boston's trade and increased the powers of the military. General Thomas Gage, who had been the supreme commander of all British forces in North America, became the new governor of Massachusetts.

General Gage decided to assert his control by seizing colonial military supplies stored at Concord, Massachusetts. The first shots of the American Revolution were fired on April 19, 1775, at Lexington, Massachusetts, about six miles from Concord. Colonial "minutemen," members of local militia who were trained to respond at a moment's notice, eventually turned back the British troops in Concord.

28

After Concord, the American militia virtually held the British army besieged on Boston's narrow peninsula. The next major battle of the war took place in June 1775 in Charlestown, north of Boston. The colonists had occupied Breed's Hill, a strategic location, and Gage sought to dislodge them. British troops suffered severe casualties, but eventually forced the Americans to retreat.

In a July 1775 letter, Captain John Chester described his role in the battle that became known as Bunker Hill.

Just after dinner on Saturday . . . , I was walking out from my lodgings, quite calm and composed, and all at once the drums beat to arms, and bells rang, and a great noise in Cambridge. Captain Putnam came by on full gallop. "What is the matter?" says I.

"Have you not heard?"

"No."

"Why, the regulars are landing at Charlestown," says he, "and father says you must all meet and march immediately to Bunker Hill to oppose the enemy."

I waited not, but ran and got my arms and ammunition, and hastened to my company (who were in the church for barracks) and found them nearly ready to march. We soon marched, with our frocks and trousers on over our other clothes (for our company is in uniform wholly blue, turned up with red), for we were loath to expose ourselves by our dress, and down we marched. I imagined we arrived at the hill near the close of the battle. When we arrived, there was not a company with us in any kind of order; although, when we first set out, perhaps three regiments were by our side and near us, but here they were scattered, some behind rocks and hay-cocks, and thirty men perhaps behind an apple tree, and frequently twenty men round a wounded man, retreating, when not more than three or four could touch him to advantage. Others were retreating, seemingly without any excuse, and some said they had left the fort with leave of the officers, because they had been all night and day on [duty], without sleep, victuals, or drink, and some said they had no officers to head them, which indeed seemed to be the case.

At last I met with a considerable company who were going off rank and file. I called to the officer that led them and asked why he retreated. He made me no answer. I halted my men and told him if he went on, it should be at his peril. He still seemed regardless of me. I then ordered my men to make ready. They immediately cocked and declared if I ordered they would fire. Upon that they stopped short, tried to excuse themselves, but I could not tarry to hear him, but ordered him forward, and he complied.

We were then very soon in the heat of action. Before we reached the summit of Bunker Hill, and while we were going over the Neck, we were in imminent danger from the cannon shot, which buzzed around us like hail. The musquetry began before we passed the Neck, and when we were on the top of the hill, and during our descent to the foot of it on the south, the small as well as cannon shot were incessantly whistling by us. We joined our army on the right of the center, just by a poor stone fence, two or three feet high, and very thin, so that the bullets came through. Here we lost our regularity, as every company had done before us, and fought as they did, every man loading and firing as fast as he could.

"We Renounce Our Connection with a Kingdom of Slaves"

Independence Resolution of the Town Meeting

Malden, Massachusetts

Now in open warfare with Great Britain, the colonies had to decide whether to break forever with the mother country or merely seek reforms in Parliament's rule over them. In May 1776, the Massachusetts House of Representatives anticipated that the Continental Congress might soon declare independence and asked the inhabitants of each town if they would "solemnly engage, with their lives and fortunes, to support [Congress] in the measure." The town of Malden's response rivals Thomas Jefferson's declaration in its eloquence.

At a legal meeting of the inhabitants of the town of Malden (Mass.), May 27, 1776, it was voted unanimously that the following instructions be given to their representative. . . .

Sir: A resolution of the hon. house of representatives, calling upon the several towns in this colony to express their minds in respect to the important question of American independence, is the occasion of our now instructing you. The time was, sir, when we loved the king and the people of Great Britain with an affection truly filial; we felt ourselves interested in their glory; we shared in their joys and sorrows; we cheerfully poured the fruit of all our labors into the lap of our mother country, and without reluctance expended our blood and our treasure in their cause.

These were our sentiments toward Great Britain while she continued to act the part of a parent state; we felt ourselves happy in our connection with her, nor wished it to be dissolved, but our sentiments are altered; it is now the ardent wish of our soul that America may become a free and independent state.

A sense of unprovoked injuries will arouse the resentment of the most peaceful. Such injuries these colonies have received from Britain. Unjustifiable claims have been made by the king and his minions to tax us without our consent; these claims have been prosecuted in a manner cruel and unjust to the highest degree. The frantic policy of administration hath induced them to send fleets and armies to America; that, by depriving us of our trade, and cutting the throats of our brethren, they might awe us into submission, and erect a system of despotism in America, which should so far enlarge the influence of the crown as to enable it to rivet their shackles upon the people of Great Britain.

This plan was brought to a crisis upon the ever memorable nineteenth of April. We remember the fatal day! The expiring groans of our countrymen yet vibrate on our ears, and we now behold the flames of their peaceful dwellings ascending to Heaven! We hear their blood crying to us from the ground for vengeance. . . . The manner in which the war has been prosecuted has confirmed us in these sentiments; piracy and murder, robbery and breach of faith, have been conspicuous in the conduct of the king's troops. Defenseless towns have been attacked and destroyed; the ruins of Charlestown, which are daily in our view, daily reminds us of this. The cries of the widow and the orphan demand our attention; they demand that the hand of pity should wipe the tear from their eye, and that the word of their country should avenge their wrongs. We long entertained hope that the spirit of the British nation would once more induce them to assert their own and

30

our rights, and bring to condign [deserved] punishment the elevated villains who have trampled upon the sacred rights of men and affronted the majesty of the people. We hoped in vain; they have lost their love of freedom; they have lost their spirit of just resentment. We therefore renounce with disdain our connection with a kingdom of slaves; we bid a final adieu to Britain.

Could an accommodation now be effected, we have reason to think that it would be fatal to the liberties of America; we should soon catch the contagion of venality and dissipation which hath led Britons to lawless domination. Were we placed in the situation we were in 1763; were the powers of appointing to offices and commanding the militia in the hands of governors, our arts, trade, and manufactures would be cramped; nay, more than this, the life of every man who has been active in the cause of his country would be endangered.

For these reasons, as well as many others which might be produced, we are confirmed in the opinion that the present age would be deficient in their duty to God, their posterity, and themselves if they do not establish an American republic. This is the only form of government which we wish to see established, for we can never be willingly subject to any other King than he who, being possessed of infinite wisdom, goodness, and rectitude, is alone fit to possess unlimited power.

"A Natural and Unalienable Right to Freedom"

Denouncing America's Contradictions

Massachusetts Slave Petition

During the revolutionary period, many slaves signed petitions that applied the language of the Declaration of Independence to their own quest for freedom. Reprinted here is one such petition submitted to the Massachusetts legislature in 1777.

To the Honorable Counsel and House of Representatives for the state of Massachusetts in General Court assembled, January 13, 1777.

The petition of a great number of blacks detained in a state of slavery in the bowels of a free and Christian country humbly show that your petitioners apprehend that they have in common with all other men a natural and unalienable right to that freedom which the Great Parent of the Universe has bestowed equally on all mankind and which they have never forfeited by any compact or agreement whatever. They were unjustly dragged by the hand of cruel power from their dearest friends and some of them even torn from the embraces of their tender parents—from a populous, pleasant, and plentiful country, and in violation of the laws of nature and of nations and in defiance of all the tender feelings of humanity brought here to be sold like beasts of burden and like them condemned to slavery for life, among a people professing the mild religion of Jesus. . . .

[Imitating] the laudable example of the good people of these states, your petitioners have long and patiently waited [for responses to] petition after petition by them presented to the legislative body of this state and cannot but with grief reflect that their success has been but too similar. They cannot but express their astonishment that it has never been considered that every principle from which America has acted in the course of their unhappy difficulties with Great Britain pleads stronger than a thousand arguments in favor of your petitioners. They therefore humbly beseech your honors to give this petition its due weight and consideration and cause an act of the legislature to be passed whereby they may be restored to the enjoyments of that which is the natural right of all men, and their children who were born in this land of liberty may not be held as slaves after they arrive at the age of 21 years, so [that] the inhabitants of this state no longer [may be charged] with the inconsistency of acting themselves the part which they condemn and oppose in others.

"Starvation Here Rioted in Its Glory"

Winter at Valley Forge

James Sullivan Martin

In December 1777, General George Washington's army of 11,000 men made its winter quarters at Valley Forge, Pennsylvania. About 2,500 of the ill-fed, poorly clothed troops died during the harsh winter. Nonetheless, drilled by European officers, the army emerged a better fighting force. According to one Hessian major, only "the spirit of liberty" kept the army together. James Sullivan Martin, a Connecticut private, gave a vivid account of the ordeal at Valley Forge.

Soon after the British had quit their position on Chestnut Hill [Philadelphia], we left this place, and after marching and countermarching back and forward some days, we crossed the Schuylkill in a cold, rainy, and snowy night, upon a bridge of wagons set end to end and joined together by boards and planks, and after a few days' more maneuvering, we at last settled down at a place called "the Gulf" (so named on account of a remarkable chasm in the hills), and here we encamped some time, and here we [almost] encamped forever—for starvation here rioted in its glory. But, lest the reader should be disgusted at hearing so much said about "starvation," I will give him something that, perhaps, may in some measure alleviate his ill humor.

While we lay here there was a Continental thanksgiving ordered by Congress, and as the army had all the cause in the world to be particularly thankful, if not for being well off, at least that it was no worse, we were ordered to participate in it. We had nothing to eat for two or three days previous, except what the trees of the fields and forests afforded us. But we must now have what Congress said—a sumptuous thanksgiving to close the year of high living we had now nearly seen brought to a close. Well—to add something extraordinary to our present stock of provisions—our country, ever mindful of its suffering army, opened her sympathizing heart so wide, upon this occasion, as to give us something to make the world stare. And what do you think it was, reader? Guess. You cannot guess, be you as much of a Yankee as you will. I will tell you: it gave each and every man *half a gill* [about one-fourth cup] of rice and a *tablespoon full* of vinegar!

After we had [received] this extraordinary superabundant donation, we were ordered out to attend a meeting and hear a sermon delivered upon the occasion. We accordingly went, for we could not help it. I heard a sermon, a "thanksgiving sermon," what sort of one I do not know now, nor did I at the time I heard it. I had something else to think upon; my belly put me in remembrance of the fine thanksgiving dinner I was to partake of when I could get it. I remember the text, like an attentive lad at church. I can still remember that; it was this: "And the soldiers said unto him, 'And what shall we do?' And he said unto them, 'Do violence to no man, nor accuse any one falsely.'" The preacher ought to have added the remainder of the sentence to have made it complete: "And be content with your wages." But that would not do, it would be too apropos; however, he heard it as soon as the service was over; it was shouted from a hundred tongues.

Well, we had got through the services of the day and had nothing to do but to return in good order to our tents and fare as we could. As we returned to our camp, we passed by our commissary's quarters. All his stores, consisting of a barrel about two-thirds full of hocks of fresh beef, stood directly in our way, but there was a sentinel guarding even that; however, one of my messmates purloined a piece of it, four or five pounds perhaps. I was exceeding glad to see him take it; I thought it might help to eke out our thanksgiving supper, but, alas! how soon my expectations were blasted! The sentinel saw him have it as soon as I did and obliged him to return it to the barrel again. So I had nothing else to do but to go home and make out my supper as usual, upon a leg of nothing and no turnips.

The army was now not only starved but naked; the greatest part were not only shirtless and barefoot, but destitute of all other clothing, especially blankets. I procured a small piece of raw cowhide and made myself a pair of moccasins, which kept my feet (while they lasted) from the frozen ground, although, as I well remember, the hard edges so galled my ankles while on a march that it was with much difficulty and pain that I could wear them afterwards, but the only alternative I had was to endure this inconvenience or to go barefoot, as hundreds of my companions

had to, till they might be tracked by their blood upon the rough frozen ground. But hunger, nakedness, and sore shins were not the only difficulties we had at that time to encounter; we had hard duty to perform and little or no strength to perform it with.

The army continued at and near the Gulf for some days, after which we marched for Valley Forge in order to take up our winter quarters. We were now in a truly forlorn condition—no clothing, no provisions, and as disheartened as need be. We arrived, however, at our destination a few days before Christmas. Our prospect was indeed dreary. In our miserable condition, to go into the wild woods and build us habitations to *stay* (not to *live*) in, in such a weak, starved, and naked condition, was appalling in the highest degree, especially to New Englanders, unaccustomed to such kind of hardships at home. . . .

This toy soldier of the Revolutionary War was carved around 1785.

We arrived at the Valley Forge in the evening; it was dark. There was no water to be found, and I was perishing with thirst. I searched for water till I was weary and came to my tent without finding any. Fatigue and thirst, joined with hunger, almost made me desperate. I felt at that instant as if I would have taken victuals or drink from the best friend I had on earth by force. I am not writing fiction; all are sober realities. Just after I arrived at my tent, two soldiers, whom I did not know, passed by; they had some water in their canteens which they told me they had found a good distance off, but could not direct me to the place as it was very dark. I tried to beg a draught of water from them, but they were as rigid as Arabs. At length I persuaded them to sell me a drink for three pence, Pennsylvania currency, which was every cent of property I could then call my own, so great was the necessity I was then reduced to.

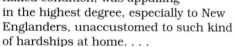

"Damn It, Boys, You—You Know What I Mean. Go On!"

Life with the Swamp Fox

Captain Tarleton Brown

After the British captured Charleston, South Carolina, in 1780, a guerrilla commander known as the "Swamp Fox," Frances Marion, helped keep the American cause alive by raiding the coastal marsh country with his band of irregulars.

Captain Tarleton Brown of South Carolina described in his memoirs what it was like to serve with Marion.

Overtaking General Marion at Kingstree, Black River, S.C., we immediately united with his troops. Marion's route lay then between the Santee and Little Pedee rivers, and being desirous to intercept and defeat Colonel Watts, who was then marching at the head of 400 men between Camden and Georgetown, every arrangement and preparation was made to carry into execution his design. All things being now ready, Watts appeared in sight at the head of his large force, and as they marched down the road with great show and magnificence (hoping, no doubt, to terrify and conquer the country), they spied us, at which time the British horse sallied forth to surround us.

Marion, with his characteristic shrewdness and sagacity, discovered their maneuvers, anticipated their object, and retreated to the woods, some four or five hundred yards, and prepared for them. In a few moments they came dashing up, expecting to find us all in confusion and disorder, but to their astonishment we were ready for the attack, and perceiving this, they called a halt, at which time Marion and Horry ordered a charge. Colonel Horry stammered badly, and on this occasion he leaned forward, spurred his horse, waved his sword, and ran fifty or sixty yards, endeavoring to utter the word "charge" and finding he could not, bawled out, "Damn it, boys, you—you know what I mean. Go on!" . . .

For prudence sake, Marion never encamped over two nights in one place, unless at a safe distance from the enemy. He generally commenced the line of march about sunset, continuing through the greater part of the night. By this policy he was enabled effectually to defeat the plans of the British and to strengthen his languishing cause. For while . . . one army was encamping and resting in calm and listless security, not dreaming of danger, the other, taking advantage of opportunity and advancing through the sable curtains of the night unobserved, often effectually vanquished and routed their foes. It was from the craftiness and ingenuity of Marion, the celerity with which he moved from post to post, that his enemies gave to him the significant appellation of the "Swamp Fox." Upon him depended almost solely the success of the provincial army of South Carolina, and the sequel has proven how well he performed the trust reposed in him. His genuine love of country and liberty, and his unwearied vigilance and invincible fortitude, coupled with the eminent success which attended him through his brilliant career, has endeared him to the hearts of his countrymen, and the memory of his deeds of valor shall never slumber so long as there is a Carolinian to speak his panegyric.

34

"An Extraordinary Instance of Virtue in a Female Soldier"

The Story of Deborah Sampson

Herman Mann

Deborah Sampson (1760-1827), an indentured servant in Massachusetts, disguised herself as a man and enlisted in the Continental Army in 1781 as Robert Shurtleff. Her secret was discovered after she was wounded in battle, and she was honorably discharged in 1783, eventually receiving a military pension.

Sampson told her story to Herbert Mann, who published a greatly embellished version of it in 1797. Mann included the following story that appeared in a New York newspaper on January 10, 1784.

Deborah Sampson served in the Revolutionary War by disguising herself as a man. When she died, her husband received a military pension as her "widow," the only man to do so in the revolutionary era.

An extraordinary instance of virtue in a female soldier has occurred lately in the American army, in the Massachusetts line: . . . a lively, comely young nymph, 19 years of age, dressed in man's apparel, has been discovered, and what redounds to her honor, she has served in the character of a soldier for nearly three years undiscovered. During this time, she displayed much alertness, chastity, and valor: having been in several engagements and received two wounds, a small shot remaining in her to this day. She was a remarkable, vigilant soldier on her post, always gained the applause of her officers, was never found in liquor, and always kept company with the most temperate and upright soldiers. For several months, this gallantress served with credit in a general officer's family. A violent illness, when the troops were at Philadelphia, led to the discovery of her sex. She has since been honorably discharged from the army, with a reward, and sent to her connections, who, it appears, live to the eastward of Boston at a place called Meduncock.

The cause of her personating a man, it is said, proceeded from the rigor of her parents, who exerted their prerogative to induce her marriage with a young gentleman against whom she had conceived a great antipathy, together with her being a remarkable heroine and warmly attached to the cause of her country; in the service of which it must be acknowledged, she gained reputation, and, no doubt, will be noticed in the history of our grand revolution. . . .

"The American Flag Waving Majestically in the Faces of Our Adversaries"

Digging Trenches at Yorktown

James Sullivan Martin

French and American forces combined at Yorktown, Virginia, to defeat the British in the final battle of the American Revolution. After a siege that began on October 6, 1781, General Cornwallis, British commander in the south, was forced to surrender his 8,000 troops on October 19 to the three-pronged attack of George Washington, French leaders Rochambeau and Lafayette, and the French fleet of the Comte de Grasse. James Sullivan Martin of Connecticut, a private at Valley Forge and now a sergeant at Yorktown, helped dig the trenches for the final siege.

We now began to make preparations for laying close siege to the enemy. We had holed him, and nothing remained but to dig him out. Accordingly, after taking every precaution to prevent his escape, . . . on the fifth of October we began to put our plans into execution.

One-third part of all the troops were put in requisition to be employed in opening the trenches. A third part of our sappers and miners were ordered out this night to assist the engineers in laying out the works. It was a very dark and rainy night. However, we repaired to the place and began by following the engineers and laying laths of pine wood end to end upon the line marked out by the officers for the trenches. We had not proceeded far in the business before the engineers ordered us to desist and remain where we were, and be sure not to straggle a foot from the spot while they were absent from us.

In a few minutes after their departure, there came a man alone to us, having on a surtout [overcoat], as we conjectured (it being excessively dark), and inquired for the engineers. We now began to be a little jealous for our safety, being alone and without arms and within forty rods of the British trenches. The stranger inquired what troops we were, talked familiarly with us a few minutes, when, being informed which way the officers had gone, he went off in the same direction, after strictly charging us, in case we should be taken prisoners, not to discover to the enemy what troops we were. We were obliged to him for his kind advice, but we considered ourselves as standing in no great need of it, for we knew as well as he did that sappers and miners were allowed no quarters, at least are entitled to none by the laws of warfare, and of course should take care, if taken and the enemy did not find us out, not to betray our own secret.

In a short time the engineers returned and the aforementioned stranger with them; they discoursed together sometime, when, by the officers often calling him "Your Excellency," we discovered that it was General Washington. Had we dared, we might have cautioned him for exposing himself so carelessly to danger at such a time, and doubtless he would have taken it in good part if we had. But nothing ill happened to either him or ourselves.

It coming on to rain hard, we were ordered back to our tents, and nothing more was done that night. The next night, which was the sixth of October, the same men were ordered to the lines that had been there the night before. We this night completed laying out the works. The troops of the line were there ready

"It Would Not Do for the Men to Fight and Starve Too"

A Camp-Follower's Account of Yorktown

Sarah Osborn

Sarah Osborn was one of thousands of "camp followers," women who traveled with the revolutionary army, cooking and cleaning for the soldiers. Her husband had enlisted without her consent and insisted that she accompany him. To qualify for his pension, she told her story of being at Yorktown in a deposition, which has been changed here to read in the first person.

We marched immediately for a place called Williamsburg, . . . myself alternately on horseback and on foot. There arrived, we remained two days till the army all came in by land and then marched for Yorktown. . . . The [New] York troops were posted at the right, the Connecticut troops next, and the French to the left. In about one day or less than a day, we reached the place of encampment about one mile from Yorktown. . . . My attention was arrested by the appearance of a large plain between us and Yorktown and an entrenchment thrown up. I also saw a number of dead Negroes lying round their encampment, whom I understood the British had driven out of the town and left to starve, or were first starved and then thrown out. I took my stand just back of the American tents, say about a mile from the town, and busied myself washing, mending, and cooking for the soldiers, in which I was assisted by the other females. Some men washed their own clothing. I heard the roar of the artillery for a number of days, and the last night the Americans threw up entrenchments; it was a misty, foggy night, rather wet but not rainy. . . . I cooked and carried in beef, bread, and coffee (in a gallon pot) to the soldiers in the entrenchment.

On one occasion when I was thus employed carrying in provisions, I met General Washington, who asked me if I "was not afraid of the cannonballs?"

I replied, . . . "It would not do for the men to fight and starve too."

with entrenching tools and began to entrench, after General Washington had struck a few blows with a pickaxe, a mere ceremony that it might be said, "General Washington with his own hands first broke ground at the siege of Yorktown." . . .

I do not remember exactly the number of days we were employed before we got our batteries in readiness to open upon the enemy, but think it was not more than two or three. The French, who were upon our left, had completed their batteries a few hours before us but were not allowed to discharge their pieces till the American batteries were ready. . . .

Our flagstaff was in the ten-gun battery, upon the right of the whole.

I was in the trenches the day that the batteries were to be opened; all were upon the tiptoe of expectation and impatience to see the signal given to open the whole line of batteries, which was to be the hoisting of the American flag in the ten-gun battery. About noon the much-wished-for signal went up. I confess I felt a secret pride swell my heart when I saw the "star-spangled banner" waving majestically in the very faces of our implacable adversaries; it appeared like an omen of success to our enterprise, and so it proved in reality.

Nationalism and Sectionalism

🐦 In 1782, the Continental Congress approved a design for the Great Seal of the United States, containing the Latin motto *e pluribus unum:* "from many, one." Americans hoped that the thirteen colonies, so different in geography, population, and economic life, would be able to unite as effectively in peace as they had in war. 🐦 Yet political factions soon emerged in the new nation. The Federalist party, stronger in the northern states, favored a powerful national government to support the growth of commerce and industry. The Democratic-Republican (or Republican) party, stronger in the southern and western regions, favored agricultural interests and advocated state sovereignty—an issue that plagued the nation. Delegates from the New England states even considered secession in objection to the War of 1812. But after the war, a nationalist spirit dominated American politics—at least for a while. 🐦 Party politics resurged in the 1820s and 1830s. Democratic-Republicans became the Democrats, as they rallied

...Listing continued on next page

around southerner Andrew Jackson, who was elected president in 1828. Because Jackson opposed a national bank and protective tariffs, he faced opposition from northern business interests, who allied with reformers to create the Whig party. Yet when South Carolina threatened to secede in protest against high tariffs, Jackson stood firmly behind the union. ❦ Politicians in the 1850s finally found it impossible to reconcile the interests of the North, South, and West over the issue of extending slavery to the western territories. The Whig party crumbled over the issue. Northern Democrats favored popular sovereignty, but slaveowning Democrats in the South demanded more absolute protection by law. The new Republican party opposed any extension of slavery. Its candidate, Abraham Lincoln, was elected president in 1860 with support from the North. Southerners seceded in response, believing that their interests could no longer be protected within the American political system. Only a bloody civil war restored the union. In 1865, America began once more to strive for the goal stated in its motto, *e pluribus unum.*

"What Then Is the American?"

A Farmer Describes the New Nation

J. Hector St. John de Crèvecoeur

Published in 1782, Letters from an American Farmer *was an extremely popular collection of essays written by a French-American farmer and naturalist, J. Hector St. John de Crèvecoeur. When a new nation was born in the Treaty of Paris of 1783, the book helped define its soul.*

America is not composed, as in Europe, of great lords who possess everything and of a herd of people who have nothing. Here are no aristocratical families, no courts, no kings, no bishops, no ecclesiastical dominion, no invisible power giving to a few a very visible one; no great manufacturers employing thousands, no great refinements of luxury. The rich and the poor are not so far removed from each other as they are in Europe. . . .

In this great American asylum, the poor of Europe have by some means met together, and in consequence of various causes; to what purpose would they ask one another what countrymen they are? Alas, two-thirds of them had no country. Can a wretch who wanders about, who works and starves, whose life is a continual scene of sore affliction or pinching penury, can that man call England or any other kingdom his country? A country that had no bread for him, whose fields procured him no harvest, who met with nothing but the frowns of the rich, the severity of the laws, with jails and punishments, who owned not a single foot of the extensive surface of this planet? No! Urged by a variety of motives, here they came. Everything has tended to regenerate them: new laws, a new mode of living, a new social system. Here they are become men; in Europe they were as so many useless plants, wanting vegetative mold and refreshing showers. They withered, and were mowed down by want, hunger, and war, but now by the power of transplantation, like all other plants they have taken root and flourished! Formerly they were not numbered in any civil lists of their country, except in those of the poor; here they rank as citizens. . . .

What attachment can a poor European emigrant have for a country where he had nothing? The knowledge of the language, the love of a few kindred as poor as himself, were the only cords that tied him. His country is now that which gives him land, bread, protection, and consequence. *Ubi panis ibi patria* [where bread, there country] is the motto of all emigrants. What then is the American, this new man? He is either a European, or the descendant of a European, hence that strange mixture of blood, which you will find in no other country. I could point out to you a family whose grandfather was an Englishman, whose wife was Dutch, whose son married a French woman, and whose present four sons have now four wives of different nations. *He* is an American, who, leaving behind him all his ancient prejudices and manners, receives new ones from the new mode of life he has embraced, the new government he obeys, and the new rank he holds. He becomes an American by being received in the broad lap of our great *Alma Mater.* Here individuals of all nations are melted into a new race of men, whose labors and posterity will one day cause great changes in the world. . . .

The American is a new man, who acts upon new principles; he must therefore entertain new ideas and form new opinions. From involuntary idleness, servile dependence, penury, and useless labor, he has passed to toils of a very different nature, rewarded by ample subsistance. This is an American. . . .

"The Great Men Are Going to Get All We Have"

An Interview with Participants in Shays' Rebellion

Massachusetts Centinal

The new nation needed a new government. Its first constitution, the Articles of Confederation, had in 1777 created a weak central government that proved unable to meet the country's crises.

From late 1786 to early 1787, a group of farmers in western Massachusetts—many of whom had fought in the Revolution—protested against high taxes and farm fore-closures. In what came to be known as Shays' Rebellion, the protesters closed down courthouses and attempted to capture a federal arsenal. Although the

Daniel Shays (left) and Job Shattuck (right), leaders of Shays' Rebellion, were featured on the cover of Bickerstaff's Boston Almanack in 1787.

state militia was able to quell the uprising, Shays' Rebellion convinced many people that a stronger national government was necessary and paved the way for the Constitutional Convention of 1787.

The Massachusetts Centinal [sic] printed an interview with some Shaysites on October 25, 1786. They made the same argument later used against the Constitution: that the government was dominated by affluent classes at the expense of working people.

I find it to be a general inquiry wherefore were the late risings of the people . . . in rebelling against the commonwealth. What influenced them to thus rise and oppose government? What did they aim at thereby? Some are apt to think these hard questions, and a general answer that the people were uneasy and did this to manifest their uneasiness doesn't satisfy the minds of the inquisitive. As therefore I was present with them at the late rising, went

through all their ranks, conversed with almost every one, and penetrated to the secret recesses of their souls, benevolence induces me to answer the foregoing inquiries of the people, and to open the minds of the insurgents as they were opened to me as I penetrated into them.

. . . I inquired of an old ploughjogger the confessed aim of the people of that assembly. He said, "To get redress of grievances." I asked, "What grievances?"

He said, "We all have grievances enough; I can tell you mine. I have labored hard all my days, and fared hard. I have been greatly abused, been obliged to do more than my part in the war, been loaded with class-rates, town-rates, province-rates, continental-rates, and all rates [taxes], lawsuits, and have been pulled and hauled by sheriffs, constables, and collectors, and had my cattle sold for less than they were worth. I have been obliged to pay, and nobody will pay me. I have lost a great deal by this man and that man and t'other man, and the great men are going to get all we have, and I think it is time for us to rise and put a stop to it, and have no more courts, nor sheriffs, nor collectors, nor lawyers. I design to pay no more, and I know we have the biggest party, let them say what they will." . . .

I next asked a pert lad, who was hard by him, the cause of his rising. The lad (who fancied himself a deep politician) made a long harangue upon governors, and jobbers, and lawyers, and judges, and sheriffs, and counsellors, and deputies, and senators, and justices, and constables, . . . and treasurers, and salaries, and fees, and pensions, and such as one has ten times too much, and such has five times too much, and the continent owes so much, and the state so much, and the town so much, and the great men pocket up all the money and live easy, and we work hard, and we can't pay it, and we won't pay it.

I found many youths among them equally versed in political knowledge. Thus I went from rank to rank, through all the mobility. I sounded their leaders, and (whether willing or unwilling) I got the secrets of their hearts. . . .

"Her Baby Strapped to Her Back"

A Frontiersman Remembers Sacajawea

Finn Burnett

In 1803, the United States doubled its size by purchasing the Louisiana territory from France. President Thomas Jefferson commissioned Meriwether Lewis and William Clark to explore the vast region. From 1804 to 1806, they travelled about 8,000 miles through the Missouri and Columbia river basins to the Pacific Ocean.

Assisting Lewis and Clark were the French interpreter Charbonneau and his Shoshoni wife, Sacajawea. Only 16, Sacajawea gave birth to a son shortly before the expedition set forth and carried him on her back during the journey. Included in the biography of Wyoming frontiersman Finn Burnett is a recollection of Sacajawea, changed here to read in the first person. While historians disagree about the identity of the real Sacajawea, the details of the expedition recounted by Burnett are largely correct.

Sacajawea, who was probably the outstanding Indian woman in the West, came to the Shoshoni reservation late in the fall of 1871. I, through more than ten years of living among the Shoshoni, knew her always by her original name of "Sacajawea," which signified "Boat Woman" or "Boat Pusher," although she was known among her intimates as "Wad-ze-wipe," meaning "Lost Woman."

All that I ever knew of the Lewis and Clark expedition, I heard from the lips of

Sacajawea. She told me of her capture on the Madison fork of the Missouri River; how she was gathering berries with several other Shoshoni girls and squaws when they were captured by a war-party of Mandans.

She had been adopted by her captors and became the wife of a French trader named Charbonneau when she was 16 years of age. Her first child was born two months before Lewis and Clark started up the Missouri River, and when her husband joined with the expedition, she accompanied him with her baby strapped to her back.

She described the boat trip up the Missouri and on the Madison fork as far as it was navigable. She told of their leaving the boats, that they had no horses, and that all the Indians east of the Rocky Mountains, with the lone exception of the Shoshoni tribe, were hostile to those redskins living on the western slopes. The only hope that the expedition had of reaching the Snake River, and so make their way to the Pacific coast, was to establish communication with the western tribes through some friendly Shoshoni. . . .

Finally, when they had managed to contact [one party of] these Indians, Sacajawea was overjoyed to discover her brother, Chief Cameahwait, among them. After a joyful reunion, she began to talk the language of her childhood again and told them that the white men wished to cross the mountains. She explained that Lewis and Clark needed Shoshoni for guides and a sufficient number of ponies to transport their provisions and equipment to the headwaters of the Columbia River.

Chief Cameahwait took the party with him to the main Shoshoni village and held a general council of all the chieftains. There was a feast of happy welcoming for Sacajawea, and ponies and guides were given to the expedition when they pushed onward.

They encountered terrible hardships on the western slope. Game was very scarce, and soon the party was reduced to the extremity of eating the dogs which had followed the expedition. The Shoshoni guides were disgusted with the white men for consuming these animals, for they would rather die of hunger than eat these camp scavengers.

It is interesting to note that although the Sioux, Cheyenne, Arapaho, and the other plains Indians living east of the Rocky Mountains considered dog flesh to be a great delicacy, the Shoshoni ridiculed the fashion and declared that only dogs would eat their kind.

When the party arrived at the Snake River, they were able to purchase canoes from the Indians who lived in that vicinity and continued down the stream.

During the years that I knew her, Sacajawea never tired of telling her people of the different tribes and portions of the country that she visited with the expedition.

Her stories were not always believed. Once, she told of a great fish, evidently a whale, which lay on the beach along the coast. It had either drifted there with the tide, or had been killed by Indians along the shore. The Shoshoni at the agency could not realize that a fish could attain the proportions that she related. . . .

Then Sacajawea would tell them of the seals which lived in great numbers along the coast. The Shoshoni believed these to be people who inhabited caves under the water. . . . They could believe that people lived under water, but not that fish could grow to be as huge as was described by Sacajawea. . . .

Sacajawea went on to say that when the boats of the expedition had reached the mouth of the Columbia River, the water had become very rough, and it was with the greatest difficulty that their light boats were kept afloat. Her account of the size of the waves was also disbelieved by her listeners.

Then, she told of their return after a winter spent on the coast: of how the expedition was divided when it reached the Rocky Mountains, and, while Charbonneau had guided Lewis with one portion over their original trail to the Madison River, Sacajawea had taken Clark and the remainder of the party across the country

44

to Clark Fork, and on to the Yellowstone River.

She told of their arrival at Clark Fork: how difficult it had been to find logs there which were large enough to use in the construction of the usual size of canoe, and of how they overcame the difficulty by making two small boats, connecting them, and decking them over in pairs. In these peculiar vessels, she recounted that they had transported their equipment down the river and had united with Lewis near the mouth of the Yellowstone River.

Her return to her own people several years after the termination of the Lewis and Clark expedition was a story of great hardship. . . . I was never able to establish definitely the number of years which elapsed between the date of the Lewis and Clark expedition and that of her return to the Shoshoni. . . . [I]t was very possible that she may have visited with the Comanche for a number of years. . . . At any rate, it was generally known that she was living with her son, Bazil, and his family near Fort Bridger in 1868, at the same time that the treaty was made which ceded the present Shoshoni reservation to the Shoshoni Indians.

Sacajawea died in 1884 and was buried in the Indian burying ground west of the Shoshoni agency.

Later, some controversy arose over an Indian woman who was buried somewhere in Dakota, and who had been the wife of Charbonneau, and who was therefore supposed to be Sacajawea. She probably had been a girl companion, one of those Shoshoni children who had been stolen from their berry picking by the Mandans.

She might very possibly have been [another] wife of Charbonneau, as that Frenchman was a great marrying man. Sacajawea had been his third wife. . . .

There were older men of the Shoshoni tribe at that time in Wyoming who could establish the identity of the Sacajawea whom they knew on the Shoshoni reservation as being the sister of Chief Cameahwait, and it is a matter of historical record that the sister of this great chieftain was a guide for Lewis and Clark on their expedition. There was never any question of her absolute identity in her own tribe by those who had known her from babyhood.

"With the Smoke of That Town"

A Pottawatomie Chief Recalls the Battle of Tippecanoe

Shabbona

In the early 1800s, Native American tribes along the western frontier attempted to unite against white settlers under the leadership of the Shawnee chief Tecumseh and his twin brother, The Prophet. General William Henry Harrison defeated the Shawnees in 1811 at their stronghold, Prophet's Town, near the Tippecanoe River in Indiana. The Battle of Tippecanoe was a prelude to the War of 1812, in which many tribes allied with the British. Chief Shabbona, of the Pottawatomie tribe, remembers that battle in the excerpt printed here.

It was fully believed among the Indians that we should defeat General Harrison, and that we should hold the line of the Wabash and dictate terms to the whites. . . .

Our young men said: We are ten to their one. If they stay upon the other side, we will let them alone. If they cross the Wabash, we will take their scalps or drive them into the river. They cannot swim. Their powder will be wet. The fish will eat their bodies. The bones of the white men will lie upon every sand bar. Their flesh will fatten buzzards. These white soldiers are not warriors. One half of them are calico peddlers. The other half can only shoot squirrels. They cannot stand before men. They will all run when we make a noise in the night like wild cats fighting for their young. . . .

Such were the opinions and arguments of our warriors. They did not appreciate the great strength of the white men. I knew their great war chief [Harrison] and some of his young men. He was a good man, very soft in his words to his red children, as he called us; and that made some of our men with hot heads mad. I listened to his soft words, but I looked into his eyes. They were full of fire. I knew that they would be among his men like coals of fire in the dry grass. The first wind would raise a great flame. I feared for the red men that might be sleeping in its way.

. . . Our women and children were in the town only a mile from the battlefield waiting for victory and its spoils. They wanted white prisoners. The Prophet had promised that every squaw of any note would have one of the white warriors to use as her slave, or to treat as she pleased.

Oh how these women were disappointed! Instead of slaves and spoils of the white men coming into town with the rising sun, their town was in flames, and women and children were hunted like wolves or driven into the river and swamps to hide.

With the smoke of that town and the loss of that battle, I lost all hope of the red men being able to stop the whites. . . .

"To Surrender to a Private"

Fighting in the Battle of New Orleans

A Kentucky Soldier

While still an infant nation, the United States was caught in the middle of a bitter war between Great Britain and France in the early 1800s. Neither European power respected U.S. neutrality. Congress finally declared war on Great Britain in June 1812, after an address by President James Madison. Madison cited three reasons for war: British impressment, or seizure by force, of American seamen; interference with neutral American shipping; and incitement of Native Americans on the frontier. The War of 1812 would determine whether the United States could truly be an independent nation.

The final battle in the War of 1812 was fought at New Orleans on January 8, 1815. Under the command of General Andrew Jackson, American forces consisting primarily of the Louisiana militia and volunteers from Tennessee and Kentucky routed the British. Although fought two weeks after a treaty ending the war had been signed, the Battle of New Orleans helped establish America's independence and made Andrew

46

Jackson a popular hero. This anonymous Kentucky soldier described the battle from the front lines.

The official report said the action lasted two hours and five minutes, but it did not seem half that length of time to me. It was so dark that little could be seen, until just about the time the battle ceased. The morning had dawned to be sure, but the smoke was so thick that everything seemed to be covered up in it. Our men did not seem to apprehend any danger, but would load and fire just as fast as they could, talking, swearing, joking all the time. All ranks and sections were soon broken up. . . .

At one time I noticed, a little on our right, a curious kind of a chap named Ambrose Odd, one of Captain Higdon's company, and known among the men by the nickname of "Sukey," standing coolly on the top of the breastworks and peering into the darkness for something to shoot at. The balls were whistling around him and over our heads, as thick as hail, and Colonel Slaughter . . . ordered him to come down. The colonel told him there was policy in war, and that he was exposing himself too much. Sukey turned around, holding up the flap of his old broad rimmed hat with one hand to see who was speaking to him, and replied: "Oh! never mind Colonel—here's Sukey—I don't want to waste my powder, and I'd like to know how I can shoot until I see something?" Pretty soon after, Sukey got his eye on a red coat and, no doubt, made a hole through it, for he took deliberate aim, fired, and then coolly came down to load again.

During the action, a number of the Tennessee men got mixed with ours. One of them was killed about five or six yards from where I stood. I did not know his name. A ball passed through his head, and he fell against Ensign Weller. I always thought, as did many others who were standing near, that he must have been accidently shot by some of our own men. . . .

It was near the close of the firing. . . . [T]here was a white flag raised on the opposite side of the breastwork, and the firing ceased.

Andrew Jackson (far right) led a ragtag army of backwoodsmen, Creole militiamen, Native Americans, and African Americans at the Battle of New Orleans. Jackson earned the nickname "Old Hickory" from his troops because he was as hard and tough as hickory wood.

. . . [T]he flag had been raised by a British officer wearing epaulets. It was told he was a major. He stepped over the breastwork and came into our lines.

Among the Tennesseans who had got mixed with us during the fight, there was a little fellow whose name I do not know, but he was a cadaverous looking chap and went by that of Paleface. As the British officer came in, Paleface demanded his sword. He hesitated about giving it to him, probably thinking it was derogatory to his dignity to surrender to a private all over begrimed with dust and powder, and that some officer should show him the courtesy to receive it. Just at that moment, Colonel Smiley came up and cried, "Give it up—give it to him in a minute." The British officer quickly handed his weapon to Paleface, holding it in both hands and making a very polite bow.

A good many others came in just about the same time. Among them I noticed a very neatly dressed young man, standing on the edge of the breastwork and offering his hand, as if for someone to assist him. He appeared to be about nineteen or twenty years old and, as I should judge from his appearance, was an Irishman. He held his musket in one hand while he was offering the other. I took hold of his musket and set it down, and then giving him my hand, he jumped down quite lightly.

As soon as he got down, he began trying to take off his cartouch box, and then I noticed a red spot of blood on his clean white under jacket. I asked him if he was wounded; he said that he was and he feared pretty badly. . . .

Just then one of the Tennesseans, who had run down to the river as soon as the firing ceased for water, came along with some in a tin coffeepot. The wounded man observed him, asked if he would please give him a drop. "Oh yes," said the Tennessean, "I will treat you to anything I've got." The young man took the coffeepot and swallowed two or three mouthfuls out of the spout. He then handed back the pot, and in an instant we observed him sinking backward. We eased him down against the side of a tent, when he gave two or three gasps and was dead. He had been shot through the breast. . . .

When the smoke cleared away and we could obtain a fair view of the field, it looked at first glance like a sea of blood. It was not blood itself which gave it this appearance, but the red coats in which the British soldiers were dressed. Straight out before our position, for about the width of

space which we supposed had been occupied by the British column, the field was entirely covered with prostrate bodies. In some places they were lying in piles of several, one on top of the other. . . .

When we first got a fair view of the field in our front, individuals could be seen in every possible attitude. Some lying quite dead, others mortally wounded, pitching and tumbling about in the agonies of death. Some had their heads shot off, some their legs, some their arms. Some were laughing, some crying, some groaning, and some screaming. There was every variety of sight and sound. Among those that were on the ground, however, there were some that were neither dead nor wounded. A great many had thrown themselves down behind piles of slain for protection. As the firing ceased, these men were every now and then jumping up and either running off or coming in and giving themselves up.

Among those that were running off, we observed one stout looking fellow, in a red coat, who would every now and then stop and display some gestures toward us that were rather the opposite of complimentary. Perhaps fifty guns were fired at him, but as he was a good way off, without effect. "Hurrah, Paleface! Load quick and give him a shot. The infernal rascal is patting his butt at us!" Sure enough, Paleface rammed home his bullet, and taking a long sight, he let drive. The fellow, by this time, was two to three hundred yards off. . . . Paleface . . . drew sight on him and then ran it along up his back until the sight was lost over his head, to allow for the sinking of the ball in so great a distance, and then let go. As soon as the gun cracked, the fellow was seen to stagger. He ran forward a few steps, and then pitched down on his head and moved no more.

"It Was the People's Day"

Witnessing the Inauguration of Andrew Jackson

Margaret Bayard Smith

Andrew Jackson's popularity after the Battle of New Orleans fueled his political career. By the 1820s, most states had eliminated property requirements for voting, and Jackson emerged as a champion of the common man. Jackson campaigned for the "producing class" of farmers and wage earners and against the "special privileges" of the wealthy. Although he was defeated in the presidential election of 1824, he won in 1828.

This portrait of Andrew Jackson appeard on his campaign materials.

Jackson's inauguration on March 4, 1829, was the first in which "the people" played a significant role. Massive crowds surrounded the Capitol and overran the White House. In a letter to her son, Margaret Bayard Smith, a Washington socialite, reported on the inauguration with a mixture of pride and apprehension.

The inauguration . . . was one grand whole—an imposing and majestic spectacle . . . , one of moral sublimity. Thousands and thousands of people, without distinction of rank, collected in an immense mass around the Capitol, silent, orderly, and tranquil, with their eyes fixed on the front of the Capitol, waiting the appearance of the president. . . . The door from the Rotunda opens, preceded by the marshall, surrounded by the judges of the Supreme Court, the old man [Jackson] with his grey hair, that crown of glory, advances, bows to the people, who greet him with a shout that rends the air. The cannon, from the heights around from Alexandria and Fort Washington, proclaim the [oath] he has taken and all the hills around reverberate the sound. It was grand; it was sublime! An almost breathless silence succeeded and the multitude

was still—listening to catch the sound of his voice, though it was so low as to be heard only by those nearest to him. After reading his speech, the oath was administered to him by the chief justice. The marshall presented the Bible. The president took it from his hand, pressed his lips to it, laid it reverently down, then bowed again to the people. Yes, to the people in all their majesty—and had the spectacle closed here, even Europeans must have acknowledged that a free people, collected in their might, silent and tranquil, restrained solely by a moral power, without a shadow around of military force, was majesty, rising to sublimity, and far surpassing the majesty of kings and princes, surrounded with armies and glittering in gold. . . .

[But at the White House reception following the inauguration,] what a scene did we witness!! The *majesty of the people* had disappeared, and [instead] a rabble, a mob . . . scrambling, fighting, romping. . . . The president, after having literally been nearly pressed to death . . . escaped to his lodgings at Gadsby's. Cut glass and bone china to the amount of several thousand dollars had been broken in the struggle to get refreshments. . . . Ladies fainted, men were seen with bloody noses. . . . Ladies and gentlemen only had been expected at this [reception], not the people *en masse*.

But it was the people's day, and the people's president. . . .

God grant the people do not put down all rule and rulers. I fear . . . as they have been found in all ages and countries where they get power in their hands, that of all tyrants, they are the most ferocious, cruel, and despotic. The . . . rabble in the president's house brought to my mind descriptions I had read of the mobs in the Tuileries and at Versailles.

"Forced to Return to the Savage Life"

Fighting Removal from Their Native Lands

Protest of the Cherokee Nation to Congress

During the Jacksonian era, one consequence of universal suffrage for white males was that people without property now had the political means to try to get it. In the Southeast, federal and state officials expanded white settlement by removing the "Five Civilized Tribes" (Cherokees, Chickasaws, Choctaws, Creeks, and Seminoles) to new lands west of the Mississippi River in present-day Oklahoma.

The Cherokees—who had adopted many ways of plantation life, including owning slaves—tried to use the legal system to fight removal. In Cherokee Nation v. Georgia (1831), the Supreme Court ruled in favor of the Cherokees, stating in the words of Chief Justice John Marshall that Native American tribes were "domestic dependent nations" with territorial rights guaranteed by the United States. But President Andrew Jackson responded, "John Marshall has made his decision; now let him enforce it."

Under the Indian Removal Act of 1830, U.S. agents negotiated with the tribes to exchange their eastern lands for holdings in the west. A few Cherokees were pressured into signing the Treaty of New Echota (the Cherokee capital), which the rest of the tribe regarded as fraudulent. The Cherokee Nation's protest to Congress in 1836, drafted by Chief John Ross, was to no avail. About 4,000 Cherokees (more than one in four) died on the "Trail of Tears," a forced march from their native lands to Oklahoma.

50

The Cherokees were happy and prosperous under a scrupulous observance of treaty stipulations by the government of the United States, and from the fostering hand extended over them they made rapid advances in civilization, morals, and in the arts and sciences. Little did they anticipate that when taught to think and feel as the American citizen, and to have with him a common interest, they were to be *despoiled by their guardian,* to become strangers and wanderers in the land of their fathers, forced to return to the savage life, and to seek a new home in the wilds of the far west, and that without their consent. An instrument purporting to be a treaty with the Cherokee people has recently been made public by the president of the United States that will have such an operation, if carried into effect. This instrument, [Cherokees declare] before the civilized world and in the presence of Almighty God, is fraudulent, false upon its face, made by unauthorized individuals without the sanction and against the wishes of the great body of the Cherokee people. . . .

If it be said that the Cherokees have lost their national character and political existence, as a nation or tribe, by state legislation [Georgia had passed such a law], then the president and Senate can make no treaty with them. But if they have not, then no treaty can be made for them, binding, without and against their will. . . . If treaties are to be thus made and enforced, deceptive to the Indians and to the world, purporting to be a contract, when, in truth, wanting the assent of one of the pretended parties, what security would there be for any nation or tribe to retain confidence in the United States? . . .

. . . [O]wing to the intelligence of the Cherokee people, they have a correct knowledge of their own rights, and they well know the illegality of those oppressive measures which have been adopted for their expulsion by state authority. Their devoted attachment to their native country has not been, nor can ever be, eradicated from their breast. This, together with the implicit confidence they have been taught to cherish in the *justice, good faith, and magnanimity of the United States,* also, their firm reliance on the generosity and friendship of the American people, have formed the anchor of their hope and upon which alone they have been induced and influenced to shape their peaceful and manly course, under some of the most trying circumstances any people have been called to witness and endure.

For more than *seven long years* have the Cherokee people been driven into the necessity of contending for their just rights, and they have struggled against fearful odds. Their means of defense being altogether within the grasp and control of their competitors, they have at last been trampled under foot. Their resources and means of defense have been seized and withheld. The treaties, laws, and Constitution of the United States, their bulwark and only citadel of refuge, put beyond their reach; unfortunately for them, the protecting arm of the commander-in-chief of these fortresses has been withdrawn from them. The judgments of the judiciary branch of the government in support of their rights have been disregarded and prostrated; and their petitions for relief, from time to time before Congress, been unheeded. Their annuities withheld; their printing press, affording the only clarion through which to proclaim their wrongs before the American people and the civilized world, has been seized and detained at the instance of and agent of the United States.

An attorney at law, employed by them to defend the rights of the suffering Cherokees before the courts of Georgia, has been induced to desert his clients' cause, under expectations of being better paid, at their expense, by taking sides against them. . . . Is there to be found in the annals of history a parallel case to this? By this treaty all the lands, rights, interests, and claims, of whatsoever nature, of the Cherokee people east of the Mississippi are pretended to be ceded to the United States for the pittance of $5,600,000. . . . The Cherokee Territory, within the limits of North Carolina, Georgia, Tennessee, and Alabama, is estimated to contain *ten million acres.* It embraces a

"We Are a Separate People!"

Respecting Cherokee Culture

Corn Tassel

After the Revolutionary War, the U.S. government negotiated new treaties with the Cherokees, who had allied them-selves with the British. Corn Tassel, a Cherokee chief of that era, decried the incessant demands by white settlers for more land. He also criticized attempts to "civilize" the Cherokees. But even once Cherokees had been "civilized" by the 1830s, their land was still not safe.

It is a little surprising that when we enter into treaties with our brothers, the whites, their whole cry is *more land!* . . .

[W]ere we to inquire by what law or authority you set up a claim, I answer, none! Your laws extend not into our country, nor ever did. You talk of the law of nature and the law of nations, and they are both against you.

Indeed, much has been advanced on the want of what you term civilization among the Indians, and many proposals have been made to us to adopt your laws, your religion, your manners, and your customs. But we confess that we do not yet see the pro-priety or practicability of such a reformation, and should be better pleased with beholding the good effect of these doctrines in your own practices than with hearing you talk about them. . . .

You say, why do not the Indians till the ground and live as we do? May we not, with equal propriety, ask why the white people do not hunt and live as we do? . . .

The great God of Nature has placed us in different situations. It is true that he has endowed you with many superior advan-tages, but he has not created us to be your slaves. *We are a separate people!*

---

are many extensive and valuable improvements made upon the lands by the native Cherokee inhabitants and those adopted as Cherokee citizens by inter-marriages.

The Cherokee population has recently been reported by the War Department to be 18,000, according to a census taken by agents appointed by the government. These people have become civilized and adopted the Christian religion. Their pursuits are pastoral and agri-cultural, and in some degree mechanical. Their stocks of cattle, however, have become greatly reduced in numbers within the past few years, owing to the unfortunate policy which has thrown upon this territory a class of white and irresponsible settlers, who, disregarding all laws and treaties so far as the rights of the Cherokees are con-cerned, and who have been actuated more from the sordid impulses of avarice than by any principle of moral obligation or of justice, have by fraud and force made Cherokee property their own. . . .

. . . For the surrender then of a territory containing about ten million acres, . . . [t]he sum of $5,600,000 only is proposed to be paid: the price given for the lands at this rate would not exceed thirty cents per acre. Will Georgia accept the whole amount for that portion within her limits? . . .

. . . The Cherokees cannot resist the power of the United States, and should they be driven from their native land, then they will look in melancholy sadness upon the golden chain presented by President Wash-ington to the Cherokee people as emblemat-ical of the brightness and purity of the friendship between the United States and the Cherokee nation.

large portion of the finest lands to be found in any of the states and a salubrity of cli-mate unsurpassed by any. . . .

The entire country is covered with a dense forest of valuable timber, also abounding in inexhaustible quarries of marble and limestone. Above all, it pos-sesses the most extensive regions of the precious metal known in the United States. The riches of the gold mines are incalculable. . . .

. . . Independent of all these natural advantages and invaluable resources, there

"Not One Can Read Intelligibly"

The Beginnings of Public Education

Letters from a New Teacher

The Jacksonian Era created access to education along with access to the ballot. Few communities supported free schooling before 1820, but by 1850 education had become a major responsibility of local governments. Reformers like Horace Mann of Massachusetts argued that education was "the great equalizer of the conditions of men."

As part of this movement, Catharine Beecher, author of A Treatise on Domestic Economy (1841), trained seventy young women in Hartford, Connecticut, to be "missionary teachers." Sent to new communities in western states such as Illinois, Michigan, and Tennessee, these teachers were to be moral and religious leaders as well as instructors. Printed here are letters to Beecher from one of them.

Dear Miss B—:

I address you with many pleasant and grateful recollections of the intercourse it was my privilege to enjoy with yourself and the other ladies associated with you at Hartford—a privilege that every day makes more precious.

We arrived safely, after a pleasant journey, and I am now located in this place, which is the county-town of a newly organized county. The only church built here is Catholic. Presbyterians, Campbellites, Baptists, and Methodists are the chief denominations. The last are trying to build a church and have preaching once a fortnight. The Sabbath is little regarded, and is more a day for diversion than devotion.

I board with a physician, and the house has only two rooms. One serves as the kitchen, eating, and sitting room; the other, where I lodge, serves also as the doctor's office, and there is no time, day or night, when I am not liable to interruption.

My school embraces both sexes and all ages from five to seventeen, and not one can read intelligibly. They have no idea of the proprieties of the schoolroom, or of study, and I am often at a loss to know what to do for them. Could you see them, your sympathies would be awakened, for there are few but what are ragged and dirty in the extreme. Though it is winter, some are without stockings, and one delicate little girl came in with stockings and no shoes. The first day, I felt like having a thorough ablution of both the room and the occupants, they were so filthy.

I had to wait two weeks before I could get three broken panes mended and a few poor benches brought in. My furniture consists now of these benches, a single board put up against the side of the room for a writing-desk, a few bricks for andirons, and a stick of wood for shovel and tongs. I have been promised a blackboard, but I find that promises are little to be relied on. The first week I took a severe cold by being obliged to keep both doors open to let out the smoke. The weather is much colder than I expected, and the houses are so poor, we felt the cold much more. . . .

[from another letter]

Many thanks for your letter. . . . In reply to your questions, I would say that books might be loaned here to some extent with advantage. I have lent your *Domestic Economy* around and have received applications for six copies from those who will pay.

I have a married woman and two of her children now attending my school as pupils. She is anxious to have me form a reading circle to meet once a week. . . .

I think *some money* would much promote my usefulness here, in purchasing suitable books to read in such a circle and to loan; also to furnish school-books to some of my poor children who can get none. Maps are needed much, and some simple apparatus would greatly add to the attraction of the school and the usefulness of the teacher. I have *four* from one family, and another of seventeen is coming, and none of them ever were in a school before. Something to interest and aid such would help me much. I need slates, pencils, and paper, and sometimes I would buy a pair of shoes for a poor child who has none. . . .

The people promised that, if I would stay, they would build me a schoolhouse, but since I have consented to remain, I hear nothing about it. There is a great deal to be done here, and I cannot but hope I may be the instrument of good to this people, and if it is but little, I shall not regret the privations or sacrifices I may suffer.

"A Free Boy in a Free State"

Escape on the Underground Railroad

James Williams

Abolitionist organizations grew as part of the reform movement during the antebellum period. The Underground Railroad, a secret network of free black Americans and white northerners, helped many runaway slaves escape to the North or to Canada. This account of life on the Underground Railroad was written in 1873 by James Williams, who had changed his slave name of John Thomas Evans.

I, John Thomas, was born in Elkton, Cecil County, Maryland, April 1st, A.D. 1825, in the house of my master, William Hollingsworth, being born a slave. I remained with him until I was 13 years of age, when I took one of his blooded mares and made my escape. Whilst riding, I met a number of men, one of whom said to me: "Little boy, where are you going?" "I am going to Mr. Cuche's Mill." "Who do you belong to?" "I belong to Mr. William Hollingsworth." . . .

Ere I arrived at Mr. Cuche's Mill, I met a little boy. I said to him, "Little boy, what is the name of the next town beyond Mr. Cuche's Mill?" He told me, "New London Cross Roads." Ere I arrived there I met a white man. He accosted me thus: "Boy, who do you belong to?" I told him that I belonged to Mr. William Hollingsworth. "Where are you going to now?" "I am going to New London."

At New London I met a schoolboy. I asked him, "Where is the line that divides Maryland from Pennsylvania?" He said, "New London is the line." I asked him, "What is the name of the next town?" He said, "Eaton Town." On my way out I met another man; he said to me, "Where are you going?" I answered, "To Eaton Town." He said, "Where are you from?" I said, "Cuche's Mill." He asked me if I belonged to Mr. Cuche. I said, "Yes." . . .

When I arrived at Eaton Town, I asked a little boy what the name of the next town was. He said, "Russelville." I asked him if any colored families lived there. He said, "Yes, Uncle Sammy Glasgow." He advised me to stop there. He asked me where I belonged. I said, "New London Cross Roads." And for fear that he would ask to whom I belonged, I whipped up my horse and went my way. I was then a few miles in Pennsylvania, and

I felt that I was a free boy and in a free state.

I met a man, and he asked me where I was going. I said, "Russelville, to Uncle Sammy Glasgow." He asked me if I was a free boy. I said, "Yes." He said, "You look more like one of those little runaway niggers than anything else that I know of." I said, "Well, if you think I am a runaway, then you had better stop me, but I think you will soon let me go."

I then went to Russelville, and asked for Sammy Glasgow, and a noble old gentleman came to the door, and I asked him if he could tell me the way to Somerset, and he pointed out the way. I asked him if he knew any colored families there. He said, "Yes." He told me of one William Jourden, the first house that I came to, on my left hand. This Jourden was my stepfather; he married my mother, who had run away years before. . . .

I stayed one night at my mother's, and in the morning . . . they carried me to one Asa Walton, who lived at Penningtonville, Pennsylvania, and he took me on one of his fastest horses and carried me to one Daniel Givens, a good old abolitionist, who lived near Lancaster City; and I traveled onward from one to another . . . until I got to a place of refuge. This way of travel was called the Underground Railroad.

At the age of sixteen I commenced my labors with the underground road. The way that we used to conduct the business was this: A white man would carry a certain number of slaves for a certain amount, and if they did not all have money, then those that [did] had to raise the sum that was required. We used to communicate with each other in this [way]: one of us would go to the slaves and find out how many wanted to go, and then we would inform the party who was to take them, and some favorable night they would meet us out in the woods; we would then blow a whistle, and the man in waiting would answer, "All right." He would then take his load and travel by night, until he got into a free state.

Then I have taken a covered wagon, with as many as fourteen in, and if I met anyone that asked me where I was going, I told them that I was going to market. I became so daring that I went within twenty miles of Elkton. At one time the kidnappers were within one mile of me; I turned the corner of a house and went into some bushes, and that was the last they saw of me. . . .

"They Had to Go Through or Die"

Remembering Harriet Tubman

William Still

Harriet Tubman (1821–1913) was the most famous leader of the Underground Railroad. In 1849, she escaped from slavery and subsequently led about 300 more slaves to freedom—earning the title "the Moses of her people." She could be ruthless to prevent frightened fugitives from turning back, as William Still points out. A leader of the Philadelphia abolitionist movement and a child of former slaves, Still kept detailed records of all passengers on the Underground Railroad who came his way.

Harriet Tubman had been their "Moses." . . . She had faithfully gone down into Egypt and had delivered these six bondmen by her own heroism. Harriet was a woman of no pretensions; indeed, a more ordinary specimen of

Harriet Tubman (far left) poses in this photograph with some of the 300 slaves she helped escape to freedom.

humanity could hardly be found among the most unfortunate-looking farm hands of the South. Yet, in point of courage, shrewdness, and disinterested exertions to rescue her fellow men, by making personal visits to Maryland among the slaves, she was without her equal.

Her success was wonderful. Time and again she made successful visits to Maryland on the Underground Railroad and would be absent for weeks at a time, running daily risks while making preparations for her safety, but she seemed wholly devoid of personal fear. . . .

While she thus manifested such utter personal indifference, she was much more watchful with regard to those she was piloting. Half of her time, she had the appearance of one asleep, and would actually sit down by the roadside and go fast asleep when on her errands of mercy through the South. Yet, she would not suffer one of her party to whimper once about "giving out and going back," however wearied they might be from hard travel day and night.

She had a very short and pointed rule or law of her own, which implied death to any who talked of giving out and going back. Thus, in an emergency she would give all to understand that "times were very critical and therefore no foolishness would be indulged on the road." That several who were rather weak-kneed and faint-hearted were greatly invigorated by Harriet's blunt and positive manner and threat of extreme measures, there could be no doubt.

After having once enlisted, "they had to go through or die." Of course Harriet was supreme, and her followers generally had full faith in her and would back up any word she might utter. So when she said to them that "a live runaway could do great harm by going back, but that a dead one could tell no secrets," she was sure to have obedience. . . . [H]er success in going into Maryland as she did was attributable to her adventurous spirit and utter disregard of consequences. Her like it is probable was never known before or since.

"A Disappointed Woman"

Speaking Out for Women's Rights

Lucy Stone

The women's rights movement was closely linked to that of abolition. When they were denied admittance to an antislavery conference because they were women, Elizabeth Cady Stanton and Lucretia Mott organized the first American women's rights convention, held in 1848 at Seneca Falls, New York. Attended by abolitionist Frederick Douglass, that convention issued a "Declaration of Sentiments," modeled after the Declaration of Independence, which declared that "all men and women are created equal."

One of the most popular speakers for women's rights was Lucy Stone (1818–1893). A Massachusetts native, she attended the first American college to admit women, Oberlin College in Ohio. In 1855, she married reformer Henry Blackwell, but only after they drafted a new marriage contract protesting current laws that made a wife subject to her husband. Moreover, she kept her given name upon marriage, leading to the creation of the Lucy Stone League to popularize the practice. Lucy Stone delivered this speech in October 1855 at a national women's rights convention in Cincinnati, Ohio.

The last speaker alluded to this movement as being that of a few disappointed women. From the first years to which my memory stretches, I have been a disappointed woman. When, with my brothers, I reached forth after the sources of knowledge, I was reproved with "It isn't fit for you; it doesn't belong to women." Then there was but one college in the world where women were admitted, and that was in Brazil. I would have found my way there, but by the time I was prepared to go, one was opened in the young state of Ohio—the first in the United States where women and negroes could enjoy opportunities with white men.

I was disappointed when I came to seek a profession worthy an immortal being—every employment was closed to me, except those of the teacher, the seamstress, and the housekeeper. In education, in marriage, in religion, in everything, disappointment is the lot of woman. It shall be the business of my life to deepen this disappointment in every woman's heart until she bows down to it no longer. I wish that women, instead of being walking showcases, instead of begging of their fathers and brothers the latest and gayest new bonnet, would ask of them their rights.

The question of woman's rights is a practical one. The notion has prevailed that it was only an ephemeral idea; that it was but women claiming the right to smoke cigars in the streets and to frequent barrooms. Others have supposed it a question of comparable intellect; others, still, of sphere.

Too much has already been said and written about woman's sphere. Trace all the doctrines to their source, and they will be found to have no basis except in the usages and prejudices of the age. This is seen in the fact that what is tolerated in women in one country is not tolerated in another. In this country women may hold prayer-meetings, etc., but in Mohammedan countries it is written upon their mosques, "Women and dogs, and other impure animals, are not permitted to enter."

Wendell Phillips says, "The best and greatest thing one is capable of doing, that is his sphere." I have confidence in the Father to believe that when He gives us the capacity to do anything He does not make a blunder. Leave women, then, to find their sphere. And do not tell us before we are born even, that our province is to cook dinners, darn stockings, and sew on buttons.

We are told woman has all the rights she wants, and even women, I am ashamed to say, tell us so. They mistake the politeness of men for rights—seats while men stand in this hall tonight, and their adulations; but these are courtesies. We want rights. The flour-merchant, the house-builder, and the postman charge us no less on account of our sex, but when we endeavor to earn money to pay all these, then, indeed, we find the difference.

Man, if he have energy, may hew out for himself a path where no mortal has ever trod, held back by nothing but what is in himself; the world is all before him, where to choose, and we are glad for you, brothers, men, that it is so. But the same society that drives forth the young man keeps woman at home—a dependent— working little cats on worsted and little dogs on punctured paper. But if she goes out heartily and bravely to give herself to some worthy purpose, she is out of her sphere and she loses caste.

Women working in tailor shops are paid one-third as much as men. Someone in Philadelphia has stated that women make fine shirts for twelve and a half cents apiece; that no woman can make more than nine a week, and the sum thus earned, after deducting rent, fuel, etc., leaves her just three and a half cents a day for bread. Is it a wonder that women are driven to prostitution? Female teachers in New York are paid fifty dollars a year, and for every situation there are five hundred applicants.

I know not what you believe of God, but I believe He gave yearnings and longings to be filled and that He did not mean all our time should be devoted to feeding and clothing the body. The present condition of women causes a horrible perversion of the marriage relation. It is asked of a lady, "Has she married well?" "Oh, yes, her husband is rich." Woman must marry for a home, and you men are the sufferers by this; for a woman who loathes you may marry you because you have the means to get money which she cannot have. But when woman can enter the lists with you and make money for herself, she will marry you only for deep and earnest affection.

"I Never Cared Much for Machinery"

Life in the Lowell Mills

Lucy Larcom

Through New England's textile mills, industrial technology was introduced to the United States from England, where the Industrial Revolution began. Samuel Slater, an English immigrant, started America's first cotton thread mill in Pawtucket, Rhode Island, in 1790. Francis Cabot Lowell and other investors created the "Waltham system" of large-scale textile manufacturing in Waltham, Massachusetts, in 1813.

The Waltham system drew its labor pool from the daughters of New England farm families. In mills like those in Lowell, Massachusetts, young women lived highly regulated lives in company-owned dormitories. Yet they also achieved a new measure of independence. Lucy Larcom (1824-1893) began working at the Lowell mills at the age of 11, after her father's death left the family in financial hardship.

I went to my first day's work in the mill with a light heart. The novelty of it made it seem easy, and it really was not hard just to change the bobbins on the spinning-frames every three-quarters of an hour or so, with half a dozen other little girls who were doing the same thing. When I came back at night, the family began to pity me for my long, tiresome day's work, but I laughed and said, "Why, it is nothing but fun. It is just like play."

And for a while it was only a new amusement; I liked it better than going to school and "making believe" I was learning when I was not. And there was a great deal of fun mixed with it. We were not occupied more than half the time. The intervals were spent frolicking around the spinning-frames, teasing and talking to the older girls, or entertaining ourselves with games and stories in a corner, or exploring, with the overseer's permission, the mysteries of the carding-room, the dressing-room, and the weaving-room.

I never cared much for machinery. The buzzing and hissing of pulleys and rollers and spindles and flyers around me often grew tiresome. I could not see into their complications, or feel interested in them. But in a room below us we were sometimes allowed to peer in through a sort of blind door at the great waterwheel that carried the works of the whole mill. It was so huge that we could only watch a few of its spokes at a time, and part of its dripping rim, moving with a slow, measured strength through the darkness that shut it in. It impressed me with something of the awe which comes to us in thinking of the great Power which keeps the mechanism of the universe in motion. . . .

There were compensations for being shut in to daily toil so early. The mill itself had its lessons for us. But it was not and could not be the right sort of life for a child, and we were happy in the knowledge that, at the longest, our employment was only to be temporary.

When I took my next three months at the grammar school, everything there was changed, and I too was changed. The teachers were kind and thorough in their

59

These English women worked at textile mills very similar to those in America, such as the Lowell mills.

to tend some frames that stood directly in front of the river windows, with only them and the wall behind me, extending half the length of the mill. . . .

The printed regulations forbade us to bring books into the mill, so I made my windowseat into a small library of poetry, pasting its side all over with newspaper clippings. . . .

Some of the girls could not believe that the Bible was meant to be counted among the forbidden books. We all thought that the Scriptures had a right to go wherever we went, and that if we needed them anywhere, it was at our work. I evaded the law by carrying some leaves from a torn Testament in my pocket. . . .

The last window in the row behind me was filled with flourishing houseplants—fragrant-leaved geraniums, the overseer's pets. They gave that corner a bowery look; the perfume and freshness tempted me there often. Standing before that window, I could look across the room and see girls moving backwards and forwards among the spinning frames, sometimes stooping, sometimes reaching up their arms, as their work required, with easy and not ungraceful movements. On the whole, it was far from being a disagreeable place to stay in. The girls were bright looking and neat, and everything was kept clean and shining. The effect of the whole was rather attractive to strangers. . . .

. . . Still, we did not call ourselves ladies. We did not forget that we were working girls, wearing coarse aprons suitable to our work, and that there was some danger of our becoming drudges. I know that sometimes the confinement of the mill became very wearisome to me. In the sweet June weather I would lean far out of the window, and try not to hear the unceasing clash of the sound inside. Looking away to the hills, my whole stifled being would cry out, "Oh, that I had wings!" Still I was there from choice, and "The prison unto which we doom ourselves,/ No prison is."

instruction, and my mind seemed to have been ploughed up during that year of work, so that knowledge took root in it easily. It was a great delight to me to study, and at the end of the three months the master told me that I was prepared for the high school.

But alas! I could not go. The little money I could earn—one dollar a week, besides the price of my board—was needed in the family, and I must return to the mill. It was a severe disappointment to me, though I did not say so at home. . . .

. . . I went back to my work, but now without enthusiasm. I had looked through an open door that I was not willing to see shut upon me.

I began to reflect upon life rather seriously for a girl of twelve or thirteen. What was I here for? What could I make of myself? Must I submit to be carried along with the current and do just what everybody else did? No, I knew I should not do that, for there was a certain Myself who was always starting up with her own original plan or aspiration before me, and who was quite indifferent as to what people generally thought. . . .

At this time I had learned to do a spinner's work, and I obtained permission

60

. . . I defied the machinery to make me its slave. Its incessant discords could not drown the music of my thoughts if I would let them fly high enough. Even the long hours, the early rising, and the regularity enforced by the clangor of the bell were good discipline for one who was naturally inclined to dally and to dream, and who loved her own personal liberty with a willful rebellion against control. Perhaps I could have brought myself into the limitations of order and method in no other way. . . .

The girls who toiled together at Lowell were clearing away a few weeds from the overgrown track of independent labor for other women. They practically said, by numbering themselves among factory girls, that in our country no real odium could be attached to any honest toil that any self-respecting woman might undertake. I regard it as one of the privileges of my youth that I was permitted to grow up among those active, interesting girls, whose lives were not mere echoes of other lives, but had principle and purpose distinctly their own. Their vigor of character was a natural development. The New Hampshire girls who came to Lowell were descendants of the sturdy backwoodsmen who settled that state scarcely a hundred years before. Their grandmothers had suffered the hardships of frontier life, had known the horror of savage warfare when the beautiful valleys of the Connecticut and the Merrimack were threaded with Indian trails from Canada to the white settlements. Those young women did justice to their inheritance. They were earnest and capable, ready to undertake anything that was worth doing. My dreamy, indolent nature was shamed into activity among them. They gave me a larger, firmer ideal of womanhood. . . .

We used to sometimes see it claimed, in public prints, that it would be better for all of us mill girls to be working in families, at domestic service, than to be where we were.

Perhaps the difficulties of modern housekeepers did begin with the opening of the Lowell factories. Country girls were naturally independent, and the feeling that at this new work the hours they had of everyday leisure were entirely their own was a satisfaction to them. They preferred it to going out as "hired help." It was like a young man's pleasure in entering upon business for himself. Girls had never tried that experiment before, and they liked it. It brought out in them a dormant strength of character which the world did not previously see, but now fully acknowledges. . . .

My return to mill work [after spending some time with her sister's family] involved making acquaintance with a new kind of machinery. The spinning room was the only one I had hitherto known anything about. Now my sister Emilie found a place for me in the dressing room, beside herself. It was more airy, and fewer girls were in the room, for the dressing frame itself was a large, clumsy affair that occupied a great

---

"A Slave at Morn, A Slave at Eve"

Decrying the Factory System

Thomas Man

A language teacher in Providence, Rhode Island, Thomas Man published this poem, "Picture of a Factory Village," in 1833. It compared wage labor to slavery and charged that Britain, where the factory system originated, was once again threatening American liberty.

> For Liberty our fathers fought,
> Which with their blood, they dearly bought,
> The factory system sets at naught.
> A slave at morn, a slave at eve,
> It doth my innermost feelings grieve;
> The blood runs chilly from my heart,
> To see fair Liberty depart;
> And leave the wretches in their chains,
> To feed a vampire from their veins.

deal of space. Mine seemed to me as unmanageable as an overgrown spoilt child. It had to be watched in a dozen directions every minute, and even then it was always getting itself and me into trouble. I felt as if the half-live creature, with its great, groaning joints and whizzing fan, was aware of my incapacity to manage it; indeed, I had never liked, and never could learn to like, any kind of machinery. And this machine finally conquered me. It was humiliating, but I had to acknowledge that there were some things I could not do, and I retired from the field, vanquished. . . .

The paymaster asked, when I left, "Going where you can earn more money?"

"No," I answered, "I am going where I can have more time." . . .

Freedom to live one's life truly is surely more desirable than any earthly acquisition or possession. . . . I never went back again to the bondage of machinery and a working day thirteen hours long.

"So Many of You Contending for Your Rights"

The Labor Movement Begins

A Lowell Factory Worker

The factory system increased class consciousness among workers, giving birth to the labor movement. In the 1840s, workers formed the Lowell Female Labor Reform Association to demand a ten-hour day and protest speed ups (increasing a machine's operating rate), stretch outs (increasing the number of machines a worker operated), and reduced wages. Its newspaper, The Voice of Industry, *denounced the tyranny of capitalism. This letter was printed on April 24, 1846.*

Sister Operatives:

. . . I am now in the "City of Spindles," out of employment. . . . It would be useless to attempt to portray the hardships and privations which are daily endured, for all that have toiled within the factory walls must be well acquainted with the present system of labor, which can be properly termed slavery.

I am a peasant's daughter, and my lot has been cast in the society of the humble laborer. I was drawn from the home of my childhood at an early age, and necessity obliged me to seek employment in the factory. . . . I have heard with the deepest interest of your flourishing association of which you are members, and it rejoices my heart to see so many of you contending for your rights, and making efforts to elevate the condition of your fellow brethren and raising them from their oppressed and degraded condition, and seeing rights restored which God and Nature designed them to enjoy.

Do you possess the principles of Christianity? Then do not remain silent, but seek to ameliorate the condition of every fellow being. Engage laboriously and earnestly in the work, until you see your desires accomplished. Let the proud aristocrat, who has tyrannized over your rights with oppressive severity, see that there is ambition and enterprise among the "spindles," and show a determination to have your plans fully executed. Use prudence and discretion in all your ways; act independently and no longer be a slave to petty tyrants, who, if they have an opportunity, will encroach upon your privileges.

Some say that "Capital will take good care of labor," but don't believe it; don't trust them. Is it not plain that they are trying to deceive the public, by telling them that your task is easy and pleasant, and that there is

no need of reform? Too many are destitute of feeling and sympathy, and it is a great pity that they are not obliged to toil one year, and then they would be glad to see the "Ten Hour Petition" brought before the legislature. This is plain, but true language.

Probably you meet with many faithless and indifferent ones. If you have a spark of philanthropy burning within your bosom, show them the errors of their ways; make them understand it; tell them that it is through the influence of the laboring community that these things are to be accomplished. . . .

Read and patronize the *Voice,* and circulate the "Ten Hour Petition" among all classes, and may God strengthen you in your efforts; may you continue on in courage and perseverance until oppression and servitude may be entirely extinguished from our land, and thus, do honor to yourselves, and good to your country.
—*A Lowell Factory Girl*

"The Truth About This Country"

Letters Home from New Immigrants

Alice Barlow
David Davies

The northern work force had changed dramatically by the 1850s due to the rising number of immigrants, primarily from Ireland and Germany. But other groups from northern Europe also sought refuge in the United States—with mixed results. Printed here are two letters written home from Pennsylvania, one by an English woman and the other by a Welsh man.

August 13th, 1818

I write to say we are all in good health, and hope this will find you so. . . . Tell my brother John I think he would do very well here; my husband can go out and catch a bucket of fish in a few minutes, and John brings as many apples as he can carry, when he comes from school; also cherries, grapes, and peaches. We get as much bread as we can eat in a day, for seven pence; although now it is called dear.

Dear mother, I wish you were all as well off as we now are: there is no want of meat and drink here. We have a gallon of spirits every week, and I have a bottle of porter per day myself. In short, I have everything I could wish. . . . Tell little Adam, if he was here, he would get puddings and pies every day.

Tell my old friends I shall be looking for them next spring, and also tell my brother John and sister Ann, if they were here, they would know nothing of poverty. I live like an Indian Queen. . . .

Manufacturing is improved; weavers can get 31 shillings and 6 pence per week; children nine or ten years old get 6 shillings 9 pence, and from twelve to thirteen, 9 shillings in the factory where my husband works. William Latham is the manager of a carpet manufactory and has 2 pounds 14 shillings a week. Respects to all inquiring friends.
—Your affectionate daughter,
Alice Barlow

February 17, 1834

I did not think a year ago that I would be writing to you from America. I left Wales with others on 3 August 1833. We took two months to cross the sea which seemed like two years. . . .

It is some comfort to me that hundreds of my fellow countrymen are as unfortunate as I am or else I do not know what would become of me. I cannot blame anyone but myself because nothing would do but that I should come to America.

It is coal work here and that very stagnant at present and the outlook is poor that any improvement will take place for a long time. . . . This makes everyone here want to return home. I wish that I could persuade Welsh people to believe the truth about this country.

There is no acre to be had under 10 shillings and that covered by trees and a wilderness. If a young man lived for fifty years he could not gather all the stones from off it even if he worked every day. If you spent a year here seeing nothing but poor cottages in the woods with the chimneys smoking so that Welsh people could not breathe in them and the jolly Welsh women were losing their rosy cheeks and smiling eyes, what would your feelings be? You would sigh for the lovely land that you had left.

—*David Davies*

"To Shut Out the Foreigners"

Natives Versus Immigrants

Daily Plebeian
Champion of American Labor

Nativism arose in response to increased immigration before the Civil War. Nativists feared immigrants because they competed for jobs, causing wages to drop due to the larger labor pool. Nativists even formed their own political party, the American party (or Know-Nothings). Newspapers in the 1840s reflected the conflict between immigrants and nativists, as demonstrated by this campaign circular and letter to the editor printed in New York papers.

Look at the hordes of Dutch and Irish thieves and vagabonds roaming about our streets, picking up rags and bones, pilfering sugar and coffee along our wharves and slips, and whatever our native citizens happen to leave in their way. Look at the English and Scotch pick-pockets and burglars crowding our places of amusement, steamboat landings, and hotels. Look at the Italian and French mountebanks roaming the streets of every city in the Union with their dancing monkeys and hand-organs, all as an excuse for the purpose of robbing us of our property the first favorable opportunity. Look at the wandering Jews crowding our business streets with their shops as receptacles for stolen goods, encouraging thievery and dishonesty among our citizens. Look at the Irish and Dutch grocers and rum-sellers monopolizing the business which properly belongs to our own native and true-born citizens.

—*Daily Plebeian*

You intend to shut out the foreigners or naturalized citizens of this country from any benefit that will arise from your plans to get better wages. . . . You use the term *American* very often, and nothing at all is said about *naturalized citizens*. But if you think to succeed without the aid of foreigners you will find yourself mistaken, for we are strong and are getting stronger every day. And though we feel the effects of competition from these men who are sent here from the poorhouses of Europe, yet if you don't include us to get better wages by shutting off such men, why, you needn't expect our help.

—*Champion of American Labor*

64

"A Plantation as a Piece of Machinery"

Excerpts from a Planter's Diary

Bennet H. Barrow

Unlike the North, the South depended on agriculture rather than industry for its livelihood. At the heart of this economy were the plantation system and slavery, although wealthy planters were in the minority. Of the almost 400,000 southern families who owned slaves before the Civil War, one-third owned just one slave, and only about 10,000 planters owned more than 50 slaves. For African Americans, however, plantation life was the common experience: less than 5 percent lived on small farms with one or two slaves, whereas 25 percent lived on plantations with more than 50 slaves.

Bennet H. Barrow (1811-1854) was a typical planter, raising cotton in Louisiana on a large scale. His diary included rules by which he ran his plantation. Indeed, his insistence on order and regularity paralleled that of factory owners in the North.

The very security of the plantation requires that a general and uniform control over the people of it should be exercised. Who are to protect the plantation from the intrusion of ill-designed persons when everybody is abroad? Who can tell the moment when a plantation might be threatened with destruction by fire—could the flames be arrested if the Negroes are scattered throughout the neighborhood seeking their amusement? . . .

To render this part of the rule justly applicable, however, it would be necessary that such a settled agreement should exist on the plantation as to make it unnecessary for a Negro to leave it—or to have a good plea for doing so. You must therefore make him as comfortable at home as possible, affording him what is essentially necessary for his happiness—you must provide for him yourself and by that means create in him a habit of perfect dependence on you. Allow it once to be understood by a Negro that he is to provide for himself, and you that moment give him an undeniable claim on you for a portion of his time to make this provision, and should you from necessity, or any other cause, encroach upon his time, disappointment and discontent are seriously felt.

If I employ a laborer to perform a certain quantum of work per day, and I agree to pay him a certain amount for the performance of said work when he has accomplished it, I of course have no further claim on him for his time or services—but how different is it with a slave. Who can calculate the exact profit or expense of a slave one year with another? If I furnish my Negro with every necessary of life, without the least care on his part—if I support him in sickness, however long it may be, and pay all his expenses, though he does nothing; if I maintain him in his old age, when he is incapable of rendering either himself or myself any service, am I not entitled to an exclusive right to his time? Good feelings and a sense of propriety would always prevent unnecessary employment on the Sabbath, and policy would check any exaction of excessive labor in common.

I never give a Negro a pass to go from home without he first states particularly where he wishes to go and assigns a cause for his first desiring to be absent. If he offers a good reason, I never refuse. Some think that after a Negro has done his work it is an act of oppression to confine him to the plantation, when he might be strolling about the neighborhood for his amusement and recreation—this is certainly a mistaken humanity. Habit is everything. The Negro who is accustomed to remain constantly at home is just as satisfied with the society on the plantation as that which he would find elsewhere, and the very restrictions laid upon him being equally imposed on others, he does not feel them, for society is kept at home for them.

No rule that I have stated is of more importance than that relating to Negroes marrying out of the plantation. It seems to me, . . . it is utterly impossible to have any method or regularity when men and women are permitted to take wives and husbands indiscriminately off the plantation. . . .

A plantation might be considered as a piece of machinery; to operate successfully, all of its parts should be uniform and exact and the impelling force regular and steady, and the master, if he pretended at all to attend to his business, should be their impelling force. If a master exhibits no extraordinary interest in the proceedings on his plantation, it is hardly to be expected that any other feelings but apathy could exist with his Negroes, and it would be unreasonable for him to expect attention and exaction from those who have no other interest than to avoid the displeasure of their master. In the different departments on the plantation, as much distinction and separation are kept up as possible with a view to create responsibility. The driver has a directed charge of everything, but there are subordinate persons who take the more immediate care of the different departments. . . .

Most of the above rules . . . I have adopted since 1833—and with success. Get your Negroes once disciplined and planting is a pleasure—a H[ell] without it.

"No Man Has Ever Labored More Faithfully"

An Overseer Writes to a Planter

John Evans

White overseers helped planters manage their lands. The plantations with the worst reputations for cruelty were often those run by overseers on behalf of absentee owners. These landless whites found work by supervising another's property, but they were often subject to restrictions similar to those imposed on the slaves they oversaw—as these letters from overseer John Evans to planter George Noble Jones make clear.

April 2, 1852

Mr. Jones, Sir,
I wrote you on the twentieth of March and directed my letter to Newport, R.I. I will inform you that I am getting on finely now with my business. I finished planting cotton today at nine o'clock. Now the crop is all planted. I have cleared up and ditched a nice pond and planted it in rice. I will be ready to go to ploughing and hoeing corn about the sixth of this month. The first cotton that I planted is coming up fine. . . .

You directed me to send you all of the names of the Negroes on Chemoonie [Plantation] in families, which I will do in my next letter, which will be on the fifteenth of this [month]. Jim asked me to let him have

Slaves work while an overseer watches. In the plantation system, which considered slaves to be property, an experienced field hand was valued at $600 to $800.

more years, and I think it is to my interest always to know in due time what I am going to do another year. So if we don't agree to live together, why it will give us both a chance to look around. . . .

. . . Should I take a notion to marry, you must give me leave to get a wife. I don't know that I shall ever marry, but I merely mention this so we will know what to depend upon. I would not think of getting a wife without your consent. I think if I had a wife I could get along better. I would have someone to help nurse the sick women and so forth.

January 10, 1856

Mr. Jones,
Sir, as we disagreed the other day at your house about the business of the plantation, you appeared to be so much dissatisfied with my management of your business you will not perhaps be much surprised when I inform you that I have come to the conclusion to quit your employment. For you will doubtless recollect perfectly well the fact of my having always told you that I would live with no man who was not satisfied with the manner in which I manage his business. I have always endeavored to do you justice, and although I say it, no man has ever labored more faithfully for another than I have for you.

Your Negroes behave badly behind my back and then run to you, and you appear to believe what they say. From circumstances that have happened I am led to believe that I run great risks of my life in the case of Jacob. When I mentioned it to you that my life had been threatened by him, you seemed to pay no attention to it whatever.

I have always been accustomed to having my friends to see me, and the indul-

Martha for a wife, so I have gave them leave to marry. Both of them are very smart, and I think they are well matched. Also Lafayette Renty asked for leave to marry Lear; I also gave them leave. Rose, Renty's other wife, says that she don't want to live with Renty on the account of his having so many children, and they were always quarreling so I let them separate. Lear says she is willing to help Renty take care of his children. I will send the load of cotton to Newport on the eighth of this month.

I believe I have written you all of the news from Chemoonie.

Sept. 9, 1854

Mr. George Jones,
. . . My object in writing to you is principally this—it is not a great while before my term will be up with you. So I think it is always best for both parties to know in due time what we will do another year. I am poor and expect to follow overseeing a few

gence of it never for a moment caused me to neglect the business committed to my charge. And now when I am married and might naturally expect the friends of my wife and self to visit us in a reasonable manner, your expression about this matter the other day at your house was enough to let me know that you did not want my friends to come and see me. Taking all these circumstances into due considera-tion, I think I am but acting right when I seek to dissolve the connection that has existed between us for nine years, and in doing so I wish you to believe that I am moved by no unfriendly feelings whatever, but solely by a regard for my own interest. You will be pleased to come over early in the morning and let us settle and get your keys. You owe me a little on the taxes I paid for you in 1855.

"A Cruel Mistress"

A Southern Woman Speaks Out Against Slavery

Angelina Grimké Weld

Not all southerners supported slavery. Angelina and Sarah Grimké, sisters from a prominent South Carolina family, lectured widely in the North for abolitionist groups. Published in 1839, Angelina Grimké Weld's first-hand testimony illustrated the corrosive effects of slavery not only upon slaves, but upon slaveholders.

But it is not alone for the sake of my poor brothers and sisters in bonds, or for the cause of truth, and right-eousness, and humanity, that I testify. The deep yearnings of affection for the mother that bore me, who is still a slave-holder, both in fact and in heart; for my brothers and sisters (a large family circle), and for numerous other slaveholding kin-dred in South Carolina, constrain me to speak; for even were slavery no curse to its victims, the exercise of arbitrary power works such fearful ruin upon the hearts of *slaveholders* that I should feel impelled to labor and pray for its overthrow with my last energies and latest breath.

I think it important to premise that I have seen almost nothing of slavery on *plantations.* My testimony will have respect exclusively to the treatment of *"houseservants,"* and chiefly those belong-ing to the first families in the city of Charleston, both in the religious and in the fashionable world. . . .

I will first introduce the reader to a woman of the highest respectability—one who was foremost in every benevolent enterprise, and stood for many years, I may say, at the *head* of the fashionable elite of the city of Charleston, and afterwards at the head of the religious and moral society there. . . . This lady used to keep cowhides, or small paddles (called "pancake sticks"), in four different apartments in her house so that when she wished to punish, or to have punished, any of her slaves, she might not have the trouble of sending for an instrument of torture. For many years, one or other, and *often* more of her slaves, were flogged *every day,* particularly the young slaves about the house, whose faces were slapped or their hands beat with the "pancake stick" for every trifling offense— and often for no fault at all.

But the floggings were not all; the scoldings and abuse daily heaped upon them all, were worse: "fools" and "liars," "sluts" and "husseys," "hypocrites" and "good-for-nothing creatures" were the *com-mon* epithets with which her mouth was filled when addressing her slaves, adults as well as children. Very often she would take

a position at her window, in an upper story, and scold at her slaves while working in the garden, at some distance from the house. . . . I have known her thus on the watch, scolding for more than an hour at a time, in so loud a voice that the whole neighborhood could hear her, and this without the least apparent feeling of shame. . . .

After the "revival" in Charleston in 1825, she opened her house to social prayer meetings. The room in which they were held in the evening, and where the voice of prayer was heard around the family altar, and where she herself retired for private devotion thrice each day was the very place in which, when her slaves were to be whipped with the cowhide, they were taken to receive the infliction. And the wail of the sufferer would be heard where, perhaps only a few hours previous, rose the voices of prayer and praise.

This mistress would occasionally send her slaves, male and female, to the Charleston workhouse to be punished. One poor girl, whom she sent there to be flogged and who was accordingly stripped naked and whipped, showed me the deep gashes on her back—I might have laid my whole finger in them—*large pieces of flesh had actually been cut out by the torturing lash.* She sent another female slave there, to be imprisoned and worked on the tread-mill. This girl was confined several days and forced to work the mill while in a state of suffering from another cause. For ten days or two weeks after her return, she was lame from the violent exertion necessary to enable her to keep the step on the machine. She spoke to me with intense feeling of this outrage on her, as a *woman.* Her men servants were sometimes flogged there, and so exceedingly offensive has been the putrid flesh of their lacerated

Taken in 1862 after Union troops arrived, this photograph of American slaves is one of the few still in existence.

backs, for days after the infliction, that they would be kept out of the house—the smell arising from their wounds being too horrible to be endured. They were always stiff and sore for some days and not in a condition to be seen by visitors.

This professedly Christian woman was a most awful illustration of the ruinous influence of arbitrary power upon the temper—her bursts of passion upon the heads of her victims were dreaded even by her own children, and very often all the pleasure of social intercourse around the domestic board was destroyed by her ordering the cook into her presence and storming at him when the dinner or break-fast was not prepared to her taste, and in the presence of all her children, command-ing the waiter to slap his face. . . .

It was common for her to order broth-ers to whip their own sisters and sisters their own brothers, and yet no woman vis-ited among the poor more than she did or gave more liberally to relieve their wants. This may seem perfectly unaccountable to a northerner, but these seeming contradic-tions vanish when we consider that over *them* she possessed no arbitrary power; they were always presented to her mind as unfortunate sufferers, towards whom her sympathies most freely flowed. She was ever ready to wipe the tears from *their* eyes and open wide her purse for *their* relief, but the others were her *vassals*, thrust down by public opinion beneath her feet, to be at her beck and call, ever ready to serve in all humility her whom God in his providence had set over them—it was their *duty* to abide in abject submission, and hers to *compel* them to do so—*it was thus that she reasoned.* . . .

Southern mistresses sometimes flog their slaves themselves, though generally one slave is compelled to flog another. Whilst staying at a friend's house some years ago, I one day saw the mistress with a cowhide in her hand, and heard her scolding in an undertone her waiting man, who was about twenty-five years old. Whether she actually inflicted the blows I do not know, for I hastened out of sight and hearing. It was not the first time I had seen a mistress thus engaged. I know she was a cruel mistress. . . .

The utter disregard of the comfort of the slaves in *little* things can scarcely be conceived by those who have not been a *component part* of slaveholding communities. Take a few particulars out of hundreds that might be named. In South Carolina mosquitos swarm in myriads more than half the year—they are so excessively annoying at night that no family thinks of sleeping without nets or "mosquito bars" hung over their bedsteads, yet slaves are never provided with them unless it be the favorite old domestics who get the cast-off pavilions; and yet these very masters and mistresses will be so kind to their *horses* as to provide them with *fly nets*. . . .

Only two meals a day are allowed the house slaves—the *first at twelve* o'clock. If they eat before this time, it is by stealth, and I am sure there must be a good deal of suffering among them from *hunger,* and particularly by children. Besides this, they are often kept from their meals by way of punishment. No table is provided for them to eat from. They know nothing of the comfort and pleasure of gathering round the social board—each takes his plate or tin pan and iron spoon and holds it in the hand or on the lap. I *never* saw slaves seated round a *table* to partake of any meal. . . .

The sufferings to which slaves are subjected by separations of various kinds cannot be imagined by those unacquainted with the working out of the system behind the curtain. Take the following instances. . . .

Persons who own plantations and yet live in cities often take children from their parents as soon as they are weaned and send them into the country, because they do not want the time of the mother taken up by attendance upon her own children, it being too valuable to the mistress. As a *favor,* she is, in some cases, permitted to go see them once a year. So, on the other hand, if field slaves happen to have children of an age suitable to the convenience of the master, they are taken from their parents and brought to the city. Parents are almost never consulted as to the disposition to be made of their children; they have as little control over them as have domestic animals over the disposal of their young. Every natural and social feeling and affection are violated with indifference; slaves are treated as though they did not possess them.

Another way in which the feelings of slaves are trifled with and often deeply wounded is by changing their names, if at the time they are brought into a family there is another slave of the same name, or if the owner happens, for some other reason, not to like the name of the newcomer. I have known slaves very much grieved at having the names of their children thus changed, when they had been called after a dear relation. Indeed it would be utterly impossible to recount the multitude of ways in which the *heart* of the slave is continually lacerated by the total disregard of his feelings as a social being and a human creature. . . .

In the course of my testimony I have entered somewhat into the *minutiae* of slavery, because this is a part of the subject often overlooked and cannot be appreciated by any but those who have been witnesses, and entered into sympathy with the slaves as human beings. Slaveholders think nothing of them, because they regard their slaves as *property,* the mere instruments of their convenience and pleasure. *One who is a slaveholder at heart never recognizes a human being in a slave.* . . .

70

"Father and Mother Could Not Save Me"

A Slave Child's View of Plantation Life

Jacob Stroyer

Jacob Stroyer grew up on a large plantation in South Carolina. He was eventually emancipated and became a minister in Salem, Massachusetts. Stroyer published an account of his slave years, My Life in the South, *in 1885.*

Father had a surname, Stroyer, which he could not use in public, as the surname Stroyer would be against the law; he was known only by the name of William Singleton, because that was his master's name. So the title Stroyer was forbidden him, and could be used only by his children after the emancipation of the slaves.

There were two reasons given by the slaveholders why they did not allow a slave to use his own name, but rather that of the master. The first was that if he ran away, he would not be so easily detected by using his own name as if he used that of his master instead. The second was that to allow him to use his own name would be sharing an honor which was due only to his master, and that would be too much for a Negro, said they, who was nothing more than a servant. So it was held as a crime for the slave to be caught using his own name, which would expose him to severe punishment.

Mother's name was Chloe. She belonged to Colonel M. R. Singleton too; she was a field hand, and was never sold, but her parents were once. The family from which Mother came, the most of them had trades of some kind; some were carpenters, some blacksmiths, some house servants, and others were made drivers over the other Negroes.

Most of them had trades of some kind, but she had to take her chance in the field with those who had to weather the storm. But my readers are not to think that those having trades were free from punishment, for they were not; some of them had more troubles than the field hands.

At times the overseer, who was a white man, would go to the shop of the blacksmith or carpenter and would pick a quarrel with him, so as to get an opportunity to punish him. He would say to the Negro, "Oh, ye think yourself as good as ye master, ye ——." Of course he knew what the overseer was after, so he was afraid to speak; the overseer, hearing no answer, would turn to him and cry out, "Ye so big yer can't speak to me, ye ——," and then the conflict would begin, and he would give that man such a punishment as would disable him for two or three months. The merciless overseer would say to him, "Ye think because ye have a trade ye are as good as ye master, ye ——, but I will show ye that ye are nothing but a nigger."

I did not go to the sandhill, or summer seat, my allotted time, but stopped on the plantation with Father, as I said that he used to take care of horses and mules. I was around with him in the barnyard when but a small boy; of course that gave me an early relish for the occupation of hostler, and soon I made known my preference to Colonel Singleton, who was a sportsman and had fine horses. And, although I was too small to work, the Colonel granted my request; hence I was allowed to be numbered among those who took care of the fine horses, and learned to ride. But I soon found that my new occupation demanded a little more than I cared for.

It was not long after I had entered my new work before they put me upon the back of a horse which threw me to the ground almost as soon as I reached his back. It hurt me a little, but that was not the worst of it, for when I got up there was a man standing near with a switch in hand, and he immediately began to beat me. Although I was a very bad boy, this was the first time I had been whipped by anyone except Mother and Father, so I cried out in a tone of voice as if I would say, this is the first and last whipping you will give me when Father gets hold of you.

When I got away from him I ran to Father with all my might, but soon my expectation blasted, as Father very coolly said to me, "Go back to your work and be a good boy, for I cannot do anything for you." But that did not satisfy me, so I went on to Mother with my complaint and she came out to the man who whipped me. He was a groom, a white man whom master hired to train his horses, as he was a man of that trade. Mother and he began to talk, then he took a whip and started for her, and she ran from him, talking all the time. I ran back and forth between Mother and him until he stopped beating her. After the fight between the groom and Mother, he took me back to the stable yard and gave me a severe flogging. And although Mother failed to help me at first, still I had faith that when he took me back to the stable yard and commenced whipping me, that she would come and stop him, but I looked in vain for she did not come.

Then the idea first came to me that I, with my dear father and mother and the rest of my fellow Negroes, was doomed to cruel treatment through life, and was defenseless. But when I found that Father and Mother could not save me from punishment, as they themselves had to submit to the same treatment, I concluded to appeal to the sympathy of the groom, who seemed to have full control over me. But my pitiful cries never touched his sympathy, for things seemed to grow worse rather than better; so I made up my mind to stem the storm the best I could.

One day, about two weeks after Boney Young and Mother had the conflict, he . . . gave me a first-class flogging.

That evening when I went home to Father and Mother, I said to them, "Mr. Young is whipping me too much now; I shall not stand it, I shall fight him." Father said to me, "You must not do that, because if you do he will say that your mother and I advised you to do it, and it will make it hard for your mother and me, as well as for yourself. You must do as I told you, my son; do your work the best you can, and do not say anything." I said to Father, "But I don't know what I have done that he should whip me; he does not tell me what wrong I have done, he simply calls me to him and whips me when he gets ready."

Father said, "I can do nothing more than pray to the Lord to hasten the time when these things shall be done away; that is all I can do." When Mother stripped me and looked at the wounds that were upon me, she burst into tears, and said, "If he were not so small I would not mind it so much; this will break his constitution. I am going to master about it, because I know he will not allow Mr. Young to treat this child so."

And I thought to myself that had Mother gone to master about it, it would have helped me some, for he and she grew up together and he thought a great deal of her. But Father said to Mother, "You better not go to master, for while he might stop the child from being treated badly, Mr. Young may revenge himself through the overseer, for you know that they are very friendly to each other." So said Father to Mother, "You would gain nothing in the end; the best thing for us to do is to pray much over it, for I believe that the time will come when this boy with the rest of the children will be free, though we may not live to see it."

"Santa Claus Brought Me These New Clothes"

A Slave's Christmas

Harriet Jacobs

Writing under the pseudonym of Linda Brent, Harriet Jacobs wrote Incidents in the Life of a Slave Girl, *published in 1861. It depicted slavery from a woman's point of view and related the many ways that black families tried to ease the burden of slavery for one another. For seven years, Harriet Jacobs hid from the unwanted attentions of her master in her grandmother's attic, watching her children grow up without her. Jacobs eventually escaped to New York, and her children were later emancipated and reunited with her.*

Christmas was approaching. Grandmother brought me materials, and I busied myself making some new garments and playthings for my children. Were it not that hiring day [January 1, when slaves were hired out to other masters] is near at hand, and many families are fearfully looking forward to the probability of separation in a few days, Christmas might be a happy season for the poor slaves. Even slave mothers try to gladden the hearts of their little ones on that occasion.

Benny and Ellen [her children] had their Christmas stockings filled. Their imprisoned mother could not have the privilege of witnessing their surprise and joy. But I had the pleasure of peeping at them as they went into the street with their new suits on. I heard Benny ask a little playmate whether Santa Claus brought him anything. "Yes," replied the boy, "but Santa Claus ain't a real man. It's the children's mothers that put things into the stockings." "No, that can't be," replied Benny, "for Santa Claus brought Ellen and me these new clothes, and my mother has been gone this long time."

How I longed to tell him that his mother made those garments, and that many a tear fell on them while she worked!

Every child rises early on Christmas morning to see the Johnkannaus. With-out them, Christmas would be shorn of its greatest attraction. They consist of companies of slaves from the plantations, generally of the lower class. Two athletic men, in calico wrappers, have a net thrown over them, covered with all manner of bright-colored stripes. Cow's tails are fastened to their backs, and their heads are decorated with horns. . . . A box, covered with sheepskin, is called the gumbo box. A dozen beat on this, while others strike triangles and jawbones, to which bands of dancers keep time. For a month previous they are composing songs, which are sung on this occasion.

These companies, of a hundred each, turn out early in the morning, and are allowed to go round till twelve o'clock, begging for contributions. Not a door is left unvisited where there is the least chance of obtaining a penny or a glass of rum. . . .

Christmas is a day of feasting, both with white and colored people. Slaves who are lucky enough to have a few shillings are sure to spend them for good eating, and many a turkey and pig is captured, without saying, "By your leave, sir." Those who cannot obtain these cook a 'possum or a racoon, from which savory dishes can be made. My grandmother raised poultry and pigs for sale, and it was her established custom to have both a turkey and a pig roasted for Christmas dinner.

"Absolute Democracy in Country Places"

An Eastern Emigrant's View of Michigan

Caroline S. Kirkland

American settlers continually pushed the frontier farther west. Beginning in the late 1700s, they moved from the eastern seaboard into the North-west Territory, land north of the Ohio River and east of the Mississippi River. The Louisiana Purchase further expanded America's western boundaries in 1803. And in the 1820s, Americans began to settle in the Mexican territory of Texas, leading to the Mexican-American War of 1846-47. This expansionism prompted New York magazine editor John L. O'Sullivan to write in 1845 that it was the "manifest destiny" of the United States to overtake the entire continent. By 1860, U.S. territory stretched from coast to coast.

Caroline S. Kirkland, writing under a pseudonym, published an account in 1839 of her emigration to Michigan. Unlike many western set-tlers, she was well-to-do. Her comparison of eastern and western habits illustrates the new kinds of communities that emerged on the frontier, away from established traditions and institutions.

No settlers are so uncomfortable as those who, coming with abundant means as they suppose to be com-fortable, set out with a determination to live as they have been accustomed to. They soon find that there are places where the "almighty dollar" is almost powerless; or rather, that powerful as it is, it meets with its conqueror in the jeal-ous pride of those whose services must be had in order to live at all.

It would be in vain to pretend that this state of society can ever be agreeable to those who have been accustomed to the more rational arrangements of the older world. The social character of the meals, in particular, is quite destroyed by the constant presence of strangers whose manners, habits of thinking, and social connections are quite different from your own, and often exceedingly repugnant to your taste. Granting the correctness of

the opinion which may be read in their countenances that they are "as good as you are," I must insist that a greasy cook-maid, or a redolent stableboy can never be, to my thinking, an agreeable table companion—putting pride, that most ter-rific bugbear of the woods, out of the question.

Some of my dear theorizing friends in the civilized world had dissuaded me from bringing a maid with me.

"She would always be discontented and anxious to return; and you'll find plenty of good farmer's daughters ready to live with you for the sake of earning a little money."

Good souls! how little did they know of Michigan! I have since that day seen the interior of many a wretched dwelling, with almost literally nothing in it but a bed, a chest, and a table; children ragged to the last degree, and potatoes the only

74

fare; but never yet saw I one where the daughter was willing to own herself obliged to live out at service. She would "hire out" long enough to buy some article of dress perhaps, money to pay the doctor, or for some special reason; but never as a regular calling, or with an acknowledgment of inferior standing.

This state of things appalled me at first, but I have learned a better philosophy since. I find no difficulty now in getting such aid as I require, . . . though there is always a desire of making an occasional display of independence. Since living with one for wages is considered by common consent a favor, I take it as a favor; and, this point once conceded, all goes well. . . .

To be sure, I had one damsel who . . . was highly offended because room was not made for her at table with guests from the city, and that her company was not requested for tea visits. . . .

I took especial care to be impartial in my own visiting habits, determined at all sacrifice to live down the impression that I felt *above* my neighbors. In fact, however we may justify certain exclusive habits in populous places, they are strikingly and confessedly ridiculous in the wilderness. What can be more absurd than a feeling of proud distinction, where a stray spark of fire, a sudden illness, or a day's contretemps may throw you entirely upon the kindness of your humblest neighbor? If I treat Mrs. Timson with neglect today, can I with any face borrow her broom tomorrow? And what would become of me if, in revenge for my declining her invitation to tea this afternoon, she should decline to do my washing on Monday?

"Mother wants your sifter," said Miss Ianthe Howard, a young lady of six year's standing, attired in a tattered calico thickened with dirt, her unkempt locks straggling from underneath that hideous substitute for a bonnet so universal in the western country, a dirty cotton handkerchief, which is used, *ad nauseum,* for all sorts of purposes.

"Mother wants your sifter, and she says she guesses you can let her have some sugar and tea, 'cause you've got plenty."

This excellent reason, "'cause you've got plenty," is conclusive as to sharing with your neighbors. Whoever comes into Michigan with nothing will be sure to better his condition, but woe to him that brings with him anything like an appearance of abundance, whether of money or mere household conveniences. To have them and not be willing to share them in some sort with the whole community is an unpardonable crime. . . . [Y]our wheelbarrows, your shovels, your utensils of all sorts belong not to yourself but to the public, who do not think it necessary to even *ask* a loan, but take it for granted. . . .

The better classes of English settlers seem to have left their own country with high-wrought notions of the unbounded freedom to be enjoyed in this, and it is with feelings of angry surprise that they learn after a short residence here that this very universal freedom abridges their own liberty to do as they please in their individual capacity; that the absolute democracy which prevails in country places imposes as heavy restraints upon one's free will in some particulars, as do the overbearing pride and haughty distinctions of the old world in others. . . .

"Oro! Oro! Oro!!!"

Discovering Gold in California

John Augustus Sutter

As a result of the Mexican-American War, the United States acquired California from Mexico. Initially, life changed little for Californians, but with the discovery of gold at Sutter's Mill in 1848, a flood of eastern emigrants followed.

John Augustus Sutter, originally from Switzerland, owned the mill where gold was discovered at the junctions of the Sacramento and American rivers. In 1854, he described the event that forever changed California—and America.

I was sitting one afternoon just after my siesta, engaged, by-the-bye, in writing a letter to a relation of mine at Lucerne, when I was interrupted by Mr. Marshall, a gentleman with whom I had frequent business transactions, bursting into the room. From the unusual agitation in his manner I imagined that something serious had occurred, and, as we involuntarily do in this part of the world, I at once glanced to see if my rifle was in its proper place. . . .

When he had recovered himself a little, he told me that, however great my surprise might be at his unexpected reappearance, it would be much greater when I heard the intelligence he had come to bring me. "Intelligence," he added, "which if properly profited by, would put both of us in possession of unheard-of wealth—millions and millions of dollars, in fact." I frankly own, when I heard this, that I thought something had touched Marshall's brain, when suddenly all my misgivings were put at an end by his flinging on the table a handful of scales of pure virgin gold.

I was fairly thunderstruck and asked him to explain what all this meant, when he went on to say that according to my instructions, he had thrown the mill wheel out of gear to let the whole body of the water in the dam find a passage through the tail race, which was previously too narrow to allow the water to run off in sufficient quantity, whereby the wheel was prevented from efficiently performing its work. By this alteration the narrow channel was considerably enlarged, and a mass of sand and gravel carried off by the force of the torrent. Early in the morning after this took place, Mr. Marshall was walking along the left bank of the stream when he perceived something which he at first took for a piece of opal—a clear transparent stone, very common here—glittering on one of the spots laid bare by the sudden crumbling away of the bank.

He paid no attention to this, but while he was giving directions to the workmen, having observed several similar glittering fragments, his curiosity was so far excited that he stooped down and picked one of them up. "Do you know," said Mr. Marshall to me, "I positively debated within myself two or three times whether I should take the trouble to bend my back to pick up one of the pieces and had decided on not doing so when further on, another glittering morsel caught my eye—the largest of the pieces now before you. I condescended to pick it up, and to my astonishment found that it was a thin scale of what appears to be pure gold." . . .

At the conclusion of Mr. Marshall's account, and when I had convinced myself from the specimens he had brought with him that it was not exaggerated, I felt as much excited as himself. I eagerly inquired if he had shown the gold to the work people at the mill and was glad to hear that he had not spoken to a single person about it. We agreed not to mention the circumstance to any one and arranged to set off early the next day for the mill.

On our arrival, just before sundown, we poked the sand around in various places and before long succeeded in collecting between us more than an ounce of gold, mixed up with a good deal of sand. I stayed at Mr. Marshall's that night, and the next day we proceeded some little distance up the South Fork, and found that gold existed along the whole course, not only in the bed of the main stream, where the [water] had subsided, but in every little dried-up creek and ravine. . . .

Notwithstanding our precautions not to be observed, as soon as we came back to the mill we noticed by the excitement of the working people that we had been dogged about, and to complete our disappointment, one of the Indians who had worked at the gold mine in the neighborhood of La Paz cried out in showing us some specimens picked up by himself, *"Oro! Oro! Oro!!!"*

"Across the Plains in a Prairie Schooner"

The 1849 Gold Rush

Catherine Haun

People streamed westward to California in the gold rush of 1849. These "forty-niners" left established homes in the Midwest and East to pursue their dreams of getting rich quick.

Catherine Haun, a new bride, left Iowa with her lawyer husband hoping to find enough gold in California to pay off old debts. The Hauns were from middle-class families and well educated, and they were lucky enough to join a large and experienced wagon train. Catherine Haun dictated this account to her daughter many years afterward.

Early in January of 1849 we first thought of emigrating to California. It was a period of national hard times, and we being financially involved in our business interests near Clinton, Iowa, longed to go to the new El Dorado and "pick up" gold enough with which to return and pay off our debts. . . .

Full of the energy and enthusiasm of youth, the prospects of so hazardous an undertaking had no terror for us. Indeed, as we had been married but a few months, it appealed to us as a romantic wedding tour.

The territory bordering upon the Mississippi River was, in those days, called "the West" and its people were accustomed to the privations and hardships of frontier life. It was mostly from their ranks that were formed the many companies of emigrants who traveled across the plains, while those who came to California from the Eastern states usually chose the less strenuous ocean voyage by way of the Isthmus of Panama or around the Horn.

At that time the "gold fever" was contagious and few, old or young, escaped the malady. On the streets, in the fields, in the workshops, and by the fireside, golden California was the chief topic of conversation. Who were going? How was best to "fix up" the "outfit"? What to take as food and clothing? Who would stay at home to care for the farm and womenfolks? Who would take wives and children along? Advice was handed out quite free of charge and often quite free of common sense. However, as two heads are better than one, all proffered ideas helped as a means to the end. The intended adventurer diligently collected

Prospectors who rushed to California after the discovery of gold in 1848 were known as "forty-niners."

The two-horse spring wagon was our bedroom and was driven by [Mr. Haun]—on good stretches of road by myself. A hair mattress, topped off with one of feathers and laid on the floor of the wagon with plenty of bedding made a very comfortable bed after a hard day's travel. . . .

The pockets of the canvas walls of the wagon held everyday needs and toilet articles, as well as small firearms. The ready shotgun was suspended from the hickory bows of the wagon camp. A ball of twine, an awl, and buckskin strings for mending harness, shoes, etc., were invaluable. It was more than three months before we were thoroughly equipped and on April 24, 1849, we left our comparatively comfortable homes—and the uncomfortable creditors—for the uncertain and dangerous trip, beyond which loomed up, in our mind's eye, castles of shining gold. . . .

At the end of a month we reached Council Bluffs, having only travelled across the state of Iowa, a distance of about 350 miles, every mile of which was beautifully green and well watered. . . .

As Council Bluffs was the last settlement on the route, we made ready for the final plunge into the wilderness by looking over our wagons and disposing of whatever we could spare. . . .

For the common good each party was "sized up" as it were. People insufficiently supplied with guns and ammunition were not desirable but, on the other hand, wagons too heavily loaded might be a hindrance. Such luxuries as rocking chairs, mirrors, washstands, and corner what-nots were generally frowned upon, and when their owners insisted upon carrying them they had to be abandoned before long on the roadside and were appropriated by the Indians who were always eager to get anything that might be discarded. . . .

Our caravan had a good many women and children, and although we were probably longer on the journey owing to their presence, they exerted a good influence, as

their belongings and after exchanging such articles as were not needed for others more suitable for the trip, begging, buying, or borrowing what they could, with buoyant spirits started off.

Some half dozen families of our neighborhood joined us and probably about twenty-five persons constituted our little band. . . .

Eight strong oxen and four of the best horses on the farm were selected to draw our four wagons—two of the horses were for the saddle. Two wagons were filled with merchandise which we hoped to sell at fabulous prices when we should arrive in the "land of gold." The theory of this was good but the practice—well, we never got the goods across the first mountain. Flour ground at our own gristmill and bacon of home-curing filled the large, four-ox wagon while another was loaded with barrels of alcohol. The third wagon contained our household effects and provisions. The former consisted of cooking utensils, two boards nailed together, which was to serve as our dining table, some bedding, and a small tent. We had a very generous supply of provisions. All meats were either dried or salted, and vegetables and fruit were dried, as canned goods were not common sixty years or more ago. For luxuries we carried a gallon each of wild plum and crabapple preserves and blackberry jam. . . .

78

the men did not take such risks with Indians and thereby avoided conflict; were more alert about the care of the teams and seldom had accidents; more attention was paid to cleanliness and sanitation; and, lastly but not of less importance, the meals were more regular and better cooked, thus preventing much sickness, and there was less waste of food. . . .

. . . [W]e reached Sacramento on November 4, 1849, just six months and ten days after leaving Clinton, Iowa. We were all in pretty good condition. . . .

Although very tired of tent life, many of us spent Thanksgiving and Christmas in our canvas houses. I do not remember ever having happier holiday times. For Christmas dinner we had a grizzly bear steak for which we paid $2.50, one cabbage for $1.00 and—oh horrors—some more *dried* apples! And for a Christmas present the Sacramento River rose very high and flooded the whole town! . . . It was past the middle of January before we . . . reached Marysville—there were only a half dozen houses, all occupied at exorbitant prices. Someone was calling for the services of a lawyer to draw up a will, and my husband offered to do it, for which he charged $150.

This seemed a happy omen for success and he hung out his shingle, abandoning all thought of going to the mines. As we had lived in a tent and had been on the move for nine months, traveling 2,400 miles we were glad to settle down and go housekeeping in a shed that was built in a day of lumber purchased with the first fee. The ground was given us by some gamblers who lived next door, and upon the other side, for neighbors, we had a real live saloon. I never have received more respectful attention than I did from these neighbors.

Upon the whole I enjoyed the trip, [in] spite of its hardships and dangers and the fear and dread that hung as a pall over every hour. Although not so thrilling as were the experiences of many who suffered in reality what we feared, but escaped, I like every other pioneer love to live over again in memory those romantic months, and revisit, in fancy, the scenes of the journey.

"When the Last Red Man Shall Have Perished"

A Native American Mourns His People

Chief Seattle

Western expansion came at a price, and that price was paid by Native Americans. Driven from their lands, they were forced to live on federal reservations.

Chief Seattle, who led several tribes in the Pacific Northwest, gave this speech to hundreds of people, native and white, in 1854 on the site of the future city of Seattle. He addressed Governor Isaac I. Stevens, who had recently returned from Washington authorized to buy Native American lands and establish reservations.

Dr. Henry A. Smith supposedly took notes when Chief Seattle's speech was being delivered. Smith's version was published in 1887, but some historians question its authenticity. Several other versions of Chief Seattle's speech have since appeared, but Smith's is the most reliable. This account differs only slightly from Smith's original.

There was a time when our people covered the land as the waves of a wind-ruffled sea cover its shell-paved floor, but that time long since passed away with the greatness of tribes that are now but a mournful memory. I will not dwell on, nor mourn over, our untimely decay, nor reproach my paleface brothers with hastening it as we too may have been somewhat to blame.

Youth is impulsive. When our young men grow angry at some real or imaginary wrong, and disfigure their faces with black paint, it denotes that their hearts are black, and that they are often cruel and relentless, and our old men and old women are unable to restrain them. Thus it has ever been. Thus it was when the white men first began to push our forefathers further westward. But let us hope that the hostilities between us may never return. We would have everything to lose and nothing to gain. Revenge by young men is considered gain, even at the cost of their own lives, but old men who stay at home in times of war, and mothers who have sons to lose, know better.

Our good father at Washington—for I presume he is now our father as well as yours, since King George has moved his boundaries further north—our great and good father, I say, sends us word that if we do as he desires he will protect us. His brave warriors will be to us a bristling wall of strength, and his wonderful ships of war will fill our harbors so that our ancient enemies far to the northward—the Hydas and Tsimpsians—will cease to frighten our women,

Chief Seattle led the Duwamish and other related tribes in the Puget Sound area of Washington.

children, and old men. Then in reality will he be our father and we his children.

But can that ever be? Your God is not our God! Your God loves your people and hates mine. He folds his strong protecting arms lovingly about the paleface and leads him by the hand as a father leads his infant son, but He has forsaken His red children—if they really are His. . . .

How then can we be brothers? How can your God become our God and renew our prosperity and awaken in us dreams of returning greatness? If we have a common heavenly father, He must be partial—for He came to His paleface children. We never saw Him. . . . No, we are two distinct races with separate origins and separate destinies. There is little in common between us.

To us the ashes of our ancestors are sacred and their resting place is hallowed ground. You wander far from the graves of your ancestors and seemingly without regret. Your religion was written upon tables of stone by the iron finger of your God so that you could not forget. The Red Man could never comprehend nor remember it. Our religion is the traditions of our ancestors—the dreams of our old men, given them in solemn hours of night by the Great Spirit and the visions of our sachems, and is written in the hearts of our people.

Your dead cease to love you and the land of their nativity as soon as they pass the portals of the tomb and wander away beyond the stars. They are soon forgotten and never return. Our dead never forget the beautiful world that gave them being. They still love its verdant valleys, its murmuring rivers, its magnificent mountains, sequestered vales and verdant lined lakes and bays, and ever yearn in tender, fond affection over the lonely hearted living, and often return from the Happy Hunting Ground to visit, guide, console, and comfort them.

Day and night cannot dwell together. The Red Man has ever fled the approach of the White Man, as the morning mist flees before the morning sun.

However, your proposition seems fair, and I think that my people will accept it and will retire to the reservation you offer them. Then we will dwell apart in peace, for the words of the Great White Chief seem to be the words of nature speaking to my people out of dense darkness.

It matters little where we pass the remnant of our days. They will not be many. The Indian's night promises to be dark. Not a single star of hope hovers above his horizon. Sad-voiced winds moan in the distance. Grim fate seems to be on the Red Man's trail, and wherever he goes he will hear the approaching footsteps of his fell destroyer and prepare stolidly to meet his doom, as does the wounded doe that hears the approaching footsteps of the hunter.

A few more moons, a few more winters, and not one of the descendants of the mighty hosts that once moved over this broad land or lived in happy homes, protected by the Great Spirit, will remain to mourn over the graves of a people—once more powerful and hopeful than yours. But why should I mourn at the untimely fate of my people? Tribe follows tribe, and nation follows nation, like the waves of the sea. It is the order of nature, and regret is useless. Your time of decay may be distant, but it will surely come, for even the White Man whose God walked and talked with him as friend with friend, cannot be exempt from the common destiny. We may be brothers after all. We will see. . . .

And when the last Red Man shall have perished, and the memory of my tribe shall have become a myth among the White Men, these shores will swarm with the invisible dead of my tribe, and when your children's children think themselves alone in the field, the store, the shop, upon the highway, or in the silence of the pathless woods, they will not be alone. . . . The White Man will never be alone. Let him be just and deal kindly with my people, for the dead are not powerless.

"The Funeral of Liberty"

Enforcing the Fugitive Slave Law

Charles E. Stevens

Westward expansion exacerbated sectional tensions. Each new western state threatened to upset the balance between the slaveholding South and the free North. California's quest for statehood led to the Compromise of 1850, in which California was admitted as a free state but slaveholders were given the protection of the Fugitive Slave Act. Under this law, black persons accused of being escaped slaves were returned from free territory to their alleged owners without a trial by jury or being allowed to cross-examine witnesses or testify on their own behalf.

In 1854, Anthony Burns was arrested in Boston and ordered to be returned to the Virginia plantation from which he had escaped. Antislavery citizens of Massachusetts vigorously opposed the decision, verging on open conflict with U.S. armed forces. An eyewitness here describes Burns's transport to the ship that would return him to slavery.

At eleven o'clock, Court Square presented a spectacle that became indelibly engraved upon the memories of men. The people had been swept out of the square and stood crowded together in Court Street, presenting to the eye a solid rampart of living beings. At the eastern door of the Court House stood the cannon, loaded, with its mouth pointed full upon the compact mass. By its side stood the officer commanding the detachment of United States troops, gazing with steady composure in the same direction. It was the first time that the armed power of the United States had ever been arrayed against the people of Massachusetts. Men who witnessed the sight, and reflected upon its cause, were made painfully to recognize the fact, before unfelt, that they were the subjects of two governments. . . .

At length, about two o'clock, the column was formed in the square. First came a detachment of United States artillery, fol-lowed by a platoon of United States Marines. After these followed the armed civil posse of the marshal, to which succeeded two platoons of Marines, [which] brought up the rear. When this arrangement was completed, Burns, accompanied by an officer on each side with arms interlocked, was conducted from his prison through a passage lined with soldiers, and placed in the centre of the armed posse. . . .

The route from the courthouse to the wharf had by this time become thronged with a countless multitude. It seemed as if the whole population of the city had been concentrated upon this narrow space. In vain the military and police had attempted to clear the street; the carriage-way alone was kept vacant. On the sidewalks in Court and State Streets, every available spot was occupied; all the passages, windows, and balconies, from basement to attic, overflowed with gazers, while the roofs of the buildings were

82

black with human beings. It was computed that not less than fifty thousand people had gathered to witness the spectacle.

At different points along the route were displayed symbols significant of the prevailing sentiment. A distinguished member of the Suffolk Bar, whose office was directly opposite the courtroom and who was at the time commander of the Ancient and Honorable Artillery, draped his windows in mourning. The example was quickly followed by others. From a window opposite the Old State House was suspended a black coffin, upon which was the legend, "The Funeral of Liberty." At a point farther on toward the wharf, a venerable merchant had caused a rope to be stretched from his own warehouse across State Street to an opposite point, and the American Flag, draped in mourning, to be suspended therefrom with the union down. . . .

Along this Via Dolorosa [literally, "sorrowful way"; refers to the route Jesus travelled to his crucifixion], with its cloud of witnesses, the column now began to move. No music enlivened its march; the dull tramp of the soldiers on the rocky pavements and the groans and hisses of the bystanders were the only sounds. . . . In its progress, it went past the Old State House. . . . Just below, it passed over the ground where, in the massacre of 1770, fell [Crispus] Attucks, the first Negro martyr in the cause of American liberty.

"He Was Seated on His Coffin"

The Execution of John Brown

David Hunter Strother

The growing conflict between pro- and antislavery forces led to widespread violence from 1854 to 1856 in Kansas, which had been opened for settlement. One of the principal figures in "Bleeding Kansas" was John Brown, a militant abolitionist who killed five proslavery settlers. Three years later, on October 16, 1859, John Brown and a small band of followers captured the federal arsenal at Harpers Ferry, in present-day West Virginia (created in 1863 after it refused to join the Confederacy with the rest of Virginia). Brown hoped to arm slave uprisings throughout the region.

But federal troops under the command of Colonel Robert E. Lee of Virginia easily quelled the revolt. Brown was convicted of treason against Virginia and hanged. At his execution, John Brown gave one of his guards this note: "I, John Brown, am now quite certain that the crimes of this guilty land will never be purged away but with blood." David Hunter Strother, a reporter for Harper's Weekly, *witnessed Brown's execution.*

On Friday, December 2, the notorious John Brown was executed at Charlestown, Virginia, according to the sentence of the law. . . .

At eleven o'clock, escorted by a strong column of soldiers, the prisoner entered the field. He was seated in a furniture wagon on his coffin with his arms tied down above the elbows, leaving the forearms free. The driver with two others occupied the front seat while the jailer sat in the after part of the wagon. I stood with

a group of half a dozen gentlemen near the steps of the scaffold when the prisoner was driven up. He wore the same seedy and dilapidated dress that he had at Harpers Ferry and during his trial, but his rough boots had given place to a pair of particolored slippers, and he wore a low-crowned, broad-brimmed hat (the first time I had ever seen him with a hat).

He had entirely recovered from his wounds and looked decidedly better and stronger than when I last saw him. As he neared the gibbet, his face wore a grim and grisly smirk which, but for the solemnity of the occasion, might have suggested ideas of the ludicrous. He stepped from the wagon with surprising agility and walked hastily toward the scaffold, pausing a moment as he passed our group to wave his pinioned arm and bid us good morning. I thought I could observe in this a trace of bravado—but perhaps I was mistaken, as his natural manner was short, ungainly, and hurried.

He mounted the steps of the scaffold with the same alacrity, and there as if by previous arrangement, he immediately took off his hat and offered his neck for the halter, which was promptly adjusted by Mr. Avis, the jailer. A white muslin cap or hood was then drawn over his face, and the sheriff, not remembering that his eyes were covered, requested him to advance to the platform. The prisoner replied in his usual tone, "You will have to guide me there."

The breeze disturbing the arrangement of the hood, the sheriff asked his assistant for a pin. Brown raised his hand and directed him to the collar of his coat where several old pins were quilted in. The sheriff took the pin and completed his work.

He was accordingly led forward to the drop, the halter hooked to the beam, and the officers supposing that the execution was to follow immediately took leave of him. In doing so, the sheriff inquired if he did not want a handkerchief to throw as a signal to cut the drop. Brown replied, "No, I don't care; I don't want you to keep me waiting unnecessarily."

These were his last words, spoken with that sharp nasal twang peculiar to him, but spoken quietly and civilly, without impatience or the slightest apparent emotion. In this position he stood for five minutes or more, while the troops that composed the escort were wheeling into the positions assigned them. . . .

During all these movements no sound was heard but the quick, stern words of military command, and when these ceased a dead silence reigned. . . . The sheriff struck the rope a sharp blow with a hatchet, the platform fell with a crash—a few convulsive struggles and a human soul had gone to judgment.

"Maybe It Won't Be Such a Picnic"

An Indiana Farm Boy Hears of Fort Sumter

Theodore Upson

Opposing any extension of slavery in the western territories, Abraham Lincoln was elected president in 1860. Southern states seceded in response, believing they could no longer protect their interests within the political system established by the U.S. Constitution. On December 20, 1860, South Carolina became the first state to leave the Union. By February 1861, six more had followed, and they all voted to form the Confederate States of America. Four more states would eventually join.

84

Many Northerners favored allowing the "erring sisters" to depart in peace. But on April 12, 1861, when Confederate guns fired upon the federal garrison at Fort Sumter in South Carolina, the Civil War began. Theodore Upson—who had relatives in both North and South—was harvesting corn when he heard the news. He believed his southern kin would fight bravely: the war would be no picnic.

Father and I were husking out some corn. We could not finish before it wintered up. When William Cory came across the field (he had been down after the mail), he was excited and said, "Jonathan, the Rebs have fired upon and taken Fort Sumter." Father got white and couldn't say a word.

William said, "The president will soon fix them. He has called for 75,000 men and is going to blockade their ports, and just as soon as those fellows find out that the North means business, they will get down off their high horse."

Father said little. We did not finish the corn and drove to the barn. Father left me to unload and put out the team and went to the house. After I had finished, I went in to dinner. Mother said, "What is the matter with Father?" He had gone right upstairs. I told her what we had heard. She went to him. After a while, they came down. Father looked ten years older.

We sat down to the table. Grandma wanted to know what was the trouble. Father told her, and she began to cry. "Oh my poor children in the South! Now they will suffer! God knows how they will suffer! I knew it would come! Jonathan, I told you it would come!"

"They can come here and stay," said Father.

"No, they will not do that. There is their home. There they will stay. Oh, to think that I should have lived to see the day when brother should rise against brother."

She and mother were crying, and I lit out for the barn. I do hate to see women cry.

We had another meeting at the schoolhouse last night; we are raising money to take care of the families of those who enlist. A good many gave money; others subscribed. The Hulper boys have enlisted and Steve Lampman and some others. I said I would go, but they laughed at me and said they wanted men not boys for this job; that it would all be over soon; that those fellows down South are big bluffers and would rather talk than fight.

Young boys enlisted on both sides as drummers, and some were killed in battle.

I am not so sure about that. I know the Hale boys would fight with their fists at any rate, and I believe they would fight with guns, too, if needs be. I remember how Charlie would get on our Dick and ride on a gallop across our south field, cutting mullein heads with his wooden sword, playing they were Indians or Mexicans (his father was in the Mexican War), and he looked fine. To be sure there was no danger, but I feel pretty certain he could fight. Maybe it won't be such a picnic as some say it will. . . .

Mother had a letter from the Hales. Charlie and his father are in their army, and Dayton wanted to go but was too young. I wonder if I were in our army and they should meet me, would they shoot me? I suppose they would.

85

"Can Such a Population Be Subjugated?"

Arguing the Southern Cause

Henry William Ravenel

Southerners believed they were fighting for their liberty, however ironic that proposition might be for slaveowners. Poor whites, who had little economic stake in the war, fought to defend their homes—although many saw it as a "rich man's war, poor man's fight." Henry William Ravenel, who belonged to a prominent South Carolina family, set forth in his journal the viewpoint of the aristocratic South.

The *New York Herald* speaks of raising 50,000 men and speedily conquering a peace. Easier said than done. We can do the same if necessary—and fighting for our liberty and our homes, we have no doubt of the issue. All good men should ardently desire a return of peace, but it must be upon terms honorable to us and our rights. I fear the Northern people have an impression that we are unable to cope with them, from inferiority in numbers, want of necessary means, and that our slave population is an element of weakness. It may be necessary therefore that they should be disabused of such impressions, and learn to appreciate and understand us better.

If we *must* pass through the terrible ordeal of war to teach them this lesson, so be it. It may be best in the end. We put our trust in the God of battles and the impartial dispenser of justice, and are willing to abide the issue. Our people are all united and stand up as one man in defense of their country. Our Negroes are contented and loyal. The old and the infirm who have not yet gone out to battle are ready to take their places in the ranks when their services are needed. Our women and children are all enthusiastic for the common defense. Can such a population be subjugated? . . .

. . . We have never sought to assail the Northern people in any way—we have only asked to be let alone. We have been satisfied, in the sight of God and of our approving conscience, that our institutions were sanctioned by justice and religion, that mutual benefits were secured to both races inhabiting our Southern states, that our very existence as a people was staked upon its preservation, and that it has the sanction of natural as well as revealed religion.

They have refused to permit us to remain in peace with them, and now that we have decided as a last effort of self-preservation to establish a government for ourselves, they insolently threaten us with subjugation. We have desired to separate from them in peace, and have offered to negotiate on friendly terms the manner of separation. They have rejected all our overtures and have answered us with insult and defiance. They appeal to arms. We will meet them, putting our trust in Him who is the Father of us all and in whose hands are the destinies of His people.

"A Pure Love of My Country Has Called Upon Me"

Reflections on the Union Cause

Major Sullivan Ballou

Initially, Northerners believed they were fighting to preserve the Union, the system of government for which their ancestors had fought the Revolutionary War. Major Sullivan Ballou of Rhode Island was stationed in Washington, D.C., in mid-July of 1861. Sensing that battle was impending, Ballou set forth his reasons for defending the Union in a love letter to his wife.

The first major battle of the Civil War was fought at Bull Run Creek, near the town of Manassas, Virginia, on July 21, 1861. Sure of a Union victory, citizens of the federal capital—only twenty-five miles away—brought picnic lunches to observe the fighting. But by late afternoon, Union forces had been totally defeated. Major Ballou was killed in the battle.

My very dear Sarah:

The indications are strong that we shall move in a few days—perhaps tomorrow. Lest I should not be able to write again, I feel impelled to write a few lines that may fall under your eye when I shall be no more. . . .

I have no misgivings about, or lack of confidence in the cause in which I am engaged, and my courage does not halt or falter. I know how strongly American civilization now leans on the triumph of the government, and how great a debt we owe to those who went before us through the blood and sufferings of the Revolution. And I am willing—perfectly willing—to lay down all my joys in this life, to help maintain this government, and to pay that debt. . . .

I cannot describe to you my feelings on this calm summer Sabbath night, when two thousand men are sleeping around me, many of them enjoying perhaps the last sleep before that of death, while I am suspicious that death is creeping around me with his fatal dart, as I sit communing with God, my country, and thee. I have sought most closely and diligently and often in my heart for a wrong motive in thus hazarding the happiness of those I love, and I could find none. A pure love of my country and of the principles I have so often advocated before the people—another name of Honor that I love more than I fear death—has called upon me and I have obeyed.

Sarah, my love for you is deathless. It seems to bind me with mighty cables that nothing but omnipotence could break; and yet my love of country comes over me like a strong wind and bears me unresistibly on with all these chains to the battlefield.

The memories of the blissful moments I have spent with you come creeping over me, and I feel most gratified to God and to you that I have enjoyed them so long. And hard it is for me to give them up and burn to ashes the hopes of future years, when, God willing, we might still have lived and loved together, and seen our sons grown up to honorable manhood around us. I have, I know, but few and small claims upon Divine Providence, but something whispers to me—perhaps it is the wafted prayer of my little Edgar—that I shall return to my loved ones unharmed. If I do not, my dear Sarah, never forget how much I love you, and when my last breath escapes me on the battlefield, it will whisper your name. Forgive my many faults and the many pains I have caused you. How thoughtless and foolish I have oftentimes been! How gladly would I wash out with my tears every little spot upon your happiness, and struggle with all the misfortunes of this world to shield you and your children from harm. But I cannot. I must watch you from the spirit-land and hover near you, with your precious little freight, and wait with sad patience, till we meet to part no more.

But, O Sarah! If the dead can come back to this earth and flit unseen around those they loved, I shall always be near you; in the gladdest days and in the darkest nights, advised to your happiest scenes and gloomiest hours, *always, always*. And if there be a soft breeze upon your cheek, it shall be my breath; as the cool air fans your throbbing temple, it shall be my spirit passing by. Sarah, do not mourn me dead; think I am gone and wait for thee, for we shall meet again. . . .

"Men Mutilated in Every Imaginable Way"

Nursing the Wounds from Shiloh

Kate Cumming

In the western theater of the war, Union commander Ulysses S. Grant sought to establish control of the Tennessee and Cumberland rivers. He won major victories in February 1862 at Fort Henry and Fort Donelson in Tennessee. But Confederate forces from Corinth, Mississippi, crossed into Tennessee and on April 6 surprised Union troops at a small Methodist church named Shiloh. The Confederate attack was repelled after two days of battle, but Grant's victory was costly and he was criticized for being unprepared.

Shiloh was the first battle with massive casualties—about 25,000. In that single battle, more Americans died than in all previous U.S. wars combined. Kate Cumming served as a nurse in Corinth, where the Confederate wounded at Shiloh eventually arrived.

April 11, 1862. . . . My heart beat high with expectation as we neared Corinth. As I had never been where there was a large army and had never seen a wounded man, except in the [railroad] cars as they passed, I could not help feeling a little nervous at the prospect of now seeing both. . . .

. . . Mrs. Ogden tried to prepare me for the scenes which I should witness upon entering the wards. But alas! Nothing that I had ever heard or read had given me the faintest idea of the horrors witnessed here. . . . Gray-haired men, men in the pride of manhood, beardless boys, Federals and all, mutilated in every imaginable way, lying on the floor just as they were taken from the battlefield; so close together that it was almost impossible to walk without stepping on them. I could not command my feeling enough to speak, but thoughts crowded upon me. Oh, if the authors of this cruel and unnatural war could but see what I saw there, they would try and put a stop to it! To think, that it is man who is working all this woe upon his fellow man. What can be in the minds of our enemies, who are now arrayed against us who have never

harmed them in any way, but simply claim our own and nothing more! May God forgive them, for surely they know not what they do.

This was no time for recrimination; there was work to do, so I went at it to do what I could. If I were to live a hundred years, I should never forget the poor sufferers' gratitude for every little thing done for them. A little water to drink or the bathing of their wounds seemed to afford them the greatest relief. . . .

April 18. . . . Dr. Smith has taken charge of this hospital. I think that there will be a different order of things now. He is having the house and yard well cleaned. Before this, it was common to have amputated limbs thrown into the yard and left there. . . .

April 23. A young man whom I have been attending is going to have his arm cut off. Poor fellow! I am doing all I can to cheer him. He says that he knows that he will die, as all who have had limbs amputated in this hospital have died. It is said that the reason is that none but the very worst cases are left here, and they are too far gone to survive the shock which the operation gives the frame. The doctors seem to think that the enemy poisoned their musket balls, as the wounds inflame terribly. Our men do not seem to stand half so much as the Northerners. Many of the doctors are quite despondent about it and think that our men will not be able to endure the hardships of camp life and that we may have to succumb on account of it, but I trust that they are mistaken. None of the prisoners have died; this is a fact that can not be denied, but we have had very few of them in comparison with the number of our own men.

April 24. Mr. Isaac Fuquet, the young man who had his arm cut off, died

These Union nurses were better equipped than their Confederate sisters due to the efforts of the U.S. Sanitary Commission. In addition to providing medical supplies, this civilian organization improved sanitary conditions in army camps to prevent the spread of diseases. Of about 600,000 Civil War deaths, more than half were due to diseases.

today. He lived only a few hours after his amputation. . . .

The amputating table for this ward is at the end of the hall, near the landing of the stairs. When an operation is to be performed, I keep as far away from it as possible. Today, just as they had got through with Mr. Fuquet, I was compelled to pass the place, and the sight I there beheld made me shudder and sick at heart. A stream of blood ran from the table into a tub in which was the arm. It had been taken off at the socket, and the hand, which but a short time before grasped the musket and battled for the right, was hanging over the edge of the tub, a lifeless thing. . . .

"The Whole Landscape Turned Red"

Fighting at Antietam

David Thompson

In the bloodiest single day of the war—September 17, 1862—Union forces scored a technical victory at Antietam Creek near Sharpsburg, Maryland. About 23,000 soldiers were killed or wounded (compared to only 6,000 American casualties on D-Day in World War II). David Thompson, of New York, recalled the intense fighting.

About noon the battle began afresh. This must have been Franklin's men of the Sixth Corps, for the firing was nearer, and they came up behind the center. Suddenly a stir beginning far up on the right, and running like a wave along the line, brought the regiment to its feet. A silence fell on everyone at once, for each felt that the momentous "now" had come. Just as we started I saw, with a little shock, a line-officer take out his watch to note the hour, as though the affair beyond the creek were a business appointment which he was going to keep. . . .

. . . After long waiting, it became noised along the line that we were to take a battery that was at work several hundred yards ahead on the top of a hill. . . .

. . . Now and then a bullet from them cut the air over our heads, but generally they were reserving their fire for that better shot which they knew they would get in a few minutes. The battery, however, whose shots at first went over our heads, had depressed its guns so as to shave the surface of the ground. Its fire was beginning to tell.

I remember looking behind and seeing an officer riding diagonally across the field—a most inviting target—instinctively bending his head down over his horse's neck, as though he were riding through a driving rain. While my eye was on him, I saw between me and him a rolled overcoat with its straps on bound into the air and fall among the furrows. One of the enemy's

Mathew Brady, the most famous photographer of the Civil War, opened an exhibition in late September 1862 entitled "The Dead of Antietam." Included was this photograph of "Bloody Lane," a sunken road where Confederate soldiers had been trapped. Wrote The New York Times *of the exhibit: "Mr. Brady has done something to bring to us the terrible reality and earnestness of the war. If he has not brought bodies and laid them in our dooryards and along [our] streets, he has done something very like it."*

grape-shot had plowed a groove in the skull of a young fellow and had cut his overcoat from his shoulders. He never stirred from his position, but lay there face downward—a dreadful spectacle. A moment after, I heard a man cursing a comrade for lying on him heavily. He was cursing a dying man.

As the range grew better, the firing became more rapid, the situation desperate and exasperating to the last degree. Human nature was on the rack, and there burst forth from it the most vehement, terrible swearing I have ever heard. Certainly the joy of conflict was not ours that day. The suspense was only for a moment, however, for the order to charge came just after. Whether the regiment was thrown into disorder or not, I never knew. I only remember that as we rose and started, all the fire that had been held back so long was loosed.

In a second the air was full of the hiss of bullets and the hurtle of grape-shot. The mental strain was so great that I saw at that moment . . . the whole landscape for an instant turned slightly red. I see again, as I saw it then in a flash, a man just in front of me drop his musket and throw up his hands, stung into vigorous swearing by a bullet behind the ear. Many men fell going up the hill, but it seemed to be all over in a moment, and I found myself passing a hollow where a dozen wounded men lay—among them our sergeant-major, who was calling me to come down. He had caught sight of the blanket rolled across my back, and called me to unroll it and help to carry from the field one of our wounded lieutenants.

When I returned from obeying this summons, the regiment was not to be seen. It had gone in on the run, what there was left of it, and had disappeared in the cornfield about the battery. There was nothing to do but lie there and await developments. Nearly all the men in the hollow were wounded, one man—a recruit named Devlin, I think—frightfully so, his

"What Is All This About?"

Questioning the War

R. M. Collins

A Confederate lieutenant in a later battle voiced sentiments similar to those of Union soldier David Thomas at Antietam.

As we lay there watching the bright stars and listening to the twitter of the little birds in their nests, many a soldier asked himself the questions: What is all this about? Why is it that 200,000 men of one blood and one tongue, believing as one man in the fatherhood of God and the universal brotherhood of man, should in the nineteenth century of the Christian era be thus armed with all the improved appliances of modern warfare and seeking one another's lives? We could settle our differences by compromising and all be at home in ten days.

arm being cut short off. He lived a few minutes only. All were calling for water, of course, but none was to be had.

We lay there till dusk, perhaps an hour, when the fighting ceased. During that hour, while the bullets snipped the leaves from a young locust tree growing at the edge of the hollow and powdered us with the fragments, we had time to speculate on many things—among others, on the impatience with which men clamor, in dull times, to be led into a fight. We heard all through the war that the army "was eager to be led against the enemy." It must have been so, for truthful correspondents said so, and editors confirmed it. But when you came to hunt for this particular itch, it was always the next regiment that had it. The truth is, when bullets are whacking against tree trunks and solid shot are cracking skulls like eggshells, the consuming passion in the breast of the average man is to get out of the way. Between the physical fear of going forward and the moral fear of turning back, there is a predicament of exceptional awkwardness from which a hidden hole in the ground would be a wonderfully welcome outlet.

"Sweet Land of Liberty"

Celebrating the Emancipation Proclamation

Thomas Wentworth Higginson

Preserving the Union, not freeing the slaves, had been President Lincoln's principal goal when the Civil War began. He told abolitionists: "If I could save the Union without freeing any slave, I would do it; if I could save it by freeing all the slaves, I would do it; and if I could save it by freeing some and leaving others alone, I would also do that."

But gradually Lincoln realized that freeing the slaves was a "military necessity" to defeat the South. Lincoln issued his Emancipation Proclamation on September 22, 1862—five days after Antietam. However, it freed only those slaves in Confederate states not under Union control. By this limited measure, Lincoln hoped to keep slaveholding border states loyal to the Union while at the same time crippling the South.

The Emancipation Proclamation took effect on January 1, 1863. Thomas Wentworth Higginson, a white Unitarian minister from an aristocratic Massachusetts family, commanded the Union's First South Carolina Volunteers, an all-black regiment. In his camp diary, Higginson described the regiment's New Year's Day celebration and local slaves' reaction to first hearing the news of freedom.

The services began at half past eleven o'clock, with prayer by our chaplain, Mr. Fowler, who is always, on such occasions, simple, reverential, and impressive. Then the president's proclamation was read by Dr. W. H. Brisbane, a thing infinitely appropriate, a South Carolinian addressing South Carolinians, for he was reared among these very islands and here long since emancipated his own slaves. Then the colors were presented to us by the Rev. Mr. French, a chaplain who brought them from the donors in New York. All this was according to the program.

Then followed an incident so simple, so touching, so utterly unexpected and startling, that I can scarcely believe it on recalling, though it gave the keynote to the whole day. The very moment the speaker had ceased, and just as I took and waved the flag, which now for the first time meant anything to these poor people, there suddenly arose, close beside the platform, a strong male voice (but rather cracked and elderly), into which two women's voices instantly blended, singing, as if by an impulse that could no more be repressed than the morning note of the song-sparrow:

> "My country, 'tis of thee,
> Sweet land of liberty,
> Of thee I sing!"

People looked at each other, and then at us on the platform, to see whence came this interruption not set down in the bills. Firmly and irrepressibly the quavering voices sang on, verse after verse. Others of the colored people joined in; some whites on the platform began, but I motioned them to silence. I never saw anything so electric; it made all other words cheap. It seemed the choked voice of a race at last unloosed. . . . Just think of it! The first day they had ever had a country, the first flag they had ever seen which promised anything to their people. . . .

"Grant Under Fire"

The March Toward Vicksburg

S. H. M. Byers

Union control of the Mississippi River was thwarted by the town of Vicksburg. Situated atop high bluffs along the Mississippi side of the river, this "Gibraltar of the Confederacy" was impregnable to Union naval forces. "Vicksburg is the key," said President Lincoln. "The war can never be brought to a close until the key is in our pocket."

In a bold plan, Grant's troops crossed the river south of the city, abandoning their supply lines, and in May 1863 they won five battles while marching toward Vicksburg. Union corporal S. H. M. Byers observed Grant under fire at one of those battles, Champion's Hill. Grant would eventually be appointed commander of all Union forces in March 1864, after Lincoln had failed in six attempts to find a winning general in the east.

It was a very hot day, and we had marched hard, slept little, and rested none. Among the magnolias on Champion's Hill, the enemy turned on us. We were in that most trying position of soldiers, being fired on without permission to return the shots. . . .

"Colonel, move your men a little by the left flank," said a quiet though commanding voice.

On looking around, I saw immediately behind us Grant, the commander in chief, mounted on a beautiful bay mare and followed by perhaps half a dozen of his staff. For some reason he dismounted, and most of his officers were sent off, bearing orders, to other quarters of the field. It was Grant under fire.

The rattling musketry increased on our front and grew louder, too, on the left flank. Grant had led his horse to the left and thus kept near the company to which I belonged. He now stood leaning complacently against his favorite steed, smoking the stump of a cigar. His was the only horse near the line and must, naturally, have attracted some of the enemy's fire. I am sure everyone who recognized him wished him away, but there he stood—clear, calm, and immovable. I was close enough to see his features. Earnest they were, but sign of inward movement there was none. It was the same cool, calculating face I had seen before; the same careful, half-cynical face I afterward saw busied with affairs of state.

Whatever there may have been in his feelings there was no effort to conceal; there was no pretense, no trick. Whatever that face was, it was natural. A man close by me had the bones of his leg shattered by a ball and was being helped to the rear. His cries of pain attracted Grant's attention, and I noticed the curious though sympathizing shades that crossed his quiet face as the bleeding soldier seemed to look toward him for help. . . .

Grant passed along the lines after the fight as we stood in the narrow roads. Every hat was in the air, and the men cheered till they were hoarse. But speechless and almost without a bow he pushed on past, like an embarrassed man hurrying to get away from some defeat. Once he stopped near the colors and, without addressing himself to anyone in particular, said, "Well done!"

"Surrounded by a Circle of Fire"

Enduring the Siege of Vicksburg

A Union Woman

Union forces could not take Vicksburg directly, so they dug in for a long siege. So did the citizens of Vicksburg. To protect themselves from Union shelling, they dug caves into the hillsides. The siege lasted six weeks, and the residents were reduced to eating rats by the time the city surrendered on July 4, 1863. Vicksburg would not celebrate Independence Day again for almost 100 years. This anonymous Union woman, married to a Vicksburg man, details the terrors of the siege.

May 28. Since that day [May 17] the regular siege has continued. We are utterly cut off from the world, surrounded by a circle of fire. . . . People do nothing but eat what they can get, sleep when they can, and dodge the shells. There are three intervals when the shelling stops, either for the guns to cool or for the gunners' meals, I suppose: about eight in the morning, the same in the evening, and at noon. In that time we have both to prepare and eat ours. Clothing cannot be washed or anything else done. . . .

At all the caves I could see from my high perch, people were sitting, eating their poor suppers at the cave door, ready to plunge in again. As the first shell again flew they dived, and not a human being was visible. The sharp crackle of the musketry firing was a strong contrast to the scream of the bombs. I think all the dogs and cats must be killed or starved: we don't see any more pitiful animals prowling around. . . .

I am so tired of cornbread, which I never liked, that I eat it with tears in my eyes. We are lucky to get a quart of milk daily from a family near who have a cow they hourly expect to be killed. I send five dollars to market each morning, and it buys a small piece of mule meat. Rice and milk is my main food; I can't eat the mule meat. We boil the rice and eat it cold with milk for supper. Martha [her slave] runs the gauntlet to buy the meat and milk once a day in a perfect terror. . . .

July 3. Today we are down in the cellar again, shells flying as thick as ever; provisions so nearly gone, except the hogshead of sugar, that a few more days will bring us to starvation indeed. Martha says rats are hanging dressed in the market for sale with mule meat: there is nothing else. The officer at the battery told me he had eaten one yesterday. . . .

July 4. It is evening. All is still. Silence and night are once more united. . . .

But I must write the history of the last twenty-four hours. . . . When supper was eaten, . . . it was just six, and we crossed the street to the cave opposite. As I crossed, a mighty shell flew screaming right over my head. It was the last thrown in Vicksburg. We lay on our pallets waiting for the expected roar, but no sound came except the chatter from neighboring caves, and at last we dropped asleep. . . . I awoke at dawn stiff. . . . Everyone was expressing surprise at the quiet. We started for home and met the editor of the *Daily Citizen* [the local newspaper, which had been printing on wallpaper]. H. [her husband] said, "This is strangely quiet, Mr. L."

"Ah, sir," shaking his head gloomily, "I'm afraid the last shell has been thrown into Vicksburg."

"Why do you fear so?"

"It is surrender."

94

"An Expression of Sadness I Had Never Before Seen"

Lee After Gettysburg

General John Imboden

When Grant laid siege to Vicksburg, Confederate President Jefferson Davis wanted General Robert E. Lee to send troops to the city's defense. But Lee had another plan. Invade the North, he argued, and Union troops would be forced to respond, easing the pressure on Vicksburg. Davis agreed, and Lee's Army of Northern Virginia headed for Pennsylvania. On July 1, 1863, they met Union forces at Gettysburg. The three-day battle was the bloodiest of the war, with 51,000 casualties.

The climax of the battle came on July 3, when Lee ordered General George Pickett's division to attack the Union lines on Cemetery Ridge. To do so, Pickett's men had to cross a large open area beneath the well-fortified Union positions. More than half of Pickett's 13,000 troops were killed or wounded. Afterwards, the Confederate Army retreated to Virginia, never again to penetrate the North. Lee blamed himself for the defeat and offered to resign, but Jefferson Davis refused. Confederate General John Imboden here describes Lee's suffering in the aftermath of Pickett's Charge.

When night closed the struggle, Lee's army was repulsed. We all knew that the day had gone against us, but the full extent of the disaster was only known in high quarters. The carnage of the day was generally understood to have been frightful. . . . All felt and appreciated the momentous consequences to the cause of Southern independence. . . .

It was a warm summer's night; there were few campfires, and the weary soldiers were lying in the luxuriant grass of the beautiful meadows, discussing the events of the day, speculating on the morrow, or watching that our horses did not straggle off while browsing. About eleven o'clock a horseman came to summon me to General Lee. . . . When we reached the place indicated, a single flickering candle, visible from the road through the open front of a common wall-tent, exposed to view Generals Lee and [A. P.] Hill seated on camp stools with a map spread upon their knees. . . . General Lee directed me to go back to his headquarters and wait for him. I did so, but he did not make his appearance until about one o'clock, when he came riding alone, at a slow walk, and evidently wrapped in profound thought.

When he arrived, there was not even a sentinel on duty at his tent, and no one of his staff was awake. The moon was high in the clear sky, and the silent scene was unusually vivid. As he approached and saw us lying on the grass under a tree, he spoke, reined in his jaded horse, and essayed to dismount. The effort to do so betrayed so much physical exhaustion that I hurriedly rose and stepped forward to assist him, but before I reached his side he had succeeded in alighting, and threw his arm across the saddle to rest, and fixing his eyes upon the ground leaned in silence and almost motionless upon his equally weary horse, the two forming a striking and never-to-be-forgotten group.

The moon shone full upon his massive features and revealed an expression of

"This Iron Rain of Death"

Shelling on Cemetery Hill

Warren Lee Gross

To prepare the way for Pickett's Charge, Confederate artillery bombarded Union positions at Cemetery Hill and Cemetery Ridge. The shelling was so massive that Warren Lee Gross, a Union private, felt that constellations were colliding above him.

We were sheltered behind a stone wall which was struck, splintered, and crushed. The men clung close to the ground, taking advantage of its inequalities for protection.

Right, left, and rear of us, caissons were exploded—scudding fragments of wheels, woodwork, shell, and shot sent a hundred feet into the air like the eruption of a volcano.

Only eighty guns of the Union artillery could be crowded upon the ridge with which to make reply. For an hour and a half, crash followed crash. The enemy used railroad iron and various other missiles besides the ordinary ones. Shells from the Wentworth guns came with a humming sound like a spinning wheel in motion. Some of the shot shrieked and hissed; some whistled; some came with muffled growl; some with howls like rushing, circling winds. Some spat and sputtered; others uttered unearthly groans or hoarsely howled their mission of death. Holes like graves were gouged in the earth by exploding shells. The flowers in bloom upon the graves at the cemetery were shot away. Tombs and monuments were knocked to pieces, and ordinary gravestones shattered in rows.

If a constellation of meteoric worlds had exploded above our heads, it would have scarcely been more terrible than this iron rain of death furiously hurled upon us. Over all these sounds were heard the shrieks and groans of the wounded and dying. The uproar of the day previous seemed silence when compared to this inferno.

sadness that I had never before seen on his face. Awed by his appearance I waited for him to speak until the silence became embarrassing, when, to break it and change the silent current of his thoughts, I ventured to remark, in a sympathetic tone, and in allusion to his great fatigue: "General, this has been a hard day on you."

He looked up, and replied mournfully, "Yes, it has been a sad, sad day to us," and immediately relapsed into his thoughtful mood and attitude. Being unwilling to intrude upon his reflections, I said no more. After perhaps a minute or two, he suddenly straightened up to his full height, and turning to me with more animation and excitement of manner than I had seen in him before, for he was a man of wonderful equanimity, he said in a voice tremulous with emotion:

"I never saw troops behave more magnificently than Pickett's division of Virginians did today in that grand charge upon the enemy. And if they had been supported as they were to have been— but, for some reason not yet fully explained to me, were not—we would have held the position and the day would have been ours." After a moment's pause he added in a loud voice, in a tone almost of agony, "Too bad! *Too bad! Oh! Too bad!*"

I shall never forget his language, his manner, and his appearance of mental suffering.

96

"Northern Rebels Help Southern Ones"

Witnessing the New York City Draft Riots

Anna Dickinson

In the summer of 1863, President Lincoln issued a call for troops under the first federal draft law, which had been passed by Congress in March. Included in the draft pool were all men between the ages of 20 and 45, and those inducted had to serve three years. However, the law favored the rich because any man who could afford a $300 "commutation fee" or could hire a substitute was exempt.

In northern cities, Irish immigrants particularly objected to the law. They competed with blacks for low-paying jobs and resented fighting for their rivals' freedom. On July 12, 1863, the names of the first draftees in New York City appeared in the newspapers beside the lists of soldiers killed at Gettysburg. On July 13, a three-day riot began that focused its violence on blacks. Anna Dickinson, an antislavery writer, watched in horror as her city burned.

On the morning of Monday, the thirteenth of July [1863], began this outbreak, unparalleled in atrocities by anything in American history and equaled only by the horrors of the worst days of the French Revolution. Gangs of men and boys, composed of railroad employees, workers in machine shops, and a vast crowd of those who lived by preying upon others, thieves, pimps, professional ruffians, the scum of the city, jailbirds, or those who were running with swift feet to enter the prison doors, began to gather on the corners and in streets and alleys where they lived. . . .

A body of these, five or six hundred strong, gathered about one of the enrolling offices in the upper part of the city, where the draft was quietly proceeding, and opened the assault upon it by a shower of clubs, bricks, and paving stones torn from the streets, following it up by a furious rush into the office. Lists, records, books, the drafting wheel, every article of furniture or work in the room was rent in pieces and strewn about the floor or flung into the streets. . . .

. . . And then, finding every portable article destroyed—their thirst for ruin growing by the little drink it had had—and

believing, or rather hoping, that the officers had taken refuge in the upper rooms, set fire to the house, and stood watching the slow and steady lift of flames, filling the air with demoniac shrieks and yells, while they waited for the prey to escape from some door or window, from the merciless fire to their merciless hands. . . .

. . . With difficulty and pain the inoffensive tenants escaped from the rapidly spreading fire, which, having devoured the house originally lighted, swept across the neighboring buildings till the whole block stood a mass of burning flames. The firemen came up tardily and reluctantly, many of them of the same class as the miscreants who surrounded them and who cheered at their approach, but either made no attempt to perform their duty or so feeble and farcical a one as to bring disgrace upon a service they so generally honor and ennoble. . . .

The work was begun, continued, gathering in force and fury as the day wore on. Police stations, enrolling offices, rooms or buildings used in any way by government authority or obnoxious as representing the dignity of law, were gutted, destroyed, then left to the mercy of the flames. . . . Before night fell it was no

"A Hundred Thousand Colored Troops"

The Attack on Fort Wagner

Lewis Douglass

On July 18, 1863, only three days after the New York draft riots ended, the all-black Massachusetts Fifty-Fourth Regiment attacked Fort Wagner, South Carolina. More than 40 percent of the 600 men fell in battle, including their white commander, Colonel

By 1865, one out of ten Union soldiers was black.

Robert Gould Shaw. Their bravery paved the way for other black troops, and by the war's end 185,000 black men—most of the men former slaves—had joined the Union Army. However, these men received less pay, food, and medical attention than their white counterparts. Lewis Douglass, a soldier in the Fifty-Fourth and son of famed abolitionist Frederick Douglass, described the battle at Fort Wagner in a letter to his fiancée.

My Dear Amelia:

I have been in two fights and am unhurt. I am about to go in another, I believe, tonight. Our men fought well on both occasions. The last was desperate—we charged that terrible battery on Morris Island known as Fort Wagner and were repulsed with a loss of [many] killed and wounded. I escaped unhurt from amidst that perfect hail of shot and shell. It was terrible. . . . Should I fall in the next fight killed or wounded, I hope to fall with my face to the foe. . . .

My regiment has established its reputation as a fighting regiment—not a man flinched, though it was a trying time. Men fell all around me. A shell would explode and clear a space of twenty feet. Our men would close up again, but it was no use; we had to retreat, which was a very hazardous undertaking. How I got out of that fight alive I cannot tell, but I am here. My dear girl, I hope again to see you. I must bid you farewell should I be killed. Remember, if I die, I die in a good cause. I wish we had a hundred thousand colored troops—we would put an end to this war.

others, with clubs and weapons in their hands, prowling round apparently with no definite atrocity to perpetrate, but ready for any iniquity that might offer, and, by way of pastime, chasing every stray police officer or solitary soldier or inoffensive Negro who crossed the line of their vision. These three objects—the badge of a defender of the law, the uniform of the Union army, the skin of a helpless and outraged race—acted upon these madmen as water acts upon a rabid dog.

Late in the afternoon a crowd which could have numbered not less than ten thousand, the majority of whom were ragged, frowzy, drunken women, gathered about the Orphan Asylum for Colored Children—a large and beautiful building and one of the most admirable and noble charities of the city. When it became evident from the menacing cries and groans of the multitude that danger, if not destruction, was meditated to the harmless and inoffensive inmates, a flag of truce appeared, and an appeal was made in their behalf by the principal to every sentiment of humanity which these beings might possess—a vain appeal! . . .

longer one vast crowd collected in a single section, but great numbers of gatherings, scattered over the whole length and breadth of the city, some of them engaged in actual work of demolition and ruin,

Then on the front of the steps, in the midst of these drunken and infuriated thousands, [the fire department chief] stood up and besought them, if they cared nothing for themselves nor for those hapless orphans, that they would not bring lasting disgrace upon the city by destroying one of its noblest charities, which had for its object nothing but good.

He was answered on all sides by yells and execrations and frenzied shrieks of "Down with the nagurs!" coupled with every oath and every curse that malignant hate of the blacks could devise and drunken Irish tongues could speak. It had been decreed that this building was to be razed to the ground. The house was fired in a thousand places, and in less than two hours the walls crashed in, a mass of smoking, blackened ruins, whilst the children wandered through the streets, a prey to beings who were wild beasts in everything save the superior ingenuity of man to agonize and torture his victims. . . .

The next morning's sun rose on a city which was ruled by a reign of terror. Had the police possessed the heads of Hydra . . .

they would have been powerless against the multitude of opposers. . . . The mayor, seeing that civil power was helpless to stem this tide, desired to call the military to his aid and place the city under martial law, but was opposed by the governor—a governor who, but a few days before, had pronounced the war a failure and not only predicted but encouraged this mob rule. . . .

It was absurd and futile to characterize this new reign of terror as anything but an effort on the part of Northern rebels to help Southern ones at the most critical moment of the war, with the state militia and available troops absent in a neighboring commonwealth and the loyal people unprepared. These editors and their coadjutors, men of brains and ability, were of that most poisonous growth—traitors to the government and the flag of their country—renegade Americans.

"Rich Man's War, Poor Man's Fight"

Conscription in the Confederate Army

Private Sam Watkins

In April 1862, the Confederate Congress passed the first national draft in American history—preceding Union conscription by almost a year. Private Sam Watkins, a soldier in the First Tennessee Regiment, recalled the impact of the draft on Confederate morale in a memoir written after the war.

The histories of the Lost Cause are all written out by "big bugs," generals and renowned historians, and like the fellow who called a turtle a "cooter," being told that no such word as cooter was in Webster's dictionary, remarked that he had as much right to make a dictionary as Mr. Webster or any other man, so have I to write a history.

But in these pages I do not pretend to write the history of the war. I only give a few sketches and incidents that came under the observation of a "high private" in the rear ranks of the rebel army. Of

course, the histories are all correct. They tell of great achievements of great men, who wear the laurels of victory, have grand presents given them, high positions in civil life, presidents of corporations, governors of states, official positions, etc., and when they die, long obituaries are published telling their many virtues, their distinguished victories, etc., and when they are buried, the whole country goes in mourning and is called upon to buy an elegant monument to erect over the remains of so distinguished and brave a general, etc. But in the following pages I propose to tell

"Our Son Is Not More Dear to Us"

Robert Lincoln Goes to War

Elizabeth Keckley

Elizabeth Keckley, a black seamstress and personal maid to Mary Todd Lincoln, saw the most intimate aspects of life inside the White House. She witnessed President Lincoln's grief at the death of his young son, Willie, as well as his insistence that his older son, Robert, should not be spared the wartime fate of other mothers' sons—like Keckley's own.

I never saw a man so bowed down with grief. . . . Great sobs choked his utterance. He buried his head in his hands, and his tall frame was convulsed with emotion. I stood at the foot of the bed, my eyes full of tears, looking at the man in silent, awe-stricken wonder. . . . I did not dream that his rugged nature could be so moved. . . .

Previous to this I had lost my son. . . . [H]e went to the battlefield with the three-months troops and was killed in Missouri. . . . It was a sad blow to me, and the kind womanly letter that Mrs. Lincoln wrote to me when she heard of my bereavement was full of golden words of comfort. . . .

Robert would come home every few months, bringing new joy to the family circle. He was very anxious to quit school and enter the army, but the move was sternly opposed by his mother.

"We have lost one son, and his loss is as much as I can bear, without being called upon to make another sacrifice," she would say when the subject was under discussion.

"But many a poor mother has given up all her sons," mildly suggested Mr. Lincoln, "and our son is not more dear to us than the sons of other people are to their mothers."

"That may be, but I cannot bear to have Robert exposed to danger. His services are not required in the field, and the sacrifice would be a needless one."

"The services of every man who loves his country are required in this war. You should take a liberal instead of a selfish view of the question, mother."

Argument at last prevailed, and permission was granted Robert to enter the army.

battle, which always disorganizes an army, what wonder is it that some men had to be shot merely for discipline's sake? And what wonder that General [Braxton] Bragg's name became a terror to deserters and evil doers? Men were shot by scores, and no wonder the army had to be reorganized. Soldiers had enlisted for twelve months only and had faithfully complied with their volunteer obligations; the terms for which they had enlisted had expired, and they naturally looked upon it that they had a right to go home. They had done their duty faithfully and well. They wanted to see their families; in fact, wanted to go home anyhow. War had become a reality; they were tired of it. A law had been passed by the Confederate States Congress called the conscript act. A soldier had no right to volunteer. . . . He was conscripted.

From this time on 'til the end of the war, a soldier was simply a machine, a conscript. It was mighty rough on rebels. We cursed the war, we cursed Bragg, we cursed the Southern Confederacy. All our pride and valor had gone, and we were sick of war and the Southern Confederacy.

A law was made by the Confederate States Congress about this time allowing

of the fellows who did the shooting and killing, the fortifying and ditching, the sweeping of the streets, the drilling, the standing guard, picket and vedette, and who drew (or were to draw) eleven dollars per month and rations, and also drew the ramrod and tore the cartridge. . . .

. . . [A]fter our lax discipline on the road to and from Virginia, and after a big every person who owned twenty Negroes to go home. It gave us the blues; we wanted twenty Negroes. Negro property suddenly became very valuable, and there was raised the howl of "rich man's war, poor man's fight." The glory of the war, the glory of the South, the glory and the pride of our volunteers had no charms for the conscript. . . .

Their last hope had set. They hated war. To their minds the South was a great tyrant, and the Confederacy a fraud. They were deserting by thousands. They had no love or respect for General Bragg. When men were to be shot or whipped, the whole army was marched to the horrid scene to see a poor trembling wretch tied to a post and a platoon of twelve men drawn up in line to put him to death, and the hushed command of "Ready, aim, fire!" would make the soldier, or conscript, I should say, loathe the very name of Southern Confederacy.

And when some miserable wretch was to be whipped and branded for being absent ten days without leave, we had to see him kneel down and have his head shaved smooth and slick as a peeled onion, and then stripped to the naked skin. Then a strapping fellow with a big rawhide would make the blood flow and spurt at every lick, the wretch begging and howling like a hound, and then he was branded with a red hot iron with the letter D on both hips, when he was marched through the army to the music of the "Rogue's March." It was enough. None of General Bragg's soldiers ever loved him.

"I Should Like to Hang a Yankee Myself"

Sherman's March Through Georgia

Eliza Andrews

The Union mounted two great offensives in 1864. In the East, Grant launched an all-out attack to force Lee's surrender in Virginia. In the West, General William Tecumseh Sherman marched from Tennessee into Georgia, capturing Atlanta on September 2. His victory ensured President Lincoln's reelection in November.

Sherman then undertook a "march to the sea," cutting a wide swath of destruction from Atlanta to Savannah designed to bring the war home to civilians. "We cannot change the hearts of these people of the South," said Sherman, "but we can make war so terrible . . . and make them so sick of war that generations [will] pass away before they again appeal to it." In her wartime diary, Eliza Andrews recorded Sherman's impact on her state.

December 24, 1864. About three miles from Sparta we struck the "burnt country," as it is well named by the natives, and then I could better understand the wrath and desperation of these poor people. I almost felt as if I should like to hang a Yankee myself. There was hardly a fence left standing all the way from Sparta to Gordon. The fields were trampled down and the road was lined with carcasses of horses, hogs, and cattle that the invaders, unable either to consume or to carry away with them, had wantonly shot down to starve out the people and prevent them from making their crops. The stench in some places was unbearable; every few hundred yards we had to hold our noses or stop them with cologne Mrs. Elzey had given us, and it proved a great boon. The dwellings that

were standing all showed signs of pillage, and on every plantation we saw the charred remains of the ginhouse and packing screw, while here and there lone chimney stacks, "Sherman's sentinels," told of homes laid in ashes.

The infamous wretches! I couldn't wonder now that these poor people should want to put a rope round the neck of every red-handed "devil of them" they could lay their hands on. Hayricks and fodder stacks were demolished, corncribs were empty, and every bale of cotton that could be found was burned by the savages. I saw no grain of any sort except little patches they had spilled when feeding their horses and which there was not even a chicken left in the country to eat. A bag of oats might have lain anywhere along the road without danger from the beasts of the field, though I cannot say it would have been safe from the assaults of hungry men.

Crowds of soldiers were tramping over the road in both directions; it was like traveling through the streets of a populous town all day. They were mostly on foot, and I saw numbers seated on the roadside greedily eating raw turnips, meat skins, parched corn—anything they could find, even picking up the loose grains that Sherman's horses had left. . . .

Before crossing the Oconee at Milledgeville, we ascended an immense hill from which there was a fine view of the town, with Governor Brown's fortifications in the foreground and the river rolling at our feet. The Yankees had burned the bridge, so we had to cross on a ferry. There was a long train of vehicles ahead of us, and it was nearly an hour before our turn came, so we had ample time to look about us.

On our left was a field where thirty thousand Yankees had camped hardly three weeks before. It was strewn with the debris they had left behind, and the poor people of the neighborhood were wandering over it, seeking for anything they could find to eat, even picking up grains of corn that were scattered around where the Yankees had fed their horses. We were told that a great many valuables were found there at first, plunder that the invaders had left behind, but the place had been picked over so often by this time that little now remained except tufts of loose cotton, piles of half-rotted grain, and the carcasses of slaughtered animals, which raised a horrible stench. Some men were plowing in one part of the field, making ready for next year's crop.

"My Heart Aches for the Poor Wretches"

Union Prisoners Suffer at Andersonville

Eliza Andrews

Neither side was prepared to deal with prisoners of war. Union and Confederate forces routinely exchanged prisoners until 1863 when Grant realized that the South had more to gain by the process. The most notorious Confederate prison was an open stockade at Andersonville, Georgia, where about one-third of all prisoners died. Eliza Andrews's tour of the prison in January 1865 softened her hard feelings toward Yankees.

102

Although matters have improved somewhat with the cool weather, the tales that are told of the condition of things there last summer are appalling. Mrs. Brisbane heard all about it from Father Hamilton, a Roman Catholic priest from Macon who has been working like a good Samaritan in those dens of filth and misery. It is a shame to us Protestants that we have let a Roman Catholic get so far ahead of us in this work of charity and mercy. Mrs. Brisbane says Father Hamilton told her that during the summer the wretched prisoners burrowed in the ground like moles to protect themselves from the sun. It was not safe to give them material to build shanties as they might use it for clubs to overcome the guard. These underground huts, he said, were alive with vermin and stank like charnel houses [funeral vaults].

Many of the prisoners were stark naked, having not so much as a shirt to their backs. He told a pitiful story of a Pole who had no garment but a shirt, and to make it cover him better, he put his legs into the sleeves and tied the tail around his neck. The others guyed him so on his appearance, and the poor wretch was so disheartened by suffering, that one day he deliberately stepped over the dead line and stood there 'til the guard was forced to shoot him. But what I can't understand is that a Pole, of all people in the world, should come over here and try to take away our liberty when his own country is in the hands of oppressors. One would think that the Poles, of all nations in the world, ought to sympathize with a people fighting for their liberties.

Father Hamilton said that at one time the prisoners died at the rate of a hundred and fifty a day, and he saw some of them die on the ground without a rag to lie on or a garment to cover them. Dysentery was the most fatal disease, and as they lay on the ground in their own excrements, the smell was so horrible that the good father says he was often obliged to rush from their presence to get a breath of pure air. It is dreadful.

My heart aches for the poor wretches, Yankees though they are, and I am afraid God will suffer some terrible retribution to fall upon us for letting such things happen. If the Yankees ever should come to southwest Georgia and go to Andersonville and see the graves there, God have mercy on the land! And yet what can we do? The Yankees themselves are really more to blame than we, for they won't exchange these prisoners, and our poor, hard-pressed Confederacy has not the means to provide for them when our own soldiers are starving in the field. Oh, what a horrible thing war is when stripped of all its pomp and circumstance!

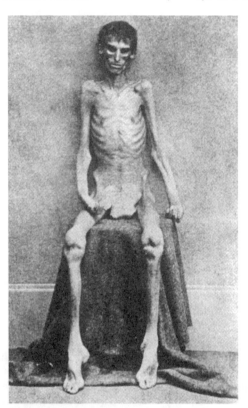

This photograph of a Union prisoner of war from Belle Isle, the Confederate prison at Richmond, demonstrates the horrific conditions many prisoners endured.

"I Accept These Terms"

Lee Surrenders

Colonel Charles Marshall

In mid-1864, Grant managed to trap Lee at Petersburg, Virginia, a rail center south of the Confederate capital at Richmond. From June 1864 to April 1865, Grant laid siege to Petersburg. On April 2, 1865, both Petersburg and Richmond fell. Lee retreated to the west, but Grant cut off his escape. On April 9, Lee surrendered to Grant at Appomattox Courthouse, Virginia. Colonel Charles Marshall, an aide to Lee, witnessed the event.

We struck up the hill towards Appomattox Courthouse. There was a man named McLean who used to live on the first battlefield of Manassas, at a house about a mile from Manassas Junction. He didn't like the war, and having seen the first battle of Manassas, he thought he would get away where there wouldn't be any more fighting, so he moved down to Appomattox Courthouse. General Lee told me to go forward and find a house where he could meet General Grant, and of all people, whom should I meet but McLean. I rode up to him and said, "Can you show me a house where General Lee and General Grant can meet together?" He took me into a house that was all dilapidated and that had no furniture in it. I told him it wouldn't do.

Then he said, "Maybe my house will do!" He lived in a very comfortable house, and I told him I thought that would suit. I had taken the orderly along with me, and I sent him back to bring General Lee and [Colonel] Babcock, who were coming on behind. I went into the house and sat down, and after a while General Lee and Babcock came in. Colonel Babcock told his orderly that he was to meet General Grant, who was coming on the road, and turn him in when he came along. So General Lee, Babcock, and myself sat down in McLean's parlor and talked in the most friendly and affable way.

In about half an hour we heard horses, and the first thing I knew General Grant walked into the room. There were with him General Sheridan, General Ord, Colonel Badeau, General Porter, Colonel Parker, and quite a number of other officers whose names I do not recall.

General Lee was standing at the end of the room opposite the door when General Grant walked in. General Grant had on a sack coat, a loose fatigue coat, but he had no side arms. He looked as though he had had a pretty hard time. He had been riding and his clothes were somewhat dusty and a little soiled. He walked up to General Lee, and Lee recognized him at once. He had known him in the Mexican War. General Grant greeted him in the most cordial manner and talked about the weather and other things in a very friendly way. Then General Grant brought up his officers and introduced them to General Lee.

I remember that General Lee asked for General Lawrence Williams, of the Army of the Potomac. That very morning General Williams had sent word by somebody to General Lee that Custis Lee, who had been captured at Sailor Creek and was reported killed, was not hurt, and General Lee asked General Grant where General Williams was, and if he could not send for him to come and see him. General Grant sent somebody out for General Williams, and when he came, General Lee thanked him for having sent him word about the safety of his son.

After a very free talk General Lee said to General Grant: "General, I have come to meet you in accordance with my letter to you this morning to treat about the surrender of my army, and I think the best way would be for you to put your terms in writing."

General Grant said: "Yes, I believe it will."

So a Colonel Parker, General Grant's Aide-de-Camp, brought a little table over from a corner of the room, and General Grant wrote the terms and conditions of surrender on what we call field note paper—that is, a paper that makes a copy at the same time as the note is written. After he had written it, he took it over to General Lee.

General Lee was sitting at the side of the room; he rose and went to meet General Grant to take that paper and read it over. When he came to the part in which only public property was to be surrendered, and the officers were to retain their side arms and personal baggage, General Lee said: "That will have a very happy effect."

General Lee then said to General Grant: "General, our cavalrymen furnish their own horses; they are not government horses. Some of them may be, but of course you will find them out—any property that is public property, you will ascertain that, but it is nearly all private property, and these men will want to plough ground and plant corn."

General Grant answered that as the terms were written, only the officers were permitted to take their private property, but almost immediately he added that he supposed that most of the men in the ranks were small farmers, and that the United States did not want their horses.

He would give orders to allow every man who claimed to own a horse or mule to take the animal home.

General Lee having again said that this would have an excellent effect, once more looked over the letter, and being satisfied with it, told me to write a reply. General Grant told Colonel Parker to copy his letter, which was written in pencil, and put it in ink. Colonel Parker took the table and carried it back to a corner of the room, leaving General Grant and General Lee facing each other and talking together. . . .

After a while Colonel Parker got through with his copy of General Grant's letter, and I sat down to write a reply. I began it in the usual way: "I have the honor to acknowledge the receipt of your letter of such a date," and then went on to say the terms were satisfactory.

I took the letter over to General Lee, and he read it and said: "Don't say 'I have the honor to acknowledge the receipt of your letter of such a date'; he is here. Just say, 'I accept these terms.'" . . .

Then General Grant signed his letter, and I turned over my letter to General Lee and he signed it. Parker handed me General Grant's letter, and I handed him General Lee's reply, and the surrender was accomplished. There was no theatrical display about it. It was in itself perhaps the greatest tragedy that ever occurred in the history of the world, but it was the simplest, plainest, and most thoroughly devoid of any attempt at effect that you can imagine. . . .

"The Giant Sufferer"

Keeping Vigil at Lincoln's Deathbed

Gideon Welles

President and Mrs. Lincoln celebrated the Union victory by attending Ford's Theater on April 14, 1865—Good Friday. John Wilkes Booth, an alcoholic actor and Southern sympathizer, entered the president's box and shot him in the back of the head. Lincoln was taken across the street to a

boarding house, where he died on April 15—the first American president to be assassinated. Secretary of the Navy Gideon Welles was present at Lincoln's deathbed.

Six weeks earlier on March 4, Lincoln had argued in his Second Inaugural Address for a policy to end the war "with malice towards none, with charity for all." But with Lincoln died the South's hopes for a merciful peace.

The president had been carried across the street from the theater to the house of a Mr. Peterson. We entered by ascending a flight of steps above the basement and passing through a long hall to the rear, where the president lay extended on a bed, breathing heavily. Several surgeons were present—at least six, I should think more. Among them I was glad to observe Dr. Hall, who, however, soon left. I inquired of Dr. H., as I entered, the true condition of the president. He replied the president was dead to all intents, although he might live three hours or perhaps longer.

The giant sufferer lay extended diagonally across the bed, which was not long enough for him. He had been stripped of his clothes. His large arms, which were occasionally exposed, were of a size which one would scarce have expected from his spare appearance. His slow, full respiration lifted the clothes with each breath that he took. His features were calm and striking. I had never seen them appear to better advantage than for the first hour, perhaps, that I was there. After that, his right eye began to swell and that part of his face became discolored.

. . . A double guard was stationed at the door and on the sidewalk to repress the crowd, which was of course highly excited and anxious. The room was small and overcrowded. The surgeons and members of the Cabinet were as many as should have been in the room, but there were many more, and the hall and other rooms in the front or main house were full. One of these rooms was occupied by Mrs. Lincoln and her attendants. . . . About once an hour Mrs. Lincoln would repair to the bedside of her dying husband and with lamentation and tears remain until overcome by emotion.

April 15. A door which opened upon a porch or gallery, and also the windows, were kept open for fresh air. The night was dark, cloudy, and damp, and about six it began to rain. I remained in the room until then without sitting or leaving it, when, there being a vacant chair which someone left at the foot of the bed, I occupied it for nearly two hours, listening to the heavy groans and witnessing the wasting life of the good and great man who was expiring before me.

About six a.m. I experienced a feeling of faintness and for the first time after entering the room, a little past eleven, I left it and the house and took a short walk in the open air. It was a dark and gloomy morning, and rain set in before I returned to the house, some fifteen minutes [later]. Large groups of people were gathered every few rods, all anxious and solicitous. Some one or more from each group stepped forward as I passed to inquire into the condition of the president and to ask if there was no hope. Intense grief was on every countenance when I replied that the president could survive but a short time. The colored people especially—and there were at this time more of them, perhaps, than of whites—were overwhelmed with grief. . . .

A little before seven, I went into the room where the dying president was rapidly drawing near the closing moments. His wife soon after made her last visit to him. The death-struggle had begun. Robert, his son, stood with several others at the head of the bed. He bore himself well, but on two occasions gave way to overpowering grief and sobbed aloud, turning his head and leaning on the shoulder of Senator Sumner. The respiration of the president became suspended at intervals, and at last entirely ceased at twenty-two minutes past seven. . . .

President Lincoln insisted that work on the unfinished dome of the U.S. Capitol not be suspended during the war. "I take it as a sign that the Union will continue," he said. The dome was completed in time for Lincoln's second inauguration on March 4, 1865.

I went after breakfast to the Executive Mansion. There was a cheerless cold rain, and everything seemed gloomy. On the avenue in front of the White House were several hundred colored people, mostly women and children, weeping and wailing their loss. This crowd did not appear to diminish through the whole of that cold, wet day. They seemed not to know what was to be their fate since their great benefactor was dead, and their hopeless grief affected me more than almost anything else, though strong and brave men wept when I met them.

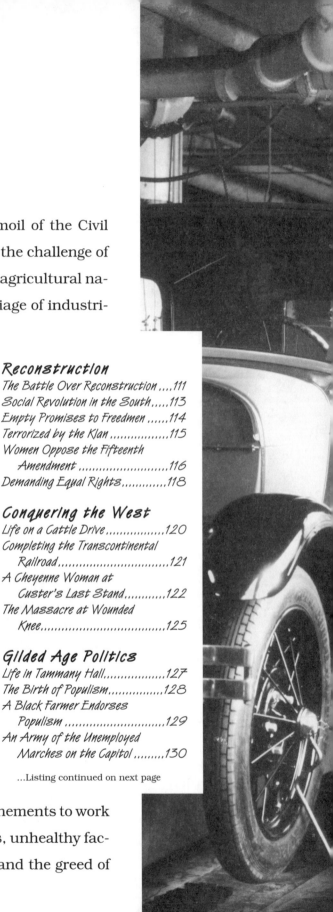

Industrializing America

❦ After the turmoil of the Civil War and Reconstruction, Americans took up the challenge of transforming the United States from a rural, agricultural nation to an urban, industrial giant. The marriage of industrialization and urbanization in the late nineteenth century affected every group in American society—for better *and* for worse. Industrialization gave farmers machinery and a national transportation system, while urbanization created new markets. Factories employed immigrants who poured into the United States. Inventors and entrepreneurs became millionaires, often returning their wealth to their communities through endowments for libraries, universities, and parks. ❦ Yet along with new opportunities came new hardships. Farmers and merchants were at the mercy of powerful railroad companies that set high shipping rates. Workers lost control of their daily tasks as mass production demanded increasing division of labor. Immigrants left dark, rat-infested tenements to work ten hours a day, six days a week in dangerous, unhealthy factories. The instability of the business cycle and the greed of

...Listing continued on next page

"robber barons" and enormous corporate trusts drove many smaller entrepreneurs out of business. As the power of corporations grew, so did their use of bribery and graft to influence politicians. ❦ By the 1890s, the problems accompanying industrialization and urbanization brought cries of outrage from all levels of American society. Farmers' alliances, workers' unions, and middle-class reform organizations all demanded that the government intervene to protect Americans from the abuses of corporations and the harshness of city life. In the early twentieth century, government began to accept more responsibility for regulating business and ensuring the welfare of its citizens. ❦ By 1900, the United States led the world in industrial production. American economic power gave the nation more influence in world politics, as the United States acquired overseas colonies to provide markets and raw materials for its industry. In 1917, the United States entered World War I to "make the world safe for democracy." But to many people—including African Americans, women, and workers—America itself had to be made safe for democracy first.

"A President Was on Trial"

The Battle Over Reconstruction

William H. Crook

Even before Abraham Lincoln's death, the president and Congress struggled over which one had ultimate control of the reconstruction of the Confederate states—that is, their readmission to the Union. The struggle intensified between Lincoln's successor, Andrew Johnson from Tennessee, who was conciliatory to the South, and the Radical Republicans in Congress, who were more punitive. Johnson attempted to readmit southern states without congressional approval, but Congress refused to seat their representatives and senators.

In March 1867, Congress passed the Reconstruction Act over Johnson's veto. The act divided the South into military districts and required states seeking readmission to ratify the Fourteenth Amendment, which gave former slaves citizenship. Fearing that Johnson would try to thwart its reconstruction program, Congress also passed the Tenure of Office Act, which prohibited the president from firing without senatorial approval officials who had been confirmed by the Senate. When Johnson nonetheless dismissed Secretary of War Edwin Stanton, who supported the congressional plan for a military reconstruction, the House of Representatives voted in February 1868 to impeach the president. William H. Crook, Johnson's bodyguard, witnessed the president's trial, which began on March 23.

When, from my seat in the gallery, I looked down on the Senate chamber, I had a moment of almost terror. It was not because of the great assemblage; it was rather in the thought that one could feel in the mind of every man and woman there that for the first time in the history of the United States a president was on trial for more than his life—his place in the judgment of his countrymen and of history. . . .

The trial lasted three weeks. The president, of course, never appeared. In that particular, the proceedings lacked a spectacular interest they might have had. Every day the president had a consultation with his lawyers. For the rest, he attended to the routine work of his position. He was absolutely calm through it all. The very night of the 23rd he gave a reception to as many of the members of Congress as would come. I was fully prepared to have the White House deserted, but instead of that it was crowded. I wondered why men who hated the president so bitterly could accept his hospitality until I came to a group of about fifteen Radicals gathered together in the East Room, where they had proceeded after paying their respects to the president. They were laughing together and teasing one another like boys.

"What are you here for?" I heard.

"And you—what are you doing here yourself?"

"Why I wanted to see how Andy takes it" was the answer. I thought to myself as I passed them that they were getting small satisfaction out of that, for no one could have seen the slightest difference in Mr. Johnson's manner. He greeted everyone as pleasantly as though it were a surprise party to congratulate him on his statesmanship. . . .

. . . [W]hile the legal lights argued, the enemies of the president were working in other ways. The Senate was thoroughly canvassed; personal argument and influence were in constant use. Every personal motive, good or bad, was played upon. Long before the final ballot, it became known how most men would probably vote. Toward the end, the doubtful ones had narrowed down to one man—Senator Ross of Kansas. Kansas, which had been the fighting-ground of rebel guerrilla and Northern abolitionist, was to have in all probability the determining vote in this contest.

Kansas was, from inception and history, abolitionist, radical. It would have been supposed that Senator Ross would vote with the Radicals. He had taken the place of James H. Lane, who had shot himself. Lane was a friend of the president, and, had he lived, in all probability would have supported him. But Ross had no such motive. It became known that he was doubtful; it was charged that he had been subject to personal influence—feminine influence.

Then the cohorts of the Senate and the House bore down upon the senator from Kansas. Party discipline was brought to bear, and then ridicule. Either from uncertainty, or policy, or a desire to keep his associates in uncertainty, Ross refused to make an announcement of his policy. In all probability he was honestly trying to convince himself. . . .

On May 16th the vote was taken.

Everyone who by any possible means could get a ticket of admission to the Senate chamber produced it early that morning at the Capitol. The floor and galleries were crowded. . . .

While the clerk was reading the legal statement of those crimes of which, in the opinion of the House of Representatives, the president was guilty, some people fidgeted and some sat with their hands tensely clasped together. At the end, the chief justice directed that the roll be called. The clerk called out:

"Mr. Anthony." Mr. Anthony rose.

"Mr. Anthony"—the chief justice fastened his eyes upon the senator—"how say you? Is the respondent, Andrew Johnson, president of the United States, guilty or not guilty of a high misdemeanor as charged in this article?"

"Guilty," answered Mr. Anthony.

A sigh went round the assemblage. Yet Mr. Anthony's vote was not in doubt. A two-thirds vote of thirty-six to eighteen was necessary to convict. Thirty-four of the senators were pledged to vote against the president. Mr. Fowler, of Tennessee, it was known, would probably vote for acquittal, although there was some doubt. Senator Ross was the sphinx; no one knew his position.

The same form was maintained with each senator in turn. When Fowler's name was reached, everyone leaned forward to catch the word.

"Not guilty," said Senator Fowler.

The tension grew. There was a weary number of names before that of Ross was reached. When the clerk called it, and Ross stood forth, the crowd held its breath.

"Not guilty," called the senator from Kansas.

It was like the bubbling over of a caldron. The Radical senators, who had been laboring with Ross only a short time before, turned to him in rage; all over the house people began to stir. The rest of the roll call was listened to with lessened interest, although there was still the chance of a surprise. When it was over and the result—thirty-five to nineteen—was announced, there was a wild outburst, chiefly groans of anger and disappointment, for the friends of the president were in the minority. . . .

I ran all the way from the Capitol to the White House. I was young and strong in those days, and I made good time. When I burst into the library, where the president sat with Secretary Welles and two other men whom I cannot remember, they were quietly talking. Mr. Johnson was seated at a little table on which luncheon had been spread in the rounding southern end of the room. There were no signs of excitement.

"Mr. President," I shouted, too crazy with delight to restrain myself, "you are acquitted!"

All rose. I made my way to the president and got hold of his hand. The other men surrounded him and began to shake his hand. The president responded to their congratulations calmly enough for the moment, and then I saw that tears were rolling down his face.

"The Experiment Is Now To Be Tried"

Social Revolution in the South

Henry W. Ravenel

One of the chief problems of Reconstruction was how to deal with the changed relationships between freed slaves and their former masters. Henry Ravenel, a South Carolina aristocrat, described in his diary during May 1865 the social revolution created by emancipation.

We still remain in doubt as to the emancipation policy. No official announcement except President Lincoln's amnesty proclamation has been published. Military officers, however, in Charleston and Mobile are prescribing in their orders the mode in which the "freed-men" are to work and the terms on which they must be engaged. I think there is no doubt emancipation will be settled policy, but whether immediate or gradual will be decided by Congress. The party in power now are radical abolitionists and will do all in their power to urge it forward. Both policy and humanity would dictate that it should be gradual, so that both parties [in] the South may accommodate themselves to so radical a change in social and political economy. And for the interest of the nation at large, this change should be gradual, and thus avoid the shock to the industrial resources of the country. Fanaticism and reason have nothing in common.

My Negroes have made no change in their behavior and are going on as they have always hitherto done. Until I know that they are legally free, I shall let them continue. If they become free by law, then the whole system must be changed. If the means which I now possess of supporting the old and the young are taken away, they must then necessarily look for their support to their own exertions. How they can support themselves at present I cannot see. Labor is more abundant (from the return of so many soldiers), and food still scarce, and money yet more scarce and difficult to be got. I have three or four of my Negroes who are only working [for] their food. If emancipation prevails, the Negro must become a laborer in the field, as the whites will soon occupy all the domestic and mechanical employments. . . . As General Gillmore's order based upon Chief Justice Chase's opinion [for the U.S. Supreme Court] announces the freedom of the Negroes, there is no further room to doubt that it is the settled policy of the country. I have today formally announced to my Negroes the fact and made such arrangements with each as the new relation rendered necessary. Those whose whole time we need get at present clothes and food, house rent, and medical attendance. The others work for themselves, giving me a portion of their time on the farm in lieu of house rent. Old Amelia and her two grand-children I will spare the mockery of offering freedom to. I must support them as long as I have anything to give.

"Forty Acres and a Mule"

Empty Promises to Freedmen

John G. Pierce

In 1865, Congress created the Freedmen's Bureau, whose purpose was to provide services to former slaves and to manage abandoned lands in the South. A rumor circulated that blacks would receive forty acres and a mule from the Freedmen's Bureau, but proposals for land redistribution were never passed. In testimony to Congress, John G. Pierce described how many former slaves were exploited through such rumors.

I can tell you from what I know and have seen myself, and also from what Negroes have told me, that they have been promised land and mules—forty acres and a mule—on diverse occasions. Many an old Negro has come to me and asked about that thing. I can illustrate it by one little thing that I saw on a visit once to Gainesville, Sumter County [Alabama]. At a barbecue there I saw a man who was making a speech to the Negroes, telling them what good he had done for them, that he had been to Washington City and had procured from one of the departments here certain pegs. I saw the pegs. He had about two dozen on his arm; they were painted red and blue. He said that those pegs he had obtained from here at great expense to himself, that they had been made by the government for the purpose of staking out the Negroes' forty acres. He told the Negroes that all he wanted was to have the expenses paid to him, which was about a dollar a peg. He told them that they could stick one peg down at a corner, then walk so far one way and stick another down, then walk so far another way and stick another down, 'til they had got the four pegs down, and that, when the four pegs were down, the Negroes' forty acres would be included in that area. And all he had to say to them was that they could stick those pegs anywhere they pleased—on anybody's land they wanted to—but not to interfere with each other. And he would advise them, in selecting the forty acres, to take half woodland and half clear, that nobody would dare to interfere with those pegs.

. . . My Negroes all express a desire to remain with me. I am gratified at the proof of their attachment. I believe it to be real and unfeigned. For the present they will remain, but in [the] course of time we must part, as I cannot afford to keep so many, and they cannot afford to hire for what I could give them. As they have always been faithful and attached to us, and have been raised as family servants, and have all of them been in our family for several generations, there is a feeling towards them somewhat like that of a father who is about to send out his children [into] the world to make their way through life.

Those who have brought the present change of relation upon us are ignorant of these ties. They have charged us with cruelty. They call us man stealers, robbers, tyrants. The indignant denial of these charges and the ill feelings engendered during thirty years of angry controversy have culminated at length in the four-year war which has now ended. It has pleased God that we should fail in our efforts for independence—and with the loss of independence, we return to the union under the dominion of the abolitionist sentiment.

The experiment is now to be tried. The Negro is not only to be emancipated, but is to become a citizen with all the rights and privileges! It produces a financial, political, and social revolution [in] the South, fearful to contemplate in its ultimate effects. Whatever the result may be, let it be known and remembered that neither the Negro slave nor his master is responsible. It has been done by those who, having political power, are determined to carry into practice the sentimental philanthropy they have so long and angrily advocated. Now that is fixed. I pray God for the great issues at stake, that he may bless the effort and make it successful—make it a blessing and not a curse to the poor Negro.

"They Have Killed My Poor Grandpappy"

Terrorized by the Klan

Charlotte Fowler

Congress's reconstruction plan required southern states to grant suffrage to black men and to disqualify former Confederate officials from voting or holding office. Many black men were elected to the new state governments created under Reconstruction. But southern secret societies, most notoriously the Ku Klux Klan, used violence to promote white supremacy and to prevent black men from voting. In her 1871 testimony to a congressional committee investigating Klan violence, Charlotte Fowler described the murder of her 70-year-old husband, Wallace Fowler.

Tell how he was killed.

The night he was killed, I was taken sick on Wednesday morning, and I laid on my bed Wednesday and Thursday. I didn't eat a mouthful. I couldn't do it, I was so sick, so he went out working on his farm. We still had a little grandchild living with me—my daughter's child. He had two little children living with him on the farm. . . . He kept coming backward and forward to the house to see how I got on and what he could do for me. I never ate nothing until Thursday night. When he came home, he cooked something for me to eat and said: "Old woman, if you don't eat something you will die." Says I: "I can't eat." Says he: "Then I will eat and feed the little baby." That is the grandchild he meant.

I says: "You take that little child and sleep in the bed; I think I have got the fever, and I don't want you to get it." He said, "No, I don't want to get the fever, for I have got too much to do." He got up and pulled off his clothes and got in bed. He came and called to the grandchild, Tody— she is Sophia—and he says: "Tody, when you are ready to come to bed, come, and grandmother will open your frock, and you can go to bed." So he laid there for about a half an hour, and then I heard the dogs. I was only by myself now, for the children were all abed. Then I got up and went into my room to my bed. I reckon I did not lay in bed a half an hour before I heard somebody by the door. It was not one person, but two—ram! ram! ram! at the door.

Immediately I was going to call him to open the door, but he heard it as quick as lightning, and he said to them: "Gentlemen, do not break the door down; I will open the door." And just as he said that they said: "God damn you, I have got you now." I was awake, and I started and got out of bed and fell down on the floor. I was very much scared. The little child followed its grandfather to the door—you know in the night it is hard to direct a child. When he said, "God damn you, I have got you now," and he said, "Don't you run," and just then I heard the report of a pistol, and they shot him down. And this little child ran back to me before I could get out and says, "Oh, grandma, they have killed my poor grandpappy."

He was such an old gentleman that I thought they just shot over him to scare him, but sure enough, as quick as I got to the door, I raised my right hand and said, "Gentlemen, you have killed a poor, innocent man." My poor old man! Says he, "Shut up." I never saw but two of them; by that time the others had vanished.

How did you know there were any others there?

The little boy that was there when they shot his grandpappy ran into the house. He was there, and when they started I heard the horses' feet going from the gate. I was then a hallooing and screaming. After they shot the old man, they came back in the house—"Chup! Chup! Chup! make up a light." I said, "I am not able to make up a light; I have been sick two days." I called to the little girl, "Is there any light there?" She says, "No." But the mantel was there where I could reach it, where they put the splinters, and I said, "Light that splinter," and she lit the splinter. He said, "Hand it here," and she handed it to him. And then he says, "March before me, march before me." That was done in the middle of my room. He says, "Hand me up your arms"—that is, the guns. Says I, "There isn't any here, sir." Says he, "Hand me up that pistol." I says, "There is none here; the old man had none in slavery and had none in all his freedom, and everybody on the settlement knows it." When he told me about the light he put that pistol up to my face—so—and says, "If you don't come here I will get you light out of this." He did that when I was a poor woman by myself. . . .

Did these men have masks on?
Only the one that shot him.
What kind of a mask?
It was all around the eyes. It was black, and the other part was white and red, and he had horns on his head. He came in the house after he killed the old man and told me about the light, and I made the little girl make a light. He took the light from her and looked over the old man. Another man came out of the gate, and looked down at the old man and dropped a chip of fire on him and burned through his shirt—burned his breast. They had shot him through the head, and every time he breathed his brains would come out. . . .

Was the old man dead when the fire was thrown on him?
He did not die until Friday between one and two o'clock, but he couldn't speak a word. He was just bleeding, and his brains and blood came out over his eyes. . . .
Did your old man belong to any party?
Yes, sir.
What party?
The Radicals.
How long did he belong to them?
Ever since they started the voting.
Was he a pretty strong Radical?
Yes, sir; a pretty strong Radical.
Did he work for that party?
Yes, sir. . . .
Did he vote at the last election?
Yes, sir.

"Asking for a Half Loaf"

Women Oppose the Fifteenth Amendment

Paulina Wright Davis

The Fifteenth Amendment caused a rift in the women's movement because it granted suffrage only to black men and did not include women. The National Woman Suffrage Association, led by Elizabeth Cady Stanton, opposed the amendment. However, the American Woman Suffrage Association, led by Lucy Stone, supported the amendment, hoping thereby to enlist the aid of the Republican party for women's suffrage after Reconstruction was over. In a letter to Stanton, Paulina Wright Davis argued that the Fifteenth Amendment should not be ratified without a proposed Sixteenth Amendment that would give women the right to vote as well.

I feel it a duty to enter my protest with yours against the Fifteenth Amendment. Last winter in Boston, I could only give my vote against it, for no Sixteenth had been proposed. It seemed almost a childish, selfish thing to do, when all the eloquence of a Boston platform was arrayed on the other side, and other women rose and said they were ready to step aside and let the colored man have his rights first. Not one said we will step aside and let the Negro woman (whom I affirm, as I ever have, is better fitted for self-government than the Negro man) have her rights before we press our claim. I could not but think it an easy thing for them to do, never having had the right they demanded. But if they truly believe that it will do for humanity what is claimed for it, I do not see why it should be called magnanimous for a woman to say, I yield to man just what he has always asserted as his, the right to rule.

You have taken a bold stand, and I thank God for it. Though still in the minority, there is hope, for with a radical truth one shall chase a thousand, and two put ten thousand to flight. And ere very long, before another convention, I trust many more will see with us that the Fifteenth Amendment, without the Sixteenth, is a compromise worse by far for the nation than any other ever passed. They could be repealed; this cannot. Once settled, the waves of corruption will swamp our little bark freighted with all humanity, the women of all shades of color and subject to every variety of tyranny and oppression, from the cramped feet of the Chinese to the cramped brains and waists of our own higher order of civilization.

It seems specially strange to those of us who as well remember the motto of the old abolitionists, "immediate and unconditional emancipation," now to hear a half measure advocated. It was that stern principle of justice which attracted and held me in the old organization when those dearest to me went into the Liberty party. I had been trained in that school which taught children that they must do right for right's sake, without hope of reward or fear of punishment, leaving the consequences with the All-Wise Ruler of events. Among the early abolitionists this uncompromising spirit was manifest, and to me it was the real gospel.

I remember well the strong opposition to some who advocated the election of John C. Fremont in 1856, among whom was Frederick Douglass. He was then denounced as a compromiser asking for a half loaf. He still asks for the half loaf, but others who stood firmly then for the whole have now come down to his plane and desire above all things to finish up the antislavery work and have the Negro man out of the way, and so give the Sixteenth Amendment the go-by, claiming manhood suffrage because it is the order of nature that man, however ignorant, debased, and brutal he may be, shall always be first because he always has been, yielding the whole argument to physical force, leaving the Negro woman wholly out of the question, giving her over to the tyranny of the husband, which is nearly, if not quite, equal to that of the master. The antislavery platform still carefully guards itself against the woman question, while on the suffrage platform the Fifteenth Amendment is considered essential.

"Put No Barriers Between Us"

Demanding Equal Rights

R. H. Cain

After the Civil War, many southern states passed black codes restricting the rights of former slaves. Congress passed the Civil Rights Act of 1875 to protect black people from discrimination in privately owned facilities open to the public. R. H. Cain, a black South Carolinian elected to the U.S. House of Representatives, argued passionately on behalf of the bill. However, the Supreme Court declared the act unconstitutional in 1883.

Why not pass the civil rights bill? Are there not 5 million men, women, and children in this country, a larger number than inhabited this country when the fathers made the tea party in Boston harbor, 5 million whose rights are as dear and sacred to them, humble though they be, as are the rights of the 30-odd million white people in this land? I am at a loss to understand the philosophy which these gentlemen have learned, how they can arrogate to themselves all rights, all liberty, all law, all government, all progress, all science, all arts, all literature, and deny them to other men formed of God equally as they are formed, clothed with the same humanity, and endowed with the same intellectual powers, but robbed by their connivance of the means of development. I say I am at a loss to understand how they can deny to us these privileges and claim them for themselves.

The civil rights bill simply declares this: that there shall be no discriminations between citizens of this land so far as the laws of the land are concerned. I can find no fault with that. The great living principle of the American government is that all men are free. We admit from every land and every nationality men to come here and under the folds of that noble flag repose in peace and protection. We assume that, whatever education his mind may have received, each man may aspire to and acquire all the rights of citizenship. Yet because, forsooth, God Almighty made the face of the Negro black, these gentle-men would deny him that right though he be a man. Born on your soil, reared here amid the toils and sorrows and griefs of the land, producing by his long years of toil the products which have made your country great, earnestly laboring to develop the resources of this land, docile though outraged, yet when the gentlemen who held them in bondage—sir, I will not repeat the dark scenes that transpired under the benign influence and direction of that class of men. . . .

And, Mr. Speaker, I am astonished that there is an apparent disposition in some quarters to give this question the go-by. "Oh," gentlemen say, "you will stir up strife in the country"—"bad blood," the gentleman from Virginia said. Well, I think there has been a good deal of "bad blood" in the South already. It seems to me that a few years ago they had some "bad blood" in the South—very bad blood. And if any one will read the transactions in the South during the last few months, he will find that the "bad blood" has not all got out of the South—bad blood stirred up, not by northern people, but by southern people themselves.

Now, I do not think there is so much bad blood between the blacks and whites. The gentleman tells us in the next breath that they have the best laborers in the country. Well, if the labor is so good why do you not treat your laborers well? If they are the best class of laborers, if they do so much, why not guarantee to them their rights? If they give you such grand products, is it not proper and just that you

This freedmen's school in Vicksburg, Mississippi, offered education to former slaves.

should accord to them the rights that belong to them in common with other men? . . .

But, Mr. Speaker, this question of civil rights is one which ought to be met plainly and fully. It ought to be made clear and plain to the whole country. What are you going to do with these people? They are here, and here they are going to stay. We are going to fight it out on this line if it takes the whole summer. Here we are, part and parcel of this Union, born here and here we expect to die. . . .

. . . I know there are prejudices, but we must expect that these will exist. Let the laws of the country be just; let the laws of the country be equitable: that is all we ask, and we will take our chances under the laws in this land. We do not want the laws of this country to make discriminations between us. Place all citizens upon one broad platform, and if the Negro is not qualified to hoe his row in this contest of life, then let him go down. All we ask of this country is to put no barriers between us, to lay no stumbling blocks in our way, to give us freedom to accomplish our destiny, that we may thus acquire all that is necessary to our interest and welfare in this country. Do this, sir, and we shall ask nothing more.

"One of the Old School Cowboys"

Life on a Cattle Drive

James H. Cook

Mining, ranching, and farming brought thousands of settlers into the West after the Civil War. In 1862, Congress passed the Homestead Act, which offered 160-acre plots to settlers who agreed to cultivate the land for five years. By 1890, western settlement had reached such an extent that the Superintendent of the Census declared that "there can hardly be said to be a frontier line."

The lone sentinel of the frontier was the cowboy. James H. Cook experienced the dangers of the cowboy's life on his first cattle drive from Texas to Kansas.

Many settlers on the Great Plains lived in houses made of sod, the grassy surface of soil.

When Mr. Roberts informed me that I was to be one of his trail waddies [cowboys], I immediately moved all my personal belongings over to his camp. I was allowed to take five of the best saddle horses which I had been riding to be used on the trail. Roberts's trail crew consisted of twelve riders and the cook, besides himself. . . .

On the morning when we were to start up the trail, all was in readiness. Those selected to go with this herd were for the most part white men. The others were well known to be good hands with cattle. About a dozen extra men were to help us for a few days while we were breaking in the herd. . . .

On the trail we were each allowed to take a pair of bed blankets and a sack containing a little extra clothing. No more load than was considered actually necessary was to be allowed on the wagon, for there would be no wagon road over most of the country which we were to traverse, and there was plenty of rough country, with creeks and steep-banked rivers to be crossed. We had no tents or shelter of any sort other than our blankets. Our food and cooking utensils were the same as those used in cow camps of the brush country. No provision was made for the care of men in case of accident. Should anyone become injured, wounded, or sick, he would be strictly "out of luck." A quick recovery and a sudden death were the only desirable alternatives in such cases, for much of the time the outfit would be far from the settlements and from medical or surgical aid. . . .

One night we were camped on a little creek that ran into the Llano River at its

head. Throughout that day we had seen a lot of fresh Indian signs. I was on the first watch with the horses. Roberts had arranged for me to be on guard with the horse herd during the early part of each evening and also just at the break of day, those hours being the Indians' favorite times for deviltry. I was known to be the best shot in that outfit, and I was expected to score straight bull's-eyes and not get "buck fever," no matter how plentiful, hideous, or dangerously close the human targets.

The country was rough and broken, and here and there were large cedar thickets or brakes. I was holding the horses pretty close to the wagon immediately after supper, and everyone noticed that the animals were very restless. In those days, for some unknown reason, a white man's horse was generally afraid of the sight or scent of an Indian, just as Indian ponies were afraid of a white man. When our animals scented Indians they sniffed the air, snorted, ran together, and showed terror by their looks and actions. At last Roberts came out where I was holding the horses and told me I had better put them into a little opening in the center of a big cedar brake near the wagon. . . .

It required all the nerve I possessed to remain there with those horses. I had to ride hard to keep them in the space: they kept snorting and trying to scatter. I circled around them as fast as I could and kept them herded in as small a space as possible. When riding on the side of the herd nearest camp, I was only about seventy-five yards from the wagon. After what seemed an age, I heard one of the boys from the cattle herd come into camp and rouse the men who were to relieve us. Frank Dennis was the man who relieved

me. He was one of the old school cowboys, and as brave a man as ever lived. . . . I started toward camp when I saw Frank advancing. . . .

Just as my foot touched the ground, I heard a couple of dozen shots in quick succession. I turned my head and could see

"He Missed the Spike"

Completing the Transcontinental Railroad

Alexander Toponce

Railroads greatly hastened western settlement. During the Civil War, Congress passed legislation to build a transcontinental railroad linking the West to the East. The bill authorized massive subsidies of land and dollars for the Union Pacific Railroad to build westward from Omaha and the Central Pacific Railroad to build eastward from Sacramento. Construction speeded up after 1865, and the two lines finally met at Promontory Point, Utah. On May 10, 1869, Alexander Toponce witnessed the driving of the golden spike that connected the railroads.

When they came to drive the last spike, Governor Stanford, president of the Central Pacific, took the sledge, and the first time he struck he missed the spike and hit the rail.

What a howl went up! Irish, Chinese, Mexicans, and everybody yelled with delight. "He missed it. Yee." The engineers blew the whistles and rang their bells. Then Stanford tried it again and tapped the spike and the telegraph operators had fixed their instruments so that the tap was reported in all the offices east and west, and set bells to tapping in hundreds of towns and cities. . . . Then Vice President T. C. Durant of the Union Pacific took up the sledge and he missed the spike the first time. Then everybody slapped everybody else again and yelled, "He missed it too, yow!" . . .

When the connection was finally made, the Union Pacific and the Central Pacific engineers ran their engines up until their pilots touched. Then the engineers shook hands and had their pictures taken, and each broke a bottle of champagne on the pilot of the other's engine and had their picture taken again.

The Union Pacific engine, the "Jupiter," was driven by my good friend, George Lashus, who still lives in Ogden.

Both before and after the spike-driving ceremony, there were speeches, which were cheered heartily. I do not remember what any of the speakers said now, but I do remember that there was a great abundance of champagne.

the flash from the guns. I fired one shot in the direction of the flashes. . . . The next moment most of the horse herd came tearing right through camp. We had ropes stretched from the wagon wheels to some trees to make a corral in which to catch horses, and the horses ran against the ropes, upsetting the wagon.

Every man in camp ran for his life into the thicket. . . .

The horses ran into the cattle herd, and away went the cattle into a big cedar brake containing many old dead trees. There was a smashing and crashing and about as great an uproar as any cowboy ever heard. The men with the cattle did not dare yell at the animals or sing to them, lest Indians locate and slip an arrow into somebody.

I lay quite still under the tree. After a time I heard Roberts's voice calling out: "Don't let 'em get away with the horses, boys! Stay with 'em! Come on, boys, where are you?!" . . . One by one I could hear the boys answer him. I did not like to get out from beneath that tree, but I did not care to be called a coward, so I joined him, although I thought it the most foolish thing we could possibly do. It was so dark that an Indian could slip up within three feet of a man and not be seen.

Frank Dennis not appearing, I made up my mind that he had been killed. I said to Roberts, "Let's go and see if we can find Frank. I know where he was riding,

and I saw the shooting." We went and searched, but could find no trace of the missing cowboy. We then wandered about until daylight. . . .

About sunrise Frank Dennis came into camp. He was a little pale, but quite cheerful. He said, "Well, fellers, good morning; we had a very pleasant night of it, didn't we?" When he swung down from his horse I saw that there was blood on his clothes, and that his hand was tied up in his handkerchief, which was soaked with blood. He then told us his story.

After I had left him, he rode around the herd a time or two. It seems that a large bunch of Indians had crawled up to within about fifteen feet of the line where he was riding, and as he passed they blazed away at him. . . . They succeeded in shooting a hole through the center of Frank's left hand, as well as in giving him two or three little flesh wounds and shooting about a dozen holes through his blanket and saddle. . . . The horse herd had scattered in every direction after passing camp. Some ran into the cattle herd, where they were held by the boys with the herd, and one bunch of horses was chased up a canyon by the Indians for some distance. The horses were unable to get out of it because of the perpendicular bluffs, and the Indians were afraid to try to drive them back down the canyon, so they had to let the animals go. As it was, the savages got away with about a fourth of our horses.

"More Indians Than I Ever Saw"

A Cheyenne Woman at Custer's Last Stand

Kate Bighead

Railroads and settlers encroached on Native American lands in the Great Plains and destroyed the buffalo that sustained tribal life. Before the Civil War, the federal policy toward Native Americans was "concentration," limiting tribes to certain areas west of the Mississippi within which they could continue their traditional ways of life. In 1867, all tribes were required to move to reservations, where they had to abandon their hunting lifestyle and instead subsist on government rations.

In 1875, the Sioux rallied their forces to oppose prospectors during the gold rush in the Black Hills of the Dakota Territory. In June 1876, Colonel George Armstrong Custer led about 250 U.S. troops to force the "hostiles" to return to the reservations. Custer's troops were annihilated near Montana's Little Big Horn River by 2,500 Sioux warriors, allied with other tribes. Kate Bighead, a Cheyenne woman, participated in Custer's last stand.

I was with the Southern Cheyennes during most of my childhood and young womanhood. I was in the camp beside the Washita River, in the country the white people call Oklahoma, when Custer and his soldiers came there and fought the Indians (November 1868). Our Chief Black Kettle and other Cheyennes, many of them women and children, were killed that day. . . .

The next spring Custer and his soldiers found us again (March 1869). We then were far westward, on a branch of what the white people call Red River, I think. That time there was no fighting. Custer smoked the peace pipe with our chiefs. He promised never again to fight the Cheyennes, so all of us followed him to a soldier fort (Fort Sill). Our people gave him the name Hi-es-tzie, meaning Long Hair.

I saw Long Hair many times during those days. One time I was close to where he was mounting his horse to go somewhere, and I took a good look at him. He had a large nose, deep-set eyes, and light-red hair that was long and wavy. He was wearing a buckskin suit and a big white hat. I was then a young women, 22 years old, and I admired him. All of the Indian women talked of him as being a fine-looking man.

My cousin, a young woman named Me-o-tzi, went often with him to help in finding the trails of Indians. She said he told her his soldier horses were given plenty of corn and oats to eat, so they could outrun and catch the Indians riding ponies that had only grass to eat. All of the Cheyennes liked her, and all were glad she had so important a place in life. After Long Hair went away, different ones of the Cheyenne young men wanted to marry her. But she would not have any of them. She said that Long Hair was her husband, that he had promised to come back to her, and that she would wait for him. . . .

I came to the Northern Cheyennes when their reservation was in the Black Hills country (1868-1874). White people found gold there, so the Indians had to move out. The Cheyennes were told they must go to another reservation, but not many of them made the change. They said it was no use, as the white people might want that reservation too. Many Cheyennes, and many Sioux also, went to live in the hunting ground between the Powder and Big Horn rivers. . . . Word was sent to the hunting Indians that all Cheyennes and Sioux must stay on their reservations in Dakota. But all who stayed on the reservations had their guns and ponies taken from them, so the hunters quit going there. . . .

. . . The chiefs . . . decided that all of us would travel together for the spring and summer hunting, as it was said that many soldiers would be coming to try to make us go back to the reservations. . . . There were more Indians in those . . . camps than I ever saw together anywhere else. . . .

The chiefs from all the camps, in council, decided we should move down the Little Big Horn River to its mouth, so our hunters could go across to the west side of the Big Horn and kill antelope in the great herds they had seen there. All of the Indians crossed to the west side of the Little Big Horn and moved the first part of the expected journey to the mouth of this stream. The plan was to stay at this camp but one night, and to go on down the valley the next day.

The next morning (June 25, 1876) I went with an Oglala woman to visit some friends among the Miniconjou Sioux, up the valley toward where was the Uncpapa camp circle, at the upper or south end of the camps. We found our women friends bathing in the river, and we joined them. Other groups, men, women, and children, were playing in the water at many places along the stream. Some boys were fishing. All of us were having a good time. It was somewhere past the middle of the forenoon. Nobody was thinking of any battle coming. A few women were taking down their lodges, getting ready for the move on down the valley that day. After a while two Sioux boys came running toward us. They were shouting: "Soldiers are coming!" . . .

I had seen other battles, in past times. I always liked to watch the men fighting. Not many women did that, and I often was teased on account of it. But this time I had a good excuse, for . . . my nephew, named Noisy Walking, had gone. I was but 29 years old, so I had not any son to serve as a warrior, but I would sing strongheart songs for the nephew. He was 18 years old. . . .

The Indians were using bows and arrows more than they were using guns. Many of them had no guns, and not many who did have them had also plenty of bullets. But even if they had been well supplied with both guns and bullets, in that fight the bow was better. As the soldier ridge sloped on all sides, and as there were no trees on it nor around it, the smoke from each gun fired showed right where the shooter was hidden. The arrows made no smoke, so it could not be seen where they came from. Also, since a bullet has to go straight out from the end of a gun, any Indian who fired his gun had to put his head up so his eyes could see where to aim it. By doing this his head might be seen by a soldier and hit by a soldier bullet. The Indian could keep himself at all times out of sight when sending arrows. Each arrow was shot far upward and forward, not at any soldier in particular, but to curve down and fall where they were. Bullets would not do any harm if shot in that way. But a rain of arrows from thousands of Indian bows, and kept up for a long time, would hit many soldiers and their horses by

falling and sticking into their heads or their backs. . . .

Lame White Man, the bravest Cheyenne warrior chief, stayed in hiding close to where [a] small band of soldiers got off their horses. From there he called to the young men, and they began creeping and dodging back to him. . . . Within a few minutes there were many hundreds of warriors wriggling along the gullies all around those soldiers. . . .

On all sides of this band of soldiers the Indians jumped up. There were hundreds of warriors, many more than one might have thought could hide themselves in those small gullies. I think there were about twenty Indians to every soldier there. The soldier horses got scared, and all of them broke loose and ran away toward the river. Just then I saw a soldier shoot himself by holding his revolver at his head, then another one did the same, and another. Right away, all of them began shooting themselves or shooting each other. I saw several different pairs of them fire their guns at the same time and shoot one another in the breast. For a short time the Indians just stayed where they were and looked. Then they rushed forward. But not many of them got to strike coup blows on living enemies. Before they could get to them, all of the white men were dead. . . .

. . . The Indians believe that the Everywhere Spirit made all of them go crazy and do this, in punishment for having attacked a peaceful Indian camp. . . .

[Editor's note: This story of mass suicide among the troops is repeated in other Native American accounts of the battle. Also, a common saying among soldiers of that time—who feared torture by their captors—was "save the last bullet for yourself."]

I went riding among the Indians at different places on the battlefield in search of Noisy Walking. I saw several different ones of the soldiers not yet quite dead. The Indians cut off arms or legs or feet of these, the same as was done for those entirely dead. A Cheyenne told me where was my nephew, down in the deep gulch halfway to the river, where had been most of the Cheyennes and Oglalas during all of the

124

first part of the battle. I went down there and found him. He had been shot through the body and had been stabbed several times. I stayed with him while a young man friend went to the camps to tell his mother. . . .

Noisy Walking died that night. Six of our Cheyenne young men now were dead. Twenty-four Sioux warriors had been killed. Many more Indians would have been killed if the Everywhere Spirit had not caused the white men to go crazy and turn their guns upon themselves. . . .

I may have seen Custer at the time of the battle or after he was killed. I do not know, as I did not then know of his being there. All of our old warriors say the same—none of them knew of him being there until they learned of it afterward at the soldier forts or the agencies or from Indians coming from the agencies.

But I learned something more about him from our people in Oklahoma. Two of those Southern Cheyenne women who had been in our camp at the Little Big

Horn told of having been on the battlefield soon after the fighting ended. They saw Custer lying dead there. They had known him in the South. While they were looking at him, some Sioux men came and were about to cut up his body. The Cheyenne women, thinking of Me-o-tzi, made signs. "He is a relative of ours," but telling nothing more about him. So the Sioux men cut off only one joint of a finger. The women then pushed the point of a sewing awl into each of his ears, into his head. This was done to improve his hearing, as it seemed he had not heard what our chiefs in the South said when he smoked the pipe with them. They told him then that if ever afterward he should break that peace promise and should fight the Cheyennes, the Everywhere Spirit surely would cause him to be killed.

Through almost sixty years, many a time I have thought of Hi-es-tzie as the handsome man I saw in the South. And I often have wondered if, when I was riding among the dead where he was lying, my pony may have kicked dirt upon his body.

"Soldiers Surrounded and Butchered Them"

The Massacre at Wounded Knee

Turning Hawk and American Horse

In the 1880s, a religious revival based on the "Ghost Dance" swept through the Great Plains tribes. They believed that through this ritual dance, the white people would disappear, the buffalo would return, and all Native Americans—both dead and living—would be reunited in a renewed land. Settlers feared the Ghost Dance movement and called on U.S. troops for assistance.

On December 29, 1890, more than 200 Sioux men, women, and children were massacred at Wounded Knee, South Dakota, while attempting to surrender. The slaughter ended three centuries of "Indian Wars" in America. Turning Hawk and American Horse, who witnessed the attack, testified to the Commissioner of Indian Affairs in Washington about the details.

125

These people [who had left the reservation] were coming towards Pine Ridge Agency [to surrender], and when they were almost on the agency they were met by the soldiers and surrounded and finally taken to the Wounded Knee Creek, and there at a given time their guns were demanded. When they had delivered them up, the men were separated from their families, from their tepees, and taken to a certain spot. When the guns were thus taken and the men thus separated there was a crazy man, a young man of very bad influence and in fact a nobody, among that bunch of Indians fired his gun, and of course the firing of a gun must have been the breaking of a military rule of some sort, because immediately the soldiers returned fire and indiscriminate killing followed. . . .

All the men who were in a bunch were killed right there, and those who escaped that first fire got into the ravine, and as they went along up the ravine, for a long distance they were pursued on both sides by the soldiers and shot down, as the dead bodies showed afterwards. The women were standing off at a different place from where the men were stationed, and when the firing began those of the men who escaped the first onslaught went in one direction up the ravine, and then the women who were bunched together at another place went entirely in a different direction through an open field, and the women fared the same fate as the men who went up the deep ravine.

. . . [T]hey turned their guns, Hotchkiss guns, etc., upon the women who were in the lodges standing there under a flag of truce. . . . There was a woman with an infant in her arms who was killed as she almost touched the flag of truce, and the women and children of course were strewn all along the circular village until they were dispatched. Right near the flag of truce a mother was shot down with her infant; the child not knowing that its mother was dead was still nursing, and that was especially a very sad sight. The women as they were fleeing with their babes on their backs were killed together, shot right through, and the women who were very heavy with child were also killed. All the Indians fled . . . , and after most all of them had been killed, a cry was made that all those who were not killed or wounded should come forth and they would be safe. Little boys who were not wounded came out of their places of refuge, and as soon as they came in sight a number of soldiers surrounded them and butchered them there.

Of course we all feel very sad about this affair. I stood very loyal to the govern-

A mass grave held the more than 200 Sioux killed at Wounded Knee.

ment all through those troublesome days, and believing so much in the government and being so loyal to it, my disappointment was very strong, and I have come to Washington with a very great blame on my heart. Of course it would have been all right if only the men were killed; we would feel almost grateful for it. But the fact of the killing of the women, and more especially the killing of the young boys and girls who are to go to make up the future strength of the Indian people, is the saddest part of the whole affair and we feel it very sorely.

"How I Got Rich by Honest Graft"

Life in Tammany Hall

George W. Plunkitt

Mark Twain referred to the late nineteenth century as the "Gilded Age" because he believed wealth was gilding the corruption of American society. At the local level, political machines—led by "bosses"—bought votes by promising immigrants food, shelter, and other needed services. Bosses also received kickbacks from people who wanted city jobs and companies that wanted city contracts. The most notorious political machine was Tammany Hall in New York City. George W. Plunkitt, a Tammany Hall boss, argued in favor of "honest graft."

Everybody is talking these days about Tammany men growing rich on graft, but nobody thinks of drawing the distinction between honest graft and dishonest graft. There's all the difference in the world between the two. Yes, many of our men have grown rich in politics. I have myself. I've made a big fortune out of the game, and I'm getting richer every day, but I've not gone in for dishonest graft—blackmailing gamblers, saloon-keepers, disorderly people, etc.—and neither has any of the men who have made big fortunes in politics.

There's honest graft, and I'm an example of how it works. I might sum up the whole thing by saying: "I seen my opportunities and I took 'em."

Just let me explain by examples. My party's in power in the city, and it's going to undertake a lot of public improvements. Well, I'm tipped off, say, that they're going to lay out a new park at a certain place.

I see my opportunity and I take it. I go to that place and I buy up all the land I can in the neighborhood. Then the board of this or that makes its plan public, and there is a rush to get my land, which nobody cared particular for before.

Ain't it perfectly honest to charge a good price and make a profit on my investment and foresight? Of course it is. Well, that's honest graft.

Or supposing it's a new bridge they're going to build. I get tipped off and I buy as much property as I can that has to be taken for approaches. I sell at my own price later on and drop some more money in the bank.

Wouldn't you? It's just like looking ahead in Wall Street or in the coffee or cotton market. It's honest graft, and I'm looking for it every day [of] the year. I will tell you frankly that I've got a good lot of it, too. . . .

I've told you how I got rich by honest graft. Now, let me tell you that most politicians who are accused of robbing the city get rich the same way.

They didn't steal a dollar from the city treasury. They just seen their opportunities and took them. That is why, when a reform administration comes in and spends a half million dollars in trying to find the public robberies they talked about in the campaign, they don't find them.

The books are always all right. The money in the city treasury is all right. Everything is all right. All they can show is that the Tammany heads of departments looked after their friends, within the law, and gave them what opportunities they could to make honest graft. Now, let me tell you that's never going to hurt Tammany with the people. Every good man looks after his friends, and any man who doesn't isn't likely to be popular. . . .

Tammany was beat in 1901 because the people were deceived into believing that it worked dishonest graft. They didn't draw a distinction between dishonest and honest graft, but they saw that some Tammany men grew rich and supposed they had been robbing the city treasury or levying blackmail on disorderly houses, or working in with the gamblers and lawbreakers.

As a matter of policy, if nothing else, why should the Tammany leaders go into such dirty business when there is so much honest graft lying around when they are in power? Did you ever consider that?

Now, in conclusion, I want to say that I don't own a dishonest dollar. If my worst enemy was given the job of writing my epitaph when I'm gone, he couldn't do more than write: "George W. Plunkitt. He Seen His Opportunities, and He Took 'Em."

"Wall Street Owns the Country"

The Birth of Populism

Mary Lease

Farmers in the South and the West faced many hardships in the 1870s, which led them to political action. Railroads charged high prices to transport farm products, deflation increased the value of farmers' debts, and expanded farm production sharply reduced prices. Many farmers blamed these economic conditions on the eastern financial establishment.

Mary Lease was one of the most popular speakers for the People's party, in which women played a significant role.

In 1891, various farmers' organizations formed the People's party, known as the Populists. In their 1892 platform, Populists advocated a shorter workday, women's suffrage, democratic reforms such as direct election of senators, and government ownership of transportation and communication lines. Mary Lease, a Kansas Populist known for admonishing farmers to "raise less corn and more hell," stated the Populist cause in this excerpt from one of her many speeches.

This is a nation of inconsistencies. The Puritans fleeing from oppression became in turn oppressors. We fought England for our liberty and put chains on 4 million blacks. We wiped out slavery and by our tariff laws and national banks began a system of white wage slavery worse than the first. Wall Street owns the country. It is no longer a government of the people, by the people, and for the people, but a government of Wall Street, by Wall Street, and for Wall Street. The great common people of this country are slaves, and monopoly is the master.

The West and South are bound and prostrate before the manufacturing East. Money rules, and our vice president is a London banker. Our laws are the output of a system which clothes rascals in robes and honesty in rags. The parties lie to us and the political speakers mislead us.

We were told two years ago to go to work and raise a big crop, that was all we needed. We went to work and plowed and planted; the rains fell, the sun shone, nature smiled, and we raised the big crop that they told us to—and what came of it? Eight-cent corn, ten-cent oats, two-cent beef, and no price at all for butter and eggs—that's what came of it. Then the politicians said we suffered from overproduction. Overproduction, when 10,000 little children, so statistics tell us, starve to death every year in the United States, and over 100,000 shop girls in New York are forced to sell their virtue for the bread their niggardly wages deny them. . . .

Kansas suffers from two great robbers, the Santa Fe Railroad and the loan companies. The common people are robbed to enrich their masters. There are 30,000 millionaires in the United States. Go home and figure out how many paupers you must have to make one millionaire with the circulation only $10 per capita. There are thirty men in the United States whose aggregate wealth is over one and one-half billion dollars. There are half a million men looking for work. There are 60,000 soldiers of the Union in poor-houses, but no bondholders. It would have been better if Congress had voted pensions to those 60,000 paupers who wore the blue and dyed it red with their blood in the country's defense than to have voted to make the bankers' bonds nontaxable and payable, interest and principal, in gold.

We want money, land, and transportation. We want the abolition of the national banks, and we want the power to make loans direct from the government. We want the accursed foreclosure system wiped out. Land equal to a tract thirty miles wide and ninety miles long has been foreclosed and bought in by loan companies of Kansas in a year. We will stand by our homes and stay by our fireside by force if necessary, and we will not pay our debts to the loan-shark companies until the government pays its debts to us. The people are at bay; let the bloodhounds of money who have dogged us thus far beware.

"Let Us Quit the Old Party"

A Black Farmer Endorses Populism

S.D.D.

Populists supported increasing the amount of money in circulation to help farmers pay their debts. To do this, they advocated using a silver standard to back federal money, rather than the strict gold standard desired by the eastern financiers—known as "goldbugs." A black Georgia farmer—identified only by his initials, S.D.D.—argued in favor of the Populist monetary policy in an 1892 letter to the editor. He also noted southern Democrats' fear that a victory by the Populist party would give African Americans more political power.

129

Ever since the reform movement began, we colored people have had more advice given us by the Democrats than we have had before or since freedom. Their advice is for us to stick to the Republican party.

In the [1884] race between [Grover] Cleveland and [James G.] Blaine, they did not give us such advice, nor in the Cleveland and [Benjamin] Harrison campaign [in 1888] did they tell us to vote the Republican ticket. But now, since the laboring men of the North, South, and West have seen their families in want of food and raiment and their children growing up without education, they have looked into the causes of their poverty. They have petitioned Congress for some measure of relief, but Congress has laughed at their petitions and told them to go home and work harder and eat less. We have gone home and worked harder and eaten less, and find ourselves in a worse condition than before.

Now we are told that we are naked and hungry because we worked too hard and made too much cotton in the South and too much wheat, corn, and meat in the West.

Now, since we could see no hope of better times through the old parties and have got together and formed a new party—a People's party—the Democrats are kicking terribly, for Colonel Livingston says it will bring about Negro supremacy—it will wipe out the color line.

Now . . . we don't want to rule the government; we don't want to come into your family; we don't want to enter your schoolhouses or your churches. But I tell you what we do want: We want equal rights at the ballot box and equal justice before the law; we want better wages for our labor and better prices for our produce; we want more money in circulation to pay for our labor or our produce; we want to lift the mortgage from the old cow and mule which they have carried till they are sway-backed; we want to school our children; and we want a chance to earn a home.

We can never realize these wants without more money in circulation.

Our old people have been working for twenty-seven years and have not got a dollar laid by for old age. But the goldbugs are laying up money every day and plenty to spare to carry elections.

The Democrats have hired such of our ministers as they could to go to work among our people to save the old Republican party. Who ever heard the like before—white Democrats hiring colored men to vote the Republican ticket?

They call the Republicans their enemies, yet they hire colored men to bring out candidates and vote the Republican ticket. The object is to defeat the People's party, so if the Democrats are beaten the Republicans will win, because they know they will be brothers when they get to Washington anyway.

It seems to be a hard thing for us colored men to give up the Republican party, but let us stop and consider: We are living in another man's house, working another man's land, and our smokehouse and meal-tub are in town.

Let us quit the old party and vote for wife and children and a chance for a home.

"The Property of the People"

An Army of the Unemployed Marches on the Capitol

Jacob S. Coxey

During the severe depression of 1894, millions of people were unemployed. Jacob S. Coxey of Ohio, a Populist, led an "army" of unemployed people in a march to Washington to demand government relief. "Coxey's Army"

advocated that money be issued to stimulate the economy and that the government create jobs with a road construction program. Coxey and others were arrested for walking on the grass of the U.S. Capitol. Anticipating such action, Coxey prepared a protest, but was not allowed to deliver it. Coxey's protest was later published in the Congressional Record.

The Constitution of the United States guarantees to all citizens the right to peaceably assemble and petition for redress of grievances, and furthermore declares that the right of free speech shall not be abridged.

We stand here today to test these guarantees of our Constitution. We choose this place of assemblage because it is the property of the people, and if it be true that the right of the people to peacefully assemble upon their own premises and utter their petition has been abridged by the passage of laws in direct violation of the Constitution, we are here to draw the eyes of the entire nation to this shameful fact. Here, rather than at any other spot upon the continent, it is fitting that we should come to mourn over our dead liberties and by our protest arouse the imperiled nation to such action as shall rescue the Constitution and resurrect our liberties.

Upon these steps where we stand has been spread a carpet for the royal feet of a foreign princess, the cost of whose lavish entertainment was taken from the public treasury without the consent or the approval of the people. Up these steps the lobbyists of trusts and corporations have passed unchallenged on their way to committee rooms, access to which we, the representatives of the toiling wealth-producers, have been denied. We stand here today in behalf of millions of toilers whose petitions have been buried in committee rooms, whose prayers have been unresponded to, and whose opportunities for honest, remunerative, productive labor have been taken from them by unjust legislation, which protects idlers, speculators, and gamblers. . . .

We stand here to remind Congress of its promise of returning prosperity should the Sherman Act [requiring U.S. purchase of silver] be repealed. We stand here to declare by our march of over 400 miles through difficulties and distress, a march unstained by even the slightest act which would bring the blush of shame to any, that we are law-abiding citizens, and as men our actions speak louder than words. We are here to petition for legislation which will furnish employment for every man able and willing to work; for legislation which will bring universal prosperity and emancipate our beloved country from financial bondage to the descendants of King George. We have come to the only source which is competent to aid the people in their day of dire distress. We are here to tell our representatives, who hold their seats by grace of our ballots, that the struggle for existence has become too fierce and relentless. We come and throw up our defenseless hands and say, help, or we and our loved ones must perish. We are engaged in a bitter and cruel war with the enemies of all mankind—a war with hunger, wretchedness, and despair, and we ask Congress to heed our petitions and issue for the nation's good a sufficient volume of the same kind of money which carried the country through one awful war and saved the life of the nation.

. . . We have assembled here in violation of no just laws to enjoy the privileges of every American citizen. We are now under the shadow of the Capitol of this great nation, and in the presence of our national legislators are refused that dearly bought privilege, and by force of arbitrary power prevented from carrying out the desire of our hearts which is plainly granted under the great Magna Carta of our national liberties.

131

"The First Step on New Soil"

A Russian Immigrant Comes to America

Mary Antin

The industrialization of the United States caused profound changes in American society. As U.S. industry grew, so did America's cities. In 1860, less than 20 percent of Americans lived in cities. By 1920, more than half were city dwellers.

America's expanding industry also created a demand for more labor. Immigrants flooded into the United States from 1880 to 1910 to meet this demand. For those like Mary Antin, America offered new hope and new freedom.

Settlement workers tried to help immigrants adapt to American customs.

Our initiation into American ways began with the first step on the new soil. My father found occasion to instruct or correct us even on the way from the pier to Wall Street, which journey we made crowded together in a rickety cab. He told us not to lean out of the windows, not to point, and explained the word greenhorn. We did not want to be greenhorns and gave the strictest attention to my father's instructions. . . .

The first meal was an object lesson of much variety. My father produced several kinds of food, ready to eat without any cooking, from little tin cans that had printing all over them. He attempted to introduce us to a queer, slippery kind of fruit which he called banana, but had to give it up for the time being. After the meal he had better luck with a curious piece of furniture on runners which he called rocking chair. There were five of us newcomers, and we found five different ways of getting into the American machine of perpetual motion and as many ways of getting out of it. . . .

In our flat we did not think of such a thing as storing the coal in the bathtub. There was no bathtub. So in the evening of the first day, my father conducted us to the public baths. As we moved along in a little procession, I was delighted with the illumination of the streets. So many lamps, and they burned until morning, my father said, and so people did not need to carry lanterns. In America, then, everything was free, as we had heard in Russia. Light was free; the streets were as bright as a synagogue on a holy day. Music was free; we had been serenaded, to our gaping delight, by a brass band of many pieces, soon after our installation on Union Place.

Education was free. That subject my father had written about repeatedly, as comprising his chief hope for us children, the essence of American opportunity, the treasure that no thief could touch, not even misfortune or poverty. It was the one thing that he was able to promise us when he sent for us; surer, safer than bread or shelter.

On our second day I was thrilled with the realization of what this freedom of education meant. A little girl from across the alley came and offered to conduct us to school. My father was out, but we five between us had a few words of English by this time. We knew the word school. We understood. The child, who had never seen us till yesterday, who could not pronounce our names, who was not much better dressed than we, was able to offer us the freedom of the schools of Boston! No application made, no questions asked, no examinations, rulings, exclusions, no machinations, no fees. The doors stood open for every one of us. The smallest child could show us the way. . . .

. . . A fairy godmother to us children was she who led us to a wonderful country called uptown, where, in a dazzlingly beautiful palace called a department store, we exchanged our hateful home-made European costumes, which pointed us out as greenhorns to the children on the street, for real American machine-made garments, and issued forth glorified in each other's eyes.

With our despised immigrant clothing we shed also our impossible Hebrew names. A committee of our friends, several years ahead of us in American experience, put their heads together and concocted American names for us all. Those of our real names that had no pleasing American equivalents they ruthlessly discarded, content if they retained the initials. . . . The name they gave me was hardly new. My Hebrew name being Maryashe in full, Mashke for short, Russianized into Marya (Mar-ya), my friends said that it would hold good in English as Mary, which was very disappointing, as I longed to possess a strange-sounding American name like the others.

I am forgetting the consolation I had in this matter of names from the use of my surname. . . . I found on my arrival that my father was Mr. Antin on the slightest provocation, and not, as in [Russia], on state occasions alone. And so I was Mary Antin and I felt very important to answer to such a dignified title. It was just like America that even plain people should wear their surnames on week days.

"How Can I Call This My Home?"

A Chinese Immigrant's Story

Lee Chew

Many immigrants faced persecution as well as opportunity in America. Chinese immigrants became even greater targets because of racial discrimination. Indeed, they were the first nationality restricted by U.S. immigration law. The Chinese Exclusion Act of 1882 totally prohibited the immigration of Chinese laborers. Lee Chew, a successful Chinese businessman in New York, told his story around 1900.

133

I worked on my father's farm till I was about 16 years of age, when a man of our tribe came back from America and took ground as large as four city blocks and made a paradise of it. . . .

The man had gone away from our village a poor boy. Now he returned with unlimited wealth, which he had obtained in the country of the American wizards. After many amazing adventures he had become a merchant in a city called Mott Street [New York's Chinatown], so it was said. . . .

Having made his wealth among the barbarians, this man had faithfully returned to pour it out among his tribesmen, and he is living in our village now very happy, and a pillar of strength to the poor.

The wealth of this man filled my mind with the idea that I, too, would like to go to the country of the wizards and gain some of their wealth, and after a long time my father consented, and gave me his blessing, and my mother took leave of me with tears, while my grandfather laid his hand upon my head and told me to remember and live up to the admonitions of the sages, to avoid gambling, bad women, and men of evil minds, and so to govern my conduct that when I died my ancestors might rejoice to welcome me as a guest on high.

My father gave me $100, and I went to Hong Kong with five other boys from our same place, and we got steerage passage on a steamer, paying $50 each. Everything was new to me. All my life I had been used to sleeping on a board bed with a wooden pillow, and I found the steamer's bunk very uncomfortable, because it was so soft. The food was different from that which I had been used to, and I did not like it at all. I was afraid of the stews, for the thought of what they might be made of by the wicked wizards of the ship made me ill. Of the great power of these people I saw many signs. The engines that moved the ship were wonderful monsters, strong enough to lift mountains. When I got to San Francisco, which was before the passage of the Exclusion Act, I was half-starved, because I was afraid to eat the provisions of the barbarians, but a few days living in the Chinese quarter made me happy again. A man got me work as a house servant in an American family, and my start was the same as that of almost all the Chinese in this country.

The Chinese laundryman does not learn his trade in China; there are no laundries in China. The women there do the washing in tubs and have no washboards or flat irons. All the Chinese laundrymen here were taught in the first place by American women just as I was taught. . . .

It was twenty years ago when I came to this country, and I worked for two years as a servant, getting at the last $35 a month. I sent money home to comfort my parents, but though I dressed well and lived well and had pleasure, going quite often to the Chinese theater and to dinner parties in Chinatown, I saved $50 in the first six months, $90 in the second, $120 in the third, and $150 in the fourth. So I had $410 at the end of two years, and I was now ready to start in business.

When I first opened a laundry it was in company with a partner, who had been in the business for some years. We went to a town about 500 miles inland, where a railroad was building. We got a board shanty and worked for the men employed by the railroads. . . . We had to put up with many insults and frauds, as men would come in and claim parcels that did not belong to them, saying they had lost their tickets, and would fight if they did not get what they asked for. Sometimes we were taken before magistrates and fined for losing shirts that we had never seen. On the other hand, we were making money. . . . When the railroad construction gang moved on, we went with them. The men were rough and prejudiced against us, but not more so than in the big eastern cities. . . .

We were three years with the railroad, and then went to the mines, where we made plenty of money in gold dust, but had a hard time, for many of the miners were wild men who carried revolvers and after drinking would come in to our place to shoot and steal shirts, for which we had to pay. One of these men hit his head hard against a flat iron and all the miners came and broke up our laundry, chasing us out of town. They were going to hang us. We lost all our property and $365 in money, which members of the mob must have found.

Luckily most of our money was in the hands of Chinese bankers in San Francisco. I drew $500 and went east to Chicago, where I had a laundry for three years, during which I increased my capital to $2,500. After that I was four years in Detroit. I went home to China in 1897, but returned in 1898, and began a laundry business in Buffalo. But Chinese laundry business now is not as good as it was ten years ago. American cheap labor in the steam laundries has hurt it.

So I determined to become a general merchant, and with this idea I came to New York and opened a shop in the Chinese quarter, keeping silks, teas, porcelain, clothes, shoes, hats, and Chinese provisions, which include sharks' fins and nuts, lily bulbs and lily flowers, lychee nuts and other Chinese dainties, but do not include rats, because it would be too expensive to import them. The rat which is eaten by the Chinese is a field animal which lives on rice, grain, and sugar cane. Its flesh is delicious. . . .

American people eat groundhogs, which are very like these Chinese rats and they also eat many sorts of food that our people would not touch. Those that have dined with us know that we understand how to live well. . . .

There is no reason for the prejudice against the Chinese. The cheap labor cry was always a falsehood. Their labor was never cheap and is not cheap now. It has always commanded the highest market price. But the trouble is that the Chinese are such excellent and faithful workers that bosses will have no others when they can get them. If you look at men working on the street, you will find an overseer for every four or five of them. That watching is not necessary for Chinese. They work as well when left to themselves as they do when someone is looking at them.

It was the jealousy of laboring men of other nationalities—especially the Irish—that raised all the outcry against the Chinese. No one would hire an Irishman, German, Englishman, or Italian when he could get a Chinese, because our countrymen are so much more honest, industrious, steady, sober, and painstaking. Chinese were persecuted not for their vices, but for their virtues. There never was any honesty in the pretended fear of leprosy or in the cheap labor scare, and the persecution continues still, because Americans make a mere practice of loving justice. They are all for money making, and they want to be on the strongest side always. They treat you as a friend while you are prosperous, but if you have a misfortune they don't know you. There is nothing substantial in their friendship.

Irish fill the almshouses and prisons and orphan asylums; Italians are among the most dangerous of men; Jews are unclean and ignorant. Yet they are all let in, while Chinese, who are sober, or duly law-abiding, clean, educated, and industrious, are shut out.

There are few Chinamen in jails and none in the poorhouses. There are no Chinese tramps or drunkards. Many Chinese here have become sincere Christians, in spite of the persecution which they have to endure from their heathen countrymen. More than half the Chinese in this country would become citizens if allowed to do so and would be patriotic Americans. But how can they make this country their home as matters are now? They are not allowed to bring wives here from China, and if they marry American women there is a great outcry.

All congressmen acknowledge the injustice of the treatment of my people, yet they continue it. They have no backbone.

Under the circumstances, how can I call this my home, and how can anyone blame me if I take my money and go back to my village in China?

135

"Is It American to Let People Starve?"

Anarchism and the Haymarket Riot

Michael Schwab

Workers began to organize to gain more control in the new industrial workplace. The first major interstate strike was the Great Railroad Strike of 1877, which affected some two-thirds of the nation's railways. In its wake, membership grew in the Knights of Labor, a union that included both skilled and unskilled workers. But in 1886, an act of violence turned public opinion strongly against the labor movement.

The Haymarket Riot occurred in Chicago at a protest against a police attack on strikers. A bomb was thrown into the crowd, killing several people. Anarchist leaders were sentenced to death for the crime, despite a lack of convincing evidence. Michael Schwab, one of the anarchists, addressed the court after his conviction.

It is not much I have to say. And I would say nothing at all if keeping silent did not look like a cowardly approval of what has been done here. To term the proceedings during the trial justice would be a sneer. Justice has not been done—more than this, could not be done. If one class is arrayed against the other, it is idle and hypocritical to think about justice. Anarchy was on trial, as the state's attorney put it in his closing speech—a doctrine, an opinion, hostile to brute force, hostile to our present murderous system of production and distribution. I am condemned to die for writing newspaper articles and making speeches. . . .

It is not violence in word or action the attorneys of the State and their urgers-on are waging war against; it is our doctrine—anarchy.

We contend for communism and anarchy—why? If we had kept silent, stones would have cried out. Murder was committed day by day. Children were slain; women worked to death; men killed inch by inch, and these crimes are never punished by law. The great principle underlying the present system is unpaid labor. Those who amass fortunes, build palaces, and live in luxury are doing these things by virtue of unpaid labor. Being directly or indirectly the possessors of land and machinery, they dictate terms to the workingman. He is compelled to sell his labor cheap or to starve. The price paid him is always far below the real value. He acts under compulsion, and they call it a free contract. This infernal state of affairs keeps him poor and ignorant, an easy prey for exploitation. . . .

What these common laborers are today, the skilled laborers will be tomorrow. Improved machinery that ought to be a blessing for the workingman under the existing conditions becomes for him a curse. Machinery multiplies the army of unskilled laborers, makes the laborer more dependent upon the men who own the land and machines. And that is the reason that socialism and communism got a foothold in this country. The outcry that socialism, communism, and anarchism are the creed of foreigners is a big mistake. There are more socialists of American birth in this country than foreigners, and that is much, if we consider that more than half of all industrial workingmen are native Americans. There are socialistic papers in a great many states edited by Americans for Americans. The capitalistic newspapers conceal that fact very carefully.

Socialism, as we understand it, means that land and machinery shall be held in common by the people. The production of goods shall be carried on by productive groups which shall supply the demands of the people. Under such a system, every human being would have an opportunity to do useful work, and no doubt would work. Some hours' work every day would suffice to produce all, according to statistics, that is necessary for a comfortable living. Time would be left to cultivate the mind and to further science and art.

That is what the socialists propose. Some say it is un-American! Well, then, is it American to let people starve and die in ignorance? Is exploitation and robbery of the poor, American? What have the great political parties done for the poor? Promised much, done nothing—except corrupting them by buying their votes on election day. A poverty-stricken man has no interest in the welfare of the community. It is only natural that in a society where women are driven to sell their honor, men should sell their votes.

But we were not only "socialists and communists," we were "anarchists." What is anarchy?

Is it not strange that when anarchy was tried, nobody ever told what anarchy was? Even when I was on the witness stand and asked the state's attorney for a definition of anarchy, he declined to give it. But in their speeches, he and his associates spoke very frequently about anarchy, and it appeared that they understood it to be something horrible—arson, rapine,

"The Wild-Eyed Agitator"

An Anarchist Assassinates President McKinley

Ohio State Journal

Anarchist Leon Czolgosz assassinated President William McKinley in September 1901. In the wake of a third presidential assassination, the Ohio State Journal *questioned whether America's tradition of liberty could survive unlimited immigration and dangerous new ideas.*

A great calamity has befallen the American people. The black pall of a great sorrow covers the land. President McKinley is dead. . . .

The great loss is all the more terrible because it has brought an unspeakable disgrace upon the American people. Three times within a generation the noblest and the best of American presidents have fallen by the hand of an assassin.

No other country in the world has such a black blot upon it in this respect as free America. Lincoln, Garfield, McKinley—three martyrs to liberty and nationality in less than forty years. Not even despotic, absolute Russia can show such a record. There is crushing humiliation in the fact.

Has it come that liberty cannot exist without license running riot? Must order-loving America, with all its freedom, its intelligence, and its abounding prosperity, admit reluctantly that its measure of liberty, in speech and press, has been too great?

Certainly the time has come when anarchy must be stamped out in America and immigration must be restricted more sharply. We have been too careless of the wild-eyed agitator spouting on the street corner; too tolerant also of the demagogue inciting class against class for party and personal advantage. Serene in our confidence in American self-control, the mad rantings of anarchy and demagogy have been passed by as harmless vaporings.

This has been a mistake. We must realize that American cities have become cosmopolitan. In their congested centers are thousands who have no true appreciation of the meaning of liberty. Greater efforts at enlightenment in these districts must be made, and with them must be enforced a greater respect for law and higher regard for public office as it typifies the whole people.

murder. . . . "Anarchy" is Greek and means, verbatim: without rulership; not being ruled. According to our vocabulary, anarchy is a state of society in which the only government is reason; a state of society in which all human beings do right for the simple reason that it is right and hate wrong because it is wrong. In such a society, no laws, no compulsion will be necessary. . . .

It is entirely wrong to use the word anarchy as synonymous with violence. Violence is one thing and anarchy another. In the present state of society, violence is used on all sides, and, therefore, we advocated the use of violence against violence, but against violence only, as a necessary means of defense. . . . I have not the slightest idea who threw the bomb on the Haymarket and had no knowledge of any conspiracy to use violence on that or any other night.

"To Make a Millionaire a Billionaire"

Life in a Company Town

Pullman Strikers

In 1894, workers at the Pullman Palace Car Company, which manufactured railroad cars, protested wage cuts and company control of housing and stores. Their town—Pullman, Illinois—was entirely owned by their employer, George Pullman. The company used an injunction to prevent the union from obstructing the railways and the mails. President Grover Cleveland finally sent troops to end the strike. This statement by the Pullman strikers was delivered at a convention of the American Railway Union.

Mr. President and Brothers of the American Railway Union: We struck at Pullman because we were without hope. We joined the American Railway Union because it gave us a glimmer of hope. Twenty thousand souls, men, women, and little ones, have their eyes turned toward this convention today, straining eagerly through dark despondency for a glimmer of heaven-sent message you alone can give us on this earth.

. . . Five reductions in wages, in work, and in conditions of employment swept through the shops at Pullman between May and December, 1893. The last was the most severe, amounting to nearly thirty percent, and our rents had not fallen. We owed Pullman $70,000 when we struck May 11. We owe him twice as much today. He does not evict us for two reasons: one, the force of popular sentiment and public opinion; the other because he hopes to starve us out, to break through in the back of the American Railway Union, and to deduct from our miserable wages when we are forced to return to him the last dollar we owe him for the occupancy of his houses.

Rents all over the city in every quarter of its vast extent have fallen, in some cases to one-half. Residences, compared with which ours are hovels, can be had a few miles away at the price we have been contributing to make a millionaire a billionaire. What we pay $15 for in Pullman is leased for $8 in Roseland; and remember that just as no man or woman of our 4,000 toilers has ever felt the friendly pressure of George M. Pullman's hand, so no man or woman of us all has ever owned or can ever hope to own one inch of George M. Pullman's land. Why, even the very streets are his. . . .

Water which Pullman buys from the city at 8 cents a thousand gallons he retails to us at 500 percent advance and claims he is losing $400 a month on it. Gas which sells at 75 cents per thousand feet in Hyde Park, just north of us, he sells for $2.25. When we went to tell him our grievances, he said we were all his "children."

Pullman, both the man and the town, is an ulcer on the body politic. He owns the houses, the schoolhouses, and churches of God in the town he gave his once humble name. The revenue he derives from these, the wages he pays out with one hand—the Pullman Palace Car Company, he takes back with the other—the Pullman Land Association. He is able by this to bid under any contract car shop in this country. His competitors in business, to meet this, must reduce the wages of their men. This gives him the excuse to reduce ours to conform to the market. His business rivals must in turn scale down; so must he. And thus the merry war—the dance of skeletons bathed in human tears—goes on, and it will go on, brothers, forever, unless you, the American Railway Union, stop it; end it; crush it out.

"You Get Off the Earth"

The Miners' Plight

Mother Jones

One of the most familiar union organizers was Mary Harris "Mother" Jones (1830-1930). Her motto was "pray for the dead and fight like hell for the living." An Irish immigrant whose father had worked on the railroads, Mother Jones became an organizer for the United Mine Workers. She marshalled miners' wives into an "army" to chase away strikebreakers with their brooms. Excerpted here is one of her many writings on behalf of miners' rights.

A few Sundays ago I attended church in a place called McDonald, on Loop Creek, in West Virginia. In the course of his sermon the preacher gave the following as a conversation that had recently taken place between him and a miner.

"I met a man last week," said the preacher, "who used to be a very good church member. When I asked him what he was doing at the present time, he said that he was organizing his fellow craftsmen of the mines."

Then, according to the preacher, the following discussion took place:

"What is the object of such a union?" asked the preacher.

"To better our condition," replied the miner.

"But the miners are in a prosperous condition now."

"There is where we differ."

"Do you think you will succeed?"

"I am going to try."

Commenting on this conversation to his congregation the preacher said: "Now I question if such a man can meet with any success. If he were only a college graduate he might be able to teach these miners something and in this way give them light, but as the miners of this creek are in a prosperous condition at the present time I do not see what such a man can do for them." Yet this man was professing to preach the doctrines of the Carpenter of Nazareth.

Let us compare his condition with that of the "prosperous" miners, and perhaps we can see why he talked as he did. At this same service he read his report for the previous six months. For his share of the wealth these miners had produced during that time, he had received $847.67, of which $46 had been given for missionary purposes. Besides receiving this money, he had been frequently wined and dined by the mine operators and probably had a free pass on the railroad. What had he done for the miners during that time? He had spoken to them twenty-six times, for which he received $32.41 a talk, and if they were all like the one I heard, he was at no expense either in time, brains, or money to prepare them. During all this time the "prosperous" miners were working ten hours a day beneath the ground amid poisonous gases and crumbling rocks. If they were fortunate enough to be allowed to toil every working day throughout the year, they would have received in return for 3,080 hours of most exhausting toil less than $400. . . .

The miner with whom this minister had been talking had been blacklisted up and down the creek for daring to ask for a chance to let his boy go to school instead of into the mines. This miner could have told the minister more about the great industrial tragedy in the midst of which he was living in five minutes than all his college training had taught him.

At the bidding of . . . stock and bondholders, often living in a foreign land, the schoolhouses of Virginia are closed to those who build them and to whom they belong by every right. The miners pay taxes, build the school, and support the officers, but if they dare even to stand upon the schoolhouse steps, a snip of a mine boss comes along with a pistol in hand and orders them off. "——— free speech," said one of them to me when I

protested, "we do not need any free speech. You get off the earth." Not only the schoolrooms, but every church or public hall is locked against us. On every school board you will find at least one company clerk or mining boss, and it is the business of this henchman of the mine owners to see to it that the school buildings are not used for public meetings by the miners.

Yet these same school buildings are used by the operators for any kind of meeting they choose and any demoralizing, degrading show that comes along has free access to them, as well as all political meetings of the old capitalist parties. But when the labor agitator or trade union organizer comes along trying to make it possible for the miner's children to go to school, the schoolhouses are tightly closed.

In some of these camps the miners are forced to pay as much as $9 a barrel for flour, 14 cents a pound for sugar, 18 cents a pound for fat pork, and $8 to $10 a month rent for a company shack, the roof of which is so poor that when it rains the bed is moved from place to place in the attempt to find a dry spot. Many a miner works his whole life and never handles a cent of money. All he earns must be spent in the "Pluck me" [company store]. Every miner has one dollar stopped for a company doctor. With 1,200 men working in a mine and a young doctor paid $300 a year, this means a nice little lump for the company. And this is the divine system the preacher was defending.

"To Defend the Bill of Rights"

The I.W.W. Fights for Free Speech

Elizabeth Gurley Flynn

One of the most radical unions was the Industrial Workers of the World (I.W.W.), whose members were known as "Wobblies." Founded in 1905, the I.W.W. advocated socialist democracy instead of capitalism. Using the slogan "One Big Union," the I.W.W. organized unskilled as well as skilled workers—unlike the American Federation of Labor (AFL), which consisted of national craft unions.

140

The Wobblies' chief base was in the West, where they organized miners and migrant workers. They conducted many free speech fights in cities that passed laws prohibiting them from organizing on street corners. The first of these was in Missoula, Montana, in 1908. Elizabeth Gurley Flynn helped organize the protest.

My first participation in an I.W.W. free-speech fight and my second arrest occurred in this little place, which was not an industrial town but was a gateway to many lumber camps and mining areas. It was surrounded by mountains; the air was clear and invigorating. It was a clean and attractive little place, the site of a state university. We held street meetings on one of the principal corners and drew large crowds, mainly the migratory workers who flocked in and out of town. We had rented as an I.W.W. hall a large roomy space in the basement of the leading theatre and were rapidly recruiting members into the organization.

The storekeepers objected to our meetings, especially the employment agencies, which we attacked mercilessly. [Editor's note: Employment agencies often defrauded migrant workers by collecting advance fees for fake jobs.] Under their pressure, the City Council passed an ordinance making street speaking unlawful. We decided to defy this ordinance as unconstitutional, a violation of the First Amendment guaranteeing freedom of speech. There were only five or six of us in town at that time. One was Frank Little, who was lynched in Butte, Montana, eight years later during World War I. When we tried to hold meetings, two were arrested the first night, who were dismissed with a warning not to speak again. Four were arrested the second night, including my husband, Jones, Frank Little, and a stranger to us, Herman Tucker.

He was employed by the U.S. Forestry Department, which had an office in a building overlooking the corner. He rushed downstairs when he saw a young logger dragged off the platform for attempting to read the Declaration of Independence. Tucker took it over, jumped on the platform, and continued to read until he was arrested. . . . Our Missoula free-speechers were sentenced to fifteen days in the county jail. Those of us who were left planned the mass tactics which were advocated in free-speech fights, of which Missoula was one of the first examples.

We sent out a call to all "footloose rebels to come at once—to defend the Bill of Rights." A steady stream of I.W.W. members began to flock in by freight cars. . . . As soon as one speaker was arrested, another took his place. The jail was soon filled, and the cellar under the firehouse was turned into an additional jail. But the excrement from the horses leaked through and made this place so unbearable that the I.W.W. prisoners protested by song and speech, night and day. They were directly across the street from the city's main hotel, and the guests complained of the uproar. The court was nearby, and its proceedings were disrupted by the noise. People came to listen to the hubbub, until finally all I.W.W.'s were taken back to the county jail.

The fire department next turned the hose on one of the meetings, but the townspeople protested vigorously against this after several people were hurt. College professors at the university took up the cudgels for free speech, especially when another woman, Mrs. Edith Frenette, and I were arrested. We were treated with kid gloves by the sheriff and his wife, although my husband had been badly beaten up in the jail by this same Sheriff Graham. . . . Butte Miners Union No. 1, the biggest local in Montana, passed a strong resolution condemning the local officials for "an un-American and unjust action in preventing men and women from speaking on the streets of Missoula" and commending "our gallant fight for free speech." They sent it to the Missoula papers, stating that my arrest had caused them to investigate the matter and adopt the resolution.

141

There were some humorous aspects to our efforts. Not all the I.W.W. workers were speakers. Some suffered from stage fright. We gave them copies of the Bill of Rights and the Declaration of Independence. They would read along slowly, with one eye hopefully on the cop, fearful that they would finish before he would arrest. One such was being escorted to jail, about two blocks away, when a couple of drunks got into a pitched battle. The cop dropped him to arrest them. When they arrived at the jail, the big strapping I.W.W. was tagging along behind. The cop said in surprise: "What are you doing here?" The prisoner retorted: "What do you want me to do—go back there and make another speech?"

Eventually, the townspeople got tired of the unfavorable publicity and excitement. The taxpayers were complaining of the cost to the little city. . . .

Finally, the authorities gave up. All cases were dropped. We were allowed to resume our meetings. We returned to our peaceful pursuit of agitating and organizing the I.W.W.

"To Give People Everything They Want"

Henry Ford's Ideas on Mass Production

Ida Tarbell

Not all industrialists were insensitive to the needs of their workers. Henry Ford used mass production to put the prices of automobiles within the reach of most Americans, including the people who made them. Ford also doubled his workers' buying power by instituting a minimum wage of five dollars for an eight-hour workday. Ida Tarbell, a journalist who had exposed corporate corruption, interviewed Ford as part of a series about what was good in American industry.

Then there was Henry Ford attacking the problem which most concerned his plant, labor turnover—in his case something like 1,200 percent. He had come into the industrial picture with his minimum wage of five dollars a day just before I began my work. In May of 1915, I set up shop for ten days in a Detroit hotel in order to study what he was doing. . . .

He was boyish and natural in off hours. Coming into the private lunchroom for officers at the plant, where I judged a place was always left for him, I saw him throw his long right leg over the back of the chair before he slid leisurely into the seat.

"I have got an idea," he said. "People complain about the doors of the car—not convenient. I am going to put a can opener into every car from now on and let them cut their own."

He delighted in the flow of Ford jokes, wanted to hear the latest, to see it in the house organ.

When he saw me, it was he who did the talking, and he seemed to be straightening out his thoughts rather than replying to my questions. When I asked him his reasons for mass production, he had a straightaway answer.

"It is to give people everything they want and then some," he said. And then he went on to enlarge in a way I have never forgotten.

"There's no reason why everybody shouldn't have everything he needs if we managed it right, weren't afraid of making too much. Our business is to make things so cheap that everybody can buy 'em. Take these shears." He picked up a handsome pair of large shears on his

Henry Ford used the moving assembly line to manufacture his automobiles, including this Model A.

desk. "They sell for three or four dollars, I guess. No reason you couldn't get them down to fifty cents. Yes, fifty cents," he repeated as I gasped. "No reason at all. Best in the world—so every little girl in the world could have a pair. There's more money in giving everybody things than in keeping them dear so only a few can have them.

"I want our car so cheap that every workman in our shop can have one if he wants it. Make things everybody can have—that's what we want to do. And give 'em money enough. The trouble's been we didn't pay men enough. High wages pay. People do more work. We never thought we'd get back our five dollars a day. Didn't think of it; just thought that something was wrong that so many people were out of work and hadn't anything saved up, and thought we ought to divide. But we got it all back right away. That means we can make the car cheaper, and give more men work. Of course when you're building and trying new things all the time you've got to have money, but you get it if you make men. I don't know that our scheme is best. It will take five years to try it out, but we are doing the best we can and changing when we strike a snag."

What it simmered down to was that if you wanted to make a business you must make men, and you must make men by seeing that they had a chance for what we are pleased to call these days a good life. And if they are going to have a good life they must not only have money but have low prices.

"An Advancing Step in Manifest Destiny"

Purchasing Alaska

The New York World

The doctrine of manifest destiny that fueled the United States' westward expansion took on an even broader scope after the Civil War. Secretary of State William H. Seward negotiated the purchase of Alaska from Russia in 1867. Alaska was ridiculed as "Seward's Folly" until gold was discovered there in 1897. However, The New York World *argued that Alaska was an important step toward the eventual acquisition of Canada as well.*

Russia has sold us a sucked orange. . . . What remains of the Russian fur trade is not of sufficient importance to justify the expense of the naval protection. . . . Russia has therefore done wisely in selling the territory and islands which to her had become useless.

But have we done wisely in buying it? If estimated by what is in itself, certainly not; if by what the purchase may hereafter lead to, perhaps yes.

When Franklin was asked the use of some new discovery in science, his reply was: "What is the use of a newborn infant? It may become a man." It is only in some prospective view that we can discover any value in this new purchase. It is almost amusing to read the comments of the effervescing quidnuncs [busybodies] who first heralded the news. They dilate on the vastness of the territory—ten or twelve times as large, they say, as the state of New York. But the greater part of it is of no more human use than so many square miles of ice in the Arctic Ocean by which it is bounded. . . . Other explosive enthusiasts think the purchase opens brilliant prospects for the China and Japan trade! As the territory can never have a population of consumers, and lies at a vast distance from the route for supplying inhabited countries, it is not very obvious how the new acquisition is to contribute mightily to the development of the Asiatic trade. . . . The small value of the territory in itself being so evident to everyone who will make the effort to look into the subject, its purchase, at the price paid, is not defensible except with a view to ulterior objects. . . .

The purchase of the Russian territory renders it morally certain that we shall some day acquire [British Columbia].

In the first place, a gap in our possessions on the Pacific Coast will always be an eyesore to the nation, whose sense of symmetry will be offended by the ragged look of the maps. The national imagination shall always require that our coastline shall be continuous, and this aspiration will sooner or later be potential. It will secure for the government efficient popular support whenever the time shall be ripe for completing what is now begun.

The acquisition [of the territory] is important because the British part of the coast is certain to follow at some day more or less remote. So long as the two nations are at peace, we can take no other steps toward its acquisition than proposals to purchase. If such proposals are rejected, we can afford to wait, since time will accomplish much for us and nothing for Great Britain. Our population and military strength on the Pacific are growing so rapidly that the seizure of the residue of the coast in the event of war will become constantly easier. If we should never have another war with Great Britain, we shall never need the territory. If we should have a war, we shall of course take it.

Looking to the future, we must regard the purchase of the Russian possessions as wise, although they are of little immediate value. It is an advancing step in that manifest destiny which is yet to give us British North America. . . .

"Into a Chute of Death"

Roosevelt and the Rough Riders

Richard Harding Davis

As U.S. industrial strength increased at the end of the nineteenth century, so did public pressure to adopt an imperialistic policy toward developing countries. Empire meant new sources of raw materials and new markets for American goods. Many Americans also believed that their moral destiny was to "give the world the life more abundant both for here and hereafter."

American business interests were heavily involved in Cuba, which revolted against Spain in 1895. Newspapers sensationalized Spanish cruelty to the Cubans and demanded that the United States intervene. Finally, when the U.S. battleship Maine *was sunk in Havana harbor in February 1898, the call for war became irresistible.*

Theodore Roosevelt resigned his position as assistant secretary of the Navy to join a volunteer cavalry unit called the Rough Riders. Although Roosevelt's charge on Cuba's San Juan Hill became legendary, like most legends the reported facts were not entirely accurate. Richard Harding Davis, a newspaper reporter, described the attack.

The situation was desperate. Our troops could not retreat, as the trail for two miles behind them was wedged with men. They could not remain where they were, for they were being shot to pieces. There was only one thing they could do—go forward and take the San Juan hills by assault. It was as desperate as the situation itself. To charge earthworks held by men with modern rifles and using modern artillery, until after the earthworks have been shaken by artillery, and to attack them in advance and not in the flanks are both impossible military propositions. But this campaign had not been conducted according to military rules, and a series of military blunders had brought

several thousand American soldiers into a chute of death, from which there was no escape except by taking the enemy who held it by the throat and driving him out and beating him down. So the generals of divisions and brigades stepped back and relinquished their command to the regimental officers and enlisted men.

"We can do nothing more," they virtually said. "There is the enemy."

Colonel Roosevelt, on horseback, broke from the woods behind the line of the Ninth [an all-black cavalry regiment] and, finding its men lying in his way, shouted: "If you don't wish to go forward, let my men pass, please." The [white] junior officers of the Ninth, with their Negroes, instantly

Artist Frederic Remington covered the Spanish-American War from the front lines. This painting depicts Theodore Roosevelt leading the charge on San Juan Hill.

They had no glittering bayonets; they were not massed in regular array. There were a few men in advance, bunched together, and creeping up a steep, sunny hill—the top of which roared and flashed with flame. The men held their guns pressed across their breasts and stepped heavily as they climbed. . . . They walked to greet death at every step, many of them as they advanced sinking suddenly or pitching forward and disappearing in the high grass, but the others waded on,

sprang into line with the Rough Riders and charged at the blue blockhouse on the right.

I speak of Roosevelt first because . . . he was, without doubt, the most conspicuous figure in the charge. . . . Roosevelt, mounted high on horseback and charging the rifle-pits at a gallop and quite alone, made you feel that you would like to cheer. He wore on his sombrero a blue polka-dot handkerchief . . . , which, as he advanced, floated out straight behind his head, like a guidon [military flag]. Afterward, the men of his regiment, who followed this flag, adopted a polka-dot handkerchief as the badge of the Rough Riders. . . .

I think the thing that impressed one the most, when our men started from cover, was that they were so few. It seemed as if someone had made an awful and terrible mistake. One's instinct was to call them to come back. You felt that someone had blundered and that these few men were blindly following out some madman's mad order. It was not heroic then; it merely seemed terribly pathetic. The pity of it, the folly of such a sacrifice was what held you.

stubbornly, forming a thin blue line that kept creeping higher and higher up the hill. It was as inevitable as the rising tide. It was a miracle of self-sacrifice, a triumph of bulldog courage, which one watched breathless with wonder. The fire of the Spanish riflemen, who still stuck bravely to their posts, doubled and trebled in fierceness, the crests of the hills crackled and burst in amazed roars and rippled with waves of tiny flame. But the blue line crept steadily up and on, and then, near the top, . . . the Spaniards . . . fired a last volley and fled before the swift-moving wave that leaped and sprang up after them.

The men of the Ninth and the Rough Riders rushed to the blockhouse together; the men of the Sixth, of the Third, of the Tenth [another black regiment] cavalries, of the Sixth and Sixteenth infantries, fell on their faces along the crest of the hills beyond and opened upon the vanishing enemy. They drove the yellow silk flags of the cavalry and the Stars and Stripes of their country into the soft earth of the trenches and then sank down and looked back at the road they had climbed and swung their hats in the air.

146

"Among the Bravest . . . of This Land"

Black Soldiers at San Juan Hill

Presley Holliday

Black soldiers played an important part in the Spanish-American War, yet they received little credit for it. Indeed, Theodore Roosevelt charged in an 1899 magazine article that black troops had attempted to retreat at San Juan Hill and that they only made good soldiers if led by white officers. Presley Holliday, a member of the Tenth Cavalry, disputed Roosevelt's claim in a black newspaper, The New York Age.

Having read in *The Age* of April 13 an editorial entitled "Our Troops in Cuba," which brings to my notice for the first time a statement made by Colonel Roosevelt, which, though in some parts true, . . . will certainly give rise to the wrong impression of colored men as soldiers, . . . and as I was an eyewitness to the most important incidents mentioned in that statement, I deem it a duty . . . to do all in my power to place the colored soldier where he properly belongs—among the bravest and most trustworthy of this land.

In the beginning, I wish to say that from what I saw of Colonel Roosevelt in Cuba and the impression his frank countenance made upon me, I cannot believe that he made that statement maliciously. I believe the colonel thought he spoke the exact truth. But did he know that of the four officers connected with two certain troops of the Tenth Cavalry, one was killed and three so seriously wounded as to cause them to be carried from the field, and the command of these two troops fell to the [black] first sergeants, who led them triumphantly to the front? Does he know that both at Las Guasima and San Juan Hill the greater part of troop B, of the Tenth Cavalry, was separated from its commanding officer by accidents of the battle and was led to the front by its first sergeant? . . .

There were frequent calls for men to carry the wounded to the rear, to go for ammunition, and as night came on, to go for rations and entrenching tools. A few colored soldiers volunteered, as did some from the Rough Riders. It then happened that two men of the Tenth were ordered to the rear by Lieutenant Fleming, Tenth Cavalry, who was then present with part of his troop for the purpose of bringing either rations or entrenching tools—and Colonel Roosevelt, seeing so many men going to the rear, shouted to them to come back, jumped up and drew his revolver, and told the men of the Tenth that he had orders to hold that line and he would do so if he had to shoot every man there to do it.

His own men immediately informed him that "you won't have to shoot those men, colonel. We know those boys." He was also assured by Lieutenant Fleming, of the Tenth, that he would have no trouble keeping them there, and some of our men shouted, in which I joined, that "we will stay with you, colonel." Everyone who saw the incident knew the colonel was mistaken about our men trying to shirk duty, but well knew that he could not admit of any heavy detail from his command, so no one thought ill of the matter. In as much as the colonel came to the line of the Tenth the next day and told the men of his threat to shoot some of their members and, as he expressed it, he had seen his mistake and found them to be far different men from what he supposed, I thought he was sufficiently conscious of his error not to make a so ungrateful statement about us at a time when the nation is about to forget our past service. . . .

And further, as to lack of qualifications for command, I will say that when our soldiers, who can and will write history, sever their connections with the regular army, and thus release themselves from their voluntary status of military lockjaw, and tell what they saw, those who now preach that the Negro is not fit to exercise command over troops and will go no further than he is led by white officers will see in print held up for public gaze, much to their chagrin, tales of those Cuban battles that have never been told outside the tent and barrack room—tales that it will not be agreeable for some of them to hear. The public will then learn that not every troop or company of colored soldiers who took place in the assaults on San Juan Hill or El Caney was urged forward by his white officer.

It is unfortunate that we had no colored officers in that campaign, and this thing of white officers for colored troops is exasperating, and I join with *The Age* in saying our motto for the future must be: "No officers. No soldiers."

"The War Against the Mosquito"

Building the Panama Canal

Albert Edwards

As a result of the Spanish-American War, the United States acquired the Philippines and Puerto Rico, among other islands. To defend these new possessions, America needed easy passage between the Atlantic and the Pacific. The U.S. government sought to build a canal across the Isthmus of Panama, then part of Colombia. When Colombia refused, the United States backed Panama in a 1903 revolt.

Construction of the canal began in 1904. One of the principal problems facing the project was yellow fever, which killed and weakened vast numbers of workers. William C. Gorgas, chief sanitary engineer, controlled yellow fever by eliminating the mosquitos that spread it. Journalist Arthur Bullard, writing under the name of Albert Edwards, described Gorgas's work.

O f all the sights on the Panama Canal, there is none more worthy of note than a dilapidated, galvanized iron ashcan [that sits on a plank across a stream]. . . .

. . . Just such an unattractive affair as the men of the Street Cleaning Department empty into their carts every morning in New York City. Only this one is uglier still, as it, like the banks of the stream, is smeared with . . . black oil.

A piece of lampwick hangs out near the bottom, and from it there falls every few seconds a drop of the blackness. Splashing into the water, it spreads out—wider and wider, till it touches each bank—into an iridescent film. It looks like the stuff they use for oiling automobile roads. It is a compound of crude carbolic acid, resin, and caustic soda called larvacide. These disreputable-looking ashcans—there are many of them all through the hills at the headwaters of each stream—have a very intimate connection with the mighty work down in the valley and with the healthy bloom on the cheeks of these village children. They are outposts—frontier stations—in the war against the mosquito. . . .

And if you talk with these men who are fighting disease—the engineer, who with transit and chain is laying out drainage ditches; the man who has the responsibility of guarding the purity of the drinking water; the rat-catcher, who strolls about with a Flobert rifle and a pocket full of poison; the red-headed young doctor who vaccinates you at Colon; or even the bacteriologist who finds his interesting researches "disturbed"—they will speak of themselves as "ditch-diggers." And no dynamite operator nor steam-shovel man will deny their right to say, "We've got sixty percent of the dirt out of Culebra Cut," or "We beat the record laying concrete at Gatun this week." . . .

The responsible head of the men who have done this marvelous work—and no words at my command can express the wonder of it—is W.C. Gorgas, chief sanitary officer. . . . Gorgas is genial and sympathetic. They say, "He can give you liquid quinine and jolly you into thinking you like it." That is just what he did to the people of Panama City and Colon during the early yellow fever epidemic. Nobody likes to have his home fumigated. The Panamanians are immune to the fever. . . . Gorgas succeeded in fumigating every house in Panama City within two weeks. He did it by jollying them—slapping the men on the shoulders, smiling at the women, and playing "one little pig went to market, one little pig stayed at home" on the toes of the babies. Even the Panamanians who are most unfriendly to Americans admit that Gorgas is a good fellow, and every child that knows him wants to sit in his lap.

Before coming here he had had charge of cleaning up Havana, and he knew how it should be done. Doubtless there were other American army doctors who had had similar experience and understood the work as well. But beyond the technique of his profession, Gorgas knew the Latin American people, their manner of life, and their prejudices. He knew how to make them swallow quinine and at least half believe they liked it. It was necessary to fumigate those houses, and we would have done it even if it had been necessary to call in the marines and proclaim martial law. But Gorgas, with his wonderful tact, did it without using force or in any way increasing the enmity to the Gringo. It was not only a remarkably effective sanitary accomplishment, but an exceedingly clever bit of diplomacy.

They tell a story about Gorgas in Cuba, and people who know him say it sounds true.

In the early days there were many who made light of the mosquito work. Gorgas went to one of his superiors for some money to carry on his campaign.

"Is it worthwhile to spend all this money just to save the lives of a few niggers?" the commandant protested.

"That's not the point, general," Gorgas shot back at him. "We're spending it to save *your* life. And that's worthwhile."

He got the money.

149

"Ignorance Is the Real Enemy"

A Muckraker Describes His Craft

Ray Stannard Baker

A new reform movement, Progressivism, gained support after 1896, when the Populists lost influence. Mostly middle-class city dwellers, Progressives believed in the ability of individuals and government to improve society. Many journalists encouraged the Progressive movement by exposing social problems, unfair business practices, and political corruption. Theodore Roosevelt labeled these reporters "muckrakers" (people who clean stables) because he believed they focused too much on the negative aspects of America. Ray Stannard Baker, a leading muckraker, reflected on his profession's impact on American society.

What I remember best about the earlier "exposure" articles—my own as well as those of Ida Tarbell, Lincoln Steffens, and others—was the extraordinary reception they had in every part of the country. . . . I think I can understand now why these exposure articles took such a hold upon the American people. It was because the country, for years, had been swept by the agitation of soapbox orators, prophets crying in the wilderness, and political campaigns based upon charges of corruption and privilege which everyone believed or suspected had some basis of truth, but which were largely unsubstantiated. . . .

What the early "exposers" did was to look at their world, *really* look at it. They reported honestly, fully, and above all interestingly what they found. And the public, now anxious and indignant, eagerly read the long and sometimes complicated and serious articles we wrote. Month after month they would swallow dissertations of ten or twelve thousand words without even blinking—and ask for more. . . .

. . . [T]he letters we received, the brick-bats as well as the bouquets, seemed highly encouraging to anyone who believed in the democratic method. They showed that ordinary men were not only willing but eager to know the truth.

We also began to receive enthusiastic responses from leaders in American public life, especially students of social, economic, or political conditions—to say nothing of argumentative letters from agitators and reformers who criticized us unmercifully for not accepting their particular brands of reform. . . . Occasionally a correspondent would ask indignantly why we ourselves remained so unmoved. I remember one letter from an angry reader, who asked how I could make such exposures without saying in plain terms that these men were thieves and traitors who ought to be in jail.

What he wanted was "red-hot invective." I remember thinking considerably about this letter, finally suggesting to my critic that if I became angry, or showed it, he wouldn't. If I "blew off," wouldn't he feel relieved, even satisfied; wouldn't he be tempted to do nothing more about it? But with the ugly facts, the complete picture, the truth, vividly and dispassionately set forth, wouldn't he and other honest men be stirred to the point of doing something about it themselves? . . .

. . . It seems to be a failing peculiarly American to begin dosing before the diagnosis is complete; we dislike to be quiet and slow; we hate to think things through. We believe in formulas and slogans; we like "drives." We have a pathetic faith in legal enactments such as the Eighteenth Amendment, and changes in the "system" such as the initiative and referendum. There may be considerable education of individual minds in the process of campaigning for such reforms, but it is astonishing how little, how very little, they change actual conditions.

I am not even sure of democracy as a universal cure—that is, if it means what it seems to mean to many people. But I am strong for democracy as a way of life—if it means what I think it ought to mean.

Ignorance is the real enemy.

"A Big Moral Movement in Democracy"

Political Reforms of Progressivism

William Allen White

Progressives introduced political reforms designed to make democracy work better. They supported direct primaries and secret ballots to prevent party bosses from controlling votes. Progressives also advocated democratic reforms such as the right of voters to propose legislation through the initiative, to approve legislation through the referendum, and to remove elected officials from office through the recall. Progressives were instrumental in securing direct election of the U.S. Senate, eventually guaranteed nationwide via the Seventeenth Amendment. William Allen White, a leading Progressive, summarized these reforms in his book The Old Order Changeth *(1910).*

Politics in America [in the late 1800s] was founded upon the boss system. At the bottom, in the smallest political unit, was the precinct boss. Delegates to local party conventions were elected from precincts or wards or townships.

The party convention in a county, town, or city was made up of from two to four hundred of such delegates. They nominated the local county, township, ward, or city candidates for the offices that composed the local government. . . . The precinct boss at the bottom of the system generally said who should go to the county, town, or city convention as delegates. . . . Half a dozen precinct bosses controlled the average county or small city. And the indomitable man among them controlled them. . . .

The extraconstitutional place of the boss in government was as the extraconstitutional guardian of business. If a telephone company desired to put its poles in the street, and the city council objected, straightway went the owner of the telephone stock to the boss. He straightened matters out. If a streetcar company was having trouble with the city street department, the manager of the street railway went to the boss, and the street department became reasonable. . . . Always business was considered. And in some exceptional cases, vice was considered business. That was because vice paid rent, and property interests could not be disturbed. . . . Money in politics was there for the purpose of protecting the rights of property under the law, as against the rights of men. So prosperity dwelt among the people. The greed of capital was rampant, the force of democracy was dormant. . . .

The movement to divorce the corporation from politics is so general that a federal law has been enacted limiting campaign contributions. And for the first time in the history of the United States the people know now exactly how much it costs to conduct a national campaign and from what sources the money comes. . . .

But the secret ballot, the direct primary, and the purged party—which are now fairly well assured in American politics—do not set the metes and bounds of progress toward self-government in this country. They are fundamental reforms, it is true, and they are the steps that are necessary before there may be any real forward movement. For it will be seen that each one of these movements is a leveling process, a tendency to make money, capital, property, wealth, or financial distinction count for nothing save as indirect influence in the ballot box. Each of these innovations, the secret ballot, the primary, and the reformed party, is a step toward democracy—a step toward the Declaration of Independence and away from the Constitution, which so feared majority rule that the majority was hedged about with checks and balances at every possible point.

In the early days of the republic, the people annulled the Constitution by getting a direct vote on the president, and thus obtained the executive branch of the government. Now they are capturing the legislative branch through the primary, which today puts over half the United States senators under the direct vote of the people. When one stops to think that in [many states] United States senators at the next election will go directly to the people for nominations, and not to the railroads and the public service corporations of their respective states—in short, not to capital as they did ten years ago—one realizes how revolutionary are the changes that are coming into our system. . . .

Indeed, the growth of fundamental democracy in this country is astonishing. Thirty years ago the secret ballot was regarded as a passing craze by professional politicians. Twenty years ago it was a vital issue in nearly every American state. Today the secret ballot is universal in American politics. Ten years ago the direct primary was the subject of an academic discussion in the University of Michigan by a young man named La Follette of Wisconsin. Now it is in active operation in over two-thirds of our American states, and over half of the American people use the direct primary as a weapon of self-government. Five years ago the recall was a piece of freak legislation in Oregon. Today more American citizens are living under laws giving them the power of recall than were living under the secret ballot when Garfield came to the White House. . . . The referendum is only five years behind the primary. . . . .

So the appearance of the recall, in the cities of a dozen states within a little over a year, should make those statesmen nervous who look forward to the time when the country will go back to the Good Old Days. . . . Whose wisdom directed it? No man's name is connected with it. No party or propaganda has been behind the movement. . . . It is growth—spiritual growth in the hearts of the American people. It is a big moral movement in democracy.

152

"God Must Work in Some Other Mine"

Decrying Child Labor

John Spargo

Progressive reformers deplored the use of child labor in American industry. They supported a national act forbidding child labor, which was passed in 1916 but declared unconstitutional by the Supreme Court in 1918. While a proposed constitutional amendment outlawing child labor failed to be ratified, the Supreme Court eventually reversed its decision in 1941. John Spargo's book, The Bitter Cry of Children, *fueled the arguments against child labor.*

American industries employed thousands of children, such as this girl who worked in a textile mill and boy who worked in a coal mine. In the 1890s, about 20 percent of children 10 to 15 years old had jobs. Many families could not survive without the wages earned by their children.

The textile industries rank first in the enslavement of children. In the cotton trade, for example, 13.3 percent of all persons employed throughout the United States are under 16 years of age. In the southern states, where the evil appears at its worst, so far as the textile trades are concerned, the proportion of employees under 16 years of age in 1900 was 25.1 percent; in Alabama the proportion was nearly 30 percent. . . . There are more than 80,000 children employed in the textile industries of the United States, according to the very incomplete census returns, most of them being little girls. In these industries conditions are undoubtedly worse in the southern states than elsewhere, though I have witnessed many pitiable cases of child slavery in northern mills which equalled almost anything I have ever seen in the South. During the Philadelphia textile workers' strike in 1903, I saw at least a score of children ranging from 8 to 10 years of age who had been working in the mills prior to the strike. One little girl of 9 I saw in the Kensington Labor Lyceum. She had been working for almost a year before the strike began, she said, and careful inquiry proved her story to be true.

When "Mother" Mary Jones started with her little "army" of child toilers to march to Oyster Bay, in order that the president of the United States might see for himself some of the little ones who had actually been employed in the mills of Philadelphia, I happened to be engaged in assisting the strikers. For two days I accompanied the little "army" on its march, and thus had an excellent opportunity of studying the children. Amongst them were several from 8 to 11 years of age, and I remember one little girl who was not quite 11 telling me with pride that she had "worked two years and never missed a day." . . .

According to the census of 1900, there were 25,000 boys under 16 years of age

153

employed in and around the mines and quarries of the United States. In the state of Pennsylvania alone—the state which enslaves more children than any other— there are thousands of little "breaker boys" employed, many of them not more than 9 or 10 years old. The law forbids the employment of children under 14, and the records of the mines generally show that the law is "obeyed." Yet in May 1905, an investigation by the National Child Labor Committee showed that in one small borough of 7,000 population, among the boys employed in breakers, 35 were 9 years old, 40 were 10, 45 were 11, and 45 were 12—over 150 boys illegally employed in one section of boy labor in one small town! . . .

Work in the coal breakers is exceedingly hard and dangerous. Crouched over the chutes, the boys sit hour after hour, picking out the pieces of slate and other refuse from the coal as it rushes past to the washers. From the cramped position they have to assume, most of them become more or less deformed and bent-backed like old men. When a boy has been working for some time and begins to get round-shouldered, his fellows say that "He's got his boy to carry round wherever he goes." The coal is hard, and accidents to the hands, such as cut, broken, or crushed fingers, are common among the boys. Sometimes there is a worse accident: a terrified shriek is heard, and a boy is mangled and torn in the machinery, or disappears in the chute to be picked out later smothered and dead. Clouds of dust fill the breakers and are inhaled by the boys, laying the foundations for asthma and miners' consumption.

I once stood in a breaker for half an hour and tried to do the work a 12-year-old boy was doing day after day, for ten hours at a stretch, for sixty cents a day. The gloom of the breaker appalled me. Outside the sun shone brightly, the air was pellucid [clear], and the birds sang in chorus with the trees and the rivers. Within the breaker there was blackness; clouds of deadly dust enfolded everything. The harsh, grinding roar of the machinery and the ceaseless rushing of coal through the chutes filled the ears. I tried to pick out the pieces of slate from the hurrying stream of coal, often missing them; my hands were bruised and cut in a few minutes. I was covered from head to foot with coal dust, and for many hours afterward I was expectorating some of the small particles of anthracite I had swallowed.

I could not do that work and live, but there were boys of 10 and 12 years of age doing it for fifty and sixty cents a day. Some of them had never been inside of a school; few of them could read a child's primer. True, some of them attended the night schools, but after working ten hours in the breaker the educational results from attending school were practically nil. "We goes fer a good time, an' we keeps de guys wots dere hoppin' all de time," said little Owen Jones, whose work I had been trying to do. How strange that barbaric patois sounded to me as I remembered the rich, musical language I had so often heard other little Owen Joneses speak in faraway Wales. As I stood in that breaker I thought of the reply of the small boy to Robert Owen. Visiting an English coal-mine one day, Owen asked a 12-year-old lad if he knew God. The boy stared vacantly at his questioner: "God?" he said, "God? No, I don't. He must work in some other mine." It was hard to realize amid the danger and din and blackness of that Pennsylvania breaker that such a thing as belief in a great all-good God existed.

"Mob Violence Has No Place"

Supporting Antilynching Laws

Ida B. Wells

African Americans faced discrimination and terror at the turn of the century. The Supreme Court upheld Jim Crow laws mandating segregation, and violent mobs lynched black citizens without a trial. Ida Wells, a black journalist, launched a national antilynching campaign. She found that almost 10,000 Americans were lynched from 1878 to 1898. Refuting the charge that lynching "is the only successful method of dealing with a certain class of crimes," namely assaults on women, Wells demonstrated that most lynchings were for misdemeanors. Violence against African Americans led to the founding in 1909 of the National Association for the Advancement of Colored People (NAACP), the nation's oldest and largest civil rights organization.

The record of the past ten years shows a surprising increase in lynchings and riot even in the North. No northern state has more frequently offended in this crime than Illinois, the state of Lincoln. . . . Since 1893 there have been sixteen lynchings within the state, including the Springfield riot. With each repetition there has been increased violence, rioting, and barbarism. The last lynching, which took place November 11 of last year in Cairo, was one of the most inhuman spectacles ever witnessed in this country.

The Negroes of Illinois have taken counsel together for a number of years over Illinois's increased lynching record. They elected one of their number to the state legislature in 1904, who secured the passage of a bill which provided for the suppression of mob violence, not only by punishment of those who incited lynchings, but provided for damages against the city and county permitting lynchings. The bill goes further and provides that if any person shall be taken from the custody of the sheriff or his deputy and lynched, it shall be prima facie evidence of failure on the part of the sheriff to do his duty. And upon that fact being made to appear to the governor, he shall publish a proclamation declaring the office of sheriff vacant, and such sheriff shall not thereafter be eligible to either election or reappointment to the office. . . . This bill passed both houses, was signed by Governor Deneen, and became a law in 1905. . . .

On the morning of November 11 last year, a double lynching was reported from Cairo, Illinois—a white man and a Negro. A white girl had been found murdered two days before. The bloodhounds which were brought led to a Negro's house three blocks away. A Negro who had stayed in that house the night before was arrested and sweated for twenty-four hours. Although the only clue found was that the gag in the girl's mouth was of the same kind of cloth as the handkerchief of the prisoner, threats of lynching him became so frequent that the sheriff took him away from the city, back in the woods twenty-five miles away.

When the mob had increased its numbers, they chartered a train, went after the sheriff, [and] brought him and his prisoner back to Cairo. A rope was thrown over [the prisoner] Will James's neck; he was dragged off the train to the main business corner of the town. The rope was thrown over a steel arch, which had a double row of electric lights. The lights were turned on and the body hauled up in view of the assembled thousands of men, women, and children. The rope broke before James was strangled to death and before hundreds of waiting bullets could be fired into his body. However, as many as could crowd around emptied their revolvers into the quivering mass of flesh as it lay on the ground. Then seizing the rope the mob dragged the corpse a mile up Washington Street, the principal thoroughfare, to where the girl's body had been found. They were followed by a jeering, hooting, laughing throng of all ages and of both sexes of white people. There they built a fire and placed this body on the flames. It was then dragged out of the fire, the head cut off and stuck on a nearby fence post. The trunk was cut open, the heart and other organs cut out, sliced up and passed around as souvenirs of the ghastly orgy and our American civilization.

Having tasted blood, a voice in the crowd said, "Let's get Salzner." Away went the mob to the county jail. Salzner, a white man, had been indicted for wife murder and was in jail awaiting trial. The suggestion is said to have come from the brother of Salzner's murdered wife. The mob demanded that the sheriff, who had repaired to his office in the jail when Will James had been taken from him an hour before, get Salzner for them. He begged them to go away, but when they began battering in the doors he telephoned the governor for troops. The lynchers got Salzner, hanged him in the courtyard in front of the jail, emptied their remaining bullets in his body, and went away. When troops reached the scene six hours later, they found, as the leading morning paper said next day, that "the fireworks were all over."

In mass meeting assembled, the Negro citizens of Chicago called on Governor Deneen to do his duty and suspend the sheriff. Two days later the sheriff's office was vacated. Ten days more and Sheriff Davis had filed his petition for reinstatement, and on December 1, argument was had before Governor Deneen both for and against the sheriff.

The sheriff's counsel, an ex-state senator and one of the leading lawyers of southern Illinois, presented the sheriff's petition for reinstatement, which declared he had done all in his power to protect the prisoners in his charge. He read letters and telegrams from judges, editors, lawyers, bankers, merchants, clergymen, the mayor of the city, captain of Company K of the state militia, his political opponents, and even the temporary incumbent of the sheriff's office himself—all wrote to urge Sheriff Davis's reinstatement. The petitions were signed by hundreds of citizens in all walks of life and the Catholic priest of Sheriff Davis's parish was present all day and sat at the sheriff's side.

As representing the people who had sent me to Cairo to get the facts, I told of the lynching, of visiting the scenes thereof, of the three days interview with the colored people of Cairo, and of reading the files of every newspaper in the city published during the lynching to find some account of the steps that had been taken to protect the prisoner. I told of the mass meeting of the Negroes of Cairo in which a resolution was passed declaring that from Tuesday morning when Will James was arrested until Thursday night when he was lynched, the sheriff had neither sworn in deputies to aid him in defending the prisoners nor called on the governor for troops. We said that a reinstatement of the sheriff would be an encouragement to mobs to hang, shoot, burn, and pillage whenever they felt inclined in the future, as they had done in the past.

Governor Deneen rendered his decision a week later, removing the sheriff. After reviewing the case he said:

> . . . Only one conclusion can be reached, and that is that the sheriff failed to take the necessary precaution for the protection of his prisoners. Mob violence has no place in Illinois. It is denounced in every line of the Constitution and in every statute. Instead of breeding respect for the law it breeds contempt.

It is believed that this decision with its slogan "Mob law can have no place in Illinois" has given lynching its death blow in this state.

"Women Fighting for Liberty"

Force-Feeding Suffragists in Prison

Rose Winslow

In 1914, war broke out in Europe between two alliance systems: the Central Powers of Germany and Austria-Hungary and the Allied Powers of France, Great Britain, and Russia. As the United States struggled to stay neutral, President Woodrow Wilson campaigned in 1916 for his second term on the theme "he kept us out of war." But in 1917, the Germans declared unrestricted submarine warfare and sank neutral American vessels. President Wilson asked Congress to declare war, arguing that "the world must be made safe for democracy."

Yet some Americans believed that "democracy should begin at home." Many women opposed the war because they were still unable to vote. When President Wilson refused to support women's suffrage, Alice Paul and her National Woman's party picketed the White House. Their cause gained publicity when they were jailed as a result and force-fed while on a hunger strike. Writing from the prison hospital, Rose Winslow—a Polish immigrant whose real name was Ruza Wenclawska—described the force-feedings. The Nineteenth Amendment, which granted women the vote, was finally ratified in 1920.

If this thing is necessary we will naturally go through with it. Force is so stupid a weapon. I feel so happy doing my bit for decency—for *our* war, which is after all, real and fundamental. . . .

The women are all so magnificent, so beautiful. Alice Paul is as thin as ever, pale, and large-eyed. We have been in solitary for five weeks. There is nothing to tell but that the days go by somehow. I have felt quite feeble the last few days— faint, so that I could hardly get my hair brushed, my arms ached so. But today I am well again. Alice Paul and I talk back and forth though we are at opposite ends of the building and a hall door also shuts us apart. But occasionally— thrills—we escape from behind our iron-barred doors and visit. Great laughter and rejoicing! . . .

My fainting probably means nothing except that I am not strong after these weeks. I know you won't be alarmed. . . .

Alice Paul is in the psychopathic ward. She dreaded forcible feeding frightfully, and I hate to think how she must be feeling. I had a nervous time of it, gasping a long time afterward, and my stomach rejecting during the process. I spent a bad, restless night, but otherwise I am all right. The poor soul who fed me got liberally besprinkled during the process. I heard myself making the most hideous sounds. . . . One feels so forsaken when one lies prone and people shove a pipe down one's stomach. . . .

This morning but for an astounding tiredness, I am all right. I am waiting to see what happens when the president realizes that brutal bullying isn't quite a

statesmanlike method for settling a demand for justice at home. At least, if men
are supine enough to endure, women—to
their eternal glory—are not. . . .

Yesterday was a bad day for me in
feeding. I was vomiting continually during
the process. The tube has developed an
irritation somewhere that is painful. . . .

. . . Don't let them tell you we take
this well. Miss Paul vomits much. I do,
too, except when I'm not nervous, as I have
been every time against my will. . . .

We think of the coming feeding all
day. It is horrible. The doctor thinks I

take it well. I hate the thought of Alice
Paul and the others if I take it well. . . .

. . . I am really all right. If this
continues very long I perhaps won't be.
I am interested to see how long our so-
called "splendid American men" will
stand for this form of discipline. . . .

All the officers here know we
are making this hunger strike that
women fighting for liberty may be considered political prisoners; we have
told them. God knows we don't want
other women ever to have to do this
over again.

"Without Negro Labor"

Compulsory Work Laws in the South

Walter F. White

*African Americans also questioned whether America was safe for demo-
cracy. Race riots broke out in East St. Louis, Illinois, and in Chester, Pennsylvania, during 1917. And in the South, the federal "work or fight" rule, requir-
ing men of draft age to be employed, was used to discriminate against black
citizens. Many African Americans moved north to take industrial jobs that
immigration could not fill due to wartime restrictions. In what became
known as the Great Migration, about one million African Americans from the
Southeast moved to the North between 1910 and 1930. Walter F. White, an
NAACP official, helped lead the protest against compulsory work laws.*

In a small town in Alabama, sixteen
miles from Montgomery, the state capital, the mayor of the town had a colored
cook. This cook one Saturday night asked
her employer for a higher wage. The mayor
refused, stating that he had never paid any
more for a cook and wasn't going to do so
now. The woman thereupon quit, and, as
the law provided, the mayor took up her
employment card, which he himself had
issued to her. The following morning a
deputy sheriff appeared at her door and
demanded that she show her work card.
Despite her explanation of the reason why
she had no card, she was arrested and on
Monday morning was brought up for trial
in the mayor's court, before the mayor

himself. She was found guilty, and fined
fourteen dollars, which fine was paid by
the mayor, who then said to her, "Go on up
to my house, work out the fine and stop
your foolishness."

This is a striking example of the
method by which certain sections of the
South have been able to improve on the
Work-or-Fight order of Provost Marshal
General Crowder. This order provided
that every able-bodied male person
between the draft ages must be engaged
in some necessary employment. At first
this only included males of a maximum
of 31 years of age. Later the Selective
Service Act was amended to include males
up to 45 years of age. But it was not suffi-

158

cient for the many employers who found that the war took from them workers they had used in civilian forms of labor, and, North and South, compulsory-work laws were passed by various states. . . .

These federal and state laws, however, referred only to men. But women's labor was also greatly in demand. The shortage of domestic servants had been felt throughout the whole of the United States, but it remained for the South to meet it in the extraordinary manner exemplified by the mayor in Alabama. Cities and towns and rural communities passed compulsory-labor ordinances and by this means met with partial success in keeping the population at its former work and sometimes at prewar low wages. . . .

In Birmingham, . . . the wife of a respectable colored man was sitting on her porch one afternoon paring potatoes for supper, waiting for her husband to come home from his work. An officer saw her, asked her if she was working, and on being told that her duties at home required all of her time and that her husband earned enough to allow her to stay at home, he arrested her for "vagrancy," taking her to the county jail. When her husband came home and was told of the arrest, he immediately went to the jail to provide bail for his wife. This he could not do as all of the officials had gone home. His wife was forced to remain in jail all night and was released on bail the following morning. This case was dismissed when brought to trial.

In Bainbridge, Decatur County, Georgia, in July, the city council passed an ordinance forcing all women (which meant all colored women), whether married or not, whose duties were only those of their homes, to work at some particular job. An officer was sent to the homes of colored people who summoned the wives of a num-

---

"Make America Safe for Democracy First"

Protesting the War

Joseph Gilbert

Congress tried to suppress opposition to the war with the Espionage Act of 1917, which punished those who aided the enemy or obstructed military recruitment, and the Sedition Act of 1918, which prohibited criticism of the U.S. government, flag, or military uniforms. Both acts were interpreted broadly by the courts to prohibit almost any criticism of the war. In 1918, Joseph Gilbert received a year in prison and a $500 fine for making the following comments.

We are going over to Europe to make the world safe for democracy, but I tell you we had better make America safe for democracy first. You say, what is the matter with our democracy? I tell you what is the matter with it: Have you had anything to say as to who should be president? Have you had anything to say as to who should be governor of this state? Have you had anything to say as to whether we should go into this war? You know you have not. If this is such a great democracy, for heaven's sake why should we not vote on conscription of men? We were stampeded into this war by newspaper rot to pull England's chestnuts out of the fire for her. I tell you, if they conscripted wealth like they have conscripted men, this war would not last over forty-eight hours.

---

ber of colored men to appear in court. There they were charged with vagrancy and fined fifteen dollars each and told that taking care of their homes was not enough work for them to be doing. On the following night an indignation meeting of the colored citizens was held, and the city authorities were told that unless this unjust and discriminatory law were repealed, the colored people would resist "to the last drop of blood in their bodies." No further arrests were made.

No record could be found of any able-bodied white woman being molested. . . .

The crux of the whole situation is found in the fact that domestic and farm labor has been affected by the new wartime conditions, and the South in large measure

159

was unable to adjust itself to a condition where its former plethora of cheap labor was wiped out. It has the opportunity now to clean house and prevent further migration by wiping out the abuses which exist. If it is attempted through the courts to hammer down wages and persecute laborers, the South may expect increasingly to lose its Negro labor. Since 1914, it is variously estimated that between 500,000 and 1,500,000 Negroes have gone north. Without Negro labor, the South will be bankrupt. With it and its great natural resources, it can become one of the richest sections of the country. It remains to be seen whether the better element among the whites can (and will) gain the ascendancy over the larger element of those who practice the policy laid down by the *Dred Scott* decision of regarding the Negro as "having no rights which a white man is bound to respect."

"Going Over the Top"

Warfare in the Trenches

Norman Roberts

The arrival of fresh American troops and supplies lifted the morale of the British and French, who were exhausted after years of fighting in the trenches. The American Expeditionary Force fought in France from June 1917 to November 1918. In his wartime diary, soldier Norman Roberts described the terror of "going over the top" of the trenches to face the enemy's gunfire.

Sept. 11, '18. Started for the front at 6 p.m. Raining and wind blowing. Very cold. All boys wet to the skin. Roads very muddy and all shot to pieces from the Germans' big guns. Very bad walking. Falling in holes to one's waist, these holes being full of water. Germans shelling this road as we advance. No one allowed to talk. All noise unnecessary prohibited. When near the woods the Germans dropped an H.E. shell near us and threw mud all over us. Believe me I was some frightened; after entering the woods the shelling was something terrible. Iron falling like hail.

Our major was there directing the placing of the men in the trenches. Dark as pitch except when a shell would explode. Some of the boys praying and some swearing. No place to swear. So dark each man had to take the other by the straps on his haversack to keep from getting lost. With that, the detail that I was with became lost but finally found the trench which we had been allotted. Some mud. Over the knees. About 12 o'clock all were in the trenches waiting for the zero hour that we were to make our attack upon Fritz [the Germans]. At 1:30 a.m. 12th the barrage of our guns broke loose upon the first line trenches, and oh what a noise there was. . . . Then the Germans came back with their guns. Oh, me, what noise and not be allowed to talk. All of us were wet and cold and *scared*. The boy sitting next to me shot himself in the foot to keep from going over the top.

Sept. 12. At 5:00 a.m. the words came down the trench to get ready for attack. Over the top we are going after Fritz. I was the fourth man of my platoon to go over. A baptism of fire was my reception in my first battle and first all-American offensive, St. Mihiel drive. This sector had been the scene of many battles during the war by the French and English troops—to capture this would mean the straightening of the line of the Allies. But

160

both had failed to take same.

Day had not broke and you could hardly tell where to go. Bullets, millions of them, flying like raindrops. Rockets and flares in all directions. Shrapnel bursting the air and sending down its deadly iron. High explosives bursting in the ground and sending forth bricks, mud, and iron to the destruction of man. Oh, what a morning. Machine gun bullets flying past you as the wind. Whistling as a bird going its travel.

Dead and wounded all around you. Comrades falling directly in front and you not allowed to assist them. The command *onward*. Every minute looking for the next to be gone to the great beyond. A mad dash for fifty feet and then look for cover. A stop for a minute and then the barrage would lift to a farther point and then another mad rush. Always leaving some of your comrades cold in the face of death. Men crying for the Almighty God to have mercy upon them. Asking the men to shoot them and place them out of their

"If We Don't Lick the Huns Now"

A Soldier's Reasons for Fighting

Private Eldon Canright

Some pacifists argued that World War I soldiers had no idea what they were fighting for. But Private Eldon Canright, in a letter home, clearly believed that he was fighting to keep his loved ones safe.

You know I have actually seen what the Huns [Germans] have done to northern France and Belgium and know what horrors and sufferings the people who lived there have gone through, and when things are going hard and I am tired and discouraged, I like to think that I am here going through all these hardships to do my bit to keep you all from experiencing the same horrors that these unfortunate people have—that if we don't lick the Huns now, and lick them to a standstill, they might at some future time try to do the same thing in America. You can laugh at me if you want to, and say I'm foolish, but that thought gives me fresh determination to carry on. There is nothing I would not do to prevent you from going through even a part of what they have had to do.

misery. Oh, what a pleading before your very eyes for death. Men making all kinds of promises to God if he would only protect them at this time.

Airplanes sweeping down upon you and firing their guns almost in your face. Barbed wire in all directions. I became tangled in this and thought surely before I could free myself that I would be killed. We have supremacy of the air during this battle. Day breaks and oh, how pleased to welcome same.

"I'm a Lady Leatherneck"

The First Female Marines

Private Martha L. Wilchinski

The U.S. Marine Corps first enlisted women during World War I, primarily as stenographers. Private Martha L. Wilchinski was one of these women, and in a letter to her fiancé she shared the good news.

Women and African Americans filled the desperate need for workers created by a decline in immigration and the loss of men to military service during World War I.

Dear Bill,

I've got the greatest news! No, I haven't thrown you over; I'm still strong for you, Bill. No, it's no use; don't try to guess. You're not used to that much mental effort, and you might get brain fag. Besides, you'd never guess, anyway. Now, listen and try to get this. I know it'll be hard at first, but it'll grow on you after a while. Are you ready? Well, then, I'm a lady leatherneck; I'm the last word in Hun hunters; I'm a real, live, honest-to-goodness Marine! The process was painful, I admit, and lasted for thirty-six hours, but I survived all right. . . . I'm not looking for sympathy or anything, but honest, I've been through an awful lot. They've done everything to me except punch my name out on my chest. That's coming soon, I guess. But I'll begin from the beginning and tell you everything. . . .

You know I always had a kind of a hunch that the Marines would realize the necessity of women some day, so I was laying low and waiting. Well, when I heard they had at last hung out a sign at the recruiting station—"Women wanted for the United States Marine Corps"—I was ready. "Mother," says I, "give me your blessing; I'm going to be one of the first to enlist." I was there when the doors opened in the morning. I was one of the first all right— the first 600! You'd think they were selling sugar or something. Well, when the crowd heard that you had to be willing to go anywhere as ordered and you had to be a cracker-jack stenog, they thinned out some. And from what was left, the lieutenant picked out twelve to go over to the colonel. . . . Well, only three of us came out alive. The others had fallen by the wayside. Then the colonel came in and told us to come over and be sworn in. I'm going to tell you something. I'm not bragging, but it isn't every private that's sworn in by a colonel. It was terribly impressive. Something kept sticking in my throat all the time. I don't know whether it was my heart or my liver. I had to swallow it several times before I could say, "I do." . . .

Bill, you never were very literary. But did you ever hear me speak of Kipling and what he said about the female of the species being more deadly than a triple titration of TNT? Well, if a regiment of Marines can make the Germans stand on their boneheads and yell *kamerad* [literally, "comrade"; the word Germans used to surrender], you can imagine what a regiment of female Marines would do. Why, those plop-eyed, yellow-skinned bounders would run so fast and furious they'd never stop for second wind until they reached Berlin.

I never received that German helmet. Are you sure you got the fellow, Bill?

I can't sign myself as affectionately as I used to, Bill. You understand, I'm a soldier now and you wouldn't want me doing anything that wasn't in the manual.

Yours till the cows come home.

"There Is No Armistice for Charley"

Nursing the Wounds of War

Shirley Millard

Shirley Millard was an American nurse at a French army hospital near the front lines. She experienced the effects of the worldwide epidemic in 1918 of influenza, a deadly disease that killed many soldiers. She also witnessed the horrible impact of a new weapon, poison gas. When peace finally came on the eleventh hour of the eleventh day in the eleventh month of 1918, Millard found herself unable to celebrate.

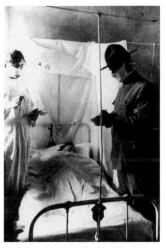

Army camps were hit hard by a worldwide flu epidemic that struck in 1918. More than 500,000 Americans died from the disease, about ten times as many as died in combat during World War I.

April 1

The big drive is over and the terrific rush has stopped, at least temporarily, but the hospital is still filled.

Most of the men are too badly wounded to be moved, although we need the space, for we are swamped with influenza cases. I thought influenza was a bad cold, something like the grippe, but this is much worse than that. These men run a high temperature, so high that we can't believe it's true, and often take it again to be sure. It is accompanied by vomiting and dysentery. When they die, as about half of them do, they turn a ghastly dark gray and are taken out at once and cremated.

November 8

More and more Americans in the death ward [for dying soldiers]. Gas cases are terrible. They cannot breathe lying down or sitting up. They just struggle for breath, but nothing can be done . . . their lungs are gone. . . . [Some are] covered with first degree burns. We try to relieve them by pouring oil on them. They cannot be bandaged or even touched. We cover them with a tent of propped-up sheets. Gas burns must be agonizing because usually the other cases do not complain even with the worst of wounds. But gas cases invariably are beyond endurance, and they cannot help crying out. . . .

November 10

Charley [a paralyzed American sergeant] died this morning. I held his hand as he went and could not keep back the tears. Near the end he saw me crying and patted my hand with his two living fingers to comfort me. I cannot describe that boy's sweetness. He took part of my heart with him. Everybody around the place was in tears.

Just after he went, someone came into the ward and said: "Armistice! The staff cars have just passed by the gate on their way to Senlis to sign an armistice!"

What a time and place to come in shouting about an armistice! I said: "Sh! Sh!"

There is no armistice for Charley or for any of the others in that ward. One of the boys began to sob. I went and talked soothingly to him, but what could I say, knowing he would die before night?

Well, it's over. I have to keep telling myself, it's over, it's over, it's over.

But there is still that letter to write to Charley's mother. I can hear commotion and shouting through the hospital as I write this. The chapel bell is ringing wildly.

I am glad it is over, but my heart is heavy as lead. Must write that letter.

One of the girls came looking for me. They have opened champagne for the staff in the dining hall. I told her to get out.

Can't seem to pull myself together.

1919-1945

Democracy and Adversity

The years of crisis from World War I through World War II gave birth to the nation in which Americans live today. New technology transformed everyday life; workers, women, and minorities strived for greater economic and political power; and the federal government began to take more responsibility for the welfare of its citizens. While dictators seized power in Europe during these years of upheaval, the United States preserved its democratic government and capitalist economy through experimentation and adaptation. During the 1920s, modern technology and mass production changed Americans' everyday lives. Electricity, automobiles, and radios became necessities rather than luxuries, and a booming economy enabled many Americans to purchase them. Advertising and the mass media encouraged the consumer culture, decreasing regional differences in the United States. A family in Newark, New Jersey, could eat the same cereal, drive the same car, and watch the same movies as a family in Lincoln, Nebraska, or Spokane, Washington. Changes in American society went much deeper than the outward signs of the consumer culture. Workers, women, and minorities,

...Listing continued on next page

who made important contributions during World War I, demanded greater economic and political power after the war. Other Americans resisted these demands, even resorting to violence. ❧ The human suffering of the Great Depression brought further changes in American life. When President Franklin Roosevelt entered office in 1933, one-fourth of the workforce was unemployed. Through Roosevelt's New Deal, the federal government substantially increased the responsibility it took for the welfare of its citizens. The legacy of Roosevelt's unprecedented twelve years as president is America's modern welfare state and an enormous federal bureaucracy, which still do much to regulate the economy and provide for the disadvantaged. ❧ Although government programs did relieve some suffering, they did not end the Depression—that came with the burst of economic activity accompanying World War II. Every American was drawn into the war effort, and when the war was over, workers, women, and minorities again hoped that the postwar era would bring rewards for their labors.

"Because I Am a Radical and an Italian"

The Trial of Sacco and Vanzetti

Nicola Sacco
Bartolomeo Vanzetti

After World War I, labor unrest at home and the spread of communism abroad led many Americans to fear a takeover by communists, or "Reds." During the "Red Scare" of 1919-20, Attorney General A. Mitchell Palmer organized the "Palmer Raids," arresting thousands of innocent people suspected of being communists and deporting hundreds of aliens.

Many radicals were of foreign ancestry, which increased the suspicion against them. In Massachusetts, Italian anarchists Nicola Sacco and Bartolomeo Vanzetti were arrested for robbery and murder in 1920 and eventually executed in 1927. Judge Webster Thayer, who referred to the defendants as "those anarchist bastards," was widely regarded as biased, and many people believed that Sacco and Vanzetti were convicted because of their political ideas. Excerpted here are Sacco and Vanzetti's final statements to the court upon sentencing.

I am not an orator. It is not very familiar with me the English language, and as I know, as my friend has told me, my comrade Vanzetti will speak more long, so I thought to give him the chance.

I never know, never heard, even read in history anything so cruel as this court. After seven years prosecuting they still consider us guilty. . . .

I know the sentence will be between two classes, the oppressed class and the rich class, and there will be always collision between one and the other. We fraternize the people with the books, with the literature. You persecute the people, tyrannize over them, and kill them. We try the education of people always. You try to put a path between us and some other nationality that hates each other. That is why I am here today on this bench, for having been the oppressed class. Well, you are the oppressor.

You know it, Judge—you know all my life, you know why I have been here, and after seven years that you have been persecuting me and my poor wife, and you still today sentence us to death. . . .

I forgot one thing which my comrade remember me. As I said before, Judge Thayer know all my life, and he know that I am never been guilty, never—not yesterday nor today nor forever.

—*Nicola Sacco*

What I say is that I am innocent, not only of the Braintree crime, but also of the Bridgewater crime. . . . That is what I want to say. And it is not all. Not only am I innocent of these two crimes, not only in all my life I have never stole, never killed, never spilled blood, but I have struggled all my life, since I began to reason, to eliminate crime from the earth.

Everybody that knows these two arms knows very well that I did not need to . . . kill a man to take the money. I can live with my two arms and live well. But besides that, I can live even without work with my arm for other people. I have had plenty of chance to live independently and to live what the world conceives to be a higher life than not to gain our bread with the sweat of our brow.

My father in Italy is in a good condition. I could have come back in Italy and he would have welcomed me every time with open arms. Even if I come back there with not a cent in my pocket, my father would have give me a possession, not to work but to make business, or to oversee upon the land that he owns. . . .

. . . [N]ot only have I struggled hard against crimes, but I have refused myself . . . the pride of life of a good position, because in my consideration it is not right to exploit man. I have refused to go in business because I understand that business is a speculation on profit upon certain people that must depend upon the businessman, and I do not consider that that is right and therefore I refuse to do that. . . .

Eugene Debs [a Socialist leader] say that not even a dog—something like that—not even a dog that kill the chickens

would have been found guilty by American jury with the evidence that the Commonwealth have produced against us. I say that not even a leprous dog would have his appeal refused two times by the Supreme Court of Massachusetts—not even a leprous dog. . . .

. . . We have proved that there could not have been another judge on the face of the earth more prejudiced and more cruel than you have been against us. We have proven that. Still they refuse the new trial. We know, and you know in your heart, that you have been against us from the very beginning, before you see us. . . .

This is what I say: I would not wish to a dog or to a snake, to the most low and misfortunate creature of the earth—I would not wish to any of them what I have had to suffer for things that I am not guilty of. But my conviction is that I have suffered for things that I am guilty of. I am suffering because I am a radical and indeed I am a radical; I have suffered because I was an Italian, and indeed I am an Italian; I have suffered more for my family and for my beloved than for myself; but I am so convinced to be right that if you could execute me two times, and if I could be reborn two other times, I would live again to do what I have done already.

—*Bartolomeo Vanzetti*

"America Belongs to Americans"

The Resurgence of the Ku Klux Klan

Hiram Evans

Immigration to the United States rose after World War I, and so did nativism. During the 1920s, the Ku Klux Klan revived itself by promoting "100 percent Americanism," gaining more than 4 million members and significant political influence in many states. Imperial Wizard Hiram Evans, a dentist from Dallas, describes the mission of the Klan in the 1920s.

The Klan can be evaluated only by starting from the point of view of what it means to the average Klansman. The real value of the Klan, or the real evil, is to be found in the needs, the purposes, and the convictions of the great mass of Americans of the old stock. It is only because the Klan has met these needs and voiced these convictions that it has won strength.

There is no possibility of trying to prove the soundness of the Klan position, or of the controlling instincts and beliefs of the common people of American descent, to any of those who insist on measuring either by the purely theoretic philosophy of cosmopolitanism: of universal equality in character, social value, and current rights. I will not attempt to argue about that doctrine. Science does not support it, and certainly the average American does not believe it. Our attitude toward the Orientals proves this, no matter what our oral professions may be, as well as does our treatment of the Negro. . . .

automatically and instinctively developed the kind of civilization which is best suited to its own healthy life and growth; and that this cannot safely be changed except by ourselves and along the lines of our own character.

Finally, we believe that all foreigners were admitted with the idea, and on the basis of at least an implied understanding,

Thousands of members of the Ku Klux Klan marched in Washington, D.C., on August 8, 1925, marking the zenith of Klan influence in the 1920s.

Neither will we argue at all about the questions of white supremacy. We may be intolerant in this, but we will not delude other races into looking forward to privileges that will, in truth, be forever denied. . . .

We believe that the pioneers who built America bequeathed to their own children a priority right to it, the control of it and of its future, and that no one on earth can claim any part of this inheritance except through our generosity. We believe, too, that the mission of America under Almighty God is to perpetuate and develop just the kind of nation and just the kind of civilization which our forefathers created.

Also, we believe that races of men are as distinct as breeds of animals; that any mixture between races of any great divergence is evil; that the American stock, which was bred under highly selective surroundings, has proved its value and should not be mongrelized; that it has

that they would become a part of us, adopt our ideas and ideals, and help in fulfilling our destiny along those lines, but never that they should be permitted to force us to change into anything else. That is the basic idea of the Klan. We hold firmly that America belongs to Americans and should be kept American.

Plain recognition of facts supports our opposition to the Roman Catholic Church. I have watched with interest the discussion whether the Roman Church is fighting Americanism, but this is another case where facts are more eloquent than any argument. The facts are that the Roman Church has always opposed the fundamental principle of liberty for which America stands. It has made certain compromises, taking advantage of the tolerance we give but which the Roman Church itself denies, and is trying through these compromises to win control of the nation. But it has made no admission that it has abandoned its old position.

Another ground for our opposition to the Roman Catholic Church is that most of its members in this country are aliens, and that the Church not only makes no effort to help them become assimilated to Americanism, but actually works to prevent this and to keep the Catholics as a group apart. . . .

The Jew the Klan considers a far smaller problem. For one thing, he is confined to a few cities and is no problem at all to most of the country. For another thing, his exclusiveness, political activities, and refusal to become assimilated are racial rather than religious, based on centuries of persecution. They cannot last long in the atmosphere of free America, and we may expect that with the passage of time the serious aspects of this problem will fade away.

To sum up: The Klan speaks for the plain people of America, who believe in an American nation, built on that unity of mind and spirit which is possible only to a homogeneous people, and growing out of the purposes, spirit, and instincts of our pioneer ancestors. We know that the melting pot has failed; the reasons are unimportant now. We believe that definite steps must now be taken to prevent ours from becoming a mongrel nation, or a milling and distraught mass of opposed groups, in which the mental and spiritual qualities that made America great will be lost forever. Therefore, we oppose all alienism in any form and the excessive liberalism that supports it. We grant to all the right to their own ideas, but we claim the same right for ourselves and a prior right to control America.

"Africa Wants You"

Promoting the Back to Africa Movement

Emily Christmas Kinch

Faced with intense prejudice and the growth of the Klan, many African Americans during the 1920s believed that their only hope was to return to Africa. Marcus Garvey, a Jamaican immigrant, founded the Universal Negro Improvement Association (UNIA) to create an independent black nation in Africa. The UNIA collapsed after Garvey was convicted of mail fraud and deported in 1927. Emily Christmas Kinch, a missionary to Africa from the African Methodist Episcopal (AME) Church, rallied support for the "Back to Africa" movement.

It is one of my great ambitions, especially since returning from Africa, to meet a group of people who have an idealism similar to my own, and that is— "Back to Africa." And somehow, in my travels throughout the United States, I feared the people had lost the vision of their opportunity—of going back to Africa and possessing the land. Is it time? Is the time ripe? Yes, it is time. It is quite time. This is the noon hour of our opportunity.

First of all, because Africa never was in a more susceptible, receptive mood for the UNIA than today. Before the worldwide war, practically every door was closed to the Negroes of America. But God has mysteriously moved on the heart of the world, and everywhere there is unrest; and because of conditions brought about through the Belgians and Germans and other nations who had a strong and powerful grip on Africa, today that grip has been gradually loosened, and everywhere the

170

African wants to know why we in America do not come home. . . .

I have never had very much use of the man or woman who said they have lost nothing in Africa. It has been a great pleasure for me to tell them they found nothing here. . . . If lynching and burning and disfranchisement and Jim Crow law has given you a disposition to remain there, then remain. But there is a land that flows with milk and honey. There is a land that would receive you gladly—a land that you have turned your back on, a land to which men have gone over and come back bringing the joyful tidings that we are fully able to go up and possess the land. Let us go forward in His name and take it.

Now if there are men of vision and men of brains and men of character and men who will gladly die for this cause, then I want you to know that there are women also who will join you and will gladly die with you that Africa might be redeemed. . . . I want you men to remember that while you are the stronger part of the great whole, that the larger numbers in this great group are the women. . . .

. . . Now then, if you want to grind out your life over the washtub, if you wish to spend the rest of your days upon the cooking table, if you are satisfied with these conditions, why, you can do nothing better than to remain here. But those of you who believe, who know that what I have said is the truth—Africa wants you. How I should have liked to be in Monrovia [Liberia] when the delegation [from UNIA] arrived there and seen the welcome which they received. The Africans waited long and patiently for the delegation that would come from the descendants of the men and women who were slaves, and they have often said to us: "Why have you stayed so long? What has civilization and freedom meant to you if not to come back and give your life. . . . [You have] bridged the rivers, thrown up skyscrapers for America, and yet you cannot go into a first-class hotel because you are black. You cannot ride in the Pullmans if you are tired, but must sit up or do the next best thing. Why not come back to Africa and make this a great country for ourselves, our children, and our children's children?" . . .

You think it is a wonderful thing to be in Harlem, but you have never enjoyed your manhood until you have walked in Liberia and have come in contact with the black president of that country and received invitations to come to the banquet that is prepared in the State House. You surely cannot go to Washington to one. And so, after all, I would rather be in Liberia tonight, all things being equal, without her trolley cars, without her subways, without her elevated system, and to feel and know that I am a woman for all of that. Black skins or short hair, money or no money, you are a man and have the opportunity of being the greatest person in that republic; for the only requirement of Liberia is that you are black. Let us therefore join hands and back up the man who is leading us out of this wilderness into the Promised Land.

"Wild Schemes to Defeat the Law"

Converting Hair Tonic to Whiskey

George Bieber

The Eighteenth Amendment—which prohibited the "manufacture, sale, or transportation of intoxicating liquors"—was ratified in 1919. Also passed in 1919, the Prohibition Enforcement Act, or Volstead Act, established the mechanisms for the implementation of Prohibition. But crafty bootleggers invented many ways to circumvent the law. George Bieber of Chicago describes how some bootleggers operated—until Prohibition was repealed by the Twenty-first Amendment in 1933.

I was fifteen when the Volstead Act went into effect, working in the Division Flower Shop on the corner of Western and Division streets. The owners weren't interested in selling flowers. They kept half a dozen bunches in the window, but if some stranger came in and placed a big order, they'd fill it through a genuine florist nearby and send it out under the Division label. That was my job, standing around in the front of the shop and handling people who actually wanted to buy flowers.

The boss was Vincent "Schemer" Drucci. They nicknamed him Schemer because of the wild schemes he was always thinking up to defeat the law. The real business of the Division Flower Shop was converting denatured alcohol into drinkable liquor. Drucci and his partners had first set up a hair tonic plant. This entitled them to buy No. 39B alcohol [which contained a nauseating agent making it unfit for human consumption].

Up to a point the Cosmo Hair Tonic Company was legitimate. They advertised widely. They even paid celebrities to endorse the product. I recall seeing on billboards: *Paul Asch*—he was a well-known bandleader—*Uses Cosmo Hair Tonic.* And they sold quite a number of bottles. Not nearly as many as their books showed, though. To deceive the government inspectors, they would sell a few hundred cases to a friendly wholesale distributor and throw in a few hundred more free as a bribe. The books would

then show sales of thousands, and on the basis of such a big volume the government would allot the company corresponding amounts of 39B alcohol.

The conversion to drinkable liquor took place in the basement of the flower shop under the direction of a chemist we all called Karl the Dutchman. . . . To fake scotch, bourbon, rye, or whatever, Karl would let the rectified alcohol stand for a few weeks in charred barrels in which authentic whiskey had been aged. I would pick up these barrels from a cooperage on Lake Street. They brought enormous prices—as high as $50 or $60 a barrel. The owner's son would help me load them onto a truck, and I remember he wore a diamond ring the shape of a barrel. Sometimes Karl used ordinary barrels in which he mixed the alcohol with shavings from charred barrels. Either way the alcohol would absorb the flavor of whiskey.

Some of Drucci's customers came from out of town, and if he figured a man was a shnook, he would sell him the

Prohibition laws were difficult to enforce because Congress did not appropriate adequate funds. Fewer than 3,000 federal agents of the Prohibition Bureau patrolled the entire United States and its borders. Here, agents pour out illegal whiskey.

liquor in a trick five-gallon can. This can had a tube soldered inside to the top and bottom. Only the tube contained whiskey. The rest of the can was filled with water to give it weight, as the shnook would discover when he got it home.

There was another unusual feature of the flower shop basement—a life-size picture of a cop. The boys used it for target practice.

"We Hear Fine Music from Boston"

Radio Expands Middle America's Horizons

Robert S. Lynd and Helen Merrell Lynd

During the 1920s, American lifestyles changed dramatically due to the widespread availability of modern technology. Sociologists Robert S. Lynd and Helen Merrell Lynd conducted a detailed study of the residents of Muncie, Indiana, in the 1920s. Their book, Middletown, *described the new patterns of behavior that emerged as a result of the radio and other consumer products. By 1930, more than one-third of American homes had a radio.*

Though less widely diffused as yet than automobile owning or movie attendance, the radio nevertheless is rapidly crowding its way in among the necessities in the family standard of living. Not the least remarkable feature of this new invention is its accessibility. Here skill and ingenuity can in part offset money as an open sesame to swift sharing of the enjoyments of the wealthy. With but little equipment one can call the life of the rest of the world from the air, and this equipment can be purchased piecemeal at the ten-cent store. Far from being simply one more means of passive enjoyment, the radio has given rise to much ingenious manipulative activity. In a count of representative sections of Middletown, it was found that, of 303 homes in 28 blocks in the "best section" of town, inhabited almost entirely by the business class, 12 percent had radios; of 518 workers' homes in 64 blocks, 6 percent had radios.

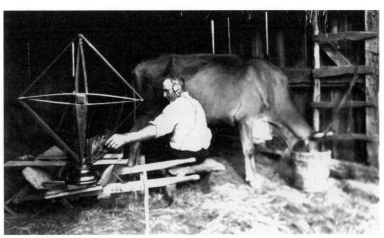

This farmer adjusts his radio while milking, indicating radio's widespread appeal during the 1920s.

As this new tool is rolling back the horizons of Middletown for the bank clerk or the mechanic sitting at home and listening to a Philharmonic concert or a sermon by Dr. Fosdick, or to President Coolidge bidding his father good night on the eve of election, and as it is wedging its way with the movie, the automobile, and other new tools into the twisted mass of habits that are living for the 38,000 people of Middletown, readjustments necessarily occur.

"Hit the Trail to Better Times!"

Automobiles Revolutionize America

Robert S. Lynd and Helen Merrell Lynd

Perhaps the greatest transformer of American life during the 1920s was the automobile. The Lynds found "Middletown" to be no exception. By 1929, automobile manufacturing was the nation's largest industry.

The automobile has apparently unsettled the habit of careful saving for some families. "Part of the money we spend on the car would go to the bank, I suppose," said more than one working-class wife. . . .

The "moral" aspect of the competition between the automobile and certain accepted expenditures appears in the remark of another businessman: "An automobile is a luxury, and no one has a right to one if he can't afford it. I haven't the slightest sympathy for any one who is out of work if he owns a car." . . .

"We'd rather do without clothes than give up the car," said one mother of nine children. "We used to go to his sister's to visit, but by the time we'd get the children shoed and dressed there wasn't any money left for carfare. Now no matter how they look, we just poke 'em in the car and take 'em along." . . .

Meanwhile, advertisements pound away at Middletown people with the tempting advice to spend money for automobiles for the sake of their homes and families:

"Hit the trail to better times!" says one such advertisement.

Another depicts a gray-haired banker lending a young couple the money to buy a car and proffering the friendly advice: "Before you can save money, you first must make money. And to make it you must have health, contentment, and full command of all your resources. . . . I have often advised customers of mine to buy cars, as I felt that the increased stimulation and opportunity of observation would enable them to earn amounts equal to the cost of their cars."

Many families feel that an automobile is justified as an agency holding the family group together. "I never feel as close to my family as when we are all together in the car," said one business-class mother, and one or two spoke of giving up country club membership or other recreations to get a car for this reason. "We don't spend anything on recreation except for the car. We save every place we can and put the money into the car. It keeps the family together," was an opinion voiced more than once.

"I don't use my car so much any more. The heavy traffic makes it less fun. But I spend seven nights a week on my radio. We hear fine music from Boston." (From a shabby man of 50.)

"Sundays I take the boy to Sunday School and come straight home and tune in. I get first an eastern service, then a Cincinnati one. Then there's nothing doing till about two-thirty, when I pick up an eastern service again and follow 'em across the country till I wind up with California about ten-thirty. Last night I heard a ripping sermon from Westminister Church somewhere in California. We've no preachers here that can compare with any of them."

"One of the bad features of radio," according to a teacher, "is that children stay up late at night and are not fit for school next day."

"We've spent close to $100 on our radio, and we built it ourselves at that," commented one of the worker's wives. "Where'd we get the money? Oh, out of our savings, like everybody else."

In the flux of competing habits that are oscillating the members of the family now toward and now away from the home, radio occupies an intermediate position. Twenty-five percent of 337 high school boys and 22 percent of 423 high school girls said that they listen more often to the radio with their parents than without them, and, as pointed out above, 20 percent of 274 boys in the three upper years of the high school answered "radio" to the question, "In what thing that you are doing at home this fall are you most interested?"—more than gave any other answer. More than one mother said that her family used to scatter in the evening, "but now we all sit around and listen to the radio."

Such comments as the following suggest their nature:

"I use time evenings listening in that I used to spend in reading."

"The radio is hurting movie going, especially Sunday evening." (From a leading movie exhibitor.)

"The Flapper Grew Bolder"

Changing Roles for Young Women

Preston William Slosson

Young women called "flappers" symbolized the carefree self-indulgence of the 1920s. They broke through many of the restraints on women—in fashion, in society, and in politics. Historian Preston William Slosson witnessed the rise of the flapper.

Women's fashions have always fluctuated. . . . But usually the new styles came by degrees, so that people could get used to them; they "evolved" like the British constitution. But during and after the war a real sartorial revolution took place. The skirt, in the old sense of the word, disappeared altogether to be replaced by a sort of tunic or kilt barely reaching the knee. . . .

With the shortening of the skirt went many other changes. Hampering petticoats were discarded, the corset was abandoned as a needless impediment to free movement, silk or "rayon" stockings became practically universal even among the poor and for a time were often rolled at the knee, sleeves shortened or vanished, and the whole costume became a sheer and simple structure, too light to be the slightest burden. . . . These simplifications of costume started with the wealthier classes but were almost immediately copied everywhere. . . . The commercial effect of these changes of style was profound. Factories which specialized in petticoats, corsets, or cotton stockings had to change their trade or go bankrupt, but the sale of silk and rayon hose more than doubled in four years, and the sale of bathing suits tripled in two. . . .

When the public had scarcely recovered from the shock of the disappearing skirt, it received another. The girls began to cut their hair. The barber shop was the last refuge of masculinity in America, the only spot which had not become "coeducational." The saloon was gone; the polls were now open to women; swimming tanks were crowded with fair mermaids; the very

prize ring had its lady guests; and nearly all men's clubs had their ladies' night. But in the barber shop the unshorn male could lean back at his ease in the great chair, unashamed in his suspenders, while the barber stuffed his mouth with lather and gave him the latest gossip of politics and baseball. This last trench was now taken. . . . [L]ong tresses were out of style; hence occasional visits to the barber shop. . . .

The flapper grew bolder. The "boyish bob" appeared, and . . . [s]oon there was no difference between a man's haircut and a woman's, unless the man were an artist or musician and wore his hair long as a professional asset. One Chicago barber shop had to advertise, "Men's custom *also* welcomed!" . . .

A third phase of the revolution in fashions, even more disturbing to the traditional than short skirts or short hair, was the freer use of cosmetics. In a way, this was a move in the opposite direction, as it represented a tendency not towards "naturalness" and freedom but towards artificiality and sophistication. . . . Bright orange rouge and lipsticks advertised as "kissproof" were used by young ladies of the most unquestionable respectability. The fashionable "suntan" was sometimes acquired at the drugstore as well as on the beach. Like the other changes in fashion, the cosmetic urge was democratic in the sense that it stopped at no class barrier. . . .

. . . "Beauty shoppes" blossomed on nearly every street of the shopping districts, their proprietors sometimes seeking to professionalize their status with the word "beauticians." Seven thousand kinds of cosmetics were on the market in 1927, a large majority of them being face creams. Fortunes were made in mud baths, labeled "beauty clay," in patent hair removers, in magic lotions to make the eyelashes long and sweeping, in soaps that claimed to nourish the skin, in hair dyes that "restored the natural color," in patent nostrums for "reducing," and in all the other half-fraudulent traps of the advertisers for the beauty seeker.

One manufacturer of dentifrice based a clever advertising campaign on the vogue of the feminine cigarette, with such headlines as "Why are Men so Unreasonable about Women Smoking?" and "Can a Girl Smoke and Still be Lovely?" arguing that since women were determined to smoke they should keep their teeth stainless by the daily use of toothpaste. Cigarette advertisers took a similar ingenious advantage of the craze for the "boyish form"—

e.g., "And now, women may enjoy a companionable smoke with their husbands and brothers—at the same time slenderizing in a sensible manner. . . . Reach for a Lucky instead of a sweet." Thus one fad supported another. . . .

Thus the flapper of the 1920s stepped onto the stage of history, breezy, slangy, and informal in manner; slim and boyish in form; covered with silk and fur that clung to her as close as onion skin; with carmined cheeks and lips, plucked eyebrows, and close-fitting helmet of hair; gay, plucky, and confident. No wonder the house rang with applause; no wonder also that faint hisses sounded from the remoter boxes and galleries. But she cared little for approval or disapproval and went about her "act," whether it were a marathon dancing contest, driving an automobile at seventy miles an hour, a Channel swim, a political campaign, or a social-service settlement.

"No Woman Can Call Herself Free"

Advocating Birth Control

Margaret Sanger

Women's new roles and a shift in sexual mores during the 1920s led to the growth of the birth control movement, led by Margaret Sanger. As a visiting nurse in New York City's immigrant neighborhoods, she witnessed the high mortality rates of mothers and their babies. Sanger was indicted in 1914 for distributing information on contraception.

In 1921, Margaret Sanger founded the American Birth Control League, which campaigned against laws restricting information about birth control. In her book Woman and the New Race *(1920), from which this excerpt is taken, Sanger maintained that "no woman can call herself free who does not own and control her body."*

The problem of birth control has arisen directly from the effort of the feminine spirit to free itself from bondage. Woman herself has wrought that bondage through her reproductive powers and while enslaving herself has enslaved

the world. The physical suffering to be relieved is chiefly woman's. Hers, too, is the love life that dies first under the blight of too-prolific breeding. Within her is wrapped up the future of the race—it is hers to make or mar. All of these consider-

176

ations point unmistakably to one fact—it is woman's duty as well as her privilege to lay hold of the means of freedom. . . .

The basic freedom of the world is woman's freedom. A free race cannot be born of slave mothers. A woman enchained cannot choose but give a measure of that bondage to her sons and daughters. No woman can call herself free who does not own and control her body. No woman can call herself free until she can choose consciously whether she will or will not be a mother.

It does not greatly alter the case that some women call themselves free because they earn their own livings, while others profess freedom because they defy the conventions of sex relationship. She who earns her own living gains a sort of freedom that is not to be undervalued, but in quality and in quantity it is of little account beside the untrammeled choice of mating or not mating, or being a mother or not being a mother. She gains food and clothing and shelter, at least, without submitting to the charity of her companion, but the earning of her own living does not give her the development of her inner sex urge, far deeper and more powerful in its outworkings than any of these externals. In order to have that development, she must still meet and solve the problem of motherhood.

With the so-called "free" woman, who chooses a mate in defiance of convention, freedom is largely a question of character and audacity. If she does attain to an unrestricted choice of a mate, she is still in a position to be enslaved through her reproductive powers. Indeed, the pressure of law and custom upon the woman not legally married is likely to make her more of a slave than the woman fortunate enough to marry the man of her choice.

Look at it from any standpoint you will, suggest any solution you will, conventional or unconventional, sanctioned by law or in defiance of law, woman is in the same position, fundamentally, until she is able to determine for herself whether she will be a mother and to fix the number of her offspring. This unavoidable situation is alone enough to make birth control, first of all, a woman's problem. On the very face of the matter, voluntary motherhood is chiefly the concern of the woman.

It is persistently urged, however, that since sex expression is the act of two, the responsibility of controlling the results should not be placed upon woman alone. Is it fair, it is asked, to give her, instead of the man, the task of protecting herself when she is, perhaps, less rugged in physique than her mate, and has, at all events, the normal, periodic inconveniences of her sex? We must examine this phase of her problem in two lights—that of the ideal, and of the conditions working toward the ideal. In an ideal society no doubt, birth control would become the concern of the man as well as the woman. The hard, inescapable fact which we encounter today is that man has not only refused any such responsibility, but has individually and collectively sought to prevent woman from obtaining knowledge by which she could assume this responsibility for herself. She is still in the position of a dependent today because her mate has refused to consider her as an individual apart from his needs. . . . Having left it to him, she is exploited, driven, and enslaved to his desires. . . .

Conditions, rather than theories; facts, rather than dreams, govern the problem. They place it squarely upon the shoulders of woman. She has learned that whatever the moral responsibility of the man in this direction may be, he does not discharge it. She has learned that, lovable and considerate as the individual husband may be, she has nothing to expect from men in the mass, when they make laws and decree customs. She knows that regardless of what ought to be, the brutal, unavoidable fact is that she will never receive her freedom until she takes it for herself. . . .

"It Was Pure Improvisation"

Life in the Jazz Age

Willie Smith

During the 1920s, African Americans popularized a uniquely American art form: jazz. Derived from a mixture of African rhythms, black spirituals, ragtime, and European harmonies, jazz music placed a strong emphasis on improvisation. Willie "the Lion" Smith, a jazz pianist, here describes the musical scene at Harlem rent parties, a common practice in which tenants would convert their homes into temporary nightclubs on the weekends to earn money to pay the rent.

Piano players called these affairs jumps or shouts, and we would get substitutes to play our regular [nightclub] jobs for us. It wasn't always easy to do this because a lot of the shouts were on a Saturday night and the bosses frowned on us getting off. We made a lot of them after our regular jobs were over for the night. . . .

It got so we never stopped, and we were up and down Fifth, Seventh, and Lenox all night long hitting the keys. We even had a booking agent—old Lippy. He'd say, "You boys wanna jump for ten or twenty?" This meant he had a couple of parties paying from ten to a double sawbuck each. On a single Saturday he'd book as many as three parties for us, and we'd alternate between them. . . .

There were, of course, some of the chitterling struts where a bunch of pianists would be in competition. Lippy was a great promoter and was always trying to steam up the guests to argue about who was the best. It sometimes got annoying, especially when you had your eyes on a good-looking chick or wanted to take time out to get in the games they always had going in one or two of the back bedrooms. But you had to stay by the keyboard to hold your own reputation for being a fast pianist.

Sometimes we got carving battles [competitions] going that would last for four or five hours. Here's how these bashes worked: the Lion would pound the keys for a mess of choruses and then shout to the next in line, "Well, all right, take it from there," and each tickler would take his turn, trying to improve on a melody. . . .

We would embroider the melodies with our own original ideas and try to develop patterns that had more originality than those played before us. Sometimes it was just a question as to who could think up the most patterns within a given tune. It was pure improvisation. . . .

The best time of all at these parties came early in the morning. Then we'd play in a slow-drag style with the drummer muffling his hides and stroking the snare lightly and politely with the brushes. Sometimes we would doctor the piano by placing newspapers behind the hammers and put tin on the felts in order to get an old-fashioned player-piano effect. This also gave us a guitar sound.

During these early hours close to dawn the dancers would grab each other tightly and do the monkey hunch or bo-hog. Their shuffling feet would give everything a weird rhythmic atmosphere. . . .

Those were happy days.

"This Was Real Panic"

Wall Street Crashes

Jonathan Norton Leonard

The U.S. economy expanded greatly in the 1920s, during which the gross national product increased by 40 percent. But as production and employment slowed in the late 1920s, the stock market continued to rise—fueled by speculators hoping to make enormous profits with little investment of real capital. On "Black Tuesday"—October 29, 1929—the market finally crashed, ushering in the Great Depression. Jonathan Norton Leonard, a journalist, witnessed the panic on Wall Street that led to its collapse.

That night [Monday, October 28] Wall Street was lit up like a Christmas tree. Restaurants, barber shops, and speakeasies were open and doing a roaring business. Messenger boys and runners raced through the streets whooping and singing at the top of their lungs. Slum children invaded the district to play with balls of ticker tape. Well-dressed gentlemen fell asleep in lunch counters. All the downtown hotels, rooming houses, even flophouses were full of financial employees who usually slept in the Bronx. It was probably Wall Street's worst night. Not only had the day been bad, but everybody down to the youngest office boy had a pretty good idea of what was going to happen tomorrow.

The morning papers were black with the story of the Monday smash. Except for rather feeble hopes that the great banks would step into the gap, they had no heart for cheerful headlines. In the inside pages, however, the sunshine chorus continued as merry as ever. Bankers said that heavy buying had been sighted on the horizon. Brokers were loud with "technical" reasons why the decline could not continue.

It wasn't only the financial bigwigs who spoke up. Even the outriders of the New Era [a theory that business would enjoy permanent growth] felt that if everybody pretended to be happy, their phoney smiles would blow the trouble away. [New York Mayor] Jimmy Walker, for example, asked the movie houses to show only cheerful pictures. *True Story Magazine,* currently suffering from delusions of grandeur, ran full-page advertisements in many papers urging all wage earners to buy luxuries on credit. That would fix things right up. McGraw-Hill Company, another publishing house with boom-time megalomania, told the public to avert its eyes from the obscene spectacle in Wall Street. What they did not observe would not affect their state of mind, and good times could continue as before.

These noble but childish dabbles in mass psychology failed as utterly as might have been expected. Even the more substantial contributions of U.S. Steel and American Can in the shape of $1 extra dividends had the same fate. Ordinarily such action would have sent the respective stocks shooting upward, but in the present mood of the public it created not the slightest ripple of interest. Steel and Can plunged down as steeply as if they had canceled their dividends entirely.

The next day, Tuesday, the 29th of October, was the worst of all. In the first half hour 3,259,800 shares were traded, almost a full day's work for the laboring machinery of the Exchange. The selling pressure was wholly without precedent. It was coming from everywhere. The wires to other cities were jammed with frantic orders to sell. So were the cables, radio, and telephones to Europe and the rest of the world. Buyers were few, sometimes wholly absent. Often the specialists stood baffled at their posts, sellers pressing around them and not a single buyer at any price.

This was real panic. It was what the banks had prevented on Thursday, had slowed on Monday. Now they were helpless. Reportedly they were trying to force their associated corporations to toss their buying power into the whirlpool, but they were getting no results. . . .

When the closing bell rang, the great bull market was dead and buried. 16,410,000 shares had changed hands. Leading stocks had lost as much as 77 percent of their peak value. The Dow Jones index was off 40 percent since September 3. Not only the little speculators, but the lordly, experienced big traders had been wiped out by the violence of the crash, and the whole financial structure of the nation had been shaken to its foundations. Many bankers and brokers were doubtful about their own solvency, for their accounting systems had broken down. The truth was buried beneath a mountain of scribbled paper which would require several days of solid work to clear away.

"No Help Wanted"

Unemployed During the Depression

E. W. Bakke

The stock market crash led to massive unemployment. In 1933, the worst year of the Depression, one-fourth of the nation's workforce was unemployed. E. W. Bakke describes what it was like to look for work during the Depression.

April 19, 1934
Decided to have a go at the state employment office. Got there at eight. Fellow I knew sitting on steps. Big sign there: "No loitering in the doorway." Janitor or someone came down and asked him to move.

"Are you going upstairs?" he asked. "If you are, go, but don't sit here." The fellow jumped; not looking at the janitor, he began a loud bluster about his father paying taxes to support the place and he could sit on the steps if he wanted to. When the janitor left, he returned to the steps for a moment. Meanwhile a group of people had gathered to see what was going on.

Asked the janitor when the manager would be in. He said, "Nine o'clock." Decided to come back. When I got back, a line had formed clear out into the street. I took my place. Officials and clerks kept coming and had a good cheery word for us as they passed. But after they had gone, many sarcastic remarks followed them like, "Gives you a nice smile, but that's all."

The manager himself drove up before the office a little past nine—appeared sore that there was no parking space in front of the office. The fellows standing outside purposely raised their voices so he could hear and made remarks such as, "Not much use coming here, they never do anything but tell you to come back in sixty days"; "What'd they ever do for me?—Nothing"; "First it was April first, then it was the fifteenth, and now it will be God knows when."

I register, but they say not much chance today; maybe a week from today. . . .

April 27

Up at seven, cup of coffee, and off to Sargent's. Like to be there when the gang comes to work, the lucky devils. Employment manager not in. Waited in his outer office. . . . Three others waiting, two reporting for compensation. Other one laid off two weeks ago and said he called at office every day. He inquired what I was doing and when I said "looking for work" he laughed. "You never work here? No? What chance you think you got when 400 like me who belong here [are] out?" Employment manager showed up at 9:30. I had waited two hours. My time has no value. A pleasant fellow; told me in a kind but snappy way business was very bad. What about the future; would he take my name? Said he referred only to the present. Nothing more for me to say, so left. Two more had drifted into office. Suppose they got the same story. Must be a lot of men in New Haven that have heard it by now. . . .

May 2

Started out at seven for New Haven Clock Shop. No one in employment office. Lady at information desk asked, "What do you want?" I told her. She wanted to know if I had worked there before and when I said, "No," she didn't even ask if I had any experience in clockmaking (which I have). And when I started to tell her so, she cut me off with "No use—sorry." Suppose she gets tired too.

From Clock Shop to E. Cowells and Co., who make auto equipment. If they want to have old men, well, I worked here in 1916 and 1917. Didn't get to see anyone here because just as you get to the hall there is a big sign, "No Help Wanted."

Having heard Seamless Rubber was working quite steady I went down there. Regular employment office furnished with one bench. Another chap, a foreigner, waiting also. In about ten minutes a fellow asked us our business and told us very politely they had no jobs even for skilled men, let alone laborers. No use to tell him I wasn't always a laborer for I never had done the skilled jobs on rubber.

Saw a sign hanging out of one place in gilt letters. "No Help Wanted." In gilt, mind you, as if to make it more permanent.

Then to Bradley-Smith candymakers, where I had also worked before. The first few days I hadn't the heart for more than a couple of tries a morning. I'm getting hardened to the word "No" now, though, and can stick it the most of the morning. Bradley-Smith has no employment office. The telephone switchboard operator is apparently instructed to switch off anyone looking for work, as she made quick work of my question. I notice no one seems to be instructed to find out if we know anything about the business or work. Firms might be passing up some good bets for their force. But apparently that isn't important now.

Walking away, met two friends out going the rounds too. They said it was useless and that they were only looking through force of habit. That's going to be me before long. Even if they hadn't said so, I'm thinking it is useless to run around like this; you appear ridiculous, and that gets your goat—or would if you kept it up too long. Wish I had some drag with someone on the inside of one of those gates. I expect it's that everyone knows they have to know someone that keeps me from having more company at the employment offices. This is what a former pal of mine who is up at Yale calls "competition in the labor market," I guess. Well, it's a funny competition and with guys you never see.

"What If Our Check Does Not Come?"

Living on Relief

Ann Rivington

The income of American families decreased by more than half from 1929 to 1932. President Herbert Hoover, who blamed the Depression on international economic problems, advocated a policy of "rugged individualism" and opposed government intervention to restore the economy.

But when Franklin Delano Roosevelt became president in 1933, he instituted government programs to combat the Depression as part of his New Deal. Among these were a national relief, or welfare, program that included both direct payments and public works projects. Ann Rivington, an unemployed music teacher pregnant with her first child, describes the trauma and humiliation of applying for relief.

The despair of a migrant farm worker and her children during the Great Depression was captured by photographer Dorothea Lange in 1936. Thousands of farm families left their lands in the mid-1930s to look for work in California when a severe drought hit the southern Great Plains, which became known as the Dust Bowl.

When I went to college I studied sociology. I was taught that hunger, squalor, dirt, and ignorance are the results of environment. Charity, therefore, is no solution. We must change the environment. In order to do this we have settlement houses, playgrounds, and social workers in the slums.

In the past year and a half I have again revised my opinion. I am no longer one of us. For all my education, my training in thrift and cleanliness, I am become one of them. My condition is shared by a large sector of the population. From my new place in society I regard the problems and misery of the poor with new eyes.

Two years ago I was living in comfort and apparent security. My husband had a good position in a well-known orchestra, and I was teaching a large and promising class of piano pupils. When the orchestra was disbanded, we started on a rapid downhill path. My husband was unable to secure another position. My class gradually dwindled away. We were forced to live on our savings.

In the early summer of 1933 I was eight months pregnant and we had just spent our last twelve dollars on one month's rent for an apartment. We found that such apartments really exist. They lack the most elementary comforts. They usually are infested with mice and bedbugs. Ours was. Quite often the ceilings leak.

What, then, did we do for food when our last money was spent on rent? In vain we tried to borrow more. So strong was the influence of our training that my husband kept looking feverishly for work when there was no work, and blaming himself because he was unable to find it. An application to the Emergency Home Relief Bureau was the last act of our desperation.

We were so completely uninformed about the workings of charitable organizations that we thought all we need do was to make clear to the authorities our grave situation in order to receive immediate attention. My husband came home with an application blank in his pocket. We filled out the application with great care. The next morning my husband started early for the bureau. He returned at about two

o'clock, very hungry and weak from the heat. But he was encouraged.

"Well, I got to talk to somebody this time," he said. "She asked me over again all the questions on that paper and more besides. Then she said to go home and wait. An investigator should be around tomorrow or day after. On account of your condition she marked the paper urgent."

The next day we waited, and all of two days more. The fourth day, which was Saturday, my husband went back to the bureau. It was closed until Monday.

On Sunday morning the Italian grocer reminded me of our bill. "It get too big," he said. We cut down to one meal a day, and toast.

Monday brought no investigator. Tuesday my husband was at the bureau again. This time he came home angry.

"They said the investigator was here Friday and we were out. I got sore and told them somebody was lying."

"But you shouldn't. Now they won't help us."

"Now they will help us. She'll be here tomorrow."

Late Wednesday afternoon the investigator arrived. She questioned us closely for more than half an hour on our previous and present situation, our personal lives, our relatives. This time we certainly expected the check. But we were told to wait.

"I'm a special investigator. The regular one will be around Friday with the check."

My husband was in a torment of anxiety. "But we can't wait till Friday. We have to eat something."

The investigator looked tired. "I must make my report. And there are other cases ahead of yours."

"Dear Mrs. Roosevelt"

A Child's Letter to the First Lady

C. V. B.

Eleanor Roosevelt used her position as First Lady to campaign actively on behalf of poor people during the Depression. She received many letters asking for help, among them one by this little Ohio girl, identified by her initials. The letter has been edited to make it more readable.

Dear Mrs. Roosevelt:
I am writing you a little letter this morning. Are you glad it [is] spring? I am, for so many poor people can raise some more to eat. You know what I am writing this letter for? Mother said Mrs. Roosevelt is just a godmother to the world, and I thought maybe you had some old clothes. You know, Mother is a good sewer, and all the little girls are getting Easter dresses. And I thought that you had some. You know Papa could wear Mr. Roosevelt's shirts and clothes I know.

My Papa likes Mr. Roosevelt, and Mother said Mr. Roosevelt carries his worries with a smile—you know he is always happy. You know we are not living on the relief—we live on a little farm. Papa did have a job and got laid [off] five years ago, so we saved and got two horses and two cows and a hog so we can . . . [have] everything to eat. Sometimes we don't have anything but we live. But you know it [is] so hard to get cloth. So I thought maybe you had some. You know what you thought was no good Mother can make over for me. I am eleven years old. I wish I could see you. I know I would like you both. . . .

We have no car or no phone or radio. Papa, he would like to have a radio but he said there [are] other things he needs more. Papa is worried about his seed oats. And one horse is not very good. But everyone has to worry. I am sending this letter with the pennies I get to take to Sunday school. Mother gives me one [each week], so it took three weeks—'cause Mother would think I better not ask for things from the First Lady. But Mother said you were an angel for doing so much for the poor. And I thought that [it] would be alright. . . .

By Monday morning we had nothing for breakfast but oatmeal, without sugar or milk. We decided we must go together to the bureau and find out what was wrong. Therefore, as soon as we had finished breakfast, we borrowed carfare from our kind neighbors and started out.

We reached the relief station a good fifteen minutes before nine, but the sidewalk was crowded with people. My husband explained to me that they were waiting to waylay the investigators on their way to work, to pour complaints and problems in their ears.

At last the doors were opened. The line crept forward. Three guards stood at the entrance, and every person in the crowd had to tell his business before he was admitted. Many were turned away. For the insistent there was the inevitable answer, "I got my orders," and the policeman within ready call.

By half-past nine we had made our way to the door.

"Room two," the guard said, handing us each a slip of paper.

The place was filled with long brown benches, crowded with our drab companions in hunger. Others were standing along the walls. The air was stifling and rank with the smell of poverty. We sat down at the end of the rear bench. Gradually we were able to slide to the end of our bench, then back along the next bench.

I watched the people around us. There they sat waiting, my fellow indigents. Bodies were gaunt or flabby, faces—some stoical, some sullen—all careworn like my husband's. What had they done, or left undone, to inherit hunger? What was this relief we were asking for? Certainly it was not *charity*. It was dispensed too grudgingly, too harshly, to be that.

When our turn came to talk to one of the women behind the desks, we were told that the checks had been held up for lack of funds and that we should go home and wait for an investigator "some time this week." We were not going to be put off in this manner. My husband told her, "We have to have something more than promises. There's no food in the house, and my wife can't live on air."

"Well, that's all I can tell you," said the woman.

"If that's all you can tell me, who knows more than you? We're not leaving without a better answer. I want the supervisor." At last the supervisor was called. "The checks will be out tomorrow night. You will get yours Thursday."

Sure enough, early Thursday afternoon the regular investigator arrived. He gave us a check for $8.50 to cover two weeks' food. We had already spent $2.00 at the grocer's. And this amount, of course, was counted off the check. But Pete was not satisfied.

"Gotta take off more. I poor too."

I shook my head. "Wait," I said, "We'll pay you, but not this time." I looked around the little shop hungrily. I was tortured by a great longing for fresh fruit.

"How much are the grapes?" I asked.

"No grapes," said Pete. "No grapes for you."

"But why not, Pete?"

"Grapes are luxury. You get beans, potatoes, onions. Poor people no eat grapes."

I was bewildered. But Pete meant what he said. He showed me a bulletin he had received from the relief bureau, listing the things allowed on the food checks of the jobless. I cannot remember all the regulations. But I do remember that only dried fruit was listed. The quantities of eggs, butter, milk, were strictly limited. No meat except salt pork, unsliced bacon, pig's liver, and other entrails. Rice, beans, potatoes, bread, onions were the main items to be sold. I saw no mention of fresh vegetables. I was highly indignant.

"Listen, Pete, my stomach isn't leather even if I have no money." I picked up a nice juicy cantaloupe and two bunches of carrots.

"These are onions and potatoes," I said, and marched out the door trailing carrot tops. . . .

Gradually the more and more deficient diet began to tell on us. We did not lose much weight—the very poor usually eat plenty of starch—but we began to suffer from debility, colds, minor infections. . . .

Meanwhile we are still living on the relief. We keep wondering, questioning. What if our check does not come next week? What when the relief bureau stops paying rents for the summer? Will we be evicted? Will our family be broken up, our little girl taken away from us? After a time these questions reach out beyond our burning personal needs. What is the cause of our suffering? Whither is it leading us, and the increasing millions like us? What is wrong with the system, the civilization that brings with it such wholesale misery? My own voice is one of many that are asking, more and more insistently.

"If a White Woman Accused a Black Man"

The Scottsboro Boys Stand Trial

Clarence Norris

The Depression exacerbated racial tensions. In Scottsboro, Alabama, nine African-American youths were accused of raping two white women. Eight of the "Scottsboro Boys" were sentenced to death, including Clarence Norris. Their convictions were overturned by the Supreme Court in Powell v. Alabama *(1932). In that case, the Court also ruled that in capital cases, the states were required to appoint counsel for poor defendants.*

Those were desperate times in the late 1920s, the beginning of the Great Depression. Make no doubt, the southern Negro was hit the hardest. It was tough to survive it all. Myself and thousands of others stole rides on freight trains and rode from city to city and town to town in search of work. It was against the law to hop those trains but the jails couldn't hold all the folks doing it, so the railroad detectives didn't pay us no mind. . . .

It was March 25, 1931, when I caught a train out of Chattanooga, Tennessee, headed for Memphis. The train was a main line southern that went from Tennessee to Georgia and Alabama, then back into Tennessee. As the train went along, more and more hobos jumped aboard, black men and white men. I had been riding for some time when the whites started throwing gravel at the blacks, talking about "All you niggers unload; get your asses offa here."

They had to be crazy. We were out in the middle of nowhere, all of us stealing a ride, and these crackers start acting like they owned the train. I wasn't getting off and some of the other black guys must have felt the same way. We fought the white boys, and it was a bloody battle too. We beat the hell out of them and made 'em get off the train. The ones that didn't want to go we throwed off. We were moving pretty fast, so when they hit the ground they would tumble quite a ways. We let one guy stay because the train started moving too fast for him to make a safe landing. We had really put it to them but they had brought it on themselves. After the fight I went back to where I had been sitting on a crosstie car.

Every now and then the train had to stop and take on water. I didn't think nothing of it when we stopped at a little place, a flag station, Paint Rock, Alabama. But when I looked up, the tracks were lined with a mob of men. They had sticks, pistols, rifles, shotguns; everything you need to murder, they had it. The fellas we had throwed off the train were there too. The mob circled the train and made us all get off. They pushed and shoved us until we were lined up in front of a building. We were surrounded by a sea of white faces, screaming, "Let's hang these black sons of bitches. Where's the rope for these niggers?"

Two men had on uniforms. I don't know if they were police, firemen, or soldiers, but they saved our lives. They asked the white boys who it was had been in the fight. The white boys answered we were all in it. The men in uniform said, "Let's take them to jail." Somebody drove up in a school bus. They put handcuffs on us nine Negroes that had been taken off and ran a rope through the handcuffs so we were connected. They put us on the bus and all the whites that could get on packed in too. We were taken to the nearest jail, in Scottsboro, Alabama. That's why we are called the Scottsboro Boys today.

They put the nine of us in a large cage by ourselves, and they locked those white hobos up somewhere in there too. This is where I made the acquaintance of the rest of the Scottsboro Boys. There were four out of Chattanooga that were friends—two brothers, Roy and Andy Wright, and Eugene Williams and Haywood Patterson. Ozie Powell, Olen Montgomery, Charlie Weems, Willie Roberson, and myself were all from different parts of Georgia. . . .

All of us were scared to death, quite natural, and we didn't know what was going to happen next. Late that evening crackers were outside the jail, hollering and screaming and cursing us. They told the sheriff to "bring those niggers out." They said they would come in and get us if we weren't released. When they crowded into the doorway the sheriff pulled his gun. He said, "If you come in here I will blow your brains out. Get away from here." You never heard such a racket then. That made them mad as hell. The sheriff turned off the lights; he wanted to move us but it was too late. The jail was surrounded.

The Alabama National Guard was called out to protect the "Scottsboro Boys" from threatened mass lynchings in 1931.

The deputies kept telling the sheriff to move us but he knew we didn't stand a chance on the street. The crowd was howling like dogs, throwing rocks and threatening to burn us out.

The sheriff called Governor Ben Miller and asked him to send in the National Guard. The governor didn't waste any time. It wasn't long before I heard the

Guard outside. They had to put something on those crackers; they cracked some heads because they wouldn't leave peaceable. After the Guard cleared the streets, they stationed themselves outside the jail and all over town. But I didn't get any sleep that night.

Next day we were taken from the cage and put in a line. The sheriff brought two women over to us. He said, "Miss Price, which one of these niggers had you?" She went down the line pointing her finger: "This one, this one, this one" . . . until she had picked out six, including me. They asked the other woman, Ruby Bates, the same question but she did not part her lips. A guard said, "Well, if those six had Miss Price, it stands to reason the others had Miss Bates." We all started talking at once: "We never did any such thing"; "No, sheriff, we didn't do that." I blurted out that it was a lie. Before I could blink, that guard struck out at me with his bayonet. I threw up my hands and he slashed my right hand open to the bone. He screamed, "Nigger, you know damn well how to talk about white women."

They shoved us back into the cage. I was scared before, but it wasn't nothing to how I felt now. I knew if a white woman accused a black man of rape, he was as good as dead. My hand was bleeding like I don't know what; my blood was running out of me like water. I tore my shirt and wrapped the rag around my hand real tight. I bled for a long time before it stopped that day, but I didn't even think about it. All I could think was that I was going to die for something I had not done. I had never seen those two women before in my life. . . .

We went to trial on April 6, 1931. The interdenominational Ministers Alliance, a group of black preachers in Chattanooga, raised $50 to hire us a lawyer. He came to see us about half an hour before the trial. He was a white man named Stephen Roddy. He looked us over and asked us which ones did the raping. He said, "Now if you boys will tell the truth, I might be able to save some of your lives." I didn't know what a lawyer was supposed to be but I knew this one was no good for us. He had liquor on his breath, and he was as scared as we were. When we got into the courtroom and the judge asked him if he was our lawyer, the man said, "Not exactly." . . .

The trials lasted for three days. There were four trials for nine men. . . .

I truly can't remember much of those trials. The judge was Alfred E. Hawkins. . . . He let it be known he thought we were guilty and a trial was a waste of time and money "for niggers." I was nervous, confused, and scared. Outside, the crowds were whooping it up, and inside the courtroom they were jumping up and down, waving guns and laughing.

I know those women took the stand and testified under oath. They put their hands on the Bible and lied and lied. They said we raped them on a bed of gravel in an open freight car. They said we used knives and hit them up the side of the head with guns to make them have sex. But the law never found no knives or guns on us because we didn't have any. . . .

All of us got the death penalty except Roy Wright. He looked so young the state didn't ask for the death of him, just life imprisonment. But his jury was divided on whether to kill him or not. So his was declared a mistrial. He was never tried again, but they kept him at Birmingham in the Jefferson County Jail for six years until he was released in 1937. He was thirteen years old.

Judge Hawkins sentenced us to die April 9, 1931. . . . I was eighteen, also Charlie Weems and Olen Montgomery; Haywood Patterson and Andy Wright were nineteen; Ozie Powell was fifteen; Willie Roberson was fourteen; and Eugene Williams was thirteen years old.

I never saw so many happy white folks. They went wild. Cheers went up all over town. They were rejoicing over our fate. There was dancing in the streets. The bands played "There'll be a Hot Time in the Old Town Tonight."

"Until That Moment, We Were Nonpeople"

The Flint Sit-Down Strike

Bob Stinson

Although economic conditions were harsh, workers still wielded some power during the Depression. In 1936-37, the United Auto Workers (UAW), a member union of the Congress of Industrial Organizations (CIO), pioneered the sit-down strike at the General Motors plant in Flint, Michigan. The sit-down strike created a tactical advantage for workers because strikers remained in the factories, at their machines, making it impossible for management to bring in strikebreakers. Bob Stinson was one of the striking workers.

The Flint sit-down happened Christmas Eve, 1936. I was in Detroit, playing Santa Claus to a couple of small nieces and nephews. When I came back, the second shift had pulled the plant. It took about five minutes to shut the line down. The foreman was pretty well astonished.

The boys pulled the switches and asked all the women who was in Cut-and-Sew to go home. They informed the supervisors they could stay, if they stayed in their office. They told the plant police they could do their job as long as they didn't interfere with the workers.

We had guys patrol the plant, see that nobody got involved in anything they shouldn't. If anybody got careless with company property—such as sitting on an automobile cushion without putting burlap over it—he was talked to. You couldn't paint a sign on the wall or anything like that. You used bare springs for a bed. 'Cause if you slept on a finished cushion, it was no longer a new cushion.

Governor Murphy said he hoped to God he would never have to use [the] National Guard against people. But if there was damage to property, he would do so. This was right down our alley, because

---

"All Friends in the Union"

Minorities and the CIO

Jim Cole

The CIO was originally a committee within the American Federation of Labor (AFL) designed to promote industrial unions, which included both unskilled and skilled workers within an industry, over craft unions, which represented only skilled workers. Fearing competition, the AFL expelled the CIO. The CIO was much more open to racial and ethnic minorities than the AFL. Jim Cole, an African-American meatcutter, describes the camaraderie created by the CIO.

I'm working in the Beef Kill section. Butcher on the chain. Been in the place twenty years, I believe. You got to have a certain amount of skill to do the job I'm doing. Long ago, I wanted to join the AFL union, the Amalgamated Butchers and Meat Cutters, they called it. They wouldn't let me in. Never said it to my face, but reason of it was plain. Negro. Just didn't want a Negro man to have what he should. That's wrong—you know that's wrong.

Long about 1937 the CIO come. Well, I tell you, we Negroes was glad to see it come. Sometimes the bosses or the company stooges try to keep the white boys from joining the union. They say, "You don't want to belong to a black man's organization. That's all the CIO is." Don't fool nobody, but they got to lie, spread lying words around. . . .

I don't care if the union don't do another lick of work raising our pay, or settling grievances about anything. I'll always believe they done the greatest thing in the world getting everybody who works in the yards together, and breaking up the hate and bad feelings that used to be held against the Negro. We all doing our work now, nothing but good to say about the CIO.

In my own local we elected our officers, and it's the same all over. We try to get every people represented. President of the local, he's Negro. First vice president, he's Polish. Second vice president, he's Irish. Other officers: Scotchman, Lithuanian, Negro, German. Many different people can't understand English very well, and we have to have union interpreters for lots of our members. But that don't make no mind; they all friends in the union, even if they can't say nothing except "Brother" and shake hands.

we invited him to the plant [to] see how well we were taking care of the place.

They'd assign roles to you. When some of the guys at headquarters wanted to tell some of the guys in the plant what was cookin', I carried the message. I was a scavenger, too.

The merchants cooperated. There'd be apples, bushels of potatoes, crates of oranges that was beginnin' to spoil. Some of our members were also little farmers; they come up with a couple of baskets of junk.

The soup kitchen was outside the plant. The women handled all the cooking, outside of one chef who came from New York. He had anywhere from ten to twenty women washing dishes and peeling potatoes in the strike kitchen. Mostly stews, pretty good meals. They were put in containers and hoisted up through the window. The boys in there had their own plates and cups and saucers. . . .

Most of the men had their wives and friends come down, and they'd stand inside the window and they'd talk. Find out how the family was, if the union supplied them with enough coal. . . .

We had a ladies' auxiliary. They'd visit the homes of the guys that was in the plant. They would find out if there was any shortage of coal or food. Then they'd maneuver around amongst themselves until they found some place to get a ton of coal. Some of them even put the arm on Consumer Power if there was a possibility of having her power shut off. . . .

Morale was very high at the time. It started out kinda ugly because the guys were afraid they put their foot in it and all they was gonna do is lose their jobs. But as time went on, they began to realize they could win this darn thing, 'cause we had a lot of outside people comin' in showing their sympathy. . . .

Nationally known people contributed to our strike fund. Mrs. Roosevelt for one.

We even had a member of Parliament come from England and address us. . . .

The men sat in there for forty-four days. Governor Murphy—I get emotional over him—was trying to get both sides to meet on some common ground. I think he lost many a good night's sleep. We wouldn't use force. Mr. Knudsen was head of General Motors and, of course, there was John L. Lewis [the leader of the CIO]. They'd reach a temporary agreement and invariably the Flint Alliance [a group of local businesses] or GM headquarters in Detroit would throw a monkey wrench in it. So every morning, Murphy got up with an unsolved problem.

John L. was as close to a Shakespearean actor as any I've ever listened to. He could get up there and damn all the adversaries—he had more command of language. He made a speech that if they shoot the boys out at the plant, they'd have to shoot him first.

There were half a dozen false starts at settlement. Finally, we got the word: *The thing is settled.* My God, you had to send about three people, one right after the other, down to some of those plants because the guys didn't believe it. Finally, when they did get it, they marched out of the plants with the flag flyin' and all that stuff.

You'd see some guys comin' out of there with whiskers as long as Santa Claus. They made a rule they wasn't gonna shave until the strike was over. Oh, it was just like . . . the Armistice delirium. . . . Everybody was runnin' around shaking everybody by the hand, saying, "Jesus, you look strange, you got a beard on you now." Women kissin' their husbands. There was a lotta drunks on the streets that night.

When Mr. Knudsen put his name to a piece of paper and says that General Motors recognizes the UAW-CIO—until that moment, we were nonpeople, we didn't even exist. That was the big one.

"Abandon Ship! Abandon Ship!"

Japan Attacks Pearl Harbor

Stephen Bower Young

The United States tried to pursue an isolationist foreign policy after World War I. However, that became more difficult as Germany, Italy, and Japan all invaded other nations. When Great Britain and France declared war on Germany in September 1939, the United States stayed neutral but provided war materials under the Lend-Lease Act.

On December 7, 1941, Japanese bombers attacked the U.S. fleet at Pearl Harbor, Hawaii. Almost 20 ships were sunk or disabled, more than 150 airplanes were destroyed, and more than 2,000 Americans were killed. Congress immediately declared war on Japan, and Germany and Italy in turn declared war on the United States. For America, World War II had finally begun. Stephen Bower Young, a mess cook, here tells of his ordeal while trapped inside his sunken ship at the bottom of Pearl Harbor.

The world was my oyster that Sunday morning in December, 1941. I was 19, breakfast was over, and liberty would be starting in an hour or so. A quick look out a second-deck porthole of our battleship, the USS *Oklahoma*, confirmed my feeling that this was going to be a glorious day. . . .

I looked at my watch. Two minutes to morning colors. I started toward my locker.

Suddenly the bugle blared over the PA system. The sound filled the compartment. The first few notes told me it was not colors or calling away a motor launch. I stopped and listened. It was the call for gun crews to man their antiaircraft stations. . . .

Again the bugle tore the air. Now it was the call to general quarters! A voice boomed throughout the ship—"All hands, man your battle stations!" What the hell was this? Drills on Sunday? They knew we were all waiting to go ashore.

The harsh, excited voice on the PA system froze us in our tracks. "All hands, man your battle stations! On the double! This is no drill! Get going—they're real bombs!"

I headed for my turret battle station. Everyone was running and pushing. The ship shuddered as she was hit somewhere forward. I stumbled, but managed to stay on my feet. The lights went out just as I reached the ladder going down to the deck below. I groped my way, and as I hit the deck the emergency lights went on dimly. Another ladder to go. Another hit. Close by, this time. The deck heaved, but I hung on. The emergency lights went out momentarily. Obviously, we were being badly hit. . . .

The powder-handling room was crowded. Indistinctly I could see the faces of my friends, frightened, anxious, and unbelieving. Standing against the bulkhead, I grabbed for support as another hit made the deck beneath us jump. Until now, we supposed they were bombs and felt almost safe below the armored deck. No one had thought yet of torpedoes tearing away a ship's side.

Then someone yelled and pointed to a spot where water was pouring in through the lower port side bulkhead. The ship was listing slightly. Horrified, we watched the water rise and felt the deck slipping from under us . . .

I clutched at the bulkhead, barely able to stay on my feet as the water flooded in. That was when the dreaded phrase was passed from man to man throughout the ship, "Abandon ship! Abandon ship!" . . .

The list rapidly increased until it seemed that the ship was almost lying on her side. With awful certainty we knew that we were sinking. Suddenly the ship lurched! The deck slipped out from under me and my hands snatched at empty air. As she rolled over, I was pitched into a mass of dead and dying and, with them, buffeted and tossed about. Then the dark waters closed over me as the ship came to rest upside down on the bottom of the harbor.

Eventually I surfaced, gulped for air, and swam desperately in the darkness, surprised to find myself alive. Random shouts mingled with cries for help; then quiet fell abruptly. Water gurgled as it made its way into the ship. I thought we were done for. . . .

There were less than twenty of us left, but, incredibly, there was no panic. The hours passed by. The water level rose inexorably, inch by awful inch. I thought of home. Days of growing up. People I had known. Long summer days of hard farm work, but with lots of time for fun. Swimming, fishing. Pleasant thoughts. Even now, in the darkness, the memories brought a smile. My family. They were a source of strength to me. . . .

My watch stopped finally. Time did not matter. I dropped it in the water with a splash. Then I took out a pocketful of

> ## "I Could See the Rising Sun"
>
> ### A Civilian Witnesses the Bombing
>
> *Cornelia MacEwen Hurd*
>
> *Cornelia MacEwen Hurd, a teacher in Honolulu, describes the view from her patio on the morning of December 7, 1941.*
>
> It was 7:55 a.m. . . . I was sitting on the veranda of our house, about 800 feet above the ocean, and it commanded a view all the way from Diamond Head to Pearl Harbor. I saw the attack; I saw the bombs that were dropped in the ocean very, very vividly. In fact, as I first saw them, before I knew about the actual attack, I still thought that it must be the Army Air Force. Then I saw that they almost hit the Royal Hawaiian Hotel, and I said to myself, that was awfully close! The splashes were like plumes, going way up into the air, going splash, splash, one after the other.
>
> Then, when I heard over the radio that Hawaii was under attack, I ran up the side of my property that had a slight elevation, and there I saw the most dreadful thing I ever saw in my life. The fire, the blasting of the ships, just one after the other, in flames! I had a good view, and I knew it so well, having been there so many years, the almost enclosed lagoon harbor. And the fire and the blaze and the noise was absolutely something I'll never forget. A Japanese plane passed right in front of my yard, not more than forty feet from where I was sitting on the veranda. It was so vivid I could see the face, the profile, and the rising sun on the plane.

change and dropped the coins absently into the water. There was a place in town where *Oklahoma* sailors met to drink beer, sing songs of the Navy, tell sea stories, dance with their girls, laugh, and fight with sailors from other ships. Remembering it, I couldn't resist saying aloud, "How about a cold beer? I'm thirsty."

"Set 'em up, all the way around," a sailor replied.

"Join the Navy and see the world— from the bottom of Pearl Harbor."

No one seemed to mind the wisecracks. It was crazy, maybe, but everyone seemed to relax a bit. . . .

Time went by. As the water rose, the air became more and more foul. I felt a longing to break the silence again.

"Willy," I said, "I'll bet you a dollar we'll suffocate before we drown."

"Okay, you're on," agreed Willy. "I say we drown first." We each produced a

191

soggy dollar bill, after which we lapsed again into silence. . . .

The hours passed. . . .

Unexpectedly, and from a great distance, came the sound of hammering. Metal against metal! Our hearts jumped. The sound stopped, and we held our breaths. It started again, closer, and died away once more. . . .

We hammered at the steel bulkhead with a dog wrench. Three dots—three dashes—three dots—SOS!! . . .

"They're trying to get us," someone said. We rapped out the SOS again. Ten of us are still alive in here. We've been here a day—a whole twenty-four hours in this awful place. We were thirty, but now we're ten. The others are gone. . . .

. . . We knocked frantically against the bulkhead! A voice was heard shouting above the clamor, "Can you stand a hole? We'll drill a small one through."

"Yes, yes, go ahead and drill!" A sailor flashed on the battle lantern. . . .

The water had risen to our knees. "Hurry! Hurry up!" we shouted as the downward cut began. I turned to look at the hatch. It was bulging inward at the center. Even that heavy metal could not withstand so great a water pressure. Would we all drown like rats at the last minute, just when rescue was at hand? It was going to be close, so close! . . .

"We're going to bend it out," a voice spoke through the bulkhead. So close, yet a world away, separated from us by a quarter of an inch of steel, or less. It was the difference between life and death. Fingers pulled at the three-sided metal cut. I pushed at it. It was bending. There was no time to complete the cutting job. Gradually the opening widened as the water pushed at us from behind. It would be just wide enough to scrape through.

"Okay! Come on through!" voices called. We entered the opening in a flood of water. Friendly hands reached for our oil-slicked bodies and pulled us into the next compartment. We were free! . . .

"Here, up on my shoulders, boy," said one of the men in the accent of the islands. He smiled and I smiled back. "Thanks a lot," was all I could say. They boosted me from man to man and from space to space up through the bottom of the ship. Finally, I emerged from out of the cold darkness into the warm sunshine of a new day. It was 0900, 8 December.

Standing on the upturned hull, I gazed about me. It was the same world I had left twenty-five hours before, but as I looked at the smoke and wreckage of battle, the sunken ships *Tennessee, West Virginia,* and *Arizona* astern of us, I felt that life would never be the same, not for me—not for any of us. . . .

"To Do What Was American"

Celebrating the Fourth of July in an Internment Camp

Mary Tsukamoto

Pearl Harbor had a special impact on Japanese Americans. Unlike citizens of German or Italian ancestry, Japanese Americans were imprisoned as security risks without any proof of disloyalty. In 1942, President Roosevelt issued an order placing more than 100,000 Japanese Americans in internment camps. They lost much of their property during relocation. In 1988 Congress officially apologized for the nation's actions and partially compensated the surviving internees. Mary Tsukamoto, whose family raised strawberries in California, endured the trauma of relocation.

192

I do remember Pearl Harbor day. I was about 27, and we were in church. It was a December Sunday, so we were getting ready for our Christmas program. We were rehearsing and having Sunday school class, and I always played the piano for the adult *Issei* [native-born Japanese] service. . . .

But after the service started, my husband ran in. He had been home that day and heard on the radio. We just couldn't believe it, but he told us that Japan attacked Pearl Harbor. I remember how stunned we were. And suddenly the whole world turned dark. . . .

A lot of little things just nagged at us and harassed us, and we were frightened, but even in that atmosphere I remember we frantically wanted to do what was American. We were Americans and loyal citizens, and we wanted to do what Americans should be doing. So we were wrapping Red Cross bandages and trying to do what we could to help our country. By May 1942, more than a hundred of our boys were already drafted. . . . We started to buy war bonds, and we took first aid classes with the rest of the *Hakujin* [Caucasian] people in the community. We went out at night to go to these classes, but we worried about being out after eight o'clock. It was a frightening time. Every little rule and regulation was imposed only on the Japanese people. There were Italian and German people in the community, but it was just us that had travel restrictions and a curfew. . . .

. . . When we left, we swept our house and left it clean, because that's the way Japanese feel like leaving a place. I can just imagine everyone's emotions of grief and anger when they had to leave, when the military police (MPs) came and told them, "Get ready right now. You've got two hours to get ready to catch this train." . . .

. . . There were tears everywhere; Grandma couldn't leave her flowers, and Grandpa looked at his grape vineyard. We urged him to get into the car and leave. I

Japanese Americans were forcibly removed from their homes on the West Coast and sent to relocation camps during World War II.

remember that sad morning when we realized suddenly that we wouldn't be free. It was such a clear, beautiful day, and I remember as we were driving, our tears. . . .

I remember one scene very clearly: On the train, we were told not to look out the window, but people were peeking out. After a long time on the train somebody said, "Oh, there's some Japanese standing over there." So we all took a peek, and we saw this dust, and rows and rows of barracks, and all these tan, brown Japanese people with their hair all bleached. They were all standing in a huddle looking at us, looking at this train going by. Then somebody on the train said, "Gee, that must be Japanese people in a camp." We didn't realize who they were before, but I saw how terrible it looked; the dust, no trees—just barracks and a bunch of people standing against the fence, looking out. Some children were hanging onto the fence like animals, and that was my first sight of the assembly center. I was so sad and discouraged looking at that, knowing that before long we would be inside too.

193

"It Takes More Than Waving a Flag to Win a War"

Sacrifices on the Home Front

Mary Speir

Military needs took precedence in the allocation of the nation's resources. The war on the home front was fought by rationing scarce items such as gasoline, tires, meat, coffee, and canned foods. Mary Speir of Westminster, Maryland, found rationing to be merely an inconvenience compared to the ultimate sacrifice she had to make.

At that time I had a different feeling than I have now. I thought maybe people should go, but I didn't want my son to go. My husband also went, but he was a grown man and knew what he was doing, and that was different. I had a very bitter feeling about taking these college boys and not training them, which they didn't do for infantry. My son was only in the infantry six weeks when he was put in the lines, which I thought was very bad. . . .

I started to do some volunteer work in Westminster, like rolling bandages, but I couldn't make it. The people I was doing it with were not in my situation at all. They were more concerned with what they were having to give up than with what was happening in Europe. I had people call me up and ask, "Do you have coupons? We can get butter tomorrow." I never stood in a line for a thing. I thought that if the men could do without it, so could I.

I was alone and was terrifically upset the morning the Episcopal rector arrived at my door and said, "I have very bad news for you." I said, "Has my son been killed?" He said, "Yes." He was 20—my only child. It ruined my life. . . .

We don't fly a flag. The flag that came back on my son's casket was given to his school. He was president of his class, and they asked for the flag. I was standing . . . on my walk one day when everybody had flags out, and a man said to me, "You're not very patriotic, are you?" And I said, "What have you done?" He didn't get it. He walked up the street and told one of the neighbors what he had said to me and that I had reacted very violently to it. They said, "Well, you certainly talked to the wrong person." I said to him, "It takes more than waving a flag to win a war."

. . . But within a few weeks somebody had already planted a garden. Soon somebody would give us a little cucumber or one tomato. Before we left in October [1942, for another relocation camp in Arkansas], the whole camp was transformed. Who but *Nihonjins* [Japanese] would leave a place like that in beauty? It was an inspiring sight. . . .

I remember another thing. We had our Fourth of July program. Because we couldn't think of anything to do, we decided to recite the Gettysburg Address as a verse choir. We had an artist draw a big picture of Abraham Lincoln with an American flag behind him. Some people had tears in their eyes; some people shook their heads and said it was so ridiculous to have that kind of thing recited in a camp. It didn't make sense, but it was our hearts' cry. We wanted so much to believe that this was a government by the people and for the people and that there was freedom and justice. So we did things like that to entertain each other, to inspire each other, to hang on to things that made sense and were right. . . .

I know many *Niseis* [native-born Americans of Japanese ancestry] who say, that was all so long ago. Let's forget it and leave well enough alone. But I just say, we were the ones that went through it—the tears and the shame and the shock. We need to leave our legacy to our children. And also our legacy to America, from our tears, what we learned.

As we arrived [at the camp in Fresno, California], there were all these people, peeking out from behind the fence wondering what group would be coming next, and, of course, looking for their friends too. Suddenly you realized that human beings were being put behind fences just like on the farm where we had horses and pigs in corrals. . . .

"Things That Only Men Had Done Before"

New Roles for Women in Wartime

Winona Espinosa

Millions of men left their civilian jobs to join the armed forces, creating opportunities for women to fill new roles. By 1945, women made up more than one-third of the nation's labor force. Illustrator Norman Rockwell painted the image of "Rosie the Riveter" to symbolize these patriotic workers. Winona Espinosa was a real-life riveter, who fastened steel plates together with bolts.

In July 1942 I left Grand Junction, Colorado, where I grew up, and came to San Diego with my brother-in-law and my sister. I was 19 and my boyfriend had joined the Army and was in Washington state. In my mind, San Diego sounded closer to Washington than Colorado, and I thought that would make it easier for us to see each other. I also wanted to do something to help the country get the war over with and I knew there were a lot of defense jobs in San Diego.

I applied for a job at Rohr Aircraft, and they sent me to a six-week training school. You learned how to use an electric drill, how to do precision drilling, how to rivet. I hadn't seen anything like a rivet gun or an electric drill motor before except in Buck Rogers funny books. That's the way they looked to me. But I was an eager learner, and I soon became an outstanding riveter.

At Rohr I worked riveting the boom doors on P-38s [a fighter plane]. They were big, long, huge doors that had three or four thicknesses of skins, and you had to rivet those skins together. Everything had to be precise. It all had to pass inspection. Each rivet had to be countersunk by hand, so you had to be very good.

I found the work very challenging, but I hated the dress. We had to wear ugly-looking hairnets that made the girls look awful. The female guards were very strict about them too. Maybe you'd try to leave your bangs sticking out but they'd come

Many American women worked in defense plants during World War II.

and make you stick them back in. You looked just like a skinhead, very unfeminine. Then you had to wear pants—we called them slacks in those days—and you never wore them prior to the war. Finally, all the women had to wear those ugly scarves. They issued them so they were all the same. You couldn't wear a colorful scarf or bandana.

I worked at Rohr for almost a year, then, when I got married and pregnant, I went back to Grand Junction for a while.

195

When I came back, I went to work for the San Diego Transit, driving buses and streetcars. I just saw a sign on a bus downtown one day that said, "I need you," and I went and applied. I hadn't even been driving very long. I only learned to drive a car after I got to San Diego, and I didn't know anything about driving a big vehicle like that. But the war really created opportunities for women. It was the first time we got a chance to show that we could do a lot of things that only men had done before.

The transit company had a three-month school. They had classroom lessons and training in the field. You had to learn the automotive aspects of the bus so that if it broke down you could call in to tell the mechanic what was wrong so he could come and fix it. You also had to learn all the bus routes.

I drove buses and streetcars for about two and a half years. In fact I was driving a bus the day the war ended. I let everybody ride my bus free that day.

"Right in the Plexiglas Nose"

Bombing Raids on Germany

Joseph Theodore Hallock

The Allied Powers (the United States, Great Britain, France, the Soviet Union, and their allies) warred against the Axis Powers (Germany, Italy, Japan, and their allies) in two theaters. In Europe and North Africa, the Allies combatted the Germans and the Italians. In the Pacific and Asia, they fought the Japanese.

In 1942, the Allies captured the Midway Islands, halting the Japanese offensive in the Pacific. For the rest of the war, the Allies used the tactic of "island-hopping" throughout the Pacific to capture strategic points held by the Japanese. In Europe, the United States joined Great Britain in 1942 to conduct bombing raids over Germany. In an interview by Brendan Gill of The New Yorker, *bombardier Ted Hallock describes life inside the B-17 bomber, known as the "Flying Fortress."*

My first raid was . . . over Ludwigshaven. Naturally, not knowing what it was going to be like, I didn't feel scared. A little sick, maybe, but not scared. That comes later, when you begin to understand what your chances of survival are. Once we'd crossed into Germany, we spotted some flak, but it was a good long distance below us and looked pretty and not dangerous: different-colored puffs making a soft, cushiony-looking pattern under our plane.

A bombardier sits right in the plexiglas nose of a Fort, so he sees everything neatly laid out in front of him, like a living-room rug. It seemed to me at first that I'd simply moved in on a wonderful show. I got over feeling sick, there was so much to watch. We made our run over the target, got our bombs away, and apparently did a good job. Maybe it was the autopilot and bombsight that saw to that, but I'm sure I was cool enough on that first raid to do my job without thinking too much about it.

Then, on the way home, some Focke-Wulfs showed up, armed with rockets, and I saw three B-17s in the different groups around us suddenly blow up and drop through the sky. Just simply blow up and drop through the sky. Nowadays, if you

196

come across something awful happening, you always think, "My God, it's just like a movie," and that's what I thought. I had a feeling that the planes weren't really falling and burning, the men inside them weren't really dying, and everything would turn out happily in the end. Then, very quietly through the interphone, our tail gunner said, "I'm sorry, sir, I've been hit."

I crawled back to him and found that he'd been wounded in the side of the head—not deeply but enough so he was bleeding pretty bad. Also, he'd got a lot of the plexiglas dust from his shattered turret in his eyes, so he was, at least for the time being, blind. The blood that would have bothered me . . . a few months before didn't bother me at all then. The Army had trained me in a given job and I went ahead and did what I was trained to do, bandaging the gunner well enough to last him back to our base. Though he was blind, he was still able to use his hands, and I ordered him to fire his guns whenever he heard from me. I figured that a few bursts every so often from his fifties would keep the Germans off our tail, and I also figured that it would give the kid something to think about besides the fact that he'd been

hit. When I got back to the nose, the pilot told me that our No. 4 engine had been shot out. Gradually we lost our place in the formation and flew nearly alone over France. That's about the most dangerous thing that can happen to a lame Fort, but the German fighters had luckily given up and we skimmed over the top of the flak all the way to the [English] Channel. . . .

When we started our missions, we were told that after twenty-five we would probably be sent home for a rest, so that was how we kept figuring things—so many missions accomplished, so many missions still to go. We worked it all out on a mathematical basis, or on what we pretended was a mathematical basis—how many months it would take us to finish our stint, how many missions we'd have to make over Germany proper, what our chances of getting shot down were. Then, at about the halfway mark, the number of missions we would have to make was raised from twenty-five to thirty. That was one hell of a heartbreaker. Supposedly, they changed the rules of the game because flying had got that much safer, but you couldn't make us think in terms of being safer. Those five extra raids might as well have been fifty.

"In All That Flying Hell"

Commanding Tanks in North Africa

Samuel Allen

After intense fighting, the Allies forced the surrender of Axis troops in North Africa in May 1943. Sergeant Samuel Allen of Ohio wrote to his family about the tank battles in North Africa. He was killed in Italy a few months later.

Dear Family:
It's an awful funny feeling, sitting there on top of your tank just waiting. You knew that not everybody was coming back and as I sat there I looked over each tank and hoped that it was all a bad dream. After you've been in an outfit ever since it was formed and lived with the

fellows as long as I have, you get to feel like one big family. You know all about each man, his wife, kids, or his girlfriend; maybe you've met his family; anyway, we've shared each other's packages from home and things like that. I know that as a tank commander you know the other five men in your crew better than your own family and

"I Feel Like It's Me Killin' 'Em"

Leading Green Troops into Battle

Ernie Pyle

Victory in North Africa paved the way for the Allied invasion of Europe. As the Soviets kept pushing the German Army westward in Europe, British and American forces began their European offensive. In July 1943, the Allies invaded Sicily and from there attacked the mainland of Italy in the fierce campaign of 1943-44. Ernie Pyle, a popular correspondent of the war, described in one of his columns the challenges faced by an American sergeant in Italy.

Buck Eversole is a platoon sergeant in an infantry company. That means he has charge of about forty front-line fighting men.

He has been at the front for more than a year. War is old to him, and he has become almost the master of it. He is a senior partner now in the institution of death.

His platoon has turned over many times as battle whittles down the old ones and the replacement system brings up the new ones. Only a handful now are veterans.

"It gets so it kinda gets you, seein' these new kids come up," Buck told me one night in his slow, barely audible western voice, so full of honesty and sincerity.

"Some of them have just got fuzz on their faces, and don't know what it's all about, and they're scared to death. No matter what, some of them are bound to get killed."

We talked about some of the other old-time noncoms who could take battle themselves, but had gradually grown morose under the responsibility of leading green boys to their slaughter. Buck spoke of one sergeant especially, a brave and hardened man, who went to his captain and asked him to be reduced to a private in the lines.

"I know it ain't my fault that they get killed," Buck finally said. "And I do the best I can for them, but I've got so I feel like it's me killin' 'em instead of a German. I've got so I feel like a murderer. I hate to look at them when the new ones come in."

it's sort of your job to see that they all come back. That's the way we feel about it: it's just your job!

Mount up! That's the call and I guess we were all glad, I know I was; you'd go nuts if you had to sit there any longer. The minute you are in the tank you become part of a machine, you have your certain job to do and hold your end up. You stop thinking about yourself and think of your job.

We moved out into the valley travelling in two inverted wedges—VV—with our platoon in support—VV. B company was to be in the same position on our left. But as we later saw, they jumped off after we did and then did not go up to the objective. As we got to the hill we (our platoon) was to swing in an arc up the valley to the right of the hill, between the hill and the moun-

tains on the right. I was to take my section up into the valley as far as I could to get at the artillery that was behind the hill.

As we moved through a large cactus patch, they opened up on us with everything they had. It seemed to me that one gun picked my tank out because there were always four shell bursts after me. The German 76.2 mm gun shoots four shots, one in the chamber and three in a clip. From then on it was just a question of outguessing them. The valley had a lot of small bunkers in it and we sort of jumped from behind one to another—if it hadn't been for those little [hillocks] we never would have made it. First they would drop four about fifty yards behind me and then four right in front of me; then it was time to move on.

198

About this time the other tank in my section ran into a land mine and blew one track off. When that happens they are usually in a mine field and you can't help them because you'd hit one yourself. But I saw the boys bail out so I knew they could make it on foot. Now the infantry came out of the wadi on our left and swung across the valley, among us. It's not very nice to watch those boys out there running in all that flying hell, but you can't watch them, you have a job to do. You can't see the guns because they are dug in and in concrete emplacements; then all at once you spot one and lay your guns on it.

Over to my left I could see two tanks burning and on my right two more in the minefield. The hill was getting closer; now and then I could see the road up ahead. There's a tall cactus fence between us and the road and a large ditch also. Boy, it's no time to get stuck now. Just then somebody stood up in the ditch—our infantry! They grinned, waved, and one of them pointed to a spot where I could get through. Thank God for the infantry!

Across the road and my friend who is shooting at me stops. I guess he can't depress his gun far enough; just then I saw a gun on my right, just next to an Arab hut, so here we go—and then I've got to get up that valley all alone now; wonder how Toth is making out in the minefield. Damn it, that gun sees me and is swinging over on me; gosh it has a barrel about fifteen feet long. But just up there ahead is another bunker. We've got to get there fast.

Safe for a minute but then Waitman phones up that our 75 mm gun is jammed. Pawling has that 37 going like a machine gun and we are in one hell of a position. If we move from behind this bunker we'll get it sure because it's only 200 yards over to that gun. Just then Lt. Maloney called on the radio, "Let's get the hell out of here, let's go home." So we back around and pull out just enough so I can see; the gun isn't there anymore. It must be our lucky day! . . .

On the way back I stopped as close to Toth as I could but I could see that I couldn't do him any good so off we go again. One of Christison's crew comes running up and tells me that I'm in the minefield also. You can see where mines are planted if you look close enough, so I got out of the tank and brought my tank through on foot; those shells were awfully close at times but we made it.

Back to our area to gas and [ammo] up. We knew that we had lost some friends and equipment out on that field. But we have found that it is best to forget all about those friends, not to talk about them—they didn't even exist.

But it is gratifying to know that we opened the way and the British are on the way to Kairouan.

I'm a great believer in luck now. Someone got that gun—and later I learned that after I crossed the road I was in one of their minefields all the way. Luck—I travelled 600 yards on it!

"We Took That Beach"

Beating the Odds in Normandy

Ernie Pyle

On June 6, 1944, Allied forces invaded France, which was under German occupation, via the beaches of Normandy. It was the largest amphibious invasion in history, involving some 4,000 ships. About one million men came ashore within two weeks of D-day (a military code for the actual date of an attack). War correspondent Ernie Pyle witnessed the aftermath of the Normandy invasion.

Due to a last-minute alteration in the arrangements, I didn't arrive on the beachhead until the morning after D-day, after our first wave of assault troops had hit the shore.

By the time we got here, the beaches had been taken and the fighting had moved a couple of miles inland. All that remained on the beach was some sniping and

ings were strewn all over these bitter sands. That plus the bodies of soldiers lying in rows as though on drill. And other bodies, uncollected, still sprawling grotesquely in the sand or half hidden by the high grass beyond the beach.

That plus an intense, grim determination of work-weary men to get this chaotic beach organized and get all the vital supplies and the reinforcements moving more rapidly over it from the stacked-up ships standing in droves out to sea.

Now that it is over, it seems to me a pure miracle that we ever took the beach at all. For some of our units it was easy, but in this special sector where I am now our troops faced such odds that our getting ashore was like my whipping Joe Louis down to a pulp.

In this column I want to tell you what the opening of the second front in this one sector entailed, so that you can know and appreciate and forever be humbly grateful to those both dead and alive who did it for you.

Ashore, facing us, were more enemy troops than we had in our assault waves. The advantages were all theirs, the disadvantages all ours. The Germans were dug into positions that they had been working on for months, although these were not yet all complete. A 100-foot bluff a couple of hundred yards back from the beach had great concrete gun emplacements built right into the hilltop. These opened to the sides instead of to the front, thus making it very hard for naval fire from the sea to reach them. They could shoot parallel with the beach and cover every foot of it for miles with artillery fire.

Then they had hidden machine-gun nests on the forward slopes, with crossfire taking in every inch of the beach. These nests were connected by networks of trenches, so that the German gunners

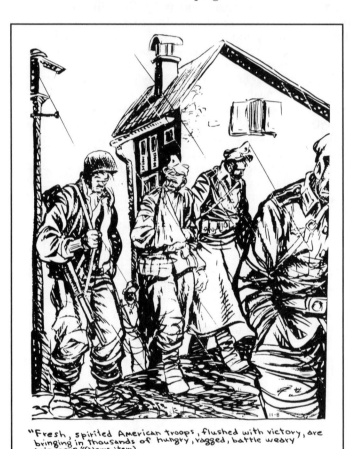

"Fresh, spirited American troops, flushed with victory, are bringing in thousands of hungry, ragged, battle weary prisoners." (News item)

Sgt. Bill Mauldin, who himself fought on the front lines, created the cartoon characters "Willie and Joe" to reflect the viewpoint of the ordinary foot soldier during World War II. Mauldin won a Pulitzer Prize for this cartoon, which contradicts the rosy picture of the war given by the press.

artillery fire, and the occasional startling blast of a mine geysering brown sand into the air. That plus a gigantic and pitiful litter of wreckage along miles of shoreline.

Submerged tanks and overturned boats and burned trucks and shell-shattered jeeps and sad little personal belong-

could move about without exposing themselves.

Throughout the length of the beach, running zigzag a couple of hundred yards back from the shoreline, was an immense V-shaped ditch fifteen feet deep. Nothing could cross it, not even men on foot, until fills had been made. And in other places at the far end of the beach, where the ground is flatter, they had great concrete walls. . . .

Our only exits from the beach were several swales or valleys, each about 100 yards wide. The Germans made the most of these funnel-like traps, sowing them with buried mines. They contained, also, barbed-wire entanglements with mines attached, hidden ditches, and machine guns firing from the slopes.

This is what was on the shore. But our men had to go through a maze nearly as deadly as this before they even got ashore. Underwater obstacles were terrific. The Germans had whole fields of evil devices under the water to catch our boats. Even now, several days after the landing, we have cleared only channels through them and cannot yet approach the whole length of the beach with our ships. Even now some ship or boat hits one of these mines every day and is knocked out of commission.

The Germans had masses of those six-pronged spiders, made of railroad iron and standing shoulder-high, just beneath the surface of the water for our landing craft to run into. They also had huge logs buried in the sand, pointing upward and outward, their tops just below the water. Attached to these logs were mines.

In addition to these obstacles they had floating mines offshore, land mines buried in the sand of the beach, and more mines in checkerboard rows in the tall grass beyond the sand. And the enemy had four men on shore for every three men we had approaching the shore.

And yet we got on. . . .

The first crack in the beach defenses was finally accomplished by terrific and wonderful naval gunfire, which knocked out the big emplacements. They tell epic stories of destroyers that ran right up into shallow water and had it out point-blank with the big guns in those concrete emplacements ashore.

When the heavy fire stopped, our men were organized by their officers and pushed on inland, circling machine-gun nests and taking them from the rear.

As one officer said, the only way to take a beach is to face it and keep going. It is costly at first, but it's the only way. If the men are pinned down on the beach, dug in and out of action, they might as well not be there at all. They hold up the waves behind them, and nothing is being gained.

Our men were pinned down for a while, but finally they stood up and went through, and so we took that beach and accomplished our landing. . . .

"Come Out Fighting"

Victories of an African-American Tanker Group

Charles A. Gates

As in previous wars, black soldiers in World War II served in segregated units, usually under white officers. Charles A. Gates was a black officer who commanded a company of the 761st Tank Battalion, the first African-American tanker group used in combat. The 761st was eventually commended for valor by the president.

I was 29 when I joined the service on April 10, 1941. I was sent to Fort Riley, Kansas. You had the Ninth and Tenth cavalries there, who established a heck of a record. I might attribute my success to the training I received from old soldiers who had no more than a fifth-grade education. Regular army men. I had noticed that every new white officer who came there was told to observe the old black sergeants.

They asked if I'd be interested in goin' to OCS. I said no, I wanted to do my twelve months and get out. The regimental commander said, "Do you know any question about the Field Manual, FM 105-dash-one?" I said yes. He said, "What are you supposed to do when a commanding officer requests you to do something?" I said, "Request in that particular case is considered as an order." He said, "Well, I'm requesting that you just sign these papers." So that's how I got stuck and ended up goin' to Officer's Training School. I did that in July of '42. Fort Knox, Kentucky.

I had been strictly an outdoors man. To be inside a building and listen to a monotone all day long, I couldn't take. I did nothing but sleep those first days. The instructor said, "You sleep in my classes, you'll not get anything but a bunch of demerits." I said I didn't want to come here anyway. After six weeks, we had our first examinations. Fifty percent of every OCS class lost in the first examination. I ended up with an average of ninety-six-point-something. So the last six weeks, they just said, Let him sleep. . . . It came as a result of the training I had gotten at Fort Riley.

I was a lieutenant at Camp Claiborne, Louisiana, until December of '42. The company commander had three platoon leaders ask me questions, to test me. I answered; they were satisfied. I then said that I have questions for them and I'll let them have a month to find the answers. They had searched every field manual and couldn't find them. So I politely told them the answers are in the field manual which they've been waiting to receive. Their manual is obsolete. I

said, "This is a lesson for you. Let us work together and we'll accomplish a hell of a lot more than we will by trying to trick one another." . . .

We went to Fort Hood, Texas, early '44. We trained against the tank destroyer outfits and consistently made monkeys out of them. They had both white and black. We established quite a reputation.

In '44, General Patton requested the best separate battalion they had left in the United States. He wanted 'em for the Third Army. We weren't in a division. Patton had made a statement that Negroes were incapable of being tankers. The equipment was too technical. And who should General Patton see when he went into the armored field? Us. Here we come, the best they had left in the United States. . . .

He viewed us for quite some time. Finally he said, "You're the first Negro tankers ever to be used in the American army in combat. I want you to establish a record for yourselves and a record for your race. I want you to make a liar out of me. When you get in combat—and you will be in combat—when you see those kraut s.o.b.'s, don't spare the ammunition." Of course, the Negroes whooped because here was a white man tellin' the Negroes to shoot white people. Well, that really tore us up. . . .

The average life of a separate tank battalion was from ten to twelve days. Then they'd just redline it out and the few men who were left were attached to somebody else. So when there was a bad spot, they'd send the separate tank battalion in the area and the division would just bypass it. You were just gun fodder really. We went 183 days without relief and damn few replacements.

We had all but ten people in the outfit were black. There were ten whites, officers. Two of 'em were company commanders. One of 'em lasted two days. The other lasted about two weeks. Then there was nothin' but Negro officers and enlisted men on the front from that day on. This was in France, Belgium, Holland, the cracking of the Siegfried Line, West Germany. We finally ended up in

Steyr, Austria. Always in combat. No other unit has any record to compare. . . .

We started out with 750 men. All through the 183 days, we had 35 men killed in action. We had 293 who received Purple Hearts. We had 60 who received Bronze Stars. We had 11 who received Silver Stars. Remember, these awards were granted through the divisions with whom we'd been attached. A division naturally is gonna take care of its own first. So for us to have received that many awards meant to me that any man who received a Bronze Star should have received a Silver Star and any man who received a Silver Star should

have received a Congressional Medal of Honor. Because we got only the crumbs. So we must have done a very creditable job. They were very well trained and disciplined. We had a job to do and they did their best. . . .

It was seldom any of this news got to the States. Most people didn't know that we had a Negro tank outfit. The campaign for a Presidential Unit Citation started back in '45. It took us thirty-three years. . . .

Our particular motto is "Come Out Fighting." After the close of hostilities, we just kept on fighting. It's just that simple.

"The Ovens Were Still Hot"

A Jewish American Witnesses Buchenwald

Philip Lief

In December 1944, a massive German attack in the Ardennes Forest of Belgium succeeded in pushing back the Allied forces after they had liberated France. Known as the Battle of the Bulge, it was the last German counteroffensive of the war. As Allied troops advanced into Germany in 1945, they liberated concentration camps in which Jews and political prisoners were being exterminated in massive numbers. Nearly 12 million people, half of them Jews, were systematically murdered. Philip Lief, a surgeon and captain in the U.S. Army, witnessed the horror at the Buchenwald camp.

We were a specialized unit called the Third Auxiliary Surgical Group composed of picked doctors, nurses, and corpsmen. The purpose of this unit was to perform surgery on the battlefield. . . .

. . . It was during [the Battle of the Bulge] that we had many German casualties who came through as they were trying to put up their counterattack. . . . [D]uring the Christmas week, I believe it was 1944, one of the SS troopers, a lieutenant colonel, came in as a casualty. I spoke to him in German. . . . The SS trooper asked me, *"Sind sie Deutsch?"* Are you German? I answered, *"Nein, ich bin ein Jude."* No, I

am Jewish. With that he gave a gasp and said nothing more.

At this time we were really hard-pressed because of the intense fighting that took place during the Battle of the Bulge. In fact, we had to retreat back to the center of Belgium because of the counterattack of the Germans. However, fortunately, the counterattack was repulsed and we were able to advance into Germany proper. On the third of April 1945, the Third Auxiliary headquarters moved to Weimar, Germany. Weimar was once the center of German culture. Men like Goethe and Schiller, Liszt and Herder had made it their home and they had left their imprint. But in the

Second World War, Weimar became noted for an entirely different brand of Teutonism. Into the prison camp at Buchenwald, in an enclosure originally built for 8,000, the Germans crowded 60,000 prisoners and gradually exterminated them. It was a spectacle of stark misery, utter degradation, and grim death. . . .

Buchenwald was approximately one mile outside of Weimar. Our hospital went

The starving survivors of Buchenwald—one of the Nazis' most notorious concentration camps—lie on their bunks, using their tin bowls as headrests.

into Buchenwald about two hours after the Germans had left. The first sight that greeted me when I entered the camp with my operating room truck was a horse and wagon. And as I looked into the contents of the wagon, I could see it was filled with human bones. One could recognize the humeri, the femurs, the spinal bones, and the pelvises and skulls of many of the deceased prisoners who had been in the camp. Where this wagon was going I really did not know, but I was horrified at this sight.

We had heard many rumors about the camps. We really didn't know too much. We had very little factual information. What we knew is what we read in the U.S. Army newspapers, what we could read from our little editions of *Time* magazine. . . . They said that there were many political prisoners and people that Hitler was trying to exterminate. In fact, they said the ovens were still hot. I myself opened one of the doors, looked inside, and could see the smoldering remains of bodies. There were about four ovens side by side in one section of Buchenwald that I visited.

Inmates from the camp were walking around without any purpose, aimlessly, almost dazed. People were malnourished, wearing the familiar striped uniforms. We went into their quarters and they were lying in the familiar type of beds, one on top of the other, bunks, four to five abreast on each shelf. These people were very emaciated, eyes were sunken into the eye sockets. . . . There were many sick inmates, and their death rate per day was approximately 145. We had a great deal of plasma with us and we would give the inmates who were terminally ill infusions of plasma. Some of the inmates couldn't wait and they opened the bottles of plasma and started to drink the plasma, although we told them that this had to be given intravenously. At autopsy many of the patients showed manifestations of marked, advanced pulmonary tuberculosis, with large cavitation in both lungs.

At first, I couldn't believe what I saw. We were . . . horrified. We also saw large piles of dead corpses, male and female without any clothes on, in large piles outside of the crematorium. We called the Army Engineers to make provisions for burying the dead as quickly as possible. The Military Police called in the civilians from Weimar to witness what we saw. Several of the people who came in said that they knew nothing of what was going on in the concentration camp.

"How Do You Think You Would Have Behaved Under Hitler?"

Looking for Good Germans

David Davidson

The concentration camps posed a disturbing question for the rest of the world: how would you have acted in Hitler's Germany? For David Davidson, who helped the U.S. Army establish anti-Nazi communications in Germany after its surrender, the question was a literal one.

Even before the last shots were fired in Europe in World War II and the dust had begun to settle over the ruins of Hitler's Thousand-Year Reich, teams of Americans in Army uniform were moving into Germany to begin sitting in judgment of the defeated enemy. . . .

I was one of these moralists in khaki. A newspaperman and radio writer in civil life, only a few days after the German surrender in May 1945, I took my place behind a battered pine desk in a bomb-cracked building in Munich. . . .

Our mission . . . was to suspend immediately every activity in public communications—press, book, and magazine publishing, radio, theater, opera, and even the circus—and root out all practitioners tainted with Nazism. Next we would search out, investigate, and license provably anti-Nazi Germans to build up a whole new democratic establishment of communications over which there would be no need to exercise censorship. . . .

The procession of Germans who came before us were, by our rough-and-ready rule of thumb, soon classified as falling into one of three categories: black, white, or gray.

Black denoted applicants with an out-and-out Nazi background and on whom little time need be wasted except for a few calculated insults to themselves and their fallen Führer. White denoted "good Germans," those who had never given in to Nazism during the Hitler era.

Gray was the tragic group, consisting of good Germans who had gone bad under pressure; people of decent anti-Nazi convictions who, because of the necessities of making a living, pursuing a career, or even staying out of the Gestapo dungeons, had finally caved in to one degree or another. . . .

Interrogating the grays was always the most painful—for the interrogator as well as for the applicant. To the grays we represented the conscience they had betrayed. And the consequences of these interrogations could be painfully dramatic. One applicant, after being faced with the record of his concessions to Nazism, killed himself.

In my case, an applicant whom I had accused of fighting Hitler "with your fist in your pocket" turned on me and shot a barbed question that stings to this day: "How do you think *you* would have behaved under Hitler?"

There was marked malnutrition throughout the entire camp. The attitude of the inmates was "what can I do for myself" for self-survival. Each one tried to look out for his own personal interests rather than the interests of the group. Apparently this had been a conditioned reflex over the time that they were there in camp. It meant that personal survival was the only way they could beat the death sentence of the Buchenwald camp.

I had studied German literature while an undergraduate at Harvard College. I knew about the culture of the German people and I could not, could not really believe that this was happening in this day and age; that in the twentieth century a cultured people like the Germans would undertake something like this. It was just beyond our imagination.

I saw the pocketbook made out of human skin that supposedly Ilse Koch, the

wife of the commandant of Buchenwald concentration camp carried about, and also saw the lampshade made out of human skin that had been stretched over a frame and used as a lampshade in her apartment. . . . There were excuses made by all the German civilian personnel that we saw, that they had no control over what was happening, that they didn't know all the facts that were going on in the camp, and the extent of the extermination in the camp. . . .

It took anywhere from a week to three weeks for most of the inmates to realize the significance of the fact that they were now among friends and Americans who had liberated the camp. They were happy to see us, but at first they distrusted everyone. They would go up for personal favors, they would ask for food, candy, chocolate, cigarettes, and these were given to them in great abundance. I'm not sure that cigarettes was a good idea for people with pulmonary tuberculosis.

They reminded me of children, of people who wanted to be cared for, of people who did not want to assume responsibility, people who had been ordered about and had become conditioned to be ordered to do certain things rather than to think for themselves. Many of them had concern for the other members of the families, as I said before, but everything was on a personal basis. The enormity of the fact that millions of Jews and political prisoners of other faiths had been exterminated could not really sink [into] their thinking. They were thinking of a very small world of their own, their immediate family, themselves and their immediate family. . . .

We tried to question the inmates themselves about what had happened and the stories would vary from day to day, even after questioning the same person, because these people were living like in a nightmare. A lot of them wanted to repress what they had seen. A lot of people didn't believe it. I myself didn't believe what I had seen. And yet there it was. We heard stories about Ilse Koch. . . . We heard how she tortured the inmates. How before they were put into the ovens she would have them hanging up naked by their thumbs. She would torture them sexually while they were hanging up naked by their thumbs before the ovens there; while they were tortured they would watch the bodies being put into the ovens. It's hard to believe these things but I think a lot of it did happen, actually did happen.

"We Swore Never to Forget"

U.S. and Soviet Troops Meet at the Elbe

Joseph Polowsky

The United States and the Soviet Union were uneasy allies in World War II. Americans opposed communism, but they believed that Hitler was an even greater evil. U.S. troops on the western front and Soviet forces on the eastern front sandwiched the Germans between them, forcing a surrender on May 8, 1945. Joseph Polowsky, an Army private, describes the meeting of the two victorious armies at the Elbe River on April 25, 1945.

I was a rifleman, private, Company G, 273rd Infantry, Third Platoon, 69th Division, First Army. We had seen plenty of action. We were in a quiet area along the Mulde River, a tributary of the Elbe. A town called Trebsen, twenty miles west of the Elbe. This was April 24.

I was called into company headquarters. They were checking on documents of Germans—suspects and former Nazis and those who wanted to be officials. I was the only man in the company who had a good working knowledge of German.

A phone call comes in from battalion headquarters. They want a patrol to be formed immediately, seven jeeps, twenty-eight men, to go about five miles in front of the lines to see if they could get some signs of the Russians. . . .

They were afraid if the two armies met at full speed, there could be casualties. Two armies, even friendly armies, going hellbent toward each other, there would be some guys who would be hurt. So Eisenhower and Zhukov decided that the two armies would stop about twenty-five miles short of each other. That's why we stopped at the Mulde and they at the Elbe. . . .

Would you believe it? There was a tremendous burst of lilacs as we [the patrol] approached the Elbe River. This exaltation of being alive, after all those days trapped in a trench war. There were even jokes that we were approaching the River Jordan, crossing into Canaan. Of course, we were saddened to learn that President Roosevelt had died about two weeks earlier. We also knew that the United Nations was being born in San Francisco on the very same day, 25th of April. Can you imagine? The very day we linked up with the Russians at the Elbe River.

It was a tremendous feeling to see the Elbe. This was about 11:30 in the morning. The Elbe is a swift-running river, about 175 yards wide. Kotzebue [the U.S. platoon leader] shot up two green flares. After about ten minutes, with shouts and the wind blowing toward the east, our voices were able to carry across the river. The Russians waved at us and gave the signal to approach their lines. The problem was getting across the river. The Germans in

retreat, the Allied forces dropping bombs along the bridges, the Russian artillery blowing up the bridges: between the three, there was no bridge to cross. . . .

At the far side of the Elbe, the Russian side, there was the remains of a steel bridge which jutted out maybe fifty yards into the river. On our side, there was a heavy chain attached to a barge and two sailboats. With a hand grenade, Kotzebue exploded the chain. About six of us piled into the sailboat. There were makeshift paddles. With tremendous effort, we managed to guide the boat into the girders protruding from the opposite side. As we climbed up, there were three Russian soldiers approaching the bank. Why were there only three? On the road ahead, we saw many Russian soldiers.

What happened was this. That bridge had been blown up at least three days. A tremendous wave of civilians, mostly Germans, a great mass, had approached the bridge, fleeing the Russians to go west. So they were piled like lumber at the bridge, along the whole bank. Fifty yards on each side was literally covered with bodies of women, old men, children. I still remember seeing a little girl clutching a doll in one hand. . . . She couldn't have been more than five or six years old. And her mother's hand in the other. They were all piled up like cordwood at the bank.

How had it happened? Who knows? Part of it was German fire, maybe Allied planes bombing the bridgehead. Probably the Russian artillery from a distance of several miles. It was a depressed area, impossible to see. It was an accident. There were so many in the war.

Actually, it was difficult for the Russians to pierce their way into meeting us. Because of the bodies. Here we are, tremendously exhilarated, and there's a sea of dead. Kotzebue, who is a very religious man, was much moved. He couldn't talk Russian. The Russians couldn't talk English.

He said, "Joe, let's make a resolution with these Russians here and also the ones on the bank: this would be an important day in the lives of the two countries and the symbolism of all the civilian dead.

"Six Feet of Earth"

The Death of FDR

Grace Tully

President Franklin Delano Roosevelt did not live to see the end of World War II. On April 12, 1945, while vacationing in Warm Springs, Georgia, the president died of a massive cerebral hemorrhage. His assistant, Grace Tully, was present at FDR's death.

I could feel a chill in my heart, a sense that this was something different from another complaint about his sinus acting up or his tummy being out of whack. I decided to go at once to the president's cottage.

By the time I reached the house, both Bruenn and Fox were with the president in his bedroom. Miss Suckley was in the living room; Miss Delano entered from the bedroom as I walked in. There were sounds of tortured breathing from the bedroom and low voices of the two men attending him. Miss Delano and Miss Suckley looked shocked and frightened; the former told me the president had finished some work with Mr. Hassett and was sitting for Madame Shoumatoff. At 1:00 the president remarked to the artist, "We have only fifteen minutes." At 1:15 he put his hand to his head and slumped backward in a coma. Prettyman and a Filipino house boy had carried him from his chair to his bedroom.

Hacky already had gotten Dr. McIntire on the phone in Washington and had put Bruenn on the line with him. At McIntire's instruction, Dr. James E. Paullin, a heart specialist in Atlanta, had been summoned. Dr. Paullin made a desperately fast automobile trip to Warm Springs and arrived while we were waiting anxiously in the living room.

Almost within seconds of Paullin's arrival, Bruenn was called again by Dr. McIntire. While on the phone he was summoned back to the bedroom. Bruenn left the line open as he disappeared into the Boss's room. In a minute or so he was back. With a tragically expressive gesture of his hands he picked up the phone again. I knew what his message was before he spoke. The president was dead.

My reaction of the moment was one of complete lack of emotion. It was as if my whole mind and sense of feeling had been swept away. The shock was unexpected and the actuality of the event was outside belief. Without a word or a glance toward the others present, I walked into the bedroom, leaned over, and kissed the president lightly on the forehead. . . .

. . . One of his last official actions had been to approve the design of a United Nations stamp, and an approval had been given over the telephone to Postmaster General Frank Walker after the Boss had studied several alternative samples. And on his bedside table was a paper-covered detective story with a page turned down at a chapter headed: "Six Feet of Earth."

Talk to them in German." As I was translating to Kotzebue in English, one of the Russians who knew German was translating to the other Russians. It was very informal, but it was a solemn moment. There were tears in the eyes of most of us. Perhaps a sense of foreboding that things might not be as perfect in the future as we anticipated. We embraced. We swore never to forget. . . .

I always felt that American-Russian relations were plagued by bad luck right from the beginning. If we had gotten publicity with the Oath of the Elbe, there would have been a certain depth in feelings. Just think of the millions who died on the Russian side and the tremendous effort on the American side, amidst all those dead women and children and that little girl clutching the doll in her hand. Nothing.

"Don't Hesitate to Fight the Japs Dirty"

Cultural Differences in Warfare

Eugene B. Sledge

After the German surrender, the Allies concentrated all their efforts on defeating Japan. Eugene B. Sledge, known to his Marine comrades as "Sledgehammer," describes the cultural—and racial—differences between how Americans fought the Germans and the Japanese.

The Japanese fought by a code they thought was right: *bushido.* The code of the warrior: no surrender. You don't really comprehend it until you get out there and fight people who are faced with an absolutely hopeless situation and will not give up. If you tried to help one of the Japanese, he'd usually detonate a grenade and kill himself as well as you. To be captured was a disgrace. . . .

Toward the end of the Okinawa campaign, we found this emaciated Japanese in the bunk of what may have been a field hospital. We were on a patrol. There had been torrential rains for two weeks. The foxholes were filled with water. This Jap didn't have but a G-string on him. About ninety pounds. Pitiful. This buddy of mine picked him up and carried him out. Laid him out in the mud. There was no other place to put him.

We were sittin' on our helmets waitin' for the medical corpsman to check him out. He was very docile. We figured he couldn't get up. Suddenly he pulled a Japanese grenade out of his G-string. He jerked the pin out and hit it on his fist to pop open the cap. He was gonna make hamburger of me and my buddy and himself. I yelled, "Look out!" So my buddy said, "You son of a bitch, if that's how you feel about it"—he pulled out his .45 and shot him right between the eyes. . . .

You developed an attitude of no mercy because they had no mercy on us. It was a no-quarter, savage kind of thing. At Peleliu, it was the first time I was close enough to see one of their faces. This Jap had been hit. One of my buddies was field-stripping him for souvenirs. I must admit it really bothered me, the guys dragging him around like a carcass. I was just horrified. This guy had been a human being. It didn't take me long to overcome that feeling. A lot of my buddies hit, the fatigue, the stress. After a while, the veneer of civilization wore pretty thin.

This hatred toward the Japanese was just a natural feeling that developed elementally. Our attitude toward the Japanese was different than the one we had toward

About 400 Navajo "code talkers" contributed to Allied victories in the Pacific by transmitting military messages in code made up of Navajo words, a code the Japanese never broke.

the Germans. My brother who was with the Second Infantry Division in the Battle of the Bulge, wounded three times, said when things were hopeless for the Germans, they surrendered. I have heard many guys who fought in Europe who said the Germans were damn good soldiers. We hated the hell of having to fight 'em. When they surrendered, they were guys just like us. With the Japanese, it was not that way. . . .

Our drill instructor at boot camp would tell us, "You're not going to Europe;

you're going to the Pacific. Don't hesitate to fight the Japs dirty. Most Americans, from the time they're kids, are taught not to hit below the belt. It's not sportsman-like. Well, nobody has taught the Japs that, and war ain't sport. Kick him in the balls before he kicks you in yours."

I've seen guys shoot Japanese wounded when it really was not necessary and knock gold teeth out of their mouths. Most of them had gold teeth. I remember one time at Peleliu, I thought I'd collect gold teeth. One of my buddies carried a bunch of 'em in a sock. What you did is you took your K-bar, a [seven-inch] fighting knife. We all had one because they'd creep into your foxhole at night. We were on Half Moon Hill in Okinawa about ten days. It happened every night.

The way you extracted gold teeth was by putting the tip of the blade on the tooth of the dead Japanese—I've seen guys do it to wounded ones—and hit the hilt of the knife to knock the tooth loose. How could American boys do this? If you're reduced to savagery by a situation, anything's pos-sible. When [Charles] Lindbergh made a trip to the Philippines, he was horrified at the way American GIs talked about the Japanese. It was so savage. We *were* savages.

When I leaned [over] to make the extraction, as the troops used to say, this navy medic, Doc Castle, God bless his soul, said, "Sledgehammer, what are you doing?" I says, "Doc, I'm gonna get me some gold teeth." He said (very softly), "You don't want to do that." I said, "All the other guys are doin' it." He says, "What would your folks think?" I said, "Gosh, my dad is a medical doctor back in Mobile; he might think it's interesting." He said, "Well, you might get germs." I said, "I hadn't thought of that, Doc." In retrospect, I realized Ken Castle wasn't worried about germs. He just didn't want me to take another step toward abandoning all concepts of decency.

I saw this Jap machine-gunner squattin' on the ground. One of our Browning automatic riflemen had killed him. Took the top of his skull off. It rained all that night. This Jap gunner didn't fall over for some reason. He was just sitting upright in front of the machine gun. His arms were down at his sides. His eyes were wide open. It had rained all night and the rain had collected inside of his skull.

We were just sittin' around on our helmets, waiting to be relieved. I noticed this buddy of mine just flippin' chunks of coral into the skull about three feet away. Every time he'd get one in there, it'd splash. It reminded me of a child throwin' pebbles into a puddle. It was just so un-real. There was nothing malicious in his action. This was just a mild-mannered kid who was now a twentieth-century savage.

"A Terrible Thing Had Been Unleashed"

Working on the Manhattan Project

Philip Morrison

The United States faced the prospect of a long and costly war against Japan. President Harry Truman, FDR's successor, made the decision to use a newly developed weapon, the atomic bomb, to hasten the end of the war. In August 1945, Japan surrendered after the United States dropped atomic bombs on the cities of Hiroshima and Nagasaki.

Known as the Manhattan Project, the U.S. effort to build an atomic weapon before the Germans did so cost $2 billion and employed hundreds of scientists. Philip Morrison was one of those scientists.

210

The folklore of the day is the physicists were approached by the Army. The Army said, We will make you rich and famous. We'll give you the wonderful opportunity to make the world's greatest explosion and all you have to forget is it's going to make a bomb to kill very many people. A Faustian bargain.

That was not the idea at all. It's a complete misapprehension. We went to the Army. I mean the scientific profession, [Albert] Einstein, the pacifist, at its head. We beat on the doors and said, We must be allowed to make this weaponry or we're going to lose the war. . . .

It was all one single enterprise, highly divided, highly complex: the Manhattan Project. . . . We knew the idea was to make the most destructive of all possible bombs. We believed Hitler was well ahead of us. . . .

By December '44, we learned unmistakably . . . that the Germans were not a threat. They could not make the atomic bomb. They were far behind and arrogant. They said, "We're well ahead of the rest of the world. The Americans can't do it. Even if Germany loses the war, we'll win the peace, because we alone control this powerful weapon." . . .

What was the right thing for us to do? It was a critical moment. The Japanese war was not yet over. Our work may bring an end to the war, save many lives, start a new world. . . .

I don't say I was antagonistic to its use, not at all. But I wondered: Is this the right thing to do? The idea of dropping it was implicit in making it. We were not certain just how. Our task was to get the bomb finished, to find out if it would work. The whole world was depending on that, we felt.

I was appointed one of the people to make sure of the details of the test in the desert. The Trinity test. There was talk of the possibility of its use over Japan. There was another suggestion that the Japanese be invited to see the test. But there was this enormous uncertainty: would it work? If it didn't work, you'd feel pretty embarrassed. . . . July 16, [1945] it went off in the desert.

The shot was set for Monday morning. I went down the Thursday before, guarded in a convoy of automobiles, carrying the core, the little ball of plutonium. I designed the ball. We assembled the bomb in the high explosive only for the second time. We were all afraid. . . .

I had a short-wave set and was responsible for listening to the radio communications from the people who would actually start it. . . . I had a microphone and I relayed the countdown. I announced it: thirty seconds, twenty seconds, ten seconds, nine, eight, seven, six. . . .

From ten miles away, we saw the unbelievably brilliant flash. That was not the most impressive thing. We knew it was going to be blinding. We wore welder's glasses. The thing that got me was not the flash but the blinding heat of a bright day on your face in the cold desert morning. It was like opening a hot oven with the sun coming out like a sunrise. It was a feeling of awe and wonder and dismay and fear and triumph, all together. The sound came a minute later. It went off in a dead silence, a great thunder.

Within a few days, I went from Los Alamos [the test site in New Mexico] to Wendover Air Force Base at Wendover, Utah. The 509th Composite Group was there. And our transport aircraft. With the core of the bomb, I flew to Tinian. That's where the B-29 bases were. They had been attacking Japan for a year.

I loaded the plane called *Bock's Car*. It had two dice, with sixes showing. It was named after Captain Bock. Somebody else loaded the other bomb on the *Enola Gay*. The takeoff was dangerous, because there was no way of rendering it safe. The airplane just had to take a chance. *Bock's Car's* bomb fell on Nagasaki three days after *Enola Gay's* fell on Hiroshima.

We heard the news of Hiroshima from the airplane itself, a coded message. When they returned, we didn't see them. The generals had them. But then the people came back with photographs. I remember looking at them with awe and terror. We knew a terrible thing had been unleashed. The men had a great party that night to celebrate, but we didn't go. Almost no

"The Damn Thing Probably Saved My Life"

From Iwo Jima to Hiroshima

Ted Allenby

Ted Allenby, a Marine, fought at the Japanese-held island of Iwo Jima in early 1945. The bloody Marine assault on the tiny island lasted six weeks and cost 20,000 American casualties. Reflecting on the battle after the war, Allenby speculates that the atomic bomb saved his life.

I enlisted in the Marine Corps. This had a good deal to do with my being homosexual. . . . How do you deal with it? You deal with it by trying to prove how rugged you are. After all, homosexuals are sissies and pansies. You're not a man. . . . I chose the Marines for that reason. It's the toughest outfit. . . .

I joined the Fourth Marine Division on Maui in Hawaii. We all lived in tents. We staged there for Iwo Jima. Tokyo Rose told us we were going there before our officers did. We picked her up on the radio all the time. When we were near Saipan, where our task force was gonna rendezvous, she said, "When the Fourth Marine Division gets to Iwo Jima, there won't be enough of it left to put in a telephone booth." Iwo Jima? Where the hell's

U.S. Marines raised the American flag on Mt. Suribachi, the highest point on Iwo Jima, when they captured the island in 1945.

that? Never heard of it before. We were told that it would be fairly easy. A small island, only eight square miles. It shouldn't be any problem. . . . We found out otherwise.

The men who landed on D-day, February 19, 1945— well, there aren't many of them left. The casualty rate was enormous. It was ghastly. Iwo was a volcanic island with very little concealment. Cover is something you hide behind—a tree, a bush, a rock. Few trees. No grass. It was almost like a piece of the moon that had dropped down to earth. . . .

[After Iwo Jima, we] were . . . planning for the landing on the Japanese mainland. Right after Hiroshima, our intelligence people told us we would have landed at Chigasaki. Ten years later I was in Japan as a Navy chaplain. One day, I got off the train at Chigasaki and walked down to the beach where we would have landed. I got a chill. It was Iwo Jima magnified a hundred times. The mountains, looking down, would have been bristling with artillery, all prezeroed on that beach. They would have wiped us out.

Right now, I'm totally against war in any form. I say yes, that bomb was a ghastly thing. I was in Hiroshima and I stood at ground zero. I saw deformities that I'd never seen before. I know there are genetic effects that may affect generations of survivors and their children. I'm aware of all this. But I also know that had we landed in Japan, we would have faced greater carnage than Normandy. It would probably have been the most bloody invasion in history. Every Japanese man, woman, and child was ready to defend that land.

The only way we took Iwo Jima was because we outnumbered them three to one. Still they held us at bay as long as they did. We'd had to starve them out, month after month after month. As it was, they were really down to eating grass and bark off trees. So I feel split about Hiroshima. The damn thing probably saved my life.

physicists went to it. We obviously killed a hundred thousand people and that was nothing to have a party about. . . .

I was of the opinion that a warning to the Japanese might work. I was disappointed when the military said you don't warn.

Realize this: the Air Force had bombed sixty-six Japanese cities and towns before the end of the war. Ninety-nine big air raids and sixty-six targets. The place was destroyed. From our point of view, the atomic bomb was not a discontinuity. We were just carrying on more of the same, only it was much cheaper. For that war, it was just one more city destroyed. We had already destroyed sixty-six; what's two more? Fire bombs and high explosives did the job on Dresden and Hamburg and Leipzig. . . .

Two among sixty-six is nothing, but each of these two big ones was only one airplane. That was the real military meaning of Hiroshima and Nagasaki. It was not that the bombs were so destructive. It was not that the bombs created radioactivity. Terrible, of course. It's that the atomic bomb, now the nuclear bomb, is cheap. . . .

At the height of its mobilization in World War II, the United States could manage to make six or eight hundred big bombers. They could visit a city and do big damage in one night. If these eight hundred came to a city several nights, they could do the damage of an atomic bomb. So, you could manage to knock off, with all your forces, a city a week. But now, a thousand cities in a night! It's the numbers. It's the cheapness.

In World War I, we saw the first application of twentieth-century science to war. . . . [T]en kilotons a day—ten thousand tons. That's a lot of bombs, a lot of shells, right?

A freight train carries 40 tons a boxcar; 40 times 250 is ten kilotons. That's a train 250 boxcars long. A mile long. Several freight trains of shells were fired off in one day by 50,000 sweating gunners shooting the shells one by one.

By 1951, the United States could do the whole World War I, which lasted a thousand nights, in one day. . . .

"Which One Might Have Been My Mother"

A Child's Memory of Hiroshima

Hideko Tamura Friedman

More than 100,000 people were killed and thousands more injured in the atomic bomb blasts at Hiroshima and Nagasaki. Hideko Tamura "Tammy" Friedman, a Hiroshima survivor, was 11 years old when the bomb exploded. She later married an American and moved to Chicago. Here she recalls the day of the explosion.

I was in my home, which happened to be a very protected kind of shelter. My grandfather was an industrialist, and we lived on a huge estate with very thick walls and beams. The house did not collapse to the ground. The thick walls protected me against the effects of radiation. Although I was affected, it was not as intensely as it might have been had I lived in a smaller house.

I was 11 years old. A few days after the bomb fell, I was looking for my mother. I was going through places, amongst the people who were not getting aid. We had

very, very little help. It was completely overwhelming to all the communities around. We had depleted resources to begin with.

People were barely having food to eat for themselves, and clothing. All I had were five grains of dried beans in my hand that I clutched all that day. I was well enough to be on my feet, but almost all the others I saw were lying in the spaces, in schoolyards and other public places.

I was going around from place to place, calling for my mother: "If you are here, if you are there, please answer me." I would have been devastated if someone answered, because I wouldn't have known what to do, to help. Yet, a child is desperately looking for her mother. Because I felt so helpless, I devised something in my head. A sort of magic.

I thought I would sing some lullabies that she loved singing, that she used to sing to me. I said in my head, God, I ask you now, would you sort of, like the wind, carry the tune and comfort her as if she could hear it? . . .

. . . [S]he is still listed among the missing, although my father ran into a woman who thought she knew where my mother might have fallen. . . .

My father went to the place where this woman took him. He said there were a number of remains. They were so burned that it was difficult to tell which one might have been my mother. So he collected little bones from each remains and brought them home and we kind of buried that as my mother. . . .

. . . I had a deep feeling of guilt, of depression about that day for a long, long time. I worked it out through hypnosis. I hypnotized myself and relived the time, the event of the Hiroshima explosion. Rather than remembering it as if I'm seeing it on the stage and hearing only loud sounds like exploding ammunition, I began to hear smaller voices and smaller sounds in the background, calling for help. That I hadn't really heard. I saw more things coming back more vividly than my actual recollection of the time. Then I was able to say that this was why I truly felt guilty. That I wasn't able to help them.

The Challenges of Power

❦ After World War II, the United States became the world's leading economic and military power. This strength enabled America to become involved in international affairs. The years after 1945 were dominated by the Cold War—a struggle for world influence between the United States and the Soviet Union. ❦ The development of nuclear weapons meant that total war between the United States and the Soviet Union would be catastrophic, thus the two powers tried to avoid direct confrontation. Instead, they fought for political, economic, and military influence around the world. The Soviet Union established control over Eastern Europe, while the United States forged strong alliances with Western Europe and Japan. The Cold War's battlefield eventually extended to Korea and Vietnam. ❦ As U.S. leaders condemned the lack of democracy in communist nations, they could no longer ignore the demands of America's minorities for equality. During the 1950s, a powerful nonviolent movement for civil rights began among African Americans in

...Listing continued on next page

the segregated South. Soon, women, Hispanics, Native Americans, and others also demanded equal rights and opportunity. ❧ In the 1980s, tensions between the United States and the Soviet Union led to an expensive arms race. ❧ But by the late 1980s, the Soviet Union and its eastern European allies were moving toward greater democracy. After the Berlin Wall fell in 1989, the republics of the Soviet Union themselves sought independence. On December 25, 1991, the Soviet Union ceased to exist. The Cold War was over. ❧ However, the end of the Cold War and emergence of the United States as the world's only superpower did not eliminate all its problems. In the decade leading up to the new millenium, Americans found themselves being asked to help keep peace in foreign lands and deal with crime, drugs, disease, and terrorism at home. Near the dawn of the twenty-first century, presidential politics took center stage as one president was impeached and a new president took office following a contentious and disputed election. The new century also ushered in a new war—a war on terrorism—perpetrated by devastating terrorist attacks on American people and property.

"Civilize 'Em With Chewing Gum!"

Reforming Hitler's Youth

Franklin M. Davis, Jr.

After World War II, the United States and the Soviet Union competed for influence in the world, in what became known as the Cold War. The United States formed an alliance with Canada and western European nations, the North Atlantic Treaty Organization (NATO), and the Soviet Union joined with eastern European nations in the Warsaw Pact. Fearing that the economic devastation of Europe after the war would make it an easy target for communist influence, the United States poured billions of dollars into rebuilding the European economy from 1948 to 1952 through the Marshall Plan, proposed and administered by Secretary of State George Marshall.

STEP ON IT, DOC!

This cartoon illustrates the fear of communist influence that spurred Congress to pass the Marshall Plan.

Postwar Germany was divided into four zones of occupation. The Soviet zone became East Germany, and the U.S., British, and French zones became West Germany. Berlin, inside the Soviet zone, was also divided among the Allied powers. West Berlin remained politically and economically tied to West Germany. Franklin M. Davis, Jr., who served in the U.S. Occupation Army, recalls how soldiers developed programs to teach democratic values to former members of Hitler's Youth.

A . . . rallying cry in the occupation [of] Germany . . . might very well have been, "Civilize 'em with chewing gum!" . . . *"Kau-gummi"* is what the German children called it, and somehow the delight of the flavorful rumination communicated itself to all ages in some mysterious way. [I]t was not unusual . . . for a soldier to see materializing before

him a ragged urchin, grubby paw extended palm up, smile beguiling, and to hear the words, *"Kau-gummi, bitte? Kau-gummi? Kau-gummi?"*

And because children have always had both a fascination and an affinity for soldiers, it is not surprising that soldiers, gum, and German children became a familiar combination, especially once the war was over and the civilian population emerged blinking from the air-raid shelters, hovels, and cellars where it had largely passed the shooting. The German children exercised a special appeal for American soldiers, even on the tougher veterans who thought they hated Germans. . . .

[P]erhaps it was because there was something so fundamentally tragic about any children—German or not—caught up in the storm of war that even the most insensitive of men felt some stirring of recognition, some sympathy with his own childhood now gone forever, or some faint chord of there-but-for-the-grace-of-American-firepower [go I]. . . .

Indeed, it was this *kau-gummi* relationship that in a very direct way caused the army to capitalize on the soldier's affinity for children, not only because a youth program offered an excellent way to keep the soldier out of trouble, but because many soldiers liked working with youngsters. Moreover, what better way to assure a lasting democracy in occupied Germany than to teach the kids what it was all about?

So the army embarked on the GYA program—German Youth Activities. The care, feeding, education, training, and management of the children of Germany in actuality represented one of the more formidable social problems facing the army in Germany. Not only were there a substantial number of war orphans, wanderers, and displaced children to be cared for, but there was also the question of reorienting and retraining the large number of children of all ages below majority who, one way or another, voluntarily or otherwise, had been caught up in the various Hitler youth programs. There was more, too, than just a humanitarian aspect to this. An idle and restless youth within the ruins of the Reich was not only a potential security threat, it was also particularly susceptible to subversive influences. . . . The army was looking ahead to the adults of tomorrow. . . .

There is little doubt that at the outset the biggest drawing cards for the GYA program were the food, shelter, and warmth available at a time when these essentials were quite scarce in Germany. There were a number of examples, however, of an imaginative approach by the army going beyond the mere handout idea. During the early period of the occupation in 1945 through 1947, some army units helped the youngsters in gardening projects, providing seeds, tools, and plowing help, and then turning the produce over to the children. The First Military Police Service Group in Frankfurt established two Niessen huts in the vicinity of the Frankfurt *Hauptbahnhof* main railroad station to shelter homeless wandering boys and girls who loitered on the fringe of the black market and the vice complex then characterizing the area. . . . All cooked and perishable army food not eaten up or usable in leftover menus was delivered twice a day to orphanages in the area as an adjunct to the Heidelberg GYA program. . . .

There is little doubt that the GYA program caught on as one of the army's greatest contributions to the occupation effort. . . . The youth program was probably the best pipeline . . . through which to pump democratic ideas and a respect for the values of individual worth and human dignity into the hearts and minds of the *Herrenvolk* [master race] who in 1948 and 1949 were emerging as the new Germany. There was a lot of mileage in the *kau-gummi*.

"We Had Not Moved An Inch"

Fighting the Cold War in Korea

James Brady

Communism spread in Asia after World War II. In 1949, communist forces won the Chinese civil war that resulted when the Japanese were expelled. Korea also was torn by war after it was divided at the thirty-eighth parallel into South Korea, backed by the United States, and North Korea, backed by the Soviet Union. In June 1950, North Korea invaded South Korea to reunify the country under communist rule.

The United Nations voted to defend South Korea, and U.S. forces led the unified command. When U.N. troops advanced into North Korea as far as the Chinese border in late 1950, Chinese forces counterattacked. Fearing war with China, President Harry Truman favored a limited war to preserve South Korea's boundaries, rather than total victory over North Korea. By July 1951, fighting had stabilized along the thirty-eighth parallel while an armistice was being negotiated.

In early 1951, Lieutenant James Brady commanded a company of Marines in the Korean cold. Here he describes Operation Clam Up, a fake withdrawal intended to lure the enemy out—with few gains. To Brady, it became a metaphor for the entire war.

The operation, bizarre as it was, went smoothly. Everyone got wet and cold and our flu worsened and a mortarman sprained an ankle climbing in the dark, but we went down the hill, sat miserably in the drifting snow as the shells clattered overhead, then climbed back to the bunkers to stand watch or go to bed. . . .

The five days of Clam Up passed. Prince and I sat in our bunker without even the luxury of a firing port to give light, coughing up lampblack from the candles we had to burn to see, reading again the one book and two magazines we had between us. My throat was still bad, but I was smoking. It was something to do. . . .

Each night we went out in turn to defecate and to empty the tin cans of urine from the day. Fortunately, my bowels were tranquil and I was able to wait for the evening stroll to the ammo box. Chafee [John Chafee, later a U.S. senator from Rhode Island] kept us informed. Apparently here and there Clam Up was actually

working, with gooks coming out of their holes, some of them venturing surprisingly high up our forward slope, reconnoitering, and going back. It was expected they would return in greater numbers, probably by night. I'd given the North Koreans credit for more sense. . . . On the fourth day, Operation Clam Up fetched the first gooks to Dog Company.

Mack Allen's people saw them first, six tiny figures like alpinists at the end of a Swiss telescope making their way slowly uphill through deep snow. . . . Toward noon the six North Koreans reached the aprons of barbed wire protecting the second platoon. They deployed belly down in the snow, and one of them fired bursts of burp-gun fire at the nearest bunkers. The marines made no reply. I could hear Allen whispering over the platoon phones, "Hold your fire, hold it."

Then they cut through the first strands of wire and began to come in. Mack reported this to Chafee, finishing by asking hoarsely, "Now?"

"Not One Knew Why They Were Dying"

Questioning the Korean War's Cost

Corporal Martin Russ

Negotiations to end the Korean War lasted two years, while fighting continued. Finally, in July 1953 an armistice was signed that recognized the thirty-eighth parallel as the border between North and South Korea. Many Americans grew frustrated with a limited war that cost lives without a clear-cut victory. Corporal Martin Russ, a Marine, voiced that frustration in his journal.

Memorial services were held yesterday at the regimental parade ground. There were thirteen companies of Marines present. A four-mile walk. General Ballard made a speech—a typical droning, platitudinous, meaningless speech. I doubt that anyone listened. A chaplain and a rabbi spoke. Isolated phrases that I remember: "in glory . . . that they will not have died in vain . . . not forgotten," etc. None of those men died gloriously. Only the ones that died while saving the lives of others did not die in vain. The most disturbing thing of all is that not one of them knew why they were dying.

I still have a book called *The Greek Way* by Edith Hamilton. I have underlined a sentence or two. "Why is the death of an ordinary man a wretched, chilling thing, which we turn from, while the death of a hero, always tragic, warms us with the sense of quickened life?" I don't know, Miss Hamilton. You tell me. You're the one who felt that sense of quickened life. I never felt it.

The roll of the dead was read off. Many, many names, some familiar. Edward Guyol. John Riley. Willy Mayfield. Waldron, Carlough. All ordinary men, no heroes.

The one word came back, and I could hear Mack shout into his phone, "Hit them now! Grenades. Give them the grenades!"

The crack of bursting grenades rolled up the hill to us, dulled by distance and by the bunker, but after four days of relative silence they sounded like Niagara Falls. Then a burp gun ripped through the explosions, followed by the heavier, slower firing of M-1s. It was over in maybe a half minute.

"Secure, secure, secure!" shouted Mack. Then to Chafee, "They're all dead, Skipper, two of them inside the wire, the rest hanging on it. Can we go out and bring them in?"

"Negative, Allen. Let me get Battalion on the line."

There was a long pause. . . . Then Chafee came on. "Leave them out there until dark and then bring them in. Battalion wants the bodies sent down after Clam Up is secured. They're pretty excited. This is about the biggest bag anyone's gotten."

They secured Clam Up the next afternoon about four. By now Mack Allen's six gooks, neatly lined up on their backs on the reverse slope near where the gook train could pick them up, were frozen stiff. Marines drifted down to look at them. Clam Up hadn't been much of an operation; all that . . . planning, and less than a dozen enemy killed all the way along the Division line. Three Marines were dead, shelling. Two more were killed around seven o'clock when, apparently in anger, the North Korean artillery slammed our lines. . . . That was the kind of war it was that winter, casualties counted on your fingers, both sides halfhearted about really starting anything, the generals assigning busywork rather than doing anything that might achieve real results. To kill a lot of people you had to lose a lot of people. I supposed some . . . believed that's precisely what we should have been doing that January and February. But the hills and the snow and the cold stopped them. . . .

A week later we were relieved and the regiment came down off the line. . . . I'd not taken off my underwear in forty-six days. . . . I was not the same man who had gone up the hill January 10. No better, or any worse, just different. In a month and a half of fighting we had not moved an inch, forward or back. A few men had died on both sides. . . . The men changed but the war did not.

220

"No American Is Safe"

The Origins of McCarthyism

John Howard Lawson

As communism spread abroad, many Americans grew more concerned about communism at home. In 1947, the Committee on Un-American Activities in the House of Representatives (HUAC) investigated the movie industry, leading to the blacklisting of suspected communists. From 1950 to 1954, Senator Joseph McCarthy campaigned to expose all communist sympathizers in the U.S. government. The term "McCarthyism" arose to describe McCarthy's practice of making sensational accusations of subversion without sufficient evidence.

John Howard Lawson, a Hollywood screenwriter and member of the Communist Party of the United States, was investigated in 1947 by HUAC, which was chaired by Representative J. Parnell Thomas. Lawson was not allowed to read the following statement he had prepared to open his testimony, although other witnesses had made such opening remarks.

For a week, this committee has conducted an illegal and indecent trial of American citizens, whom the committee has selected to be publicly pilloried and smeared. I am not here to defend myself, or to answer the agglomeration of falsehoods that has been heaped upon me; I believe lawyers describe this material, rather mildly, as "hearsay evidence." To the American public, it has a shorter name: dirt. Rational people don't argue with dirt. I feel like a man who has had truckloads of filth heaped upon him; I am now asked to struggle to my feet and talk while more truckloads pour more filth around my head. . . .

I am not going to touch on the gross violation of the Constitution of the United States, and especially of its First and Fifth amendments, that is taking place here. The proof is so overwhelming that it needs no elaboration. The Un-American Activities Committee stands convicted in the court of public opinion.

I want to speak here as a writer and a citizen.

It is not surprising that writers and artists are selected for this indecent smear. Writers, artists, scientists, educators are always the first victims of attack by those who hate democracy. The writer has a special responsibility to serve democracy, to further the free exchange of ideas. I am proud to be singled out for attack by men who are obviously—by their own admission on the record—out to stifle ideas and censor communication. . . .

. . . As a citizen I am not alone here. I am not only one of nineteen men who have been subpoenaed. I am forced to appear here as a representative of 130 million Americans because the illegal conduct of this committee has linked me with every citizen. If I can be destroyed, no American is safe. You can subpoena a farmer in a field, a lumberjack in the woods, a worker at a machine, a doctor in his office—you can deprive them of a livelihood, deprive them of their honor as Americans. . . .

[J. Parnell Thomas] is a petty politician, serving more powerful forces. Those forces are trying to introduce fascism in this country. They know that the only way to trick the American people into abandoning their rights and liberties is to manufacture an imaginary

danger, to frighten the people into accepting repressive laws which are supposedly for their protection. . . .

The struggle between thought-control and freedom of expression is the struggle between the people and a greedy unpatriotic minority which hates and fears the people. . . . [T]he attack on freedom of communication is, and has always been, an attack on the American people.

The American people will know how to answer that attack. They will rally, as they have always rallied, to protect their birthright.

"Are You Now or Have You Ever Been"

Testifying Before HUAC

Congressional Transcripts

Reprinted here are excerpts from John Howard Lawson's testimony before HUAC. Besides Lawson, the other speakers are J. Parnell Thomas, the committee's chairman, and Robert E. Stripling, its chief investigator.

Mr. Stripling: Are you a member of the Screen Writers Guild?
Mr. Lawson: The raising of any question here in regard to membership, political beliefs, or affiliation—
Mr. Stripling: Mr. Chairman—
Mr. Lawson: —is absolutely beyond the powers of this Committee. . . .
(The chairman pounding gavel.)
Mr. Lawson: It is an invasion of the right of association under the Bill of Rights of this country.
The chairman: Please be responsive to the question. . . . The chair will determine what is in the purview of this Committee.
Mr. Lawson: My rights as an American citizen are no less than the responsibilities of this committee of Congress. . . .
Mr. Stripling: Mr. Lawson, are you now or have you ever been a member of the Communist party of the United States?
Mr. Lawson: In framing my answer to that question I must emphasize the points that I have raised before. The question of communism is in no way related to this inquiry, which is an attempt to get control of the screen and to invade the basic rights of American citizens in all fields. . . .
(The chairman pounding gavel.) . . .
Mr. Lawson: The Bill of Rights was established precisely to prevent the operation of any committee which could invade the basic rights of Americans. . . .
The chairman *(pounding gavel):* We are going to get the answer to that question if we have to stay here for a week. Are you a member of the Communist party, or have you ever been a member of the Communist party? . . .
Mr. Lawson: I am framing my answer in the only way in which any American citizen can frame his answer to a question which absolutely invades his rights. . . . I have written Americanism for many years, and I shall continue to fight for the Bill of Rights, which you are trying to destroy. . . .

"Something New to Own"

Life in the Affluent Society

Lucille Windam

The postwar years were a period of great prosperity for many Americans. From 1949 to 1959, the median family income adjusted for inflation increased by 48 percent—fueling a consumer culture similar to that of the 1920s. In his book The Affluent Society *(1958), economist John Kenneth Galbraith criticized Americans' passion for consumer goods to the exclusion of education, housing, and the environment.*

Lucille Windam epitomizes the dilemma of the 1950s housewife. She is proud of her family's prosperity, yet in the midst of pursuing the best brand-name merchandise she feels "quite stale, as though I don't use my mind enough."

One fortunate thing which is important in our marriage is our fortunate change in income bracket. When we were married my husband earned $30 a week. We rented a five-room flat, . . . had a baby, etc. Now we have five children and an income of over $25,000 a year. We own our eight-room house—also a nice house on a lake. We have a sailboat, a Cris Craft, several small boats. We own our own riding horse which we keep at home. Our oldest child goes to a prep school. We have a Hammond organ in our home. . . . Our two sons at home own expensive instruments. We have and carry a lot of life insurance. Unless some disaster hits us, we see our way clear to educate all our children through prep school and college. . . .

My reaction to all this is that my husband doesn't seem content to save. He continually seeks something new to own; he doesn't keep his interest in any one thing very long. . . .

I've worked hard at making my marriage work—for my own and for my children's sake. . . . Certainly—materially—I never could attain the things I have now. Of course, the children are a great satisfaction. My job seems to swamp me sometimes but I am really very fond of my family, and I do try to treat each as a special individual so each personality is important and each child can have every advantage we can possibly give them. I can't imagine my life without children. I have no special talents, so as a career person I'm sure I would not be a great success. As a mother and homemaker, I feel I am quite successful. . . .

Because of the size of our family, we have very little personal fun—I mean no clubs or activities. I used to be very active in PTA, church (taught Sunday school), and garden club, but my last two children now 4 and 2 years old changed all this. I just stay home with them and taxi my oldest boys around. Our oldest boy, almost 15, is away at prep school, but in our rural community I have to drive someone somewhere every day. I expect to get back into community life when my younger children are in school all day. I feel quite stale, as though I don't use my mind enough.

"Race Hatred Personified"

The Murder of Emmett Till

Mamie Mobley

During World War II, more and more African Americans began to strive for equal rights. Membership in the NAACP swelled from 50,000 to 450,000, and black workers demanded equal opportunity in defense jobs. African-American soldiers returning home from the war had enjoyed equal treatment in European society and resisted going to the back of the bus again.

A massive civil rights movement swept through the United States in the 1950s and '60s. In a series of court cases, the NAACP challenged the "separate but equal" doctrine established by the Supreme Court in Plessy v. Ferguson *(1896), which upheld segregation of public facilities. Finally, in 1954, the Supreme Court ruled in* Brown v. Board of Education of Topeka, Kansas *that separate educational facilities were inherently unequal. The Court required that the nation's schools be integrated "with all deliberate speed," sparking heavy resistance.*

In the summer of 1955, young Emmett Till, a 14-year-old from Chicago, visited relatives in Mississippi. After Till reportedly whistled at a white woman in a store, the woman's relatives kidnapped and murdered him. Photographs of Till's mutilated body graphically depicted the violence of racial hatred and catalyzed national support for civil rights. Although the men were acquitted, they later admitted committing the crime to a newspaper reporter. Mamie Mobley, Emmett's mother, remembers that fateful summer.

Emmett and I were getting ready to go on our vacation. We were excited because we were driving to Omaha where some of my cousins lived. We'd set our date which was less than a week away.

But Emmett heard that Uncle Mose was in town and two of the boys that he grew up with, Uncle Mose's grandsons. They were going back to Mississippi. That's what he wanted to do. It messed up our plans completely. After a lot of pressure, my mother and I decided it would be all right to let Emmett go to Mississippi.

About three days into Mississippi, they went into a little country store. This was Money, Mississippi. They had games on the front porch and you could buy pop and candy, little junk. The boys were playing checkers and Emmett decided to go in the store and buy something. His young cousin went into the store with him. Emmett bought bubble gum and some candy.

As they came out of the store, according to the accounts I heard from some of the boys, someone asked Emmett, "How did you like the lady in the store?" They said Emmett whistled his approval. The word got back to the two men, the husband and the half-brother of that hus-

band—oh my goodness, Roy Bryant and Big Jim, W.J. Milam. . . .

It was about 2:30 the following Sunday morning that these two men stormed into my uncle's house and took my son out at gunpoint. And the rest, we don't know what really happened, but we do know how the body looked when it was finally discovered three days later. He had been shot; he had been beaten; they had wired a gin-mill fan around his neck. When the sheriff pulled Emmett from the water, the only way my uncle recognized him was by the ring on his finger.

I was successful in getting the body back to Chicago and it was then, when I looked at Emmett, I could not believe that it was even something human I was looking at. I was forced to do a bit-by-bit analysis on his entire body to make really sure that that was my son. If there was any way to disclaim that body, I would have sent that body back to Mississippi. But it was without a doubt Emmett. . . .

There was a trial. The men said they questioned Emmett and they decided he was not the boy, so they pointed him back to my uncle's house and let him go on foot. It doesn't take much to understand. You can look through certain things and see whether or not they're true.

They were acquitted within one hour and five minutes. The jury was all-male, all-white.

Mose Wright, my mother's brother-in-law, pointed out Bryant and Milam as the two men who came for Emmett: "Thar's them." It took unprecedented courage. Nothing like that had ever happened in the South before. That was an old black man, 65 years old. He stayed in the area until he was rescued by some civil-rights group and put under surveillance. One night he slept in the graveyard behind his church. He was a minister. He slept under the cotton house one night. He never spent another night in that house. No one did. . . .

That was my darkest moment, when I realized that that huge box had the remains of my son. I sent a very lovable boy on a vacation—Emmett who knew everybody in the neighborhood. They'd call for him whenever they wanted something done. "Mom, I gotta go help Mrs. Bailey." He was the block's messenger boy.

What might have been? He's never far from my mind. I was reading in Scriptures where the Lord Jesus Christ was scarred. His visage, his face, was marred beyond that of any other man, and Emmett came to me. I said, "Oh my God, what a comparison." The spirit spoke to me as plainly as I'm talking to you now. And the spirit said, "Emmett was race hatred personified. That is how ugly race hatred is."

"Now Is Your Time"

Leading the Montgomery Bus Boycott

Jo Ann Robinson

On December 1, 1955, Rosa Parks, a black seamstress, refused to give up her seat on a Montgomery, Alabama, bus to a white person and was arrested for her defiance. Parks's action triggered a yearlong boycott of city buses by black citizens and thrust one of the boycott's leaders, the Reverend Martin Luther King, Jr., into the national spotlight.

The Montgomery boycott was not spontaneous. It had been carefully planned for several years—principally by Jo Ann Robinson, an English professor who herself had been forced to take a back seat on the bus in

225

1949. Robinson and her Women's Political Council (WPC) had complained to bus officials, but to little avail. In 1955, the council developed plans for a citywide bus boycott; all they were waiting for was the right moment. Here Robinson recalls hearing the news of Rosa Parks's arrest.

Fred Gray [a local attorney] told me Rosa Parks was arrested. Her case would be on Monday. He said to me, "Jo Ann, if you have ever planned to do anything with the council, now is your time." I called all the officers of the three chapters, I called as many of the men who had supported us as I could reach, and I told them that Rosa Parks had been arrested and she would be tried. They said, "You have the plans, put them into operation." We had worked for at least three years getting that thing organized. . . .

I didn't go to bed that night. I cut stencils and took them to the college. The fellow who let me in during the night, John Cannon, is dead now, but he was in the business department. We ran off 35,000 copies. After I had talked with every WPC member in the elementary, junior high, and senior high schools to have somebody on the campus during the day so I could deliver them, I took them to school with me in my car. I taught my classes from eight o'clock to ten o'clock. When my ten o'clock class was over, I took two senior students with me and I had the flyers in my car, bundled and ready to be given out. I would drive to the place of dissemination, and a kid would be there to grab them. I was on the campus and off before anybody knew that I was there.

Most of the people got the message, but there were outlying areas that didn't. And one lone black woman, who was so faithful to her white lady, as she called it, went back to work and took one of the circulars to this woman so she would know what the blacks had planned. When the woman got it, she immediately called the media. After that, the television, the radio, the evening newspapers told those persons whom we had not reached that there would be the boycott. So the die was cast.

Monday morning, December 5, 1955, I shall never forget because many of us had not gone to bed that night. It was the day of the boycott. We had been up waiting for the first buses to pass to see if any riders were on them. It was a cold morning, cloudy, there was a threat of rain, and we were afraid that if it rained the people would get on the bus. But as the buses began to roll, and there were one or two on some of them, none on some of them, then we began to realize that the people were cooperating and that they were going to stay off the bus that first day.

"Not a Second-Class Citizen"

Integrating Little Rock Central High School

Ernest Green

On September 4, 1957, nine black students attempted to integrate Central High School in Little Rock, Arkansas. They were besieged by a mob and turned back by the Arkansas National Guard. The students were allowed to enroll three weeks later when escorted by federal troops. Ernest Green, one of the "Little Rock Nine," relates his experiences.

226

When the U.S. Supreme Court handed down its historic *Brown v. Board of Education of Topeka, Kansas* decision in 1954, I was a student in Little Rock, Arkansas, finishing the eighth grade. Little Rock had one high school for blacks, Horace Mann High School, and one for whites, Little Rock Central High School.

While I may not have understood all of the constitutional issues surrounding the *Brown* case, I did recognize it as an opportunity for ending segregation in Little Rock and for helping me get a better education. At black schools, for instance, we had to use books that had first been used by white students.

The *Brown* decision made me feel that the U.S. Constitution was finally working for me and not against me. The Fourteenth Amendment provided for equal protection and due process under the law, but it also meant I could believe I was a full citizen in this country, not a second-class citizen as segregation had made me feel.

In the spring of 1957, I was asked, along with other black students in Little Rock, to consider attending Central High School the following fall. Initially, a number of students signed up to enroll, but when fall came, only nine of us had survived the pressure to quit—and our names were published by the school board in the local newspaper. I knew this was my personal opportunity to change conditions in Little Rock. And I knew that if I didn't go, things would never change.

During the summer, rumors began to circulate that there might be violence if

the "Little Rock Nine," as we became known, tried to attend school in the fall. I didn't pay much attention to what was going on. I was too busy trying to get ready for school to begin, doing a lot of reading and studying. I believed the world wasn't going to fall apart because nine black students were going to be admitted to a school with more than 2,000 white students.

Elizabeth Eckford is threatened by a mob as she attempts to enter Little Rock Central High School in 1957.

But when we tried to attend school, we were met by an angry white mob and armed soldiers. Arkansas Governor Orval Faubus had called out the National Guard to prevent us from enrolling, defying a federal court order to integrate the Little Rock schools. Governor Faubus said he was doing this to protect the peace and tranquility of the community; obviously, my rights were secondary. It seemed strange to me at the time, and still does today, that the governor believed it was important to protect the rights of whites, but not those of blacks.

Finally, President Dwight Eisenhower called out the U.S. Army's famous 101st Airborne Division to protect us and enforce the federal court's integration order. "Mob rule cannot be allowed to override the decisions of our courts," the president declared. It was a powerful symbol that the president of the United States was willing to use his power and his might to protect nine black students and to uphold the American Constitution.

When we tried to attend school again, about 1,000 paratroopers were there to protect us. We rode to school in an army

227

station wagon, surrounded by army jeeps that were loaded with soldiers holding machine guns and drawn bayonets. It was an exciting ride to school!

Being kids, we joked about our each having our own personal soldier. When we got to the steps of Central High, the cordon of paratroopers formed a ring around us; they marched, we walked. I turned to Terrance Roberts, another one of the Little Rock Nine, and said, "I guess we'll get into school today."

Once we got inside, it was like being in a war zone. We were harassed, our books were destroyed, and our lockers were broken into several times a day. We learned not to keep anything important in them.

I was a senior that year. As graduation neared, I was surprised at the number of students who signed my yearbook, saying they admired my courage in sticking it out. But on the night of graduation, there was an eerie silence when my name was called. I didn't care that no one clapped for me. I knew that not only had I achieved something for myself, but I had broken a barrier as well.

"Ashamed to Be White"

Mississippi Freedom Summer

A Northern College Student

In 1963, more than 250,000 people marched in Washington, D.C., to support civil rights, and the next year Congress passed a landmark civil rights act. But in the state of Mississippi, little had changed. In 1964, the Student Nonviolent Coordinating Committee (SNCC) spearheaded a drive to recruit northern college students to spend their summer working for civil rights in Mississippi.

As part of "Freedom Summer," hundreds of students registered black voters, organized "freedom schools" for local children, and established community centers to provide legal and medical services. But violence marred the effort when three civil rights workers—James Chaney, a black Mississippian; Andrew Goodman, a white college student; and Michael Schwerner, a white New Yorker—disappeared in June. Their bodies were found buried in an earthen dam on August 4. Here a female student volunteer, Martha, describes her own anguish and conflict at the funeral of James Chaney.

Dear Blake,
. . . Dave [Dennis, a black civil rights worker who delivered an impassioned eulogy] finally broke down and couldn't finish, and the Chaney family was moaning, and much of the audience and I were also crying. It's such an impossible thing to describe but suddenly again, as I'd first realized when I heard the three men were missing when we were still training up at Oxford [Ohio], I felt the sacrifice the Negroes have been making for so long. How the Negro people are able to accept all the abuses of the whites—all the insults and injustices which make me ashamed to be white—and then turn around and say they wanted to love us, is beyond me.

There are Negroes who want to kill whites, and many Negroes have much

228

bitterness, but still the majority seems to have the quality of being able to look for a future in which whites will love the Negroes. Our kids [in the freedom school] talk very critically of all the whites around here and still they have a dream of freedom in which both races understand and accept each other. There is such an overpowering task ahead of these kids that sometimes I can't do anything but cry for them. I hope they are up to the task; I'm not sure I would be if I were a Mississippi Negro.

As a white northerner, I can get involved whenever I feel like it and run home whenever I get bored or frustrated or scared. I hate the attitude and position of the northern whites and despise myself when I think that way. Lately, I've been feeling homesick and longing for pleasant old Westport and sailing and swimming and my friends. I don't quite know what to do because I can't ignore my desire to go home, and yet I feel I am a much weaker person than I like to think I am because I do have these emotions. I've always tried to avoid situations which aren't so nice, like arguments and dirty houses and now maybe Mississippi.

I asked my father if I could stay down here for a whole year, and I was almost glad when he said "No," that we couldn't afford it because it would mean supporting me this year in addition to three more years of college. I have a desire to go home and read a lot and go to Quaker meetings and be by myself so I can think about all this rather than being in the middle of it all the time. But I know if my emotions run like they have in the past, that I can only take that pacific sort of life for a little while and then I get the desire to be active again and get involved with knowing other people. . . .

I am angry because I have a choice as to whether or not to work in the Movement, and I am playing upon that choice and leaving here. I wish I could talk with you 'cause I'd like to know if you ever felt this way about anything. I mean, have you ever despised yourself for your weak conviction or something? And what is making it worse is that all those damn northerners are thinking of me as a brave hero. . . .

"What Was the Point of Being Scared?"

From Sharecropper to Civil Rights Worker

Fannie Lou Hamer

One of the chief projects of Freedom Summer was the organization of the Mississippi Freedom Democratic party (MFDP), which challenged the all-white Mississippi Democratic party. In August 1964, the MFDP demanded that its delegates to the Democratic presidential convention in Atlantic City, New Jersey, be seated instead of those from the all-white party.

Fannie Lou Hamer was one of the MFDP delegates. On national television, she challenged the nation: "If the Freedom Democratic party is not seated now, I question America. . . . Is this America, the land of the free and the home of the brave, where . . . our lives be threatened daily because we want to live as decent human beings . . . ?" Hamer refused to accept a compromise that seated two of the sixty-eight MFDP delegates. Here, she describes her transformation from sharecropper to civil rights worker.

I was born October 6, 1917, in Montgomery County, Mississippi. My parents moved to Sunflower County when I was two years old, to . . . Mr. E. W. Brandon's plantation. I've been here now almost 47 years in Sunflower County. My parents were sharecroppers, and they had a big family. Twenty children. Fourteen boys and six girls. I'm the twentieth child. All of us worked in the fields, of course, but we never did get anything out of sharecropping. We'd make fifty and sixty bales [of cotton] and end up with nothing. . . .

. . . I married in 1944 and stayed on the plantation until 1962, when I went down to the courthouse in Indianola to register to vote. That happened because I went to a mass meeting one night.

Fannie Lou Hamer testifies at the 1964 Democratic National Convention.

Until then I'd never heard of no mass meeting, and I didn't know that a Negro could register and vote. Bob Moses, Reggie Robinson, Jim Bevel, and James Forman were some of the SNCC [Student Nonviolent Coordinating Committee] workers who ran that meeting. When they asked for those to raise their hands who'd go down to the courthouse the next day, I raised mine. Had it high as I could get it. I guess if I'd had any sense I'd a-been a little scared, but what was the point of being scared? The only thing they could do to me was kill me and it seemed like they'd been trying to do that a little bit at a time ever since I could remember. . . .

Well, there was eighteen of us who went down to the courthouse that day and all of us were arrested. Police said the bus was painted the wrong color—said it was too yellow. After I got bailed out, I went back to the plantation where Pap [her husband] and I lived for eighteen years. My oldest girl met me and told me that Mr. Marlow, the plantation owner,

was mad and raising sand. He had heard that I had tried to register.

That night he called on us and said, "We're not going to have this in Mississippi and you will have to withdraw. I am looking for your answer, yea or nay?" I just looked. He said, "I will give you until tomorrow morning. And if you don't withdraw you will have to leave. If you do go withdraw, it's only how I feel, you might still have to leave." So I left that same night. Pap had to stay on till work on the plantation was through. Ten days later they fired into Mrs. Tucker's house where I was staying. They also shot two girls at Mr. Sissel's. . . .

I reckon the most horrible experience I've had was in June of 1963. I was arrested along with several others in Winona, Mississippi. That's in Montgomery County, the county where I was born. . . . [T]he state highway patrolmen came and carried me out of the cell into another cell where there were two Negro prisoners. The patrolman gave the first Negro a long blackjack that was heavy. It was loaded with something, and they had me to lay down on the bunk with my face down, and I was beat. I was beat by the first Negro till he gave out. Then the patrolman ordered the other man to take the blackjack and he began to beat. That's when I started screaming and working my feet 'cause I couldn't help it. The patrolman told the first Negro that had beat me to sit on my feet. I had to hug around the mattress to keep the sound from coming out. Finally they carried me back to my cell. . . .

What I really feel is necessary is that the black people in this country will have to upset this applecart. We can no longer ignore the fact that America is *not* the "land of the free and the home of the brave." I used to question this for years— what did our kids actually fight for? They

"It Was Worth It"

Celebrating the Right to Vote

Unita Blackwell

The Voting Rights Act of 1965 helped eliminate many of the barriers to the ballot box for African Americans. By the 1980s, Mississippi had more black elected officials than any other state. Unita Blackwell, one of the MFDP delegates in 1964, addressed the Democratic National Convention in 1984, this time as mayor of Mayersville, Mississippi. For her, it invoked the memory of Fannie Lou Hamer.

I tried not to get too emotional about it, but there was a feeling that it was worth all of it that we had been through. I remember a woman told me one time when I was running for justice of [the] peace, "The reason I won't vote for you is because they going to kill you." The whites had told her that they were going to kill me, and she thought she was saving my life. And when I stood in that podium twenty years later, I was standing there for this woman, to understand that she had a right to register to vote for whomever she wanted to, and that we as a people were going to live.

Jesse Jackson spoke before me, prime time, of course. People did see me late at night, and some of those that know me know that I felt tears because Fannie Lou Hamer should have been standing there. She was standing there in us—in me, in Jesse, in all of us—because in 1964 she testified. Chaney, Schwerner, Goodman died in my state, Mississippi, for the right for me to stand there at that podium. That's what I felt, that I was standing there for all who had died, all who will live, for all the generations to come.

would go in the service and go through all of that and come right out to be drowned in the river in Mississippi. . . . I've worked on voter registration here ever since I went to that first mass meeting. In 1964 we registered 63,000 black people from Mississippi into the Freedom Democratic party. We formed our own party because the whites wouldn't even let us register. We decided to challenge the white Mississippi Democratic party at the National Convention. We followed all the laws that the white people themselves made. We tried to attend the precinct meetings and they locked the doors on us or moved the meetings, and that's against the laws they made for their ownselves.

So we were the ones that held the real precinct meetings. At all these meetings across the state we elected our representatives to go to the national Democratic convention in Atlantic City. But we learned the hard way that even though we had all the law and all the righteousness on our side—that [the] white man is not going to give up his power to us. . . .

The question for black people is not when is the white man going to give us our rights, or when is he going to give us good education for our children, or when is he going to give us jobs. If the white man gives you anything, just remember when he gets ready he will take it right back. We have to take for ourselves. . . .

"We Were Just Ordinary People"

A Child Marches in Selma

Sheyann Webb

In 1965, civil rights workers conducted a major campaign for voting rights in Selma, Alabama. Through literacy tests, limited hours for registration, and police pressure, Selma discouraged its black citizens from voting. Only about one percent of the African Americans of voting age in Selma were registered.

A fifty-mile protest march from Selma to the state capital of Montgomery was organized in March 1965. On the first try, March 7, the demonstrators were forcibly turned back by Alabama state troopers at the Edmund Pettus Bridge in Selma. A second try on March 9 was stopped pending a court hearing. On March 15, President Lyndon Johnson submitted his Voting Rights Act to Congress, boosting the marchers' cause.

Finally, on March 21, the protesters left Selma; they arrived in Montgomery four days later, 25,000 strong. One of the marchers was 9-year-old Sheyann Webb. Here she describes the confrontation at the Edmund Pettus Bridge.

Now the Edmund Pettus Bridge sits above the downtown; you have to walk up it like it's a little hill. We couldn't see the other side; we couldn't see the troopers. So we started up and the first part of the line was over. I couldn't see all that much because I was so little; the people in front blocked my view.

But when we got up there on that high part and looked down, we saw them. I remember [a] woman saying something like, "Oh, my Lord" or something. And I stepped out to the side for a second and I saw them. They were in a line—they looked like a blue picket fence—stretched across the highway. There were others gathered behind that first line and to the sides. . . . And further back were some of Sheriff Jim Clark's posse-men on their horses. Traffic had been blocked.

At that point I began to get a little uneasy about things. I think everyone did. People quit talking; it was so quiet then that all you could hear was the wind blowing and our footsteps on the concrete sidewalk.

Well, we kept moving down the bridge. I remember glancing at the water

in the Alabama River, and it was yellow and looked cold. I was told later that Hosea Williams said to John Lewis [two leaders of the march], "See that water down there? I hope you can swim, 'cause we're fixin' to end up in it."

The troopers could be seen more clearly now. I guess I was fifty to seventy-five yards from them. They were wearing blue helmets, blue jackets, and they carried clubs in their hands; they had those gas-mask pouches slung across their shoulders. The first part of the march line reached them and we all came to a stop. For a few seconds we just kept standing, and then I heard this voice speaking over the bullhorn saying that this was an unlawful assembly and for us to disperse and go back to the church.

I remember I held the woman's hand who was next to me and had it gripped hard. I wasn't really scared at that point. Then I stepped out a ways and looked again and saw the troopers putting on their masks. *That* scared me. I had never faced the troopers before, and nobody had ever put on gas masks during the downtown marches. But this one was different; we

were out of the city limits and on a highway. Williams said something to the troopers asking if we could pray . . . , and then I heard the voice again come over the bullhorn and tell us we had two minutes to disperse. . . .

. . . So the next thing I know—it didn't seem like two minutes had gone by—the voice was saying, "Troopers advance and see that they are dispersed." Just all of a sudden it was beginning to happen. I couldn't see for sure how it began, but just before it did I took another look and saw the line of the troopers moving toward us; the wind was whipping at their pants legs. . . .

Demonstrators cross the Edmund Pettus Bridge in Selma, Alabama.

All I knew is I heard all this screaming and the people were turning and I saw this first part of the line running and stumbling back toward us. At that point, I was just off the bridge and on the side of the highway. And they came running and some of them were crying out and somebody yelled, "Oh, God, they're killing us!" I think I just froze then. . . .

I remember looking toward the troopers and they were backing up, but some of them were standing over some of our people who had been knocked down or had fallen. It seemed like just a few seconds went by and I heard a shout. "Gas! Gas!" And everybody started screaming again. And I looked and I saw the troopers charging us again and some of them were swinging their arms and throwing canisters of tear gas. And beyond them I saw the horsemen starting their charge toward us. . . .

I'll tell you, I forgot about praying, and I just turned and ran. And just as I was turning, the tear gas got me; it burned my nose first, then got my eyes. I was blinded by the tears. So I began running and not seeing where I was going. I remember being scared that I might fall over the railing and into the water. I don't know if I was screaming or not, but everyone else was. People were running and falling and ducking and you could hear people scream and hear the whips swish-

ing and you'd hear them striking the people. . . . It seemed to take forever to get across the bridge. It seemed I was running uphill for an awfully long time. . . . I just knew then that I was going to die, that those horses were going to trample me. . . .

All of a sudden somebody was grabbing me under the arms and lifting me up and running. The horses went by and I kept waiting to get trampled on or hit, but they went on by and I guess they were hitting at somebody else. And I looked up and saw it was Hosea Williams who had me and he was running but we didn't seem to be moving, and I shouted at him, "Put me down! You can't run fast enough with me!" But he held on until we were off the bridge and down on Broad Street and he let me go. I didn't stop running until I got home. . . .

I could never understand the hatred some of the whites showed toward us. I was just a kid and they'd yell at me. Yet, we all prayed to the same God. I couldn't understand the hatred. I couldn't understand the segregation.

What happened here in 1965 is history now. I know that. We have to go on. But I can never forget it. I never will. . . . I'm just so happy that I could be a part of a thing that touched our souls. I am so proud of the people who did something in 1965 that was truly amazing. We were just people, ordinary people, and we did it.

233

"He Took On America for Us"

Malcolm X Speaks

Sonia Sanchez

Civil rights leaders differed on how best to pursue their goals. The Reverend Martin Luther King, Jr., supported a strategy of nonviolence, focused principally in the South, to reach the goal of integration, and he won the Nobel Peace Prize in 1964 for his efforts.

Although he began to work with King's group near the end of his life, Malcolm X initially pursued a different course. Born Malcolm Little, he adopted the "X" to denote his lost African surname and aggressively promoted black pride, especially in northern cities. As a leader of the Nation of Islam religion, Malcolm X advocated black separatism, but after he left the Nation and changed his views, he was assassinated by Nation rivals in 1965. Sonia Sanchez, a civil rights worker in New York, describes the impact Malcolm X had on many African Americans.

People quite often want to make you believe that Malcolm was some terrible, terrible man who never smiled and who was always scowling and demanding something that was obscene almost. When I first saw Malcolm on the television, he scared me also. Immediately the family said, "Turn off that television. That man is saying stuff you ain't supposed to hear." . . .

But you know when the sun comes in the window and you kind of jump up to get it, to close the blinds or pull down the shade, before you do that the sun comes in? Well, before each time we turned the television off, a little sun came in. And you'd be walking someplace and it would resonate in the air, what he said. And you would say, "No, I can't listen to that because I'm in New York CORE [Congress of Racial Equality]. I can't listen to that because they say he's a racist. So don't listen."

The first time that I really listened to Malcolm was when CORE was doing a large demonstration. And Malcolm had sent out a directive to all of the civil rights organizations that "You cannot have a demonstration in Harlem unless you invite me to speak." So in our office at 125th Street, we moaned and groaned and said,

"Who is that man? Imagine that man saying such a thing. Who does he think he is?" Of course, we had to say yes.

So we went to this big demonstration. Malcolm came with his bodyguards. . . . And I looked up and looked around determined not to look at him. Determined not to listen. But he started to talk. And I found myself more and more listening to him. . . .

When he came off the stage, I . . . walked up to him, and of course when I got to him the bodyguard moved in front. He just pushed them away. I extended my hand and said, "I liked some of what you said. I didn't agree with all that you said, but I like some of what you said." And he looked at me, held my hand in a very gentle fashion, and said, "One day you will, sister. One day you will, sister." And he smiled. After that, every time he was speaking in New York City I was there.

. . . What he said to an audience is that we are enslaved. And everyone looked at first and said, "Who? We are enslaved? We're free." And he began to tell us and explain to us in a very historical fashion just what our enslavement was about. The moment he did that, he always had some new information for you. As a consequence, he drew an audience towards him.

234

Malcolm knew how to curse you out, in a sense, and make you love him at the same time for doing it. He knew how to, in a very real sense, open your eyes as to the kind of oppression that you were experiencing. On the one hand, he would say something in a very harsh fashion. And then on the other hand, he would kiss you and hug you.

I've never seen anyone appeal to such a broad audience. . . . And he understood the bottom line is that if you tell people the truth, then it will appeal to everyone. If you tell them all about their oppression, in a fashion they ain't never heard before, then they will all gravitate towards you. He cut through all the crap. You see, what he said out loud is what African-American people had been saying . . . forever behind closed doors. The reason why initially we cut off the televisions is that we were scared. What he did was he said, "I will now"—in a very calm fashion—"wipe out fear for you." . . . When he said it in a very strong fashion and this very manly fashion, and this fashion that says I am not afraid to say what you've been thinking all these years, that's why we loved him. He said it out loud. Not behind closed doors. He took on America for us. . . .

That's why we all loved him so very much. Because he made us feel holy. And he made us feel whole. He made us feel loved. And he made us feel that we were worth something finally on this planet Earth. Finally, we had some worth.

"Poor White Trash Like Me"

Bringing Black and White Together

Peggy Terry

Urban blacks in the North had been relatively unaffected by the move to end legal segregation in the South. Their problems of de facto segregation, poverty, and neglect were not remedied by civil rights laws. In the 1960s, a wave of riots sparked by black protesters swept northern cities.

The Reverend Martin Luther King, Jr., believed that fighting poverty was the next step in the civil rights movement. He criticized President Lyndon Johnson for spending too much money on the Vietnam War and not enough on domestic problems. In late 1967, King began to organize a multiracial "Poor People's Campaign" to march on Washington. He was assassinated in Memphis, Tennessee, in 1968 while still planning the campaign. Peggy Terry, a poor white woman who once hated black people, joined in King's movement.

I knew black people were around, but I didn't know where they lived, in Oklahoma City. In Paducah [Kentucky], we lived on the edge. We could sit on the porch and hear the singing from the black church. That's where I really learned to love gospel singing. I never made friends with any of them because I was brought up in prejudice. How can you be raised in garbage and not stink from it? You pick it up. It's like the air you breathe. There wasn't anyone saying any different. Until I heard Reverend King, I never heard any black person say, "I'm as good as you are." Out in the open.

I picked it up from everyone in the family. My father never changed. In one of our trips from Kentucky to Oklahoma in

235

1929, we went there in a Model T Ford. Daddy slid the car off into a ditch. We were just laying sidewise. This old black man came by on a wagon and offered to pull Daddy out. Daddy says, "Nigger, you better get your black ass on down the road. I don't need any help from you!" Here was my mother, pregnant—she had the baby two weeks after we got there—and three other little children in the car. I was eight. I remember it was so cold. Here's this bigoted man, cutting off his nose to spite his face. That's what a lot of white people do. . . .

Funny thing, my father was a strong union man and always fought the bosses. He always spoke out and stuck up for the working man. Walked off many jobs, without a penny in his pocket. But he had this blind spot when it came to color. . . .

You don't go anywhere because you always see yourself as something you're not. As long as you can say, "I'm better than they are," then there's somebody below you can kick. But once you get over that, you see that you're not any better off than they are. In fact, you're worse off because you're livin' a lie. And it was right there, in front of us. In the cotton field, choppin' cotton, and right over in the next field, there's these black people—Alabama, Texas, Kentucky. Never once did it occur to me that we had anything in common. . . .

I was living in Montgomery, Alabama, during the bus boycott and that absolutely changed my life. It forced white people to take a look at the situation. Not all of them changed the way I did. It didn't leave you in the same comfortable spot you were in. You had to be either for it or against it. . . . I saw Reverend King beat up at the jail. He would be released on bond and they would pick him up again on some trifling thing. They just kept repeatedly doing these things.

I remember one time he came out of jail in all-white clothes. About five or six white men jumped him. . . . When I saw 'em beatin' up on Reverend King, something clicked.

When I heard he was gonna get out of jail, me and some other white women wanted to see this smart-aleck nigger. I'm so thankful I went down there that day because I might have gone all my life just the way I was. When I saw all those people beating up on him and he didn't fight back, and didn't cuss like I would have done, and he didn't say anything, I was just turned upside down. . . .

With all my feelings and what had happened in Montgomery, I was ready to take a step forward and try to [undo] all the damage. When I believe in something, I act on it. I went down and joined CORE. . . .

I enjoy picketing, too. I don't remember who we were picketing, but this really well-dressed white woman said, "Why are you out there doing this?" I had about six kids with me, mine and my girlfriend's. I said, "Well, where else could I go and be treated with this respect that I've been treated with by Reverend King, the Nobel Peace Prize winner? No white Nobel Prize winner would pay poor white trash like me the slightest attention. Reverend King does."

"You Can't Come Here"

Busing in Boston

Ruth Batson

In 1969, the Supreme Court ruled that "all deliberate speed" had not been fast enough: the nation's schools must be desegregated without delay. In Boston and other northern cities, segregation of public schools resulted from residential patterns, rather than legal prohibitions. But black schools were often inferior to white schools.

Some federal courts mandated busing students outside their neighborhoods to achieve racial balance in the schools, and the Supreme Court upheld the practice in 1971. In Boston, court-ordered busing met with intense resistance and even violence. Ruth Batson, an African-American community leader, fought for the integration of Boston's schools.

When we would go to white schools, we'd see these lovely classrooms, with a small number of children in each class. The teachers were permanent. We'd see wonderful materials. When we'd go to our schools, we would see overcrowded classrooms, children sitting out in the corridors, and so forth. And so then we decided that where there were a large number of white students, that's where the care went. That's where the books went. That's where the money went.

We formed a negotiating team. I was chair of the team. . . . [W]e decided that we would bring these complaints to the Boston School Committee. This was in 1963. . . .

We were naive. And when we got to the school committee room I was surprised to see all of the press around. We thought this is just an ordinary school committee meeting, and we made our presentation and everything broke loose. We were insulted. We were told our kids were stupid and this was why they didn't learn. We were completely rejected that night. We were there until all hours of the evening. And we left battle-scarred, because we found out that this was an issue that was going to give their political careers stability for a long time to come. . . .

After that meeting we were asked to come to a private meeting with the members of the Boston School Committee. No

press. Just us and them. And so we would sit down and we would talk.

At one point [Louise Day Hicks, the chairperson of the school committee] said, "The word that I'm objecting to is *segregation*. As long as you talk about segregation I won't discuss this." . . . Mrs. Hicks's favorite statement was, "Do you think that sitting a white child beside a black child, by osmosis the black child will get better?" That was her favorite statement.

And then there were black people and a lot of our friends who said, "Ruth, why don't we get them to fix up the schools and make them better in our district?" And, of course, that repelled us because we came through the separate but equal theory. This was not something that we believed in. Even now, when I talk to a lot of people, they say we were wrong in pushing for desegregation. But there was a very practical reason to do it in those days. We knew that there was more money being spent in certain schools, white schools—not all of them, but in certain white schools—than there was being spent in black schools. So therefore, our theory was move our kids into those schools where they're putting all of the resources so that they can get a better education. . . .

It was a horrible time to live in Boston. All kinds of hate mail. Horrible stuff. I also got calls from black people in Boston. They would call up and they'd say,

"Mrs. Batson, I know you think you're doing a good thing. And maybe where you came from there was segregation, but we don't have segregation in Boston." And I would say to them, "Well, where do I come from?" And invariably they would say South Carolina or North Carolina. Of course, now, I was born in Boston. So there were people who could not accept the fact that this horrible thing was happening to Boston, the city of culture. . . .

When [Judge] Garrity's decision came down in June of 1974, we were sunk when we heard some of the remedies, the one of busing to South Boston and Charlestown particularly, because those of us who had lived in Boston all of our lives knew that this was going to be a very, very difficult thing to pull off.

As a child I had encountered the wrath of people in South Boston. And I just felt that they were bigoted. I just felt that they made it very clear that they didn't like black people. And I was prepared for them not to want black students coming to the school. . . . I never heard any public official on the state level or on the city level come and say, "This is a good thing. We should all learn together. We should all live together." There was no encouragement from anybody. I call it complete official neglect. . . .

One of the things that I was concerned about was the fact that just because you were black, you were told that you couldn't go there. "This was my school. This was our place. You can't come here." I thought that a great educational achievement had been made to show both white and black kids that they could go anywhere they wanted to. That there should be no school in the city of Boston that would not admit a child because of their color. . . .

When you saw what the kids had to go through—I was just as proud of some of the white kids that stuck through it, because there were white families who made their kids go and stay in that school. Kids had to go through metal detectors, and police were all over the place, and there was such ridicule in the halls. I thought that the kids who went through this were just wonderful kids. And most of them weren't kids with great marks or anything. They were just kids who were determined. There was a movement. And they felt part of a movement. . . .

"Carrying Forth Democracy"

Life in the Peace Corps

Roger Landrum

Robert Burkhardt

Donna Shalala

The civil rights movement inspired many other types of activism for social justice in the 1960s. In 1961, President John F. Kennedy challenged citizens to "ask not what your country can do for you—ask what you can do for your country." Through Kennedy's Peace Corps, Americans volunteered to serve in developing countries in the hope of spreading democracy. After Kennedy was assassinated in 1963, the Peace Corps became a large part of his legacy.

I didn't go to a lot of speeches in college, but I went to hear Kennedy because someone told me he was probably going to run for president. This was in 1959. I remember him quoting the line from the Robert Frost poem that went, "miles to go before I sleep," and then dashing off the stage. It was like a meteor going through the room. I followed his campaign, and when he announced the Peace Corps idea, I wrote him a letter saying, "If you will do it, I will volunteer."

I grew up in rural Michigan and I'd never been overseas before. I was at my mother's house when the telegram came inviting me to train for Nigeria. I remember my hands were shaking as I opened it. I had never heard of Nigeria but I definitely felt I was participating in history. This was a new era of American participation in the world. Peace Corps volunteers were the frontline people making fresh contact with a whole bunch of newly independent nations. There was a sense of exhilaration about maybe carrying forth democracy and establishing new relations with Asia, Africa, and South America.

—*Roger Landrum*
(Nigeria, 1961-63)

I taught beginning English to boys between the ages of 16 and 25. I'd have fifty kids in a class and the assigned text was *Gulliver's Travels*. It was very hard to maintain continuity because whenever the weather was good, the principal would say, "Mr. Burkhardt, it's good weather. They must work the crops. When it rains they go to class. But now, they must go to the crops," and he'd yank them out of class. But what was I to do? He was the boss.

In every class I gave, there would be an agent from the Savak [Iranian secret police] sitting among the students. At first, I was very insulted by this. Hadn't they heard of the First Amendment? The other teachers would say to me, "You don't understand." In one class the students asked me what I thought of "Red China" joining the United Nations. I said that I thought China should be part of the UN—after all, it's a country. They all burst into applause and, of course, the Savak guy is busy writing down all these subversive thoughts. . . .

Being in the Peace Corps, I felt a part of this incredible pattern going on—in the

Philippines, Colombia, Kenya, Iran, Tunisia, and Guatemala—and I was just one little digit in the great wheel of history. It was a great sensation. . . .

The Iranians all knew for a fact that Lyndon Johnson had assassinated Kennedy. It happened in Texas, Johnson's home state. Who had the most to gain? He became president of the United States. I kept saying to them, "No. You don't understand." And they would just say back, "No. *You* don't understand."

—*Robert Burkhardt*
(Iran, 1962-64)

I remember staying up all night listening to the funeral on the radio. I also recall a beggar walking up to me in the street and I said, "No, I don't have any money." He said, "I don't want money. I just want to tell you how sorry I am that your young president died."

I remember how difficult it was to sleep and I remember turning cold, which is one of the first signs of shock. Kennedy was the first president we had voted for. He represented a break with the past and we had bought all that. His assassination forced us to grow up.

—*Donna Shalala*
(Iran, 1962-64)

"When You Start at the Bottom"

Giving Poor Children a Head Start

Tracy Whittaker

President Lyndon Johnson launched a "War on Poverty" in 1964 with legislation that authorized some $1 billion for programs for low-income Americans, to be administered through the Office of Economic Opportunity (OEO). One of these programs was Project Head Start, which sponsored preschools to prepare poor children for kindergarten. Tracy Whittaker, a young man from Yale working as a resource teacher, describes the obstacles faced by one Head Start center in Mississippi in 1965.

Dear Dr. Levin,
This letter is written in response to your request for an evaluation of our experience at the Holly Grove Head Start Center with a view to extending the program into the fall.

Any analysis of our center must consider what we started with—which was nothing. We held classes in the community church which had to be constantly converted to serve its dual role. We had no kitchen, no playground, no running water, and no telephone (in a very rural area that is difficult to find). The local staff was totally untrained in the operation and administration of a kindergarten.

At this writing we have a smoothly running preschool, with a capable teaching staff and a more than adequate physical plant. A kitchen and a playground was constructed entirely by volunteer workers. As the kitchen materials and its lack in the beginning absorbed about all of our petty cash and facilities money, we were thrown back on our own resources for any supplementary school supplies. While the men contributed their labor, the women made rag dolls and donated old clothes for the children's "dress-up" play. . . .

Running out of facilities money, we had to ask for contributions to outfit the kitchen with utensils. The response was

240

overwhelming—pots, large spoons, towels, etc., were freely given (from people in one of the lowest income areas in the country). It was no trip to the state park without donations of transportation and extra help. The trip is on.

To a degree, the enthusiastic community response is a reflection of gratitude for the social services provided . . . in the form of sorely needed welfare materials and the medical attention given their children. However, the response of the community is more than just gratitude, but instead the reaction of a people that have so long felt that any efforts to improve their lot were futile—doomed to failure and reprisals by an unsympathetic, hostile local autocracy. If for no other reason, Head Start would be money well spent because it serves as tangible evidence that their government in Washington is conscious of their oppressed condition and sympathetic to their advancement.

However, as important as the community unity fostered by Head Start is, it is a mere product of the larger aim of the project here at Holly Grove. The children's advancement is the standard by which this program must ultimately be evaluated. Although eight weeks is, in fact, too short a period for any accurate conclusions, I cannot but feel that we have made great progress in the development of our children. From a mass of withdrawn, repressed preschoolers who had never ridden a seesaw, worked a puzzle, drawn a picture, we have, with few exceptions, a happy, cohesive group of kids full of vitality (and now, at last, food) who spend their day creating, pretending, playing, singing, looking, listening, and wondering. We don't pretend to be a super educational machine at Holly Grove—the children didn't learn to read and write in our eight weeks. However, we did expand their limited view of life; we did provide a chance to test their intellectual and physical muscles; we did provide a transition between mother and school as the children learned to work and play with others.

Finally, and perhaps the most important of all, we tried to show these children that they were important—that we cared about what they had to say, what they did, what they made. Some of our kids can't read a word—some can't count to ten—but almost all have a measure of human dignity that they didn't have before. It is for this reason I must conclude we have succeeded admirably at Holly Grove, and it would be a sad mistake if it be denied to their successors.

If my evaluation sounds too glowing, I cannot pretend to be an uninterested observer. However, I hasten to point out that, when you start at the bottom, you can only go up. Indeed, it seems that our success at Holly Grove came almost as a matter of course. For people who have been held in semiknowledge for so long, the progress must be rapid at the beginning. And at Holly Grove, progress is our most important product. . . .

"We Want a Share"

Organizing Farmworkers in the Fields

Jessie Lopez de la Cruz

Like African Americans, Hispanic Americans suffered discrimination and took action to improve their situation in the 1960s. Using nonviolent tactics such as boycotts, Cesar Chavez organized the United Farm Workers to better working conditions for California's Hispanic farm workers. Jessie Lopez de la Cruz worked with the United Farm Workers as the first female organizer out in the fields.

The Challenges of Power

One night in 1962 there was a knock at the door and there were three men. One of them was Cesar Chavez. And the next thing I knew, they were sitting around our table talking about a union. I made coffee. Arnold had already told me about a union for the farmworkers. He was attending their meetings in Fresno, but I didn't. I'd either stay home or stay outside in the car.

But then Cesar said, "The women have to be involved. They're the ones working out in the fields with their husbands. If you can take the women out to the fields, you can certainly take them to meetings." So I sat up straight and said to myself, "That's what I want!"

When I became involved with the union, I felt I had to get other women involved. Women have been behind men all the time, always. In my sister-in-law and brother-in-law's families the women do a lot of shouting and cussing and they get slapped around. But that's not standing up for what you believe in. It's just trying to boss and not knowing how. I'd hear them scolding their kids and fighting their husbands and I'd say, "Gosh! Why don't you go after the people that have you living like this? Why don't you go after the growers that have you tired from working out in the fields at low wages and keep us poor all the time?" . . .

I was well known in the small towns around Fresno. Wherever I went to speak to them, they listened. I told them about how we were excluded from the NLRB [National Labor Relations Board] in 1935, how we had no benefits, no minimum wage, nothing out in the fields—no restrooms, nothing. I'd ask people how they felt about all these many years they had been working out in the fields, how they had been treated. And then we'd all talk about it.

They would say, "I was working for so-and-so, and when I complained about something that happened there, I was fired." I said, "Well! Do you think we should be putting up with this in this modern age? You know, we're not back in the '20s. We can stand up! We can talk back! It's not like when I was a little kid and my grandmother used to say, 'You have to especially respect the Anglos, "Yessir," "Yes, Ma'am!"' That's over. This country is very rich, and we want a share of the money those growers make [off] our sweat and our work by exploiting us and our children!" I'd have my sign-up book and I'd say, "If anyone wants to become a member of the union, I can make you a member right now." And they'd agree!

So I found out that I could organize them and make members of them. Then I offered to help them, like taking them to the doctor's and translating for them, filling out papers that they needed to fill out, writing their letters for those that couldn't write. A lot of people confided in me. Through the letter-writing, I knew a lot of the problems they were having back home, and they knew they could trust me, that I wouldn't tell anyone else about what I had written or read. So that's why they came to me.

I guess when the union found out how I was able to talk to people, I was called into Delano to one of the meetings, and they gave me my card as an organizer. I am very proud to say I was the first woman organizer out in the fields organizing the people. . . .

In Kern Country we were sprayed with pesticides. They would come out there with their sprayers and spray us on the picket lines. They have these big tanks that are pulled by a tractor with hoses attached and they spray the trees with this. They are strong like a water hose, but wider. . . .

Fresno County didn't give food stamps to the people—only surplus food. There were no vegetables, no meat, just staples like whole powdered milk, cheese, butter. At the migrant camp in Parlier the people were there a month and a half before work started, and since they'd borrowed money to get to California they didn't have any food. I'd drive them into Fresno to the welfare department and translate for them and they'd get food, but half of it they didn't eat. We heard about other counties where they had food stamps to go to the store and buy meat and milk and fresh vegetables for the children. So we began talking about getting that in Fresno.

Finally we had senate hearings at the Convention Center in Fresno. There were hundreds of people listening. I started in Spanish, and the senators were looking at each other, you know, saying, "What's going on?" So then I said, "Now, for the benefit of those who can't speak Spanish, I'll translate. If there is money enough to fight a war in Vietnam, and if there is money enough for Governor Reagan's wife to buy a $3,000 dress for the inauguration ball, there should be money enough to feed these people. The nutrition experts say surplus food is full of vitamins. I've taken a look at that food, this corn meal, and I've seen them come up and down, but you know, we don't call them vitamins, we call them weevils!" Everybody began laughing and whistling and shouting. In the end, we finally got food stamps.

"A Helluva Smoke Signal!"

The Rise of the American Indian Movement

Mary Crow Dog

Native Americans also protested for their rights in the 1960s and '70s. The American Indian Movement (AIM), founded in 1968, grew up in opposition to tribal leaders who many believed had been co-opted by white officials in the federal government's Bureau of Indian Affairs (BIA). Celebrating traditional ways, AIM took radical action to oppose mistreatment of Native Americans. Mary Crow Dog, a member of the Lakota Sioux tribe, describes the appeal of AIM to many Native Americans.

The American Indian Movement hit our reservation like a tornado, like a new wind blowing out of nowhere, a drumbeat from far off getting louder and louder. It was almost like the Ghost Dance fever that had hit the tribes in 1890, old uncle Dick Fool Bull said, spreading like a prairie fire. . . .

. . . Some people loved AIM, some hated it, but nobody ignored it. I loved it. My first encounter with AIM was at a pow-wow held in 1971 at Crow Dog's place after the Sun Dance [a Sioux ritual of self-sacrifice]. . . .

I noticed that almost all of the young men wore their hair long, some with eagle feathers tied to it. They all had on ribbon shirts. They had a new look about them, not that hangdog reservation look I was used to. They moved in a different way, too, confident and swaggering—the girls as well as the boys. . . .

One man, a Chippewa, stood up and made a speech. I had never heard anybody talk like that. He spoke about genocide and sovereignty, about tribal leaders selling out. . . . He talked about giving up the necktie for the choker, the briefcase for the bedroll, the missionary's church for the sacred pipe. He talked about not celebrating Thanksgiving, because that would be celebrating one's own destruction. He said that white people, after stealing our land and massacring us for 300 years, could not come to us now saying, "Celebrate Thanksgiving with us; drop in for a slice of turkey." He had himself wrapped up in an upside-down American flag, telling us that every star in this flag represented a state stolen from the Indians.

Then Leonard Crow Dog spoke, saying that we had talked to the white man for generations with our lips, but that he had no ears to hear, no eyes to see, no heart to

243

feel. Crow Dog said that now we must speak with our bodies and that he was not afraid to die for his people. It was a very emotional speech. Some people wept. An old man turned to me and said, "These are the words I always wanted to speak, but had kept shut up within me." . . .

Something strange happened. . . . The traditional old, full-blood medicine men joined in with us kids. Not the middle-aged adults. They were of a lost generation which had given up all hope, necktie-wearers waiting for the Great White Father to do for them. It was the real old folks who had spirit and wisdom to give us. The grandfathers and grandmothers who still remembered a time when Indians were Indians, whose own grandparents or even parents had fought Custer, gun in hand, people who for us were living links with a great past. . . .

The Trail of Broken Treaties [a march to Washington, D.C., in 1972] was the greatest action taken by Indians since the Battle of the Little Big Horn. . . .

Each caravan was led by a spiritual leader or medicine man with his sacred pipe. The Oklahoma caravan followed the Cherokees' "Trail of Tears," retracing the steps of dying Indians driven from their homes by President Andrew Jackson. Our caravan started from Wounded Knee. This had a special symbolic meaning for us Sioux, making us feel as if the ghosts of all the women and children murdered there by the Seventh Cavalry were rising out of their mass grave to go with us.

I traveled among friends from Rosebud and Pine Ridge. . . . When we arrived in Washington we got lost. We had been promised food and accommodation, but due to government pressure many church groups which had offered to put us up and feed us got scared and backed off. It was almost dawn and still we were stumbling around looking for a place to bed down. . . . [I]n the predawn light we drove around the White House, honking our horns and beating our drums to let President Nixon know that we had arrived. . . .

Somebody suggested, "Let's all go to the BIA." It seemed the natural thing to do, to go to the Bureau of Indian Affairs building on Constitution Avenue. They would have to put us up. It was "our" building after all. Besides, that was what we had come for, to complain about the treatment the bureau was dishing out to us. Everybody suddenly seemed to be possessed by the urge to hurry to the BIA. Next thing I knew we were in it. We spilled into the building like a great avalanche. Some people put up a tipi on the front lawn. Security guards were appointed. . . . Tribal groups took over this or that room. . . . Children were playing while old ladies got comfortable on couches in the foyer. A drum was roaring. . . .

The various tribal groups caucussed in their rooms, deciding what proposals to make. . . . The building had a kitchen and cafeteria, and we quickly organized cooking, dishwashing, and garbage details. Some women were appointed to watch the children, old people were cared for, and a medical team was set up. Contrary to what some white people believe, Indians are very good at improvising this sort of self-government with no one in particular telling them what to do. They don't wait to be told. I guess there were altogether 600 to 800 people crammed into the building, but it did not feel crowded.

The original caravan leaders had planned a peaceful and dignified protest. There had even been talk of singing and dancing for the senators and inviting the lawmakers to an Indian fry bread and corn soup feast. It might have worked out that way if somebody had been willing to listen to us. But the word had been passed to ignore us. The people who mattered, from the president down, would not talk to us. We were not wanted. It was said that we were hoodlums who did not speak for the Indian people. The half-blood tribal chairmen with their salaries and expense accounts condemned us almost to a man. . . .

. . . I learned that as long as we "behaved nicely" nobody gave a damn about us, but as soon as we became rowdy we got all the support and media coverage we could wish for.

We obliged them. We pushed the police and guards out of the building.

244

Some did not wait to be pushed but jumped out of the ground-floor windows like so many frogs. We had formulated twenty Indian demands. These were all rejected by the few bureaucrats sent to negotiate with us. . . . [T]he occupation turned into a siege. I heard somebody yelling, "The pigs are here." I could see from the window that it was true. The whole building was surrounded by helmeted police armed with all kinds of guns. . . .

At last the police were withdrawn and we were told that they had given us another twenty-four hours to evacuate the building. This was not the end of the confrontation. From then on, every morning we were given a court order to get out by 6:00 p.m. Came 6 o'clock and we would be standing there ready to join battle. I think many brothers and sisters were prepared to die right on the steps of the BIA building. . . .

For me the high point came not with our men arming themselves, but with Martha Grass, a simple middle-aged Cherokee woman from Oklahoma, standing up to Interior Secretary Morton and giving him a piece of her mind, speaking from the heart, speaking for all of us. She talked about everyday things, women's things, children's problems, getting down to the nitty-gritty. . . . It was good to see an Indian mother stand up to one of Washington's highest officials. "This is our building!" she told him. Then she gave him the finger.

In the end a compromise was reached. The government said they could not go on negotiating during election week,

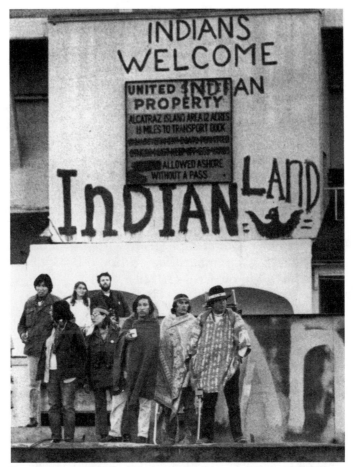

From 1969 to 1971, Native American activists occupied Alcatraz Island in San Francisco Bay—claiming that, under a Sioux treaty, the land belonged to them after the federal government had closed its prison there. The occupation proved futile.

but they would appoint two high administration officials to seriously consider our twenty demands. Our expenses to get home would be paid. Nobody would be prosecuted. Of course, our twenty points were never gone into afterward. As usual we had bickered among ourselves. But morally it had been a great victory. We had faced White America collectively, not as individual tribes. We had stood up to the government and gone through our baptism of fire. We had not run. As Russel Means put it, it had been "a helluva smoke signal!"

"Creating Herstory"

The Women's Liberation Movement

Robin Morgan

Women's longtime struggle for equal rights intensified during the 1960s and '70s. In her controversial book The Feminine Mystique *(1963), Betty Friedan argued that women had lost ground after World War II, when they were forced out of high-paying jobs and back into the "comfortable concentration camp" of the home. She advocated a role for women that transcended domestic consumerism.*

Friedan founded the National Organization for Women (NOW) in 1966, which among other things sought to have an Equal Rights Amendment added to the Constitution. Here, Robin Wright describes her own transformation into a feminist while editing a book about women's liberation, Sisterhood Is Powerful *(1970).*

This book is an action. It was conceived, written, edited, copyedited, proofread, designed, and illustrated by women. . . . During the year that it took to collectively create this anthology, we women involved had to face specific and very concrete examples of our oppression. . . .

Because of the growing consciousness of women's liberation, and, in some cases, because of articles that women wrote for the book, there were not a few "reprisals": five personal relationships were severed, two couples were divorced and one separated, one woman was forced to withdraw her article by the man she lived with; another's husband kept rewriting the piece until it was unrecognizable as her own; many of the articles were late, and the deadline kept being pushed further ahead, because the authors had so many other pressures on them—from housework to child care to jobs. More than one woman had trouble finishing her piece because it was so personally painful to commit her gut feelings to paper. We were also delayed by occurrences that would not have been of even peripheral importance to an anthology written by men: three pregnancies, one miscarriage, and one birth—plus one abortion and one hysterectomy. . . .

Speaking from my own experience, which is what we learn to be unashamed of doing in women's liberation, . . . I became, somewhere along the way, a "feminist" committed to a Women's Revolution.

. . . [W]hen I first began work on this book, . . . I was a so-called "politico," who shied away from admitting (on any but a superficial level) that I was oppressed, and who put all other causes above and ahead of my own, castigating myself with liberal guilt and doing Lady Bountiful actions about other people's oppression. This left me conveniently on top, and in a seat of relative power, because it isn't until you begin to fight in your own cause that you a) become really committed to winning, and b) become a genuine ally of other people struggling for their freedom. I also nurtured a secret contempt for other women who weren't as strong, free, and respected (by men) as I thought I was (that's called "identifying yourself with the oppressor," and it's analogous to a black person feeling compelled to have "processed" hair). Especially threatening were the women who admitted that they were simply unable to cope with the miserable situation we were all in, and needed each other and a whole movement to change that.

246

Well, somewhere during that year, I became such a woman—and it's been a radicalizing experience. I still don't fully know how it came about. Surely having a baby was part of it—the delight and excitement, and then the utter exhaustion, especially during those first three months. Surely being in women's liberation small groups—talking and action—raised my consciousness. Somehow, though, this book seems to have been most responsible. All of us who worked on it in a variety of ways had to read and think and talk about the condition of women until we began to dream about the subject, literally. The suffering and courage and humor and rage and intelligence and endurance that spilled out from the pages that came in from different women! The facts we came up against, the statistics! The history we learned, the political sophistication we discovered, the insights into our own lives that dawned on us! I couldn't believe—still can't—how angry I could become, from deep down and way back, something like a 5,000-year-buried anger.

It makes you very sensitive—raw, even, this consciousness. Everything, from the verbal assault on the street, to a "well-meant" sexist joke your husband tells, to the lower pay you get at work (for doing the same job a man would be paid more for), to television commercials, to rock-song lyrics, to the pink or blue blanket they put on your infant in the hospital nursery, to speeches by male "revolutionaries" that reek of male supremacy—everything seems to barrage your aching brain, which has fewer and fewer protective defenses to screen such things out. You begin to see how all-pervasive a thing is sexism—the definition of and discrimination against half the human species by the other half. Once started, the realization is impossible to stop, and it packs a daily wallop. *To deny that you are oppressed is to collaborate in your oppression. . . .*

This is not a movement one "joins." There are no rigid structures or membership cards. The Women's Liberation Movement exists where three or four friends or neighbors decide to meet regularly over coffee and talk about their personal lives. It also exists in the cells of women's jails, on the welfare lines, in the supermarket, the factory, the convent, the farm, the maternity ward, the streetcorner, the old ladies' home, the kitchen, the steno pool, the bed. It exists in your mind, and in the political and personal insights that you can contribute to change and shape and help its growth. It is frightening. It is very exhilarating. It is creating history, or rather, *herstory.*

"We, the Young People"

Campuses Erupt in Protest

Mark Rudd

The Vietnam War catalyzed a brewing movement among young people, which became known as the "counterculture" or "New Left," for social reform and more control over their college campuses. As the war escalated, young men were increasingly being asked to give their lives for a society whose values many did not support. This clash of values created a "generation gap" between young and old.

In 1962, Students for a Democratic Society (SDS) issued the Port Huron Statement, which challenged the status quo and decried the state of American society. In 1964, the Free Speech Movement (FSM) at the

University of California at Berkeley protested the university's ban on political activity in certain areas of campus by staging a sit-in at the administration building. And in 1968, students at Columbia University seized the president's office. Mark Rudd, a student at Columbia, explained the youth movement's goals in an open letter to Grayson Kirk, the university's president, which began with a quote by Kirk.

Our young people, in disturbing numbers, appear to reject all forms of authority, from whatever source derived, and they have taken refuge in a turbulent and inchoate nihilism whose sole objectives are destruction. I know of no time in our history when the gap between the generations has been wider or more potentially dangerous.
—*Grayson Kirk*

Dear Grayson,
Your charge of nihilism is indeed ominous; for if it were true, our nihilism would bring the whole civilized world, from Columbia to Rockefeller Center, crashing down upon all our heads. Though it is not true, your charge does represent something: you call it the generation gap. I see it as a real conflict between those who run things now—you, Grayson Kirk—and those who feel oppressed by, and disgusted with, the society you rule—we, the young people.

You might want to know what is wrong with this society, since, after all, you live in a very tight, self-created dream world. We can point to the war in Vietnam as an example of the unimaginable wars of aggression you are prepared to fight to maintain your control over your empire (now you've been beaten by the Vietnamese, so you call for a tactical retreat). We can point to your using us as cannon fodder to fight your war.

We can point out your mansion window to the ghetto below you've helped to create through your racist university expansion policies, through your unfair labor practices, through your city government and your police. We can point to this university, your university, which

trains us to be lawyers and engineers, and managers for your IBM, your Socony Mobil, your IDA, your Con Edison (or else to be scholars and teachers in more universities like this one). We can point, in short, to our own meaningless studies, our identity crises, and our revulsion with being cogs in your corporate machines as a product of and reaction to a basically sick society.

Your cry of "nihilism" represents your inability to understand our positive values. If you were ever to go into a freshman CC [Contemporary Civilization] class you would see that we are seeking a rational basis for society. We do have a vision of the way things could be: how the tremendous resources of our economy could be used to eliminate want, how people in other countries could be free from your domination, how a university could produce knowledge for progress, not waste, consumption, and destruction . . . , how men could be free to keep what they produce, to enjoy peaceful lives, to create.

These are positive values, but since they mean the destruction of your order, you call them "nihilism." In the movement we are beginning to call this vision "socialism." It is a fine and honorable name, one which implies absolute opposition to your corporate capitalism and your government; it will soon be caught up by other young people who want to exert control over their own lives and their society.

You are quite right in feeling that the situation is "potentially dangerous." For if we win, we will take control of your world, your corporation, your university and attempt to mold a world in which we and other people can live as human beings. Your power is directly threat-

Mario Savio led the Free Speech Movement (FSM) at the University of California at Berkeley. By holding a sit-in at the administration building in 1964, the FSM won its battle to end the university's ban on political activity in certain areas of campus.

ened, since we will have to destroy that power before we take over.

We begin by fighting you about your support of the war in Vietnam and American imperialism. . . . We will fight you about your control of black people in Morningside Heights, Harlem, and the campus itself. And we will fight you about the type of miseducation you are trying to channel us through. We will have to destroy at times, even violently, in order to end your power and your system—but that is a far cry from nihilism.

Grayson, I doubt if you will understand any of this, since your fantasies have shut out the world as it really is from your thinking. Vice President Truman says the society is basically sound; you say the war in Vietnam was a well-intentioned accident. We, the young people, whom you so rightly fear, say that the society is sick and you and your capitalism are the sickness.

You call for order and respect for authority; we call for justice, freedom, and socialism.

There is only one thing left to say. It may sound nihilistic to you, since it is the opening shot in a war of liberation. I'll use the words of LeRoi Jones [a militant black poet], whom I'm sure you don't like a whole lot: "Up against the wall, mother———, this is a stick-up."

Yours for freedom,
Mark

"A No-Winner from the Beginning"

Policymaking and the Vietnam War

Richard Holbrooke

After World War II, the Viet Minh, nationalist revolutionaries led by communist Ho Chi Minh, fought French colonial rule in Vietnam. When the French withdrew in defeat in 1954, an international conference divided the nation in half at the seventeenth parallel, to be reunified after elections were held in 1956. Ho Chi Minh and the Viet Minh ruled North Vietnam, and Ngo Dinh Diem ruled South Vietnam. Diem resisted holding elections to reunify Vietnam because he feared he would lose to Ho Chi Minh.

In 1954, President Dwight Eisenhower argued in his "domino theory" that if one nation was taken over by communists, surrounding nations would soon fall as well. The United States supported Diem and began sending military advisers to South Vietnam in 1955. Under President John F. Kennedy, aid to South Vietnam increased, and by the end of 1963 more than 15,000 American military advisers were stationed there. President Lyndon Johnson escalated the Vietnam War dramatically. By 1968, U.S. forces in Vietnam had grown to more than 500,000.

Richard Holbrooke, a State Department staffer, participated in the growing U.S. involvement in Vietnam. He also witnessed the persistent misinformation that sabotaged American policy there.

When I got to Saigon, I was 22 and I believed everything I had been told by the United States government. I believed that the commitment was correct—freedom of choice, self-determination, save the country from communism—and that we were doing the right thing because the U.S. government did the right thing. In those days you didn't question it. But after my Mekong Delta experiences, . . . I knew that the assessments were wrong and the reporting was perverted. I knew that the press corps' version of how things were going was correct. . . .

But the critical phase in my thinking about Vietnam did not begin until I got back to Washington in 1966. The day I went to work, our staff was called to meet with the president. I was 25, just back

from Vietnam, and I thought I knew more about the place than anyone else in the whole city. So we walk into the Cabinet Room, and of course Johnson talks for one straight hour.

He says to Komer, "Ah, Bob, I've been reading a report that they cut Route Four between Saigon and Can Tho." And he says, "You know, in Texas if the price of pigs goes up, you get thrown out of power. You lose elections. The price of pigs is power in Texas." And then he says, "Komer, I want you to get the price of pigs down by 50 percent in twenty-four hours and get that road open."

And Komer is saying, "Yes, Mr. President." And it's like Hitler at the end of World War II, moving around divisions that don't exist. Komer is being ordered to open

250

a road which is in communist control. We can't open the goddamned road. Johnson is going on and on. Then finally, after an hour of this, Johnson says, "I have another idea, Bob. You know at the end of World War II we had all these civil affairs advisers who ran occupied Germany and occupied Japan. We ought to reactivate them and get them out there to run Vietnam."

Well, I know now that Johnson said things like this all the time and all you did was say "Yes, Mr. President" and ignore him. But at the time I thought this was the president of the United States starting a policy. I suddenly had this vision of battalions of paunch-bellied, aging colonels who had run Munich in 1945 for two or three months, going to Quang Tri. This was too much for me.

I'd never talked to a president before. But I said, "Mr. President?" He looks around the table like, "Who's this punk?" So very, very carefully I say, "Mr. President, I've just come back from Vietnam and, you know, I'm a little worried about this. I'm not sure American advisers of that sort would be quite qualified. You know there are some limitations to what Americans can do in the civilian field in Vietnam." He takes off his glasses and he looks at me with that sad look of his and he says, "Son, your job is to get rid of those limitations." And he gets up and walks out of the room. That was my introduction to the White House.

But it was unforgettable, and for me it was an unforgettable time. Nothing in the world excited me more. I idolized McGeorge Bundy [national security adviser], Bob McNamara [secretary of defense], what Teddy White called the "action intellectuals." To work among them was very exciting. And they didn't know what the hell was going on in Vietnam. Worse, some of them, like Walt Rostow [an assistant to Bundy], were deliberately misrepresenting the facts, not only to the public but to themselves and the president.

There was a perversion of information that really upset and worried me. And then at the same time, I saw for the first time what I'd missed because I'd been in Vietnam— and that was the eroding base of popular support, which to the extent it still existed was dependent on the public misunderstanding the truth. Since I knew, I felt I ended up being part of the famous credibility gap. And at that point, the objectives of the United States in Vietnam came into question in my mind for the first time. . . .

The deepest and most profound error—which I certainly did not understand in the '60s—was Bob McNamara's. If Vietnam was as important to the United States as Lyndon Johnson said it was, then we should have put in much more force, much faster. If it was only as important as the resources we were devoting to it—limited manpower, constraints on the use of firepower, one-year tours which meant we never kept people there long enough to do anything—then we shouldn't have been there at all. So in a funny way, I came out of the Vietnam War neither hawk nor dove but with the simplest of things: You can't ask the American public to commit its sacred lives and treasure without having an absolutely clear readiness to achieve the objective and the objective must be clear.

Now, if you apply that standard to Vietnam, you came up with the answer that this was a no-winner from the beginning. To win the war, you had to put in triple the number of forces. You would have had to have faced the possibility of an indefinitely open-ended invasion force in North Vietnam—an occupying force. And you would have had to contemplate use of firepower even higher than the awesome levels we reached. And even that might have done nothing but flatten a small country which was not as strategically important as we claimed it was. Therefore, on the merits, the whole Vietnam adventure was misconstrued from the very beginning.

"Our Country, Right or Wrong"

Defending the Vietnam War

Joseph E. Sintoni

Americans were deeply divided over U.S. involvement in the Vietnam War. In a letter written as he was about to leave for Vietnam, where he later died, Joseph E. Sintoni justified the war to his fiancée.

Dear Angela,

This is by far the most difficult letter I shall ever write. What makes it so difficult is that you'll be reading it in the unhappy event of my death. You've already learned of my death; I hope the news was broken to you gently. God, Angie, I didn't want to die. I had so much to live for. You were my main reason for living. You're a jewel, a treasure. . . .

Please don't hate the war because it has taken me. I'm glad and proud that America has found me equal to the task of defending it.

Vietnam isn't a far-off country in a remote corner of the world. It is Sagamore, Brooklyn, Honolulu, or any other part of the world where there are Americans.

Vietnam is a test of the American spirit. I hope I have helped in a little way to pass the test.

The press, the television screen, the magazines are filled with the images of young men burning their draft cards to demonstrate their courage. Their rejection is of the ancient law that a male fights to protect his own people and his own land.

Does it take courage to flaunt the authorities and burn a draft card? Ask the men at Dak To, Con Tien, or Hill 875; they'll tell you how much courage it takes.

Most people never think of their freedom. They never think much about breathing, either, or blood circulating, except when these functions are checked by a doctor. Freedom, like breathing and circulating blood, is part of our being. Why must people take their freedom for granted? Why can't they support the men who are trying to protect their lifeblood, freedom?

Patriotism is more than fighting or dying for one's country. It is participating in its development, its progress, and its governmental processes. It is sharing the never fully paid price of the freedom which was bequeathed to us who enjoy it today. Not to squander, not to exploit, but to preserve and enhance for those who will follow after us.

Just as a man will stand by his family be it right or wrong, so will the patriot stand where Stephen Decatur stood when he offered the toast, "Our country, in her intercourse with foreign nations, may she always be in the right, but our country, right or wrong."

We must do the job God set down for us. It's up to every American to fight for the freedom we hold so dear. We must instruct the young in the ways of these great United States. We mustn't let them take these freedoms for granted.

I want you to go on to live a full, rich, productive life. I want you to share your love with someone. You may meet another man and bring up a family. Please bring up your children to be proud Americans. Don't worry about me, honey. God must have a special place for soldiers.

I've died as I've always hoped, protecting what I hold so dear to my heart. We will meet again in the future. We will. I'll be waiting for that day.

I'll be watching over you, Angie, and if it's possible to help you in some way, I will.

Feel some relief with the knowledge that you filled my short life with more happiness than most men know in a lifetime.

The inevitable, well, the last one: I love you with all my heart, and my love for you will survive into eternity.

Your Joey

"No Cause Other Than Our Own Survival"

Fighting a Different Kind of War

Philip Caputo

The Vietnam War presented a difficult challenge to the U.S. military. Instead of all-out campaigns, American soldiers were forced to fight a war of attrition against a largely unseen enemy, the Viet Cong—communist guerrillas in South Vietnam. Philip Caputo, a Marine lieutenant, describes the frustration of that kind of warfare.

For Americans who did not come of age in the early '60s, it may be hard to grasp what those years were like—the pride and overpowering self-assurance that prevailed. Most of the 3,500 men in our brigade, born during or immediately after World War II, were shaped by that era, the age of Kennedy's Camelot. We went overseas full of illusions, for which the intoxicating atmosphere of those years was as much to blame as our youth.

War is always attractive to young men who know nothing about it, but we had also been seduced into uniform by Kennedy's challenge to "ask what you can do for your country" and by the missionary idealism he had awakened in us. America seemed omnipotent then: The country could still claim it had never lost a war, and we believed we were ordained to play cop to the communists' robber and spread our own political faith around the world. . . .

So, when we marched into the rice paddies on that damp March afternoon, we carried, along with our packs and rifles, the implicit convictions that the Viet Cong would be quickly beaten and that we were doing something altogether noble and good. We kept the packs and rifles; the convictions, we lost.

The discovery that the men we had scorned as peasant guerrillas were, in fact, a lethal, determined enemy and the casualty lists that lengthened each week with nothing to show for the blood being spilled broke our early confidence. By autumn,

These soldiers of the 101st Airborne Division attempt to save the life of a wounded comrade in South Vietnam.

what had begun as an adventurous expedition had turned into an exhausting, indecisive war of attrition in which we fought for no cause other than our own survival.

Writing about this kind of warfare is not a simple task. Repeatedly, I have found myself wishing that I had been the veteran of a conventional war, with dramatic campaigns and historic battles for subject matter instead of a monotonous succession of ambushes and fire-fights. But there were no Normandies or Gettysburgs for us, no epic clashes that decided the fates of armies or nations. The war was mostly a matter of enduring weeks of expectant waiting and, at random intervals, of conducting vicious manhunts through jungles and swamps where snipers harassed us constantly and booby traps cut us down one by one.

The tedium was occasionally relieved by a large-scale search-and-destroy opera-

tion, but the exhilaration of riding the lead helicopter into a landing zone was usually followed by more of the same hot walking, with the mud sucking at our boots and the sun thudding against our helmets while an invisible enemy shot at us from distant tree lines. The rare instances when the VC [Viet Cong] chose to fight a set-piece battle provided the only excitement; not ordinary excitement, but the manic ecstasy of contact. Weeks of bottled-up tensions would be released in a few minutes of orgiastic violence, men screaming and shouting obscenities above the explosions of grenades and the rapid, rippling bursts of automatic rifles.

Beyond adding a few more corpses to the weekly body count, none of these encounters achieved anything; none will ever appear in military histories or be stud-ied by cadets at West Point. Still, they changed us and taught us, the men who fought in them; in those obscure skirmishes we learned the old lessons about fear, cowardice, courage, suffering, cruelty, and comradeship. Most of all, we learned about death at an age when it is common to think of oneself as immortal. Everyone loses that illusion eventually, but in civilian life it is lost in installments over the years. We lost it all at once and, in the span of months passed from boyhood through manhood to a premature middle age. The knowledge of death, of the implacable limits placed on a man's existence, severed us from our youth as irrevocably as a surgeon's scissors had once severed us from the womb. And yet, few of us were past 25. We left Vietnam peculiar creatures, with young shoulders that bore rather old heads.

"We Lost the Race"

Helicopters to the Rescue

Robert Mason

Helicopters played a pivotal role in the Vietnam War, as they were often the only vehicles that could penetrate the dense jungle. Robert Mason flew more than 1,000 helicopter missions in Vietnam. Here, he describes a mission to pick up critically wounded soldiers.

We finished moving the squads around by noon and returned to the hilltop for lunch and to pick up our new mission. . . . I shut down and the rotors were still turning when an aide from the tent ran out with a message.

"You got to get back up. A Jeep was just mined five klicks [kilometers] from here."

Reacher, who had just opened the cowling of the turbine to check something, slammed it shut as the four of us jumped back into the Huey [helicopter] while I lighted the fire. A medic jumped in as we got light on the skids.

The medic briefed us by talking through Reacher's microphone as we cruised over the trees at 120 knots.

"The Jeep was carrying six men from the artillery brigade. The two that were in the front seats are alive. The other four are either hurt or dead. They've got a prick-ten radio (PRC-10), so they can talk to us."

I saw the smoke ahead at the spot that matched the coordinates scribbled in ballpoint on the medic's palm. "There they are," I said.

We landed in front of the Jeep, or what was left of it. It was twisted like a child's discarded toy. . . .

A sergeant ran up to my door. He told me through my extended microphone that two of the guys in the back were still alive. "Should we put the dead on board?" His eyes were wide.

We nodded. They started loading up. The two wounded were unconscious, torn and bloody and gray.

One of the dead had had his right leg blown off with his pants. I didn't see the other body yet. . . .

I was twisted around in my seat, watching them load, directing Reacher through the intercom. The man that had lost his leg . . . lay naked on his back with the ragged stump of his leg pointing out the side door. A clump of dirt had stuck on the end of the splintered bone. . . . Riker looked sick. I don't know what I looked like. I told Reacher to move him back from the door. He could fall out. The scurrying grunts tossed a foot-filled boot onto the cargo deck. Blood seeped through the torn wool sock at the top of the boot. The medic pushed it under the sling seat.

I turned around and saw a confused-looking private walking through the swirling smoke with the head of someone he knew held by the hair.

"A head? Do we have to carry a head?" I asked Riker.

The kid looked at us, and Riker nodded. He tossed it inside with the other parts. The medic looked away as he pushed the bloody head under the seat. His heel kicked the nose.

"We can't find his body. I don't think we should stay to look for it. Is his head enough?" a grunt yelled.

"Absolutely. Plenty. Let's go," Riker answered.

I flew toward Pleiku as fast as the Huey could go. Reacher called from the pocket that "One-Leg" was sliding toward the edge of the deck. I had him tell the medic, who put his foot on One-Leg's

---

"Helping Someone Die"

A Nurse's Trauma

Dusty

About 7,500 women served in Vietnam, more than three-fourths as nurses. One of these nurses—so traumatized by her experience that she is known only by her nickname in Vietnam, Dusty—recalls the intimacy of helping a young soldier face death.

When you are sitting there working on someone in the middle of the night, and it's a 19-year-old kid who's 10,000 miles from home, and you know that he's going to die before dawn—you're sitting there checking his vital signs for him and hanging blood for him and talking to him and holding his hand and looking into his face and touching his face, and you see his life just dripping away, and you know he wants his mother, and you know he wants his father and his family to be there, and you're the only one that he's got—I mean his life is just oozing away there—well, it oozes into your soul. There is nothing more intimate than sharing someone's dying with them. This kid should have had a chance to grow up and have grandkids; he should have had a chance to die in bed with his loving family around him. Instead, he's got this second lieutenant. When you've got to do that with someone and give that person, at the age of 19, a chance to say the last things they are ever going to get to say, that act of helping someone die is more intimate than sex, it is more intimate than childbirth, and once you have done that you can never be ordinary again.

---

bloody groin. That kept him from sliding out, but the torn skin of the stump flapped in the wind, spraying blood along the outside of the ship and all over Reacher as he sat behind his machine gun.

A grunt was crying. One of the wounded, his friend, had just died. The other was just barely alive. I wanted to fly at a thousand miles an hour.

Riker called ahead so we could land at Camp Holloway without delay. We went by the tower like a flash and landed on the red cross near the newly set up hospital tent. The stretcher bearers ran out to unload the cargo.

I could see that they had been busy lately. There was a pile of American bodies outside the hospital tent.

The other wounded man died.

We had lost the race.

"Could I Take That Kind of Torture?"

Life in the Hanoi Hilton

Eugene B, "Red" McDaniel

North Vietnamese prisoner-of-war camps were notoriously brutal. The most infamous of these was the "Hanoi Hilton." During his eighty-first combat mission, pilot Eugene B. "Red" McDaniel was shot down over Hanoi in 1967. Here, he tells how he survived six years as a POW.

I arrived in the Hanoi Hilton, the main American prison camp, at about 5:30 that Sunday morning. I was put into a room which was small, windowless, and musty-smelling. I heard the iron gates clang shut behind me, and I settled down hoping to get a few hours of sleep, because right then my mind and body ached for rest. Instead an officer came in, read the camp regulations, and made the point that I was not to communicate with fellow prisoners. I felt some spark of elation in knowing that there were American prisoners here, and I thought maybe I'd get to see some of my friends who'd been shot down earlier. After a while the officer went out, and I stayed seated on the floor. . . .

Then the interrogators were there again, and I tried to point out my injuries to them. They were unmoved. "You talk, medicine later," one of them said shortly. So they went to work trying to extract military information from me. When I wouldn't come through, they put me into the ropes, a treatment I was to know and dread in the long pull ahead. They tied my wrists tight, then pulled my arms high behind me, binding me so that my shoulder bones were ready to pop. Again they questioned. For forty-five minutes to perhaps more than an hour they kept me in the ropes, and the sweat ran off me in buckets as the pain in my shoulders reached the point of sheer agony. They loosened me for a few minutes to question me again; when I didn't give them anything, it was back into the ropes.

I pretended to pass out several times in hopes they would untie me and leave me alone. But they were wise to that. At times I would bite my shoulder hard to try to transfer the pain from one area to another. . . .

Five days after torture, they let me out of the leg irons and threw me into an adjoining area outside that was called the wash area, where prisoners bathed or washed their clothes. . . .

I was six hours in that wash area trying to get some sleep, trying to ignore the pain from the irons that had clamped hard on my ankles and the ropes. . . . The question I had to face now was: Could I take that kind of torture again? And, of course, the other question: Was it so important that I refuse to answer their questions anyway? In the hours and days ahead, I was to feel this nagging question even more strongly as I listened to the screams of my fellow pilots going through the same torture, some maybe even worse. I had more coming too; I knew it. . . .

One thing I knew I had to have: communication with my own people here. I knew there were American flyers here like myself facing the same grim future and fearing the worst, either ending up telling what they did not want to tell or dying in the process of holding out. These were people like myself who wanted to live through this if at all possible. For us to do that, we had to communicate with each other, to let each other know that we were together, come what may.

Communication with each other, however, was the one occurrence that the North Vietnamese captors were taking the greatest pains to prevent. They knew, as well as I and the others did, that a man can stand more pain if he is linked with his

own kind in that suffering. The lone, isolated being becomes weak, vulnerable. I knew then that I had to make contact, no matter what it cost, and this would be my first resource. . . .

Early in June I got the camp code from Ralph Gaither and Mike Cronin by talking to them in the washroom—which, of course, was forbidden. The guards caught us. . . . But I had the code, even though much later I was to find out that both Gaither and Cronin spent seventeen days in torture for their part in that. . . .

In all of this, we simply had to take each day and move with the schedule and the routine, looking for our opportunities to communicate with others. Every day started with the morning gong at 5:00 a.m.—6:00 in the winter—and we would get up and make our bedrolls, do some exercising in the room, and be ready at 8:00 for whatever the camp commander had for us in the way of work activities. . . .

At about 10:00 we would get our first "meal," which broke nearly twenty hours of fasting—but which really didn't break it by much. It was a watery soup with a little rice. This meager food made us more tense, more conscious of our dwindling energy, more aware of how small our chances of survival were. With this demoralizing aspect of our lives, our motivation to communicate was often lessened. Food became our constant preoccupation—in our dreams, in our conversation. . . .

Any time between 2:00 and 4:00 p.m. we had our second meal of the same soup.

Then the doors were locked, and we settled down. . . . And that opened those long evening hours, when we thought the most about our families, so much so that we had to find things to do or sink into total depression. . . .

On [some] nights we would get together as a group, rather than retreat to our beds and mosquito nets, and one man would host the rest of the room for the evening. We would fantasize going to his house, and there he would serve hors d'oeuvres, then the meal—a menu we would all lovingly concoct in our imaginations. . . .

Sometimes we would take an imaginary trip in the early evening, and we would go to a city one of us had visited. Sometimes we would take our wives out, and we would go through the entire evening in our imagination—what we ate, what we did for entertainment. We learned a lot of geography then, and after a while we began to call on men in the groups who had knowledge in various fields that they could share with us, even teach us. . . .

Some nights I would retreat inside my mosquito net and count the holes in it, from right to left, up and down. I remember counting ninety-eight little squares from one end to the other on one side; each square had four hundred tiny holes. The top from left to right—the small side— had thirty-eight squares. Down the sides, forty-two squares. The holes in all these squares ran into the millions.

"No Crime Is a Crime Durin' War"

Witnessing Atrocities on Both Sides

Arthur E. "Gene" Woodley, Jr.

The year 1968 was a turning point in the Vietnam War. In January, the Viet Cong launched the Tet offensive throughout South Vietnam, even penetrating the U.S. embassy in Saigon temporarily. Although the offensive was ultimately defeated, it convinced many Americans that the war was no longer winnable.

In March 1968, troops led by Lieutenant William Calley killed 200-500 unarmed civilians in the hamlet of My Lai, even though the troops had not been fired upon. Many of the civilian bodies were found lying in a ditch, in an execution-style slaying. Calley was court-martialed in 1971 and sentenced to twenty years in prison.

While serving in Vietnam, Arthur E. "Gene" Woodley, Jr., witnessed many My Lai-type atrocities—on both sides. He describes some of the horrors that still haunt him.

I went to Vietnam as a basic naive young man of 18. Before I reached my 19th birthday, I was a animal. When I went home . . . , even my mother was scared of me. . . .

Being from a hard-core neighborhood, I decided I was gonna volunteer for the toughest combat training they had. I went to jump school, Ranger school, and Special Forces training. I figured I was just what my country needed. A black patriot who could do any physical job they could come up with. Six feet, 190 pounds, and healthy. . . .

I didn't ask no questions about the war. I thought communism was spreading, and as an American citizen, it was my part to do as much as I could to defeat the communists from coming here. Whatever America states is correct was the tradition that I was brought up in. . . .

Then came the second week of February of '69.

This was like three days after we had a helicopter go down in some very heavy foliage where they couldn't find no survivors from the air. . . . We were directed to find the wreckage, report back. Then see if we can find any enemy movement and find any prisoners.

We're headin' north. It took us ten hours to get to the location. The helicopter, it was stripped. All the weaponry was gone. There was no bodies. It looked like the helicopter had been shot out of the air. It had numerous bullet holes in it. But it hadn't exploded. The major frame was still intact. . . .

We recon this area, and we came across this fella, a white guy, who was staked to the ground. His arms and legs tied down to stakes. And he had a band around his neck that's staked in the ground so he couldn't move his head to the left or right.

He had numerous scars on his face where he might have been beaten and mutilated. And he had been peeled from his upper part of chest to down to his waist. Skinned. Like they slit your skin with a knife. And they take a pair of pliers or a instrument similar, and they just peel the skin off your body and expose it to the elements.

I came to the conclusion that he had maybe no significant value to them. So they tortured him and just left him out to die.

The man was within a couple of hours of dying on his own.

258

And we didn't know what to do, because we couldn't move him. There was no means. We had no stretcher. There was only six of us. And we went out with the basic idea that it was no survivors. We was even afraid to unstake him from the stakes, because the maggots and flies were eating at the exposed flesh so much.

The man had maggots in his armpits and maggots in his throat and maggots in his stomach. You can actually see in the open wounds parts of his intestines and parts of his inner workings bein' exposed to the weather. You can see the flesh holes that the animals— wild dogs, rats, field mice, anything—and insects had eaten through his body. With the blood loss that he had, it was a miracle that the man still alive. The man was just a shell of a person.

The things that he went through for those three days. In all that humidity, too. I wouldn't want another human being to have to go through that.

It was a heavy shock on all of us to find that guy staked out still alive. With an open belly wound, we could not give him water. And we didn't have morphine.

And he start to cryin', beggin' to die.

He said, "I can't go back like this. I can't live like this. I'm dying. You can't leave me here like this, dying."

It was a situation where it had to be remove him from his bondage or remove him from his suffering. Movin' him from

this bondage was unfeasible. It would have put him in more pain than he had ever endured. There wasn't even no use talkin' 'bout tryin' and takin' him back, because there was nothing left of him. It was that or kill the brother, and I use the term "brother" because in a war circumstance, we all brothers.

The man pleaded not only to myself but to other members of my team to end his suffering. He made the plea for about half an hour, because we couldn't decide what to do.

259

"There Aren't Any Rules"

Photographing an Execution

Eddie Adams

On a Saigon street at the height of the Tet offensive, Associated Press photographer Eddie Adams captured the execution of a Viet Cong soldier by Nguyen Ngoc Loan, chief of the South Vietnamese National Police. The photograph illustrated the media's frontline role in Vietnam, bringing the brutality of the war into America's living rooms.

Nguyen Ngoc Loan executes a Viet Cong suspect in this photograph by Eddie Adams, which won a Pulitzer Prize.

We were walking down the street when we saw the South Vietnamese police walking with this guy. We started following him because it was a prisoner, and like any photographer, you stay with a prisoner until he's out of sight. They stopped on the corner, and I was thinking, "This is boring." Just then Loan walked in out of nowhere and I saw him load his pistol. And I thought he was going to threaten the prisoner, which they always do. As soon as he raised his pistol, I raised my camera. Well, later on the U.S. military studied the picture and it turned out the moment he pulled the trigger, I pushed the shutter of my camera. It was all an accident. I just took it because I thought he was going to threaten him.

After Loan shot him, he walked over to us and said, "They killed many of my men and many of your people," and he walked away. The prisoner was later identified as a Viet Cong lieutenant. . . .

There were things a hell of a lot worse that happened in Vietnam. We had pictures that we never released. There were pictures of Americans holding heads of Viet Cong they'd chopped off. . . . Very gruesome, but this is a war. People are dying, your friends are getting blown away. In the next two minutes you could be dead. Everything is fair in love and war. There aren't any rules. It's just war.

He kept saying, "The mother———s did this to me. Please kill me. I'm in pain. I'm in agony. Kill me. You got to find 'em. You got to find 'em. Kill them sorry bastards. Kill them mother———s."

I called headquarters and told them basically the condition of the man, the pleas that the man was giving me, and our situation at that time. We had no way of bringin' him back. They couldn't get to us fast enough. We had another mission to go on.

Headquarters stated it was up to me what had to be done because I was in charge. They just said, "It's your responsibility."

I asked the team to leave.

It took me somewhere close to twenty minutes to get my mind together. Not because I was squeamish about killing someone, because I had at that time numerous body counts. Killing someone wasn't the issue. It was killing another American citizen, another GI. . . .

I put myself in his situation. In his place. I had to be as strong as he was, because he was askin' me to kill him, to wipe out his life. He had to be a hell of a man to do that. I don't think I would be a hell of a man enough to be able to do that. I said to myself, I couldn't show him my weakness, because he was showin' me his strength.

The only thing that I could see that had to be done is that the man's sufferin' had to be ended.

I put my M-16 next to his head. Next to his temple.

I said, "You sure you want me to do this?"

He said, "Man, kill me. Thank you."

I stopped thinking. I just pulled the trigger. I cancelled his suffering.

When the team came back, we talked nothing about it.

We buried him. We buried him. Very deep.

Then I cried. . . .

When we first started going into the fields, I would not wear a finger, ear, or mutilate another person's body. Until I had the misfortune to come upon [some] American soldiers who were castrated. Then it got to be a game between the communists and ourselves to see how many fingers and ears that we could capture from each other. After a kill we would cut his finger or ear off as a trophy, stuff our unit patch in his mouth, and let him die.

I collected about fourteen ears and fingers. With them strung on a piece of leather around my neck, I would go downtown, and you would get free drugs, free booze, free [sex] because they wouldn't wanna bother with you 'cause this man's a killer. It symbolized that I'm a killer. And it was, so to speak, a symbol of combat-type manhood. . . .

One night we were out in the field on maneuvers, and we seen some lights. We were investigating the lights, and we found out it was a Vietn'ese girl going from one location to another. We caught her and did what they call gang-rape her. She submitted freely because she felt if she had submitted freely she wouldn't have got killed. We couldn't do anything else but kill her because we couldn't jeopardize the mission. It was either kill her or be killed yourself the next day. If you let her go, then she's gonna warn someone that you in the area, and then your cover is blown, your mission is blown. Nothin' comes before this mission. Nothin'. You could kill [a] thousand folks, but you still had to complete your mission. The mission is your ultimate goal, and if you failed in that mission, then you failed as a soldier. And we were told there would be no prisoners. So we eliminated her. Cut her throat so you wouldn't be heard. So the enemy wouldn't know that you was in the area. . . .

After a while, it really bothered me. I started saying to myself, what would I do if someone would do something like this to my child? To my mother? I would kill 'im. Or I would say, why in the hell did I take this? Why in the hell did I do that? Because I basically became a animal. Not to say that I was involved . . . , but I had turned my back, which made me just as guilty as everybody else. 'Cause I was in charge. I was in charge of a group of animals, and I had to be the biggest animal there. I allowed things to happen. I had learned not to care. And I didn't care. . . .

With eighty-nine days left in country, I came out of the field.

At the time you are in the field you don't feel anything about what you are doin'. It's the time you have to yourself that you sit back and you sort and ponder.

What I now felt was emptiness.

Here I am. I'm still 18 years old, a young man with basically everything in his life to look forward to over here in a foreign country with people who have everything that I think I should have. They have the right to fight. . . . They fought for what they thought was right.

I started to recapture some of my old values. I was a passionate young man before I came into the Army. I believed that you respect other people's lives just as much as I respect my own. I got to thinkin' that I done killed around forty people personally and maybe some others I haven't seen in the firefights. I was really thinkin' there are people who won't ever see their children, their grandchildren.

I started seeing the atrocities that we caused each other as human beings. I came to the realization that I was committing crimes against humanity and myself. That I really didn't believe in these things I was doin'. I changed.

I stopped wearing the ears and fingers. . . .

Before I got out [of] the service, the My Lai stuff came out in the papers. Some of who had been in similar incidents in combat units felt that we were next. We were afraid that we were gonna be the next ones that was gonna be court-martialed or called upon to testify against someone or against themselves. A lot of us wiped out whole villages. We didn't put 'em in a ditch per se, but when you dead, you dead. If you kill thirty people and somebody else kills twenty-nine, and they happen to be in a ditch and the other thirty happen to be on top, who's guilty of the biggest atrocity? So all of us were scared. I was scared for a long time.

I got out January '71. Honorable discharge. Five Bronze Stars for valor. . . .

I couldn't discuss the war with my father, even though he had two tours in Vietnam and was stationed in the Mekong Delta when I was there. . . . He had a disease he caught from the service called alcoholism. He died of alcoholism. And we never talked about Vietnam.

But my moms, she brought me back 'cause she loved me. And I think because I loved her. She kept reminding me what type of person I was before I left. Of the dreams I had promised her before I left. To help her buy a home and make sure that we was secure in life.

And she made me see the faces again. See Vietnam. See the incidents. She made me really get ashamed of myself doin' the things I had done. You think no crime is a crime durin' war, 'specially when you get away with it. And when she made me look back at it, it just didn't seem it was possible for me to be able to do those things to other people, because I value life. That's what moms and grandmoms taught me as a child. . . .

I still cry.

I still cry for the white brother that was staked out.

I still cry because I'm destined to suffer the knowledge that I have taken someone else's life not in a combat situation.

I think I suffered just as much as he did. And still do. I think at times that he's the winner, not the loser.

I still have the nightmare twelve years later. And I will have the nightmare twelve years from now. Because I don't wanna forget. I don't think I should. I think that I made it back here and am able to sit here and talk because he died for me. And I'm livin' for him.

I still have the nightmare. I still cry.

I see me in the nightmare. I see me staked out. I see me in the circumstances when I have to be man enough to ask someone to end my suffering as he did.

I can't see the face of the person pointing the gun.

I ask him to pull the trigger. I ask him over and over.

He won't pull the trigger.

I wake up.

Every time.

"Who Can You Believe?"

A Disabled Veteran Protests the War

Ron Kovic

Opposition to U.S. involvement in Vietnam grew stronger as the war progressed. In October 1967, more than 100,000 Americans demonstrated against the war at the Pentagon. In May 1970, hundreds of college campuses closed down because of protests against the U.S. invasion of Cambodia, and at Kent State University the Ohio National Guard killed four demonstrators.

Demonstrators put flowers in the rifles of military police during the 1967 demonstration at the Pentagon to protest the Vietnam War.

Ron Kovic enlisted in the Marines to fight in Vietnam, serving two tours of duty. After he was disabled in combat, Kovic's initial support for the war changed into active opposition. Here he describes the "Last Patrol," a group of Vietnam veterans who demonstrated against the war at the 1972 Republican National Convention.

It was the night of Nixon's acceptance speech, and now I was on my own deep in his territory, all alone in my wheelchair in a sweat-soaked Marine utility jacket covered with medals from the war. . . .

Every once in a while someone would look at me as if I didn't belong there. But I had come almost 3,000 miles for this meeting with the president and nothing was going to prevent it from taking place.

I worked my way slowly and carefully into the huge hall, moving down one of the side aisles. "Excuse me, excuse me," I said to delegates as I pushed past them farther and farther to the front of the hall toward the speakers' podium.

I had gotten only halfway toward where I wanted to be when I was stopped by one of the convention security marshalls. "Where are you going?" he said. He grabbed hold of the back of my chair. I made believe I hadn't heard him and kept turning my wheels, but his grip on the chair was too tight and now two other security men had joined him.

"What's the matter?" I said. "Can't a disabled veteran who fought for his country sit up front?"

The three men looked at each other for a moment and one of them said, "I'm afraid not. You're not allowed up front with the delegates." . . .

In a move of desperation I swung around facing all three of them, shouting as loud as I could so Walter Cronkite and the CBS camera crew that was just above me could hear me and maybe even focus their cameras in for the six o'clock news. "I'm a Vietnam veteran and I fought in the war! Did you fight in the war?"

One of the guards looked away.

"Yeah, that's what I thought," I said. "I bet none of you fought in the war and you guys are trying to throw me out of the convention. I've got just as much right to be up front here as any of these delegates. I fought for that right and I was born on the Fourth of July."

I was really shouting now and another officer came over. I think he might have been in charge of the hall. He told me I could stay where I was if I was quiet and didn't move up any farther. I agreed with the compromise. I locked my brakes and looked for other veterans in the tremendous crowd. As far as I could tell, I was the only one who had made it in.

People had begun to sit down all around me. They all had "Four More Years" buttons, and I was surprised to see how many of them were young. I began speaking to them, telling them about the Last Patrol and why veterans from all over the United States had taken the time and effort to travel thousands of miles to the Republican National Convention. "I'm a disabled veteran!" I shouted. "I served two tours of duty in Vietnam and while on my second tour of duty up in the DMZ I was wounded and paralyzed from the chest down." I told them I would be that way for the rest of my life.

Then I began to talk about the hospitals and how they treated the returning veterans like animals, how I, many nights in the Bronx, had lain in my own shit for hours waiting for an aide. "And they never come," I said. "They never come because that man that's going to accept the nomi-

nation tonight has been lying to all of us and spending the money on war that should be spent on healing and helping the wounded. That's the biggest lie and hypocrisy of all—that we had to go over there and fight and get crippled and come home to a government and leaders who could care less about the same boys they sent over."

I kept shouting and speaking, looking for some kind of reaction from the crowd. No one seemed to want to even look at me. . . .

By then a couple of newsmen, including Roger Mudd from CBS, had worked their way through the security barricades and begun to ask me questions. . . .

. . . The camera began to roll, and I began to explain why I and the others had come, that the war was wrong and it had to stop immediately. "I'm a Vietnam veteran," I said. "I gave America my all and the leaders of this government threw me and the others away to rot in their V.A. hospitals. What's happening in Vietnam is a crime against humanity, and I just want the American people to know that we have come all the way across this country, sleeping on the ground and in the rain, to let the American people see for themselves the men who fought their war and have come to oppose it. If you can't believe the veteran who fought the war and was wounded in the war, who can you believe?"

"God Cried for Vietnam That Day"

The Fall of Saigon

Diep Thi Nguyen

Preliminary peace talks between the United States and North Vietnam began in May 1968 in Paris, but the war continued. Finally, in January 1973, a peace agreement was reached, and the last American combat troops left Vietnam that March. But two years later the North Vietnamese launched a major offensive against South Vietnam, and the United States refused to intervene. Saigon fell to the communists on April 30, 1975.

Diep Thi Nguyen tried to escape Saigon that day with her two Amerasian daughters via helicopters leaving from the American Embassy, but failed. Ten years later, they arrived in America as refugees sponsored by Jann Jansen, whose former husband was Diep's lover in Vietnam. Here Diep recalls her despair in Saigon.

Without any money, it was no use going to American Embassy, but we took what we had and left for the embassy on April 30th. . . .

We were there trying to push our children ahead of the crowds of people. Late that afternoon, helicopters come, taking people from the roof, people dashing to be first. Many people hurt. My daughters, they little and I was afraid they be trampled in the mobs. We waited all day, trying to get aboard, but we could not. People begged, pushed and begged, and there was no way. . . .

. . . One American he tell me that there would be more the next day come to take the rest of us. Someone had big laugh and ask what he was drinking. "This is the end of a culture," someone said. "This is the last day of the South Vietnamese life."

I knew that everything would be changed. I knew that I had missed my decisions [opportunities to leave] over and over, so now I would pay the price. I had so many regrets.

When I saw some Americans upstairs who did not go, I tried to go up the stairs and push the girls ahead of me. There

"He Left Me Only the Tears"

An Amerasian Child Yearns for Her Father

Mai-Uyen "Jolie" Nguyen

Mai-Uyen "Jolie" Nguyen, Diep's daughter, describes her feelings as a "bui-doi" [literally, "dust of life"], the outcast child of an American soldier who had deserted her. She was eventually reunited with her father in America, with the help of Jann Jansen.

I felt bitter toward my father who had gone away. My cousin Freddy felt bitter, too. I have never had a father to call "Daddy" and have never seen his face. That was unhappy for me. I could not understand what my American father think, why he not write me a letter to wonder about me or care about my life. Did he wonder ever if I was alive or dead? He had gone to America, leaving me in Vietnam, bequeathing me the brown hair and eyes and white skin, and he never knew what would become of me. What would he say when Vietnamese children mocked me and turned on me?

What did my father do for me? He made me, but it was nothing to him. He left me only the tears. I would think: "If I had a good father who loved me, he would make my life different. I would be happy now, and if he had not abandoned me, I would not be so miserable as this." I wanted so to write to him but did not know how to find him. Yes, I thought, he has forgotten me, but I keep his photograph and the necklace he gave me when I was two years old. It was the forbidden picture of an American soldier, but my mother had saved it and given it to me. I would never lose it or throw it away. It was all I knew of my father. . . .

were two helicopters trying very hard to land, and so many people rushed forward to be in [one] that they could not go. People fell backward, some very hurt. Helicopters were afraid then to land. Tear gasses were thrown at us to keep us away, and grenades I think were thrown to disband the many people. I think the American Marines were afraid of the panicky people.

The tear gasses made me not see. My children could not see and cried. We run inside and got water to wash our faces, and I saw the kind American soldiers in the helicopters and said: "Please save my children. They have same skin color and hair color as you."

"If he lands, he won't be able to fly off," someone said. Too many people. We had lost our decision once again.

I heard the president announce the welcome of the North Vietnam government, and I went home with tears. We lost Saigon. We lost everything. On the way home, it was rainy, and when I came in the door my daughters say that God cried for Vietnam that day. . . .

We could not leave our children, and we did not want to live with the Communist government. Minh [her sister] and I had seen the way the half-American children lived. We with the half-breed American babies knew they had no future now in Vietnam. They would be treated very bad, worse than the dog, no opportunity, no education, made fun of and badly abused.

Minh tried to poison their rice, but we cried together so much and somehow the children knew why. They wouldn't eat. . . . They were angry and afraid and did not trust us for a long time. Minh and I didn't know what to do; we were so confused. No one would protect us, we with the American children.

"Has Everyone Forgot?"

Victims of Agent Orange

Nancy Mahowald

The Vietnam War continued to inflict wounds even after the fighting stopped. In 1979, the U.S. government admitted that thousands of Vietnam veterans had been exposed to Agent Orange, a herbicide that contained the lethal carcinogen dioxin. Nancy Mahowald, whose brother Donnie served in Vietnam and later developed cancer, protested the denial of his disability benefits in this letter she left at the Vietnam Veterans Memorial in Washington, D.C.

When I was 17, Donnie . . . joined the Army.

When I was 19, he came home on leave. He told me he was going to Vietnam. I started to cry. . . .

The war is real now, not just on TV news. My brother could die there!

When I was 21, Donnie came home. Tony, my husband, doesn't have time to stop the car before I'm out and running. I am so happy! But Donnie looks pale and nervous.

I am 22, Donnie is different; he stays in his room all the time. Mom calls, she's crying, he won't talk to her at all.

Donnie has a skin cancer removed from his shoulder.

I am 23, I see Donnie every day now. He gives me a ride to work and drops my son off at the babysitter's. Don's better now, more like his old self. He's got a good job driving a truck. . . .

I am 35, I can't stand this. It's the most awful thing I've ever heard in my life. "Tony, come home, Donnie just called me. He says he has cancer in his jaw." . . .

The doctors pull most of his teeth. They tell Don if he gets a cavity, there wouldn't be any way to fix it because of the radiation.

We can see the tumor now.

The radiation is working. He can't eat, his mouth is on fire. There's no saliva. His beard will never grow back. He's so thin.

Donnie has added his name to the Agent Orange suit.

I see him every day. I can't stay away. I know it sounds awful, but I had to see him. I always felt better after. He's

---

"Perhaps Now I Can Bury You"

Grieving at America's Wailing Wall

A Vietnam Veteran

On November 13, 1982, the Vietnam Veterans Memorial was dedicated in Washington, D.C. Its V-shaped black granite wall lists the names of the 58,000 U.S. soldiers killed in Vietnam. Friends, family, and fellow soldiers began leaving mementos at "the Wall" in tribute to the dead. This anonymous letter by a Vietnam veteran to his fallen comrade was one of those offerings.

Dear Smitty,
Perhaps now I can bury you, at least in my soul. Perhaps now I won't see you night after night when the war reappears and we are once more amidst the myriad hells that Vietnam engulfed us in.

We crept "point" together and we pulled "drag" together. We lay crouched in cold mud and were drenched by monsoons. We sweated buckets and endured the heat of dry season. We burnt at least a thousand leeches off one another and went through a gallon of insect repellent a day that the bugs were irresistibly attracted to.

When you were hit, I was your medic all the way, and when I was blown fifty feet by the mortar, you were there first. When I was shaking with malaria, you wiped my brow.

We got tough, Smitty. We became hired guns, lean and mean and calloused. And after every ambush, every firefight, every "hot" chopper insertion you'd shake and get sick.

You got a bronze star, a silver star, survived eighteen months of one demon hell after another, only to walk into a booby-trapped bunker and all of a sudden you had no face or chest.

I never cried. My chest becomes unbearably painful and my throat tightens so I can't even croak, but I haven't cried. I wanted to, just couldn't.

I think I can, today. Damn, I'm crying now.
> 'Bye Smitty,
> Get some rest.

The Vietnam Veterans Memorial in Washington, D.C., is dedicated to the 2.7 million veterans of the Vietnam War and the 58,000 U.S. soldiers who died there.

going through hell, but he makes me feel better.

It's October; Don has surgery today. No one knows what to say. Donnie's joking as they close the elevator doors. . . . The doctors removed about an inch and a half of jaw bone. That's not so bad, is it?

Put your fingers up to your jaw and measure.

Oh, God, how could you let this happen to him?

Donnie's home and doing fine. It's going to take a long time to heal, but he's young and in good shape. He's going back to work. He can't taste food but maybe the taste buds will come back. He carries a little water bottle with him wherever he goes. His mouth is dry all the time.

The company he works for is going out of business. Another company is going to hire the help.

Don's out of a job. The dispatcher keeps sending Donnie out to move stoves and refrigerators. Donnie tells him that he can't do that kind of work anymore because his arm isn't strong enough since his surgery. (This company knew this when they hired him.) The dispatcher says, "Either go out on the job or walk." Donnie walks. . . .

We all tell Don to file for disability. He finally does but his claim is denied.

He's been looking for a job now for two years.

I'm angry!

I called the Vietnam veterans organization asking what I could do or where I could get help for my brother. They tell me it's hopeless. Only one veteran told me not to give up. "Keep trying," he said. "Not only for your brother, but for all of us. Tell them you're not going away."

I called the V.A. and talked to a Veteran Service Officer. . . . He . . . told me that . . . our government's stand on this is: if you take any group of people, a certain percent are going to get cancer anyway. Well, that may be, but almost half of my brother's face is missing, and it wasn't shot off. The chemicals that our government told our men to use caused this soft skin cancer in my brother. He's been wounded, only not by the enemy.

I never saw Donnie cry the whole time he was going through radiation, before or after his surgery. But he cried when he had to take money from me.

He's losing his self-respect.

I realize that Donnie's not the only Vietnam veteran in trouble, but he is the only one that's my brother.

Isn't anyone going to do anything about all these men? Has everyone forgot? Does everyone hope they'll all just go away?

268

"I Did Not Have a Choice"

Jane Roe and Abortion

Norma McCorvey

In the 1970s, the feminist movement sought greater equality for women. In 1972, Congress passed the Equal Rights Amendment, which stated that "equality of rights under the law shall not be denied . . . on account of sex," but the amendment failed to be ratified by enough states before the 1982 deadline. In 1973, the Supreme Court upheld a woman's right to choose an abortion in Roe v. Wade. *The plaintiff in that case, who used the pseudonym "Jane Roe," was Norma McCorvey. Here she describes the impact the case had on her.*

Norma McCorvey was the actual "Jane Roe" in Roe v. Wade *(1973). Plaintiffs in controversial cases often use the aliases Doe or Roe to protect their anonymity.*

The Constitution is important to me because it protects the most basic right of all—privacy, including a woman's right to control her own body. That was not true in 1969, when I sought an abortion. Poor and pregnant, I was already the young mother of a child from a broken marriage. I had no job and no permanent place to live.

I tried to find a doctor who would perform an abortion, but because the procedure was illegal, the level of professionalism among practitioners was less than that of butchers who grind up hamburger. The clinics were filthy. The equipment was antiquated. And the likelihood of life-threatening injury and infection was high. Rather than risk death at the hands of some quack, I decided to have the baby and put it up for adoption.

Through the adoption attorney, I met two young lawyers, Sarah Weddington and Linda Coffee, who were looking for a plaintiff to challenge the Texas abortion law. I was still very young and insecure, and the thought of being in the limelight scared me to death. Also, I had a 5-year-old daughter whom I did not want to entangle in my politics. So Sarah and Linda came up with the "Jane Roe" pseudonym, and I decided to accept the challenge of seeking a legal abortion.

On March 3, 1970, *Roe v. Wade* was formally filed in the Dallas court system. I was between six and seven months pregnant. The court system moved very slowly. I honestly had thought that my court case would be settled in time for me to get an abortion. . . .

In June of 1970, I went into labor at two o'clock in the morning. My water broke, and I began hemorrhaging. I asked the hospital staff if the baby was a boy or a girl, but they refused to tell me or let me see it. I became hysterical because of the way they were treating me, and they had me sedated. Later, a nurse brought the baby girl to my room, telling me it was feeding time. When she realized her mistake, she snatched the baby out of my arms.

I am bound by a confidentiality agreement with the adoption court not to speak about this child, but I can say that giving

her up was the most agonizing experience of my life. I hope that women who choose adoption today are treated with more sensitivity than I was back then.

Two and a half years later, on January 22, 1973, I read in a short article on the lower right front page of *The Dallas Times-Herald* that abortion had become legal. My initial reaction was that I had been cheated, because I did not have a choice regarding my reproductive freedom. Because I carried the "Roe baby" to birth, one of the ironies of my life is that I have never had an abortion.

For many years, I remained basically anonymous, except for occasional appearances as Jane Roe. But in 1989 I finally accepted myself as Jane Roe and stepped out of my political closet. I learned very quickly that there was a price to pay for this action. I became the target of vicious attacks. Aside from threatening letters and calls, baby clothes were thrown in my yard, my car was vandalized, and I was constantly afraid to go outside my home. Finally, late one night a car drove by and fired shotgun blasts through my front door. The first shot barely missed my head, and I now have almost no hearing in my right ear.

Decisions concerning childbearing are necessarily intimate, personal, and private. The Supreme Court recognized in 1973 that individuals, weighing their individual circumstances, make better decisions than the state. Although I never got to make that choice for myself, I'm glad that "Jane Roe" made freedom of choice possible for the women who came after her.

"The Entire Community Seemed To Be Sick!"

Living on Love Canal

Lois Marie Gibbs

Another powerful movement during the 1970s was environmentalism, epitomized by the first Earth Day celebration on April 22, 1970. That same year the Environmental Protection Agency (EPA) was created to centralize the control of pollution under one agency.

A major environmental crisis arose in 1978 when a toxic waste dump, known as Love Canal, was discovered under a neighborhood in Niagara Falls, New York. In 1980, due to the protests of Love Canal residents, Congress established a "superfund" of more than $1 billion to clean up toxic waste sites. Lois Gibbs helped organize the Love Canal protest.

Almost everyone has heard about Love Canal, but not many people know what it is all about. The Love Canal story is about a thousand families who lived near the site of an abandoned toxic chemical waste dump. More important, it is a warning of what could happen in any American community. We have very little protection against the toxic chemical wastes that threaten to poison our water, our air, and our food. The federal and state governments have agreed to move away everyone who wants to move; but they didn't at first. We had to work to achieve that goal. Love Canal is the story of how government tends to solve a problem, and of how we, ordinary citizens of the United States, can take control of our own lives by insisting that we be heard. . . .

When we moved into our house on 101st Street in 1972, I didn't even know Love Canal was there. It was a lovely neighborhood in a quiet residential area, with lots of trees and lots of children out-

side playing. It seemed just the place for our family. . . . I liked the idea of my children being able to walk to the 99th Street School. The school's playground was part of a big, open field with houses all around. Our new neighbors told us that the developers who sold them their houses said the city was going to put a park on the field.

It is really something, if you stop and think of it, that underneath that field were poisons, and on top of it was a grade school and a playground. We later found out that the Niagara Falls School Board knew the filled-in canal was a toxic dump site. We also know that they knew it was dangerous because, when the Hooker Chemical Corporation sold it to them for one dollar, Hooker put a clause in the deed declaring that the corporation would not be responsible for any harm that came to anyone from chemicals buried there. That one-dollar school site turned out to be some bargain!

Love Canal actually began for me in June 1978 with Mike Brown's articles in the Niagara Falls *Gazette.* At first, I didn't realize where the canal was. . . . Then when I found out the 99th Street School was indeed on top of it, I was alarmed. My son attended that school. . . . I decided I needed to do some investigating.

I went to my brother-in-law, Wayne Hadley, a biologist and, at the time, a professor at the State University of New York at Buffalo. He had worked on environmental problems and knew a lot about chemicals. I asked him to translate some of that jibberjabber in the articles into English. I showed Wayne Mike Brown's articles listing the chemicals in the canal and asked what they were. I was really alarmed by his answer. Some of the chemicals, he said, can affect the nervous system. Just a little bit, even the amount that's in paint or gasoline, can kill brain cells. I still couldn't believe it, but if it were true, I wanted to get Michael [her son] out of that 99th Street School. . . .

. . . I decided to go door-to-door with a petition. It seemed like a good idea to start near the school, to talk with the mothers nearest it. I had already heard that a lot of the residents near the school had been upset about the chemicals for the past couple of years. I thought they might help me. I had never done anything like this, however, and I was frightened. I was afraid a lot of doors would be slammed in my face, that people would think I was some crazy fanatic. But I decided to do it anyway. . . .

As I proceeded down 99th Street, I developed a set speech. I would tell people what I wanted. But the speech wasn't all that necessary. It seemed as though every home on 99th Street had someone with an illness. . . .

As I continued going door-to-door, I heard more. The more I heard, the more frightened I became. This problem involved much more than the 99th Street School. The entire community seemed to be sick! . . . I thought about Michael [who had epilepsy and low white blood cell count]. . . . I didn't understand how chemicals could get all the way over to 101st Street from 99th, but the more I thought about it, the more frightened I became—for my family and for the whole neighborhood. . . .

The New York State Health Department held a public meeting in June 1978. It was the first one I attended. Dr. Nicholas Vianna and some of his staff explained that they were going to do environmental and health studies. They wanted to take samples—of blood, air, and soil, as well as from sump pumps. They wanted to find out if there really was a problem. They would study only the first ring of houses, though, the ones with backyards abutting Love Canal. Bob Matthews, Niagara Falls city engineer, was there to explain the city's plan for remedial construction. They all sat in front of a big, green chalkboard on the stage in the auditorium of the 99th Street School. . . .

. . . There were about seventy-five people in that warm, humid auditorium. Everyone was hot, and we could smell the canal. The heat must have had something to do with the short tempers. . . . Dr. Vianna advised people who lived near the canal not to eat any vegetables from their gardens.

With that, [one] father became very upset. "Look—my kid can't play in the yard because her feet get burned. My neighbor's dog burns his nose in the yard. We can't eat out of the garden. What's going on here? What is this all about?"

Dr. Vianna just kept saying, "I don't know. We are investigating. It's too early to tell."

Then Bob Matthews discussed the remedial construction plan. He used the chalkboard to show us how a system of tile pipes would run the length of the canal on both sides. He said the canal was like a bathtub that was overflowing. He was talking to us as though we were children! He said it was like putting a fat woman in a bathtub, causing the water to overflow onto the floor. The tile system would collect the overflow. Then it would be pumped out and treated by filtering it through charcoal. After it had been cleaned by the charcoal, it would be pumped down to the sewers and everything would be all right. The overflow-filtering system would also draw the chemicals away from the backyards, which would be clean again. . . .

I asked him about the underground springs that feed into the canal. What would happen to them? . . . Someone else observed that the tile drains would be only twelve feet deep. "What if the chemicals are forty feet down? The canal is probably forty feet deep." Another person said there were many types of chemicals in there. How was the city engineer going to get them out? No one would, or could, give us straight answers. The audience was getting frustrated and angry. They wanted answers.

I asked Dr. Vianna if the 99th Street School was safe. He answered that the air readings on the school had come back clean. But there we were, sitting in the school auditorium, smelling chemicals! . . .

I was learning that you can't trust government to look out for your interests. If you insist to government officials strongly enough, they might do the right thing. The Niagara County Health Department and other government officials had known about the pollution problem at Love Canal for a long time but had ignored it. Maybe it was the state's fiscal deficits or the blizzard of 1977. Whatever the reason, it was ignored, and the public's health was thereby jeopardized.

"I Knew It Was Wrong"

Confessions of a Watergate Bagman

Tony Ulasewicz

A scandal unfolded during the 1970s that shook the foundations of American government and ruined the presidency of Richard Nixon. In June 1972, five people—including James McCord, security chief for Nixon's Committee to Re-elect the President (CREEP)—were arrested for the attempted burglary of the Democratic National Committee offices at the Watergate complex in Washington, D.C.

Nixon was reelected in 1972 by a landslide, but Congress set up a special committee to investigate the Watergate burglary. White House tapes eventually revealed that Nixon had been actively involved in a coverup of the crime, and the House Judiciary Committee voted to impeach the president in July 1974. On August 9, 1974, Richard Nixon became the first U.S. president to resign his office.

Tony Ulasewicz, a former police officer in New York City, worked as a private investigator for the White House. He delivered much of the money funneled through the White House to the Watergate defendants. Here he recalls his testimony before the Senate.

My Watergate souvenir is a chrome busman's money changer which sits on a bookshelf in my den and glints in the afternoon sun. In the summer of 1972, after the Watergate break-in at the Democratic National Committee headquarters, I almost wore out my pants pockets carrying the change I needed to call lawyers and some of their burglar clients to whom I was trying to deliver chunks of cash the White House wanted passed around. I bought the money changer to save my pants and clipped it on my belt. The money changer remains tagged with a label that marked it as "Exhibit 112" in the Watergate conspiracy trial held before Judge John Sirica in November 1974. I carried most of the cash around in a brown paper bag. I called it my "lunch." . . .

I made my first appearance before the Senate Watergate Committee on Wednesday, May 23 [1973]. Before stepping into the spotlight, I waited alone in a room in the New Senate Office Building. Initially, I had no idea what I was going to be asked about when I sat down before the world. While waiting to be called before the cameras, I got hungry. When I found out that I had plenty of time before I went on stage, I left to get some lunch. To avoid the curious onlookers . . . lurking in the Senate cafeteria, I walked to the railroad station.

Upon entering, I passed a newsstand, and there, on a rack, I saw something that made my heart sink. There in stone black-and-white blistering silence was my picture on the front page of the *Washington Star*. The picture was a close up, full face, and the headline, in bold black letters, read: SPY. Suddenly, I lost my appetite. I felt caged and expendable. I was no spy. I was a licensed private investigator who had broken no law and breached no confidence. I felt my guts harden like quick-drying cement. My picture had been leaked to the press. . . .

Before being called in to testify, Lenzner introduced me to [the] chief counsel to the Senate committee, Sam Dash, in front of a water cooler. Lenzner acted as if he was showing off a specimen, not a human being. The meeting with Dash was perfunctory. Dash said he was only going to ask me about the call Caulfield [a retired New York police detective who worked undercover for the White House] made to me about wanting to contact McCord right after the Watergate burglary and the call I made to McCord in January 1973 to deliver the veiled clemency message if McCord kept his mouth shut and pled guilty. That was it. Nothing more, nothing less. I understood immediately what Dash was trying to do: build a case against the president of the United States. If Nixon was behind the clemency offer to McCord, he was finished. I was just one small piece of Dash's case. He was going to try and present it like a trial lawyer in a courtroom, piece by piece, building block by building block. . . .

. . . Starting off as planned, Dash's questions centered on my anonymous contacts with McCord; these were the only specifics he asked about. When Dash finished his questions, the rest of the committee's questioning just filled time. I was surprised. Some of the things I said while answering Senator Howard Baker's questions triggered a lot of laughter, but comedy wasn't my intent. I was just being myself, as when Baker asked me if I thought my "wiremen were better than McCord's wiremen." I wasn't a wireman, but I told Baker that "any old retired man in the New York City Police Department who would become involved in a thing like that . . . would not have walked in with an army, that is for sure." . . .

The questions . . . focused primarily on how much money was involved and how I delivered it to the Watergate burglars and their lawyers. I was pressed to explain what I understood was the purpose of the money and the real purpose of the message I delivered to McCord. These . . . questions were clearly designed to get me to admit whether I knew it was "hush" money when I delivered it or an offer of White House clemency to McCord, in exchange for his silence, when I called him. These efforts were now linked to proving that the White House (and the president) tried to sabotage the Watergate investigation.

. . . Senator Inouye asked me whether I considered the activities I was involved with "were completely legal." I answered, "Yes, Sir," but when Inouye asked me whether I was aware that I was an accessory "to the crime of obstructing a criminal investigation" when I delivered the message to McCord, I answered, "Yes, I knew that it was wrong." In hindsight of course it was, and that's what I meant by my answer, but the message itself should have never existed.

"Dear President Carter"

Kids' Letters to the White House

American Children

The aftermath of the Watergate scandal helped Jimmy Carter defeat Gerald Ford for the presidency in 1976. A Democrat and Washington "outsider," Carter pledged to bring ethics back to government. The Carter presidency faced many problems: high inflation, an energy crisis, control of the Panama Canal, the arms race with the Soviet Union, and the threat of war in the Middle East. Even the youngest citizens struggled with these issues, as their letters to the president demonstrate.

Dear Mr. President Carter:
I guess you receive thousands of fan letters every day at the White House, but this is not a fan letter. This is an important letter so I hope you will read it.

I need a job very badly.

My name is Howard and I am 12 years old and I live in Dallas with my mother and my grandmother. We don't have much money and my mother gets Social Security and so does my grandmother and that is all the money we have.

When my father died, we didn't even have enough money to pay for his funeral and we had to borrow money to bury him like a good Christian.

That is why I need a job. Any kind of job. I want to help my mother and my grandmother so they can buy a new dress and we don't have to buy old bread at that bakery store because it is only five cents.

Could you please help me find a job in Dallas? I will work very hard.
Thank you,
Howard V.

Dear Mr. Carter:
I am going to try and help with the energy crisis.

Every night before I go to sleep, I am going to turn off my TV set even if my mother doesn't yell at me to do it.
Love,
Gwen S.

Dear President Carter:
Why are we going to give away the Panama Canal? I don't think we should give away the Panama Canal for 1,000 years. If we gave away the Panama Canal, then our ships won't be able to get through the canal and there will be trouble with the U.S. Navy.

274

Many Americans, including children, opposed the 1977 Panama Canal Treaties, in which the United States promised to turn over the canal to full Panamanian control in the year 2000.

The U.S.A. doesn't need any more trouble. We have enough problems in Korea, the Middle East, and the rest of the world.

So please, Mr. President, don't give away the Panama Canal for a long time. The Panama Canal is important for the U.S.A. like the Statue of Liberty and Disneyland.

> Your loyal citizen,
> Victoria J.

Dear President Jimmy Carter,
My father doesn't think you did the right thing when you decided to stop the building of the B-1 bomber. My father says that America has to be stronger than the Russians and if we don't have the B-1 bomber we won't be as strong as the Soviet Union. My father says we should never trust the Russians; even if they say they are our friends, they really aren't.

President Nixon wasn't fooled by the Russians.

President Ford wasn't fooled by the Russians.

Don't let the Russians fool you even if they write you nice letters and send you a present for your birthday.

> Your friend,
> Stephanie J.

Dear President Jimmy Carter:
Do you believe there will be a war in the Middle East between the Arabs and Israel?

If there is a war, will Americans have to fight like they did in Korea and Vietnam? Will there be a draft again so that me and my friends will have to serve in the Army like my father and my uncle?

I don't think I would want to be in the Army because I was once in the Boy Scouts for two weeks and I didn't even like that.

> Dennis J.

"Maybe Tomorrow"

Held Hostage in Iran

Bill Belk

In 1979, a revolution led by Ayatollah Khomeini, an Islamic religious leader, deposed the shah of Iran, whom the CIA had helped put in power in 1953. When the shah was admitted to the United States for medical treatment, Iranians seized the American embassy in Tehran in November 1979, taking fifty-two hostages. They were held captive for 444 days, and finally released on the day Ronald Reagan was inaugurated in 1981. It was a final slap to outgoing President Jimmy Carter, for whom the hostage crisis had become the Achilles heel of his administration.

Bill Belk was a communications officer with the American embassy in Tehran. Here he describes the conditions of his captivity, including a Christmas celebration for the hostages that the Iranians staged to get media coverage.

After we were blindfolded, they led the five of us down the hall to another room, which was all decked out for the Christmas celebration. Just before we went in the door, they took our blindfolds off. I remember the papal nuncio was there with two Iranian ministers. As soon as we walked into the room, the clergymen wanted to embrace us and kiss us on the cheek, and carry on like we were long-lost friends. You know, they were very exuberant. But that kind of greeting wasn't for me. Those guys were total strangers. We didn't even speak the same language, and their reason for being there was very different from mine. So I stood back during all of the hugging and kissing.

We were seated at a table which had cakes and fruit on it, and the papal nuncio said a few words that I couldn't understand. Then he wanted us to sing some Christmas carols, which I thought was totally ridiculous. Here we were at this table looking across the room into a television camera, and behind the camera along the back wall were about forty or fifty militants standing there with their weapons. They were all staring at us like we were monkeys in a cage. Now how can five Americans feel at ease singing Christmas carols when they're face to face with all those automatic weapons? That really blew my mind. I refused to sing. I just glowered at the militants. I wanted anyone who saw me on TV to know that I was angry. I wasn't about to pretend that I was having a good time, and that I thought this was a nice little ceremony. . . .

They let each of us deliver a short message to our families in front of the TV cameras. I said hello to my wife and told her that I was still alive. I also let her know that I had not received any mail. The whole time I was speaking, I kept glowering at the militants lined up along the back wall.

When the service was over, we were each given a present that was gift-wrapped and had our name on it. The Iranians filmed us receiving and opening these gifts. I remember there was a sweat suit and a couple of oranges in my box. Then when the television cameras were turned off, we were taken back out to the hall, blindfolded, and our gifts were taken away from us. We weren't allowed to keep them. They took that stuff and put it back on the pile with someone else's name so that there would be gifts for the next group when they came in. . . .

After the visit of the Algerian ambassador, we were all hoping that a release

276

"Peace, Like War, Is Waged"

Celebrating the Camp David Accords

Robert Maddox

The Middle East was the focus for President Carter's greatest triumph—the Camp David accords between Israel and Egypt—as well as his greatest challenge—the Iranian hostage crisis. In 1978, Carter brought together Egypt's president, Anwar Sadat, and Israel's prime minister, Menachem Begin, to discuss a peace agreement at the presidential retreat at Camp David, Maryland. After Carter personally visited both countries to lobby for peace, Israel and Egypt signed a peace treaty in March 1979. Robert Maddox, a Baptist minister who later became a speechwriter for Carter, contributed the key phrase for the signing ceremony: "Peace, like war, is waged."

Linda [his wife] and I watched the live telecast of the president's arrival back in Washington [from Egypt and Israel]. He announced then that the U.S. would host a ceremony at the White House in a short time to formally sign the agreement.

My mind began to buzz. He would need a speech for that historic ceremony. What should he say? I had run across a phrase, actually written by Walker Knight of the Baptist Home Mission Board in Atlanta, "Peace, like war, is waged." What a noble idea. That is exactly what Carter, Begin, and Sadat had done—they had "waged peace." Riding to Atlanta early one morning in the middle of March, while my children dozed in the back seat, the broad outlines of a speech began to come together in my head.

At home I went to work. For three days I wrote and rewrote. Linda read the draft and made suggestions. When it was presentable I let others read the draft, especially Edna Langford. Linda was satisfied. Edna, with tears in her eyes, said, "Send it."

I called Mary Hoyt, Mrs. Carter's press secretary, whom I had come to know over the telephone and told her what I had done. Probably to be nice, I thought, she said, "Send it to me and we will see where it goes from there."

I mailed the text that very day. Then—nothing from the White House.

But about thirty minutes before the treaty-signing ceremony, Jody Powell [the president's press secretary] called, saying, "You had better get to a television set. The president is using your speech for the signing."

My speech! Something like a hundred million people would watch that ceremony and hear the president use my words. Incredible. Sure enough, in that South Georgia drawl, he intoned my words (and Walker Knight's): "Peace, like war, is waged."

was imminent. I was sure that something was in the works, and even thought that a Christmas release was possible. But I definitely expected to be out of there by the end of the year. I was dead certain of that. But the days came and went with all of us sitting in Tehran. We were in 1981 and still in Iran. That just boggled my mind. We kept asking the guards, "Hey, what's going on in the negotiations? What's happening?"

We'd always get the same stock answer. "They're working on it." That's all

the guards would ever say. "They're working on it."

We'd ask, "Well, when is something going to happen? When are we going home?"

They'd say, "Maybe tomorrow. Do not worry. Maybe tomorrow." Or, "Soon, soon." Those were their favorite expressions. Of course, they'd been saying the exact same things back when we were being kept at the embassy. So I started getting very depressed. I was afraid that maybe the negotiations had fallen through, because the days just kept rolling by. . . .

Those first few weeks in January were particularly difficult, because we were living in such close quarters. There were six people in this one room, and a little friction among us was inevitable. We had all been in Iran for over a year now, and our nerves were frayed. We were sick and tired of being hostages. We kept hoping and hoping that we'd be released, but we were still sitting there. Because of that, the degree of frustration was intense. . . .

I remember there was a girls' preschool right next door to us, and each day would begin with these 5- and 6-year-old girls gathering on the playground to sing, *"Marg bar Amrika! Marg bar Amrika! Marg bar Carter! Marg bar Carter!"* Every morning we'd hear the teacher leading these little girls in song. It was sad to know that an adult was standing out there on the playground and teaching those children to hate. I thought that was pathetic. But that was the way it was. Instead of saying the pledge of allegiance or singing the national anthem, those kids would sing "Death to America." . . .

We arrived in Frankfurt [after being released] at some ungodly hour in the morning and were loaded onto some little buses to be driven in convoy from Frankfurt to Wiesbaden. It was probably about twenty-five miles or so to the hospital, and all along that route the streets were lined with cheering people. That just amazed me. I think every American in Germany got out of bed that morning to come out and greet us. But it wasn't just Americans. There were a lot of Germans out there, too. I was amazed that our return from Iran was such a big deal to people who didn't even know us. . . .

When we arrived in Wiesbaden, we received very warm greetings from the soldiers and patients at the hospital. A military band was playing as we walked in, and it was a very nice reception. Once again, there was a lot of hugging and kissing and shaking of hands. The band kept playing and a children's choir was singing in the lobby. It was all very festive. Very joyous.

But the thing I remember the most was the huge number of letters that were waiting for us at the hospital. They had these letters stacked in boxes there in the hallway, and there were literally thousands and thousands of them. Big huge boxes full of mail. The whole time I was in Iran I received four letters. That was it. Ahmed kept telling me, "No one is writing to you. Your wife is not writing to you." I knew that was [a lie], but in the prison I think there were times when all of us felt like we'd been left there and forgotten. But seeing all of that mail stacked up at the hospital was amazing. It gave me an idea of how much people cared. That was beautiful. . . .

When President Carter came in, it was strictly us hostages in the room, and no one else. . . . After hugging each of us, President Carter made a brief speech and discussed the financial terms of the deal that he had made to get us out. He also talked about the rescue mission. . . . President Carter is a very emotional man, and in talking about the rescue attempt he broke down and cried a couple of times. At the time, I didn't realize that eight people had died in the rescue attempt. . . . Some of the other hostages had learned some of the details while we were still in prison, but not me. I was still in the dark, and I wasn't exactly sure what all the tears were about.

"Back to Where They Were Before"

Poor and Unemployed in the 1980s

Frank Lumpkin

President Ronald Reagan ushered in a new conservative era in the 1980s. Under Reagan's presidency, the U.S. economy expanded tremendously, but many criticized Reagan's program of tax cuts for the rich and cuts in social services for the poor. Frank Lumpkin, an unemployed African-American steelworker, believed Reagan was trying to roll back the gains working people had made through the social programs of the New Deal.

They locked the gates at 3:30 with no notice, no nothin'. The company had just borrowed $80 million from the government to modernize the plant. A week before they locked the gate, they put in $300,000 worth of new equipment. New blast furnace, water treatment, continuous casting.

We figured we'd be out of work for a couple months. That was seven years ago. Chase Manhattan, who was financing the checks, put a lock on the gate: 3,600 guys knocked out without notice. Republic is down to 800 from 13,000. USX, that's U.S. Steel, had about 16,000. Now about 800. About 40,000 unemployed in this area alone. Some of the guys still got hope. We're suin' for our back pay, for our pensions, vacation pay. They didn't pay nothin'. Just closed. . . .

I started this Save Our Jobs Committee. I'm puttin' in full time, six days a week, sometimes more. We started in with this surplus food. We'd pass it out once or twice a month to workers and their families. We give out five pounds of cheese and some butter. We get some rice and honey and make them a bag and these steelworkers come around and pick it up for their families. Five hundred bags run out, just like that. . . .

A lot of the families are on welfare. What they do is pick up a little [money] here, a little there, enough for medicine. They can't put down they got it, it's illegal. A lot of guys meet their family in the park on Sunday because if they live with their family, they cut 'em off welfare.

A TV woman's comin' from New England next week. She wants to do a story on Wisconsin Steel workers and their plight. She'd like to talk to somebody who knows somebody who committed suicide. . . .

. . . To make news, you gotta have somebody jump off the bridge and commit suicide. Otherwise they don't see you. Today, if a plant goes down with 20,000, that's not news any more.

I'm invited to a conference to discuss abandoned homes. They're not abandoned; they're evicted! We've been fightin' like the devil for people to try to save homes. They put these people out. They throw their bags out, lock, stock, and bond. They board their homes up and run around hollerin': Abandoned! Who the hell abandoned them? They was put out, man!

Somethin's bound to happen. They talk about the soup lines in the thirties. What they're not talkin' about is the

279

marches. The old soldiers. People were marchin' all over the country in the thousands, in the millions. They said what happened to people, but didn't say what people were *doing*. Roosevelt didn't just do what he did out of the goodness of his heart. This world was in turmoil. It could have been a revolution then.

If Reagan thinks he's gonna roll the country back to the old days, he better think again. I see the spirit among the people. What has got to be developed is the leadership.

I been doin' this thing for seven years. We've been able to carry marches to Springfield, marches to City Hall, marches to Washington. Three, four years ago, we marched to Springfield all the way from City Hall. On the highway, all the trucks'd blow their horns, wave at us. Peoples in town, they'd know we was comin' through. An old, old senior citizen would meet us down the way and give us cool water to drink. We had about 20,000 people in Springfield. We started out with twenty. It's there, I tell ya! It's just gotta be organized, you know what I mean? . . . There's no way the people is gonna be taken back to where they were before. You can't do it. The president can do it for a while, but I do believe the pot is going to really boil. . . .

"An Upper-Class Working Girl"

Morning in America

Sugar Rautbord

Many Americans applauded President Reagan's positive outlook and optimism about the nation's future, epitomized in his "Morning in America" campaign ads. Among these was Sugar Rautbord, an affluent Chicago socialite.

I think of myself as an upper-class working girl. The handle the press has given me is "socialite." A rather peculiar word, I think, 'cause I don't know what it means. A socialite in today's world is a well-dressed fund-raiser. I can't imagine the kind of women that sat lying on their backs, looking at the ceiling, eating bonbons and rummaging through jewelry catalogues.

Socialite women meet socialite men and mate and breed socialite children so that we can fund small opera companies and ballet troupes because there is no government subsidy. And charities, of course. . . .

What the president and Mrs. Reagan have done is extraordinary at a time in our history when there was a depressed mood in this country. They came and made it positive. How can you put a value on that? After we had gone through the morass and self-hatred and all that of Vietnam, it is psychologically important that we have, A, a couple who adore each other; B, are supportive of each other; and C, a man who is a great communicator and can make things happen. If we have all these negative feelings, I don't think we can function well as an individual or as a family or as a nation. Didn't it make you feel better? That the nation itself was having a better feeling about itself?

It's not what he does; it's what he is. He's a survivor. He's a man who with one fell swoop can stop a speeding bullet. He's a superman. With one fell swoop—he almost looked like the original Superman—he could spread his cape and stop a strike. The fact that a man in his 70s could take a bullet in his lung and show no bitterness is as important as passing twenty-eight pieces of legislation. It just does something for everyone.

Let's see the beginning of the end of this business where if you're born poor, you gotta die in the slums. All these kids [around here today] can do is sell hubcaps and tires to the junkman. And steal. The answer to crime is full employment. We gotta start figurin' a way to get it. It's no mystery.

"Polish People Have Never Known Freedom"

A Solidarity Worker Immigrates to America

Jozef Patyna

During the 1980s, democratic forces fought against communist rule in eastern Europe. One of the early leaders in this movement was the Polish independent union Solidarity. Although Solidarity went underground with the martial-law crackdown of 1981, it eventually triumphed when communism fell in the late 1980s.

Jozef Patyna was a Solidarity leader in Poland. After being jailed there, he decided to emigrate with his family to the United States in 1983. Here, he comments on his life in both countries.

We arrived in Rhode Island from West Germany on December 21, 1983. It was a very cold Wednesday night, ten o'clock. We were four people, including my wife, Krystyna, our teenage daughter, Magdalena, and our 11-year-old son, Przemyslaw [Shem]. . . .

. . . I tried to tell our sponsors, "We only want three things: Show us the school for our children. Help me look for a job. And find us a decent apartment." I said, "When I have a job and am earning money, I will pay you back for everything. I don't want to be on welfare or receiving financial aid."

The sponsoring agency found us the apartment and nothing more. After the New Year holiday, my wife and the kids and I walked to the school by ourselves. It was the middle of winter, and the sidewalks were covered with snow. We only knew how to say "Good morning," "Good-bye," and "Thank you." But the principal and teachers were very kind to us. They couldn't understand Polish, but they knew what our children needed. My daughter went to high school and my son was in middle school.

Krystyna and I were anxious to find work. After a month, a Polish man told us about a local factory. We walked to the office and filled out applications. Soon the factory called my wife to work. The next day they called me. We are still working there, making safety belts for cars, parachutes, and other uses. . . .

Like many of my neighbors [in Poland], I worked in a coal mine that became part of the Solidarity Union about 1980. The Solidarity movement was the first time that Polish people felt a sense of self-determination and hope since the Germans and Soviets agreed to invade and divide Poland between them in 1939. . . .

Polish people born after the war have never known freedom. Still, the idea of freedom and democracy is what the people have an instinctive need for. People listen to Western radio. They read underground newspapers and books, which are very popular. When people buy a book and finish reading it, they exchange it with a friend. . . .

Solidarity was recognized by the Polish government as an official union in September 1980. It was the first independent union ever in a communist country. The government was unsure of what was in the minds of Polish citizens during the August strikes. So government officials said, "Okay, we'll sign this paper, the Solidarity Charter. Now, everyone go back to work. No more problems." But their plan didn't succeed. . . .

In mid-November 1981, the Solidarity leadership met in Warsaw for talks with the government about problems like food shortages and rising prices. After ten days, we decided that it was useless to continue the talks. Instead, we decided to campaign for free elections. Change could only come through a truly democratic process. And

the February 1982 national elections were just a few months away. . . .

At the end of November, the Soviet general in charge of the Warsaw Pact forces visited the Polish government. Following the Soviet visit, Jaruzelski [Poland's prime minister] made a speech threatening "a state of war." We worried that Russian tanks would charge in. . . .

On Saturday afternoon, December 12, the governor of Gdansk sent a letter to Solidarity. He gave us information about a new headquarters for the union. Everyone was happy. . . . We didn't know our "new location" would be the police jail. . . .

In March, I was hospitalized because of a problem with my heart. I was pretty ill. The authorities terminated my jail sentence in July 1982, but I remained in the hospital until August. . . .

I wanted to stay in Poland, but I was afraid for my family. The police broke down my friend's door and beat everyone, . . . wife, kids. They asked no questions. They just beat the family up, then walked out. . . .

I decided to leave the country toward the end of 1983. I came to that decision after traveling around the country for a few months and talking with friends who were living in the same circumstances as I. Though Lech Walesa [the leader of Solidari-ty] was still influential, other friends and I knew that our time in Poland was over. We had so many police problems that we were no longer effective. And we risked endangering people by meeting with them, especially underground Solidarity members. So we decided to look after our children's futures. . . .

Driving around Providence, you will see a lot of people with stickers on their car fenders. . . . I only have a "Solidarnosc" sticker. . . .

We bought the Solidarity sticker here. If people put such a sign in their window in Poland, they would be in a lot of trouble. You can be jailed for two years for such a sign.

It's kind of ironic that, after working so hard for a union in Poland, the factory where we work here doesn't have a union. It's an entirely different situation here. . . .

I am loyal to both the United States and Poland. I don't see any problem with my double loyalty, because freedom in the United States affects freedom in Poland. And the situation in Poland affects freedom in western Europe and the United States. . . .

Krystyna and I have decided that we will spend the rest of our lives in this country. This is our second homeland.

"Stop This Madness"

Joining the Nuclear Freeze Movement

Jean Gump

The 1980s saw increased tensions between the United States and the Soviet Union, leading to an intensified arms race. With that came a massive upsurge in the protests against nuclear weapons. One of the most popular proposals was that the number of nuclear weapons be frozen at their current levels.

Jean Gump, a Chicago grandmother, participated in the nuclear freeze movement by defacing a nuclear missile silo on Good Friday in 1986. She was sentenced to eight years in a federal penitentiary.

282

We commemorated the crucifixion of Christ by entering a missile silo near Holden, Missouri. We hung a banner on the outside of the chain-link fence that read: *Swords into Plowshares, An Act of Healing.* Isaiah 2, from Scriptures: We will pound our swords into plowshares and we will study war no more.

It's a Minuteman II silo, a first-strike weapon. There are 150 of these missiles. If one of these missiles were to leave the ground, it would decimate an area of seventy-two miles. And all the children and others. We wanted to make this weapon inoperable. We succeeded.

We carried three hammers, a wire clipper, three baby bottles with our blood, papers with an indictment against the United States and against the Christian church for its complicity. Ken Ripito, who is 23, and Ken Moreland, who is 25, went with me. The other two went to another silo about five miles away.

It is going to be the citizens that will have to eliminate these weapons. They were built by human hands. People are frightened of them, yet view them as our Gods of Metal. It is a chain-link fence with barbed wire on top. We have become so accustomed to these monstrosities that there are no guards. It is nondescript. If you were passing it on the road, you would see this fence. The silo itself is maybe a foot or two out of the earth. It looks like a great concrete patio. It's very innocuous.

To get through the fence, we used a wire clipper. We had practiced in the park the day before. Once we were in, I proceeded to use the blood and I made a cross on top of the silo. Underneath, I wrote the words, in black spray paint: *Disarm and Live.*

We sat down and waited in prayer. We thanked God, first of all, that we were alive. We expected a helicopter to come over and kill us terrorists. We thanked God for our successful dismantling, more or less, of this weapon. We assumed the responsibility for our actions, and we waited to be apprehended.

About forty minutes later, the soldiers arrived in an armored vehicle. There was a machine-gun turret at the top. The com-mander used a megaphone and said, "Will all the personnel on top of the silo please leave the premises with your hands raised?" So all of us personnel left the silo. . . .

They took things out of my pocket and put them on the ground. One of the items was a handkerchief. I said, "It's getting a little chilly; I think I'm getting a cold and a runny nose. I will have to get my handkerchief." It was about three feet away. The soldier said, "Don't you dare move." I said, "I'm going to get this handkerchief and I'm going to blow my nose." I did that and put the handkerchief in my pocket. The soldier said, "You have to leave your handkerchief over here." I said, "All right. But if my nose should run again, I'll go over there and I will get my handkerchief and I will blow my nose." At this point, the poor soldier looked sort of crestfallen. He was about the age of my youngest child. . . .

My children knew nothing about this. Mother's doing her thing, is what they always say. As I leave the house, they often say, "Don't get arrested, Ma." I'd been arrested five other times for civil disobedience.

I felt peace marching was fine, but what we needed was a freeze group. After campaigning in Morton Grove, we had a referendum. Five thousand voted for the freeze, two thousand against. . . .

My one daughter graduates from the University of California. I will not be there. My other daughter is getting married. I will not be there. I want more than anything in the world to be there. These are my children and I love them. But if they're going to have a world, we have to stop this madness. I think they understand that as much as I want to be with them and with my loving husband, [I can't]. . . .

I supposed my neighbors out here think I'm kind of a kook. I'm pretty ordinary. When I'm not doing these things, I'm a good cook and I have swell parties. . . .

When I started dating my husband, right after World War II, my aunt said, "Jean is going to marry a Hun." I thought, What the hell is a Hun? My husband's of German descent. We had just gotten

283

through a war and we had to hate Germans. They were bad people. We certainly had to hate the Japanese. They were bad people. Through these years, I found out there's a lot of people that I have to hate.

We have to hate the Iranians, 'cause we have to go over there and kill 'em. I had to hate the Vietnamese people. I had to hate the commies. Everybody has to hate the commies. There is no end to my nation's enemies. But I don't think they're my enemies. I think, God help me, these are people. . . .

You know, I have never been so hopeful. If I can change my way of thinking, anybody can. I don't want to be singled out as anybody special, because I'm not. We have got to have a future for our children, and we've got to make some sacrifices for it, okay?

"Equal Responsibility"

A Woman Fights in the Persian Gulf War

Rhonda Cornum

Iraq invaded its neighbor Kuwait in August 1990. In response, the United States sent more than 500,000 troops to the Persian Gulf, and war began when Iraq failed to withdraw by January 15, 1991. U.S. forces won an overwhelming victory in a matter of weeks.

Rhonda Cornum, a U.S. medical officer attached to a combat unit, served in the Persian Gulf War and was captured by Iraqi troops. Here she describes her own experiences, as well as the changing role of women in the military.

We knew by the end of December that our mission would be a major helicopter assault deep into Iraq to cut off the Republican Guard. . . . At that point, I thought the ground campaign was going to be ugly, and we were told to prepare for up to 25 percent of the combat units to be wounded or killed. One out of every four of the people I was caring for would be wounded or killed; one out of every four people I considered my friends would be hurt or dead before I went home. Those were hard numbers to turn over in my head, and it made me even more dedicated to making sure the medical side was as ready as it could be. . . .

I wasn't afraid that I would panic in combat or fail to do my job; I knew I could do it. By then my medics and I had treated enough victims of car wrecks, airplane crashes, and gunshots that I felt good about our medical skills. We had scrounged supplies and equipment from around the theater, even things we didn't have at Fort Rucker [Alabama]. Kory brought us some extra stretchers he didn't need. We borrowed big catheters from one unit and chest tubes from another. We needed the tubes to inflate collapsed lungs. I didn't have any packaged blood because most healthy young people will live a while without extra blood, as long as they have some kind of liquid volume. So IV fluid was vital to keep the remaining red blood cells circulating. . . .

The hardest part for me was trying to keep everybody else motivated and to convince them that our eighteen Apaches could handle an entire division of Iraqi tanks. For the first few days the weather was so bad that the helicopters were grounded and we were practically defenseless; we wouldn't have been able

to fly either to fight or to escape. My medics all carried M-16 rifles, and I carried my 9mm pistol, and I suppose we could have stood in the bottom of the trench and tried to fight off an attack, but the odds would not have been very good.

I did occasionally imagine having to kill another human being, but my job was to save lives, not take them. As medical people, we were allowed to defend ourselves but we were not supposed to engage the enemy. The rules were a little hazy for people assigned to combat units like we were. . . .

Part of my responsibility [after the war ended] is to understand what happened to me and help others learn from my experience. This is similar to what we always do in the Army after an exercise or an operation: an after-action report of "lessons learned." I have some lessons that I learned from my six months in Saudi Arabia and my week as a prisoner of war in Iraq. The lessons are personal, professional, and I suppose political. . . .

The war dramatized the fact that the role of women in the military already has changed. We are no longer nurses and typists serving in rear areas—there were nearly 41,000 women in the Gulf working as doctors, nurses, pilots, mechanics, truck drivers, cooks, clerks, intelligence officers, communication experts, and in a host of other specialties. There were women in every part of the theater, from the headquarters of General Schwarzkopf to a few women in the foxholes in Iraq and Kuwait. In my opinion, the war showed that America is ready for Army women, all of whom volunteered, to serve throughout the Army and not be excluded from combat jobs. Parents back home didn't miss their sons less than their daughters, and kids

Rhonda Cornum prepares for a flight on an F-16 with the Air National Guard in Montgomery, Alabama.

didn't miss their dads more or less than their moms. . . .

. . . I believe the military pays members for two things: the jobs they do and the willingness to risk their lives if called to war. . . . As a female soldier, I would resent being excluded [from combat]. We preach "equal opportunity" everywhere. I believe we should also be preaching "equal responsibility." . . .

"Serving My Country, Doing My Job"

Shot Down in Bosnia

Captain Scott O'Grady

The fall of communism in the Soviet Union and Eastern Europe brought political instability to Yugoslavia. Nationalist forces in the Yugoslav republics of Bosnia-Herzegovina, Croatia, and Slovenia fought bloody civil wars against central government forces dominated by Serbia. Some of the worst violence took place in Bosnia where thousands fell victim to death and destruction in the name of "ethnic cleansing." After a peace treaty finally ended the bloodshed in Bosnia, peacekeeping troops of the North Atlantic Treaty Organization (NATO)—including U.S. forces—were sent to the region. Working with peacekeepers on the ground, NATO warplanes patrolled a "no-fly" zone over Bosnia to make sure Serbian war planes were not operating there. However, on June 2, 1995, a surface-to-air missile launched by Bosnian Serbs brought down U.S. Air Force Captain Scott O'Grady and his F-16 fighter jet. After evading capture for six days, O'Grady was rescued by a U.S. Marine search and rescue team.

Ever since I'd ejected, I'd seen clouds in all directions—except for the cylinder of crisp blue sky right around me. I was in the hole of the doughnut, the last place I wanted to be. I could see the ground clearly in the afternoon light and knew I'd reached the level where I could be seen as well. . . .

Still high above the ground, I was passing over the highway when a car joined the truck on the road's shoulder. The wind was ruthless, pushing me on to the southeast. Under my candy-colored, twenty-eight-foot canopy, I was as conspicuous as the Goodyear blimp. I could almost feel the sets of eager eyes boring in at me.

Was I a curiosity? A target? A hostage-to-be?

I recalled what I'd been told, many times, by the intel people back in Aviano [O'Grady's home base in Italy]: there were no friendly forces in Bosnia, no safe areas, no one you could count on. This was not

World War II, when front lines meant something and the French Resistance harbored many an American pilot. This was modern warfare, where it seemed that the only thing uniting a crazy quilt of factions was a shared distrust of the U.N. peacekeepers and the NATO airpower behind them.

I'd lost count of the prayers I'd recited since my plane was hit, since that awful jolt that seemed so long ago. I'd prayed that I'd survive the missile's impact and the flames that had enveloped me; that the bubble canopy would release, allowing a safe ejection; that my seat would function and send up a working chute.

I'd been delivered all I'd asked for, and now I was asking for more. *Dear God, let me land in a safe place, without harm.*

And down by that menacing highway, they sat there waiting for me, watching and waiting for their package to arrive. . . .

The grass rustled with footsteps, coming my way. Coming with the careless noise of men who know their prey is cornered.

I burrowed my face into the dirt, but the tree root made poor cover. With no time to apply any camouflage paint, I pasted my green synthetic flight gloves over my face and ears, and I froze, barely breathing, willing myself into invisibility. . . .

The two men walked to the very edge of my hiding spot, five feet from my burrowed head, and kept going straight down the path, without a hitch in stride or conversation. . . . I don't know why they missed me—can't explain it, except that God veiled me from them.

I would win many small victories in days to come, but none more gratefully received than that one. . . .

Amid the hoopla of the days and weeks that followed [O'Grady's rescue on June 8], I was often referred to as a hero.

Every time I heard that, it made me wince. I felt like I was getting eaten alive by the Great American Celebrity Machine— getting pulled apart and put back together to satisfy some network sound bite.

For the record, I don't consider myself a hero. As I see it, I was a guy in the wrong place at the wrong time. In 70,000 [Operation] Deny Flight sorties over Bosnia, only two pilots had been shot down through June 1995; I happened to win that dubious lottery. Before the missile rudely interrupted me, I was simply serving my country, doing my job.

"Do I Chase My Job All Over the World?"

Life on the Global Assembly Line

William M. Adler

After the Cold War ended, globalization created a new economic reality in which old trade barriers were displaced by free trade agreements. One such agreement was the North American Free Trade Agreement (NAFTA), passed by Congress in 1993. Supporters of NAFTA and similar treaties say that free trade has helped create a booming American economy and will eventually boost all global economies. Opponents of globalization, including some who have led demonstrations at international economic meetings, charge that workers in poor nations are being exploited by the wealthy nations. Many American workers oppose NAFTA because they believe free trade deprives them of high-paying manufacturing jobs as U.S. companies move factories to Mexico and elsewhere seeking cheap labor.

William M. Adler, a journalist, traced the decline of U.S. manufacturing jobs during the end of the twentieth century by following the same job as it moved from the industrial Northeast to the agricultural South, and finally to Mexico—each time seeking lower labor costs. Adler's book, Mollie's Job, *tells the story of two women—Mollie James in New Jersey and Balbina Duque in Mexico—who worked the same job on what has become a global assembly line.*

This is the chronicle of [a] single job as it passed from the urban North to the rural South . . . to Mexico over the course of the past half-century and the dawn of the new one. The job in which Mollie James once took great pride, the job that fostered and valued her loyalty, enabled her to rise above humble beginnings, provide for her family—that job does not now pay Balbina Duque a wage sufficient to live on. Embedded in that core fact, and in the story of the intersecting lives and fates of Mollie and Balbina, is a larger story about fundamental changes in the economy—a story about the demise of unions and the middle class and the concurrent rise of the plutocracy; about the disposability of workers and the portability of work; about how government and Wall Street reward U.S.-based companies for closing domestic plants and scouring the globe for the lowest wages in places where human rights and labor rights are ignored; and about the ways in which "free trade" harms democracy, undermines stable businesses and communities, exploits workers on both sides of the border, both ends of the global assembly line. . . .

MagneTek closed the last of the old Universal ballast plants [a company founded in New Jersey that made fixtures for flourescent lights], in Blytheville, Arkansas, and Simpson County, Mississippi, in 1997 and 1998, respectively. On the final day at the Blytheville plant, the company treated the four hundred remaining workers (an equal number had already been laid off) to a "last supper" of fried fish, potato salad, and pickles in the employee cafeteria. For dessert there was a large chocolate sheet cake with white frosting and in blue trim, a farewell message: "MagneTek . . . So Long . . ."

After lunch, the plant's personnel director, Frank Waters, addressed the workers. "The day has arrived for all of us," Waters began, his voice cracking slightly. A large man, dressed in a long-sleeved black polo shirt, blue jeans, and tennis shoes, he took a moment to steady himself by lifting a leg on a cafeteria seat. "After tonight at midnight, you will be out of insurance from the company. You will be eligible for COBRA [the federal program that allows workers to retain their health coverage—if they pay for it]. You have sixty days to make up your mind."

Following a few questions and answers about insurance and taxes, Waters asked if there were any more questions. One woman put up her hand.

"I grew old with you in this plant," she said.

"I know," Waters replied. "Seems like we all did."

At the stroke of three-thirty the assembly-line workers punched out, sliding their photo ID cards across the electronic time clock for the last time. As I watched, an office employee motioned me aside.

"Come upstairs," she said."I want to show you something." Her name was Leila Kackley, and she had written a six-verse poem, "Plant Closure," from the perspective of the board of directors, "sixteen men in coat and tie," who decide to "move our only money-maker and spread it over Hell's half acre." An excerpt:

> *Some of it will go south of the border where the hourly wage is only a quarter . . . .*
> *All that's left is figuring out a way to stamp it "Made in the USA."*

I asked her for a signed copy, which she cheerfully inscribed with the day's gallows humor: "Thank God for NAFTA!"

Because MagneTek was moving the plant's operations to Mexico, the U.S. Department of Labor certified that the Blytheville workers were eligible for an aid program under NAFTA. The program, called NAFTA-TAA (Transitional Adjustment Assistance), extended unemployment insurance for up to a year beyond the standard twenty-six-week limit and was supposed to pay for up to two years of retraining for a new career. But according to Deanna McComb, the former chief steward of IBEW Local 1516, the program failed markedly. "It was supposed to last you up to two years depending on the type of schooling, but it didn't always happen that way. Some of them had to finish [paying tuition] on their own and nobody got a good job anyway. Most of them ended up in fast food, or part-time at Wal-Mart."

Two years after the plant closed, McComb, at the age of fifty-four, was work-

ing nights, eleven p.m. to seven a.m., as a certified nursing assistant in a nursing home. She was earning $5.80 an hour—$3.05 an hour less than she made at MagneTek. Neither she nor her husband, who was self-employed, had health insurance. "If we go somewhere for insurance, it's, well, you've got a preexisting condition and we're not going to touch you. And these hospitals around here won't take you without insurance. So where does that leave us? What are we supposed to do?" . . .

At the time the Mississippi plant closed, it had been nearly a decade since Mollie James lost her job in Paterson [New Jersey]. She had received a severance payment, after taxes, of $3,171.60—about $93 for each of the 34 years she worked. She collected unemployment benefits for six months and then enrolled in a six-month-long computer-repair school, receiving a certificate of completion and numerous don't-call-us responses to job inquiries. Mollie never again found work. She lives on Social Security and rental income from the three-family house she owns, as well as a monthly pension of $71.23 from her union, Teamsters Local 945. "That's nothing," she says. "That doesn't even pay your telephone bill. It's gone before you know it." . . .

Toward the close of 1999, two and a half years after she had encouraged me to return someday to Matamoros [Mexico], I took up Balbina Duque on her invitation. . . . She is . . . concerned with the immediate future of her job. I tell her that since I last saw her, I had paid my respects to the company's dead and dying plants in Arkansas and Mississippi. She asks if I knew that MagneTek had transferred the bulk of the Mississippi operations not to Matamoros but sixty miles upriver to Reynosa (where the company opened a plant in January 1998). The union is weaker there, she says, the wages lower. . . .

Yes, I tell Balbina, I am aware of MagneTek's expanded operations in Reynosa. I add that I'd heard recently that the company already had a thousand employees there, that it was gearing up to start a second shift, and that it had just opened an on-site day-care center.

I ask if she would consider transferring to Reynosa if the company relocated her job there.

"And what if they were to move again?" she replies. "Maybe to Juarez or Tijuana? What then? Do I chase my job all over the world?"

"I'm Still Here"

Observing World AIDS Day

Dawn Averitt

The Human Immunodeficiency Virus (HIV) is one of the deadliest pathogens in history. By 2002, nearly 40 million people worldwide were infected with HIV—more than two-thirds of those in sub-Saharan Africa.

In 1988, when she was a 19-year-old college student in Georgia, Dawn Averitt tested positive for HIV. She contracted the virus as a result of nonconsensual heterosexual sex. In 1994, she was diagnosed with full-blown Acquired Immune Deficiency Syndrome (AIDS). Dawn became a national advocate for AIDS treatment and founded the Women's Information Service and Exchange (WISE). In June 2000, she fulfilled a lifelong dream

289

by hiking the Appalachian Trail—more than 2,000 miles. That December, she wrote her friends to reflect on her 13th World AIDS Day.

Today is World AIDS Day . . . again. There is always a struggle for me to figure out exactly how to observe this day. I realized this morning that I'm not sure how long we have been marking December 1st with this weighty and auspicious burden. It seems as long as I can remember. And for me, that would mean that today marks my 13th World AIDS Day. For 13 years, on the 1st day of December I have faced the joy of being alive tainted with the guilt of survivorship.

In the early years, when HIV was my secret, my nemesis, my monster-beneath-my-bed, I acknowledged the day anxiously, painfully pondering silently whether I would be here for the next or whether I would be the reason some friend or family member would join a tear-filled candlelight vigil to remember—or worse, would not. And then the years of emergence: these were the years in the mid-90s when I was finding my voice, allowing my voice to be a channel for those who could only speak in whispers.

These were the years that the media was discovering me—a middle-class, white woman with AIDS—to put a new face on this disease. Each World AIDS Day I would patiently explain to another reporter why we "observed" World AIDS Day, not "celebrated" it. And each year, some detached but curious face would stare back at me trying to grasp the distinction. These were the years that World AIDS Day was a whirlwind of activity that left little time for reflection. WISE did free, anonymous HIV testing; I spoke at high schools, colleges, and forums; and, inevitably, there were half a dozen or more interviews before the evening ended with an emotional, gut-wrenching candlelight service somewhere.

And now it is December 1, 2000. It's another World AIDS Day. CNN will mention the horrifying statistics to which most of us have become numb. There will be some very nice services and a candlelight vigil somewhere. Those of us involved in the work will mention it to each other and remark on the travesty. But most of the world will unwittingly pass the day as any other. They will not understand or know that today is the day that we remember the beautiful, talented, caring, outrageous, and kind souls we have lost. That in remembering them we find solace and the strength to keep fighting. Fighting a battle of process and rhetoric, of acceptable losses, and miniscule gains.

I'm still here . . . and for that I am grateful. I am grateful to my family and friends, my colleagues, the thousands of people I have had the privilege to serve and represent, and the amazingly strong and courageous people who fought this fight until their time on this earth had passed. You are my strength. On the days when taking 38 pills seems too much, or the lab visits go bad, or I don't feel too good, or I have to be just another patient—you keep me fighting. And for this I thank you. Please take a moment today to remember a smile that we have shared or a battle we have won. And, if you can, find a way to share your love and concern and commitment to fight with someone else who isn't as fortunate as I am to have you all.

Thank you for fighting with me.

290

"No One Ever Asked Me to Lie"

Testifying before the Starr Grand Jury

Monica Lewinsky

On January 21, 1998, newspapers reported that President Bill Clinton had an illicit affair with Monica Lewinsky, a White House intern. Independent counsel Kenneth Starr, who was investigating President Clinton's involvement in a real estate development known as Whitewater, also investigated the Lewinsky affair. He convened a federal grand jury to determine if the president had lied about his relationship with Monica Lewinsky while testifying in a sexual harassment lawsuit brought by Paula Jones. (Jones worked for the Arkansas state government when Clinton was governor of that state.) After being granted immunity, Monica Lewinsky testified before Starr's grand jury in August 1998. In September, Starr submitted his evidence to the House of Representatives.

Bill Clinton became only the second president in U.S. history to be impeached for his behavior in office. Like President Andrew Johnson before him, President Clinton was not removed from office because the Senate could not muster the necessary two-thirds majority.

On December 19, 1998, President Clinton became the second chief executive in U.S. history to be impeached. The House of Representatives accused the president of perjuring himself in testimony to Starr's grand jury about his sexual relationship with Lewinsky and of obstructing justice in concealing evidence about the affair. On February 12, 1999, the Senate was unable to muster the necessary two-thirds majority vote to remove President Clinton from office. In her grand jury testimony, Monica Lewinsky insisted that the president had never asked her to lie about the affair nor promised her a job to keep silent.

A **JUROR:** I think that's all the questions on that topic. There is one other question. Going back to Monday night [August 17, when the President admitted he had misled the country about his affair with Lewinsky] and the President's speech, what did you want or expect to hear from the President?

A: I think what I wanted and expected were two different things. I had—I had been hurt when he referred to me as "that woman" in January [when the President denied having sexual relations with Lewinsky], but I was also glad. I was glad that he made that statement and I felt that was the best thing for him to do, was to deny this. And—but I had been hurt. I mean, it showed me how angry he was with me and I understood that. And his—the people who work for him have trashed me, they claim they haven't said anything about me, they have smeared me and they called me stupid, they said I couldn't write, they said I was a stalker, they said I wore inappropriate clothes, I mean, you all know. . . .

So I just—my family had been maligned because of a lot of their tactics and I felt that—I had wanted him to say that I was a nice, decent person and that he was sorry this had happened because I—I tried to do as much as I could to protect him. I mean, I didn't—I didn't—I didn't allow him to be put on tape that night [when she was detained by Starr's lawyers] and I didn't—and I—I felt that I waited, you know, and I would have gone to trial had—had—in my mind, had there never been a point where the office of the Independent Counsel and myself could come to—they could come to accept the truth I had to say, that that was the truth I had to give, and I'm only 24 and so I felt that I— this has been hard for me and this has been hard on my family and I just wanted him to take back—by saying something nice, he would have taken back every disgusting, horrible thing that anyone has said about me from that White House. And that was what I wanted. . . .

A JUROR: Monica, none of us in this room are perfect. We all fall and we fall several times a day. The only difference between my age and when I was your age is now I get up faster. If I make a mistake and fall, I get up and brush myself off. I used to stay there a while after a mistake. That's all I have to say.

A: Thank you. . . .

A JUROR: Could I ask one? Monica, is there anything that you would like to add to your prior testimony, either today or the last time you were here, or anything that you think needs to be amplified on or clarified? I just want to give you the fullest opportunity.

A: I would. I think because of the public nature of how this investigation has been and what the charges aired, that I would just like to say that no one ever asked me to lie and I was never promised a job for my silence.

And that I'm sorry. I'm really sorry for everything that's happened. (The witness begins to cry.) And I hate Linda Tripp [a coworker who taped Lewinsky's conversations for Starr].

A JUROR: Can I just say—I mean, I think I should seize this opportunity now, that we've all fallen short. We sin every day. I don't care whether it's murder, whether it's affairs or whatever. And we get over that. You ask forgiveness and you go on.

There's some that are going to say that they don't forgive you, but he whose sin— you know—that's how I feel about that. So to let you know from here, you have my forgiveness. Because we all fall short.

A JUROR: And that's what I was trying to say.

A JUROR: That's what it's about.

A: Thank you.

A JUROR: And I also want to say that even though right now you feel a lot of hate for Linda Tripp, but you need to move on and leave her where she is because whatever goes around comes around.

A JUROR: It comes around.

A JUROR: It does.

A JUROR: And she is definitely going to have to give an account for what she did, so you need to just go past her and don't keep her because that's going to keep you out.

A JUROR: That's right.

A JUROR: And going to keep you from moving on.

A JUROR: Allowing you to move on.

Q: MRS. IMMERGUT: [an attorney on Starr's staff]: And just to clarify, and I know we've discussed this before, despite your feelings about Linda Tripp, have you lied to this grand jury about anything with regard to Linda Tripp because you don't like her?

A: I don't think that was necessary. No. It wouldn't have been necessary to lie. I think she's done enough on her own, so . . .

Q: You would not do that just because of your feelings about her.

A: No.

"God, How Can Someone Do This To Someone else?"

Terror in Oklahoma City

Harry E. Oakes, Jr.

On April 19, 1995, the explosion of a powerful bomb concealed in a rental truck parked in front of the Alfred P. Murrah Federal Office Building in Oklahoma City killed 168 men, women, and children—the worst case of domestic terrorism in U.S. history. A 27-year-old Persian Gulf War veteran named Timothy McVeigh was captured a few days later and charged with the crime. McVeigh repeatedly justified his attack as revenge against the federal government for its 1993 handling of a standoff at the Branch Davidian religious compound near Waco, Texas. Found guilty of first-degree murder, Timothy McVeigh was executed in June 2001. Two other men were sentenced to long prison sentences in connection with the bombing.

Harry E. Oakes, Jr., a member of the International K-9 Search and Rescue (SAR) Service, was asked to bring his SAR dog Valorie to the Murrah building in the days following the explosion for the grim purpose of locating bodies of the victims. Here are his remembrances of the mission.

Today I drove up to the mountains. . . . I fought back the tears as I remembered the horrors of five years ago—our search for the victims who died in the Oklahoma City bombing. . . .

Everyone keeps telling me how horrible it must have been to be a part of that rescue effort. Seeing the cold lifeless men, women, and children lying amongst the ruins. Their bodies and body parts, and blood staining the wall, walkways, debris fields, and what was left of the ceilings. I keep telling them, it's no different than any other of the disasters we respond to, where we see and smell the same things. The only difference . . . was that this disaster was caused by human stupidity. 168 men, women, children, lost their lives because a group of people somewhere along the way lost their ability to talk, listen, and communicate. They took their built-up anger out on the innocent, forever changing our country.

I remember my first assignment when I arrived Friday night was to clear the fourth floor area. As I stepped into the tangled rebar and fractured concrete debris, I turned my head lamp on so I could see where I was walking. My lamp shined down upon a woman's remains lying directly in front of me. Her head, arms, legs were gone. Just her naked torso was laying there. . . . I took the time to cover her remains with a space blanket I had in my pack. . . . For each body we stepped around during the search, there was either a searcher, a fireman, or a police officer, standing next to the victim's remains with tears of sadness coming from their eyes. I worked my way through the assigned area and then was asked to move to the pit. The pit was the area of the structure where the children's day care had been.

We moved carefully around the debris and marked four more spots where my search dog Valorie alerted to dead human remains under the rubble. I later found out there were four dead children and six dead adults under the debris pile where Valorie alerted. . . .

. . . . All through the search efforts on Friday and Saturday my search dog partner never left my side, and through the horrors of what we found, Valorie was always ready to give love to anyone who needed it. A family member begging for us to find his daughter, a fireman who collapsed on the ground from exhaustion, a small child peering through the barrier fence with his family watching all of us work.

On our plane ride back to Oregon. . . I wrote the following words:

I look into their eyes. The living, the dead, their families, the survivors, the rescuers, the rescue dogs. We share their loss, their pain, their sorrows.

All the damage, the buildings, streets, bodies, cars, our lives, their lives, humanity. . . . and I cry, God, how can someone do this to someone else?

"Trying to Make the Best of a Very Bad Process"

Recounting the Florida Vote

Ron Gunzberger

The presidential election of 2000 was like no other. Americans who stayed up all night watching election returns saw the checkmark in the winner's column switch repeatedly. The rest woke up the morning following the election to find that Texas governor George W. Bush held about a 500-vote lead over Vice President Al Gore in Florida and that the man who won that state's recount would win the presidency. Thus, election officials in four Florida counties found themselves scrambling to hand-count thousands of ballots even as lawsuits and counter-suits challenged the methods by which they were counting and their right to count at all. After the U.S. Supreme Court ruled that further recounting of ballots in Florida must stop, that state's electoral votes went to Bush, giving him the victory.

Observing the circus-like atmosphere surrounding the manual recount in Broward County, Florida—where his mother was serving as one of three election commissioners—was Ron Gunzberger. Gunzberger, an attorney and political journalist, and founder of www.Politics1.com—a non-partisan Web site devoted to informing the American electorate—added the following observations and comments to his daily on-line journal.

Ah, the traditional Thanksgiving dinner. Because my mother didn't have time this year to cook for the holiday, we instead were dining out in a nice, intimate restaurant. . . . Maybe I need to start the story a few days earlier.

My mother, you see, is Broward County Commissioner Suzanne Gunzberger (D). As Chair of the County Commission, it was her turn to serve as a member of the county's Election Canvassing Board. So, in a period of two weeks, she went from being an obscure, local politician and former school teacher . . . to being one of the most recognizable local politicians in America—revered by Democrats and despised by Republicans. . . .

I'm going to try to simply report on the colorful, raucous, surreal political circus I observed and heard over the course of the final days of the important Broward County manual recount. . . .

Eatin' Chads. In the first two days of the count, Republicans lobbed allegations

that Democratic observers—and even some counters—were "eating chads" or otherwise manipulating the ballots to force chads to drop to the floor. . . . Within another two days, no one cared anymore about the chads on the floor. . . . As for the eating of chads, I can attest that I never saw anyone eat them (except for me). I'm not certain about the best way to prepare chads, having never seen a chad recipe. . . . I ate a few and can tell you that, despite what you've heard, they taste nothing like chicken. . . .

"I'm Ready for my Close Up, Mr. DeMille." Both parties paraded in political celebrities for brief appearances. The Democrats sat their folks off to the side in the jury box, while the Republicans tried to give each of their people a turn as an official recount observer at the main table with the Board. . . .

The Pattern . . . and the Perception. While the perception was that the three board members were often split 2-1 (my mother and [County] Judge [Robert] Lee viewed as pro-Gore and [Circuit] Judge [Bob] Rosenberg viewed as pro-Bush), the reality was that the Board voted 3-0 on at least 80 percent of all of the ballots. Still, the Republicans constantly complained . . . that my mother was clearly pro-Gore ("I see a very slight but clear indent at #3 with one corner partially dislodged and light coming through just slightly at the corner if you hold it up. This is clearly a Gore vote."). The Democrats, meanwhile, complained that Judge Rosenberg was taking instructions from the GOP and intentionally trying to delay the process with his lengthy examinations of each individual ballot in order to miss the [Florida] Secretary of State's [Katherine Harris] new certifying deadline for the revised totals ("[look at ballot, remove eyeglasses, look at ballot up close again] this ballot appears to be a ballot that has been voted success- fully in other races on the ballot . . . [long pause, use magnifying glass] . . . no vote in the Presidential race . . . [long pause, hold the ballot up to the ceiling light again] . . . no reasonable certainty so this is a 'no vote' [put eyeglasses on again]"). Judge Lee, who as chair would vote last, usually just remarked quickly during splits: "I agree with the Commissioner" or "I agree with Judge Rosenberg."

Election officials in four Florida counties counted thou- sands of ballots by hand in an effort to determine the final tally in that state's 2000 presidential election.

Back in the Streets. The Bush and Gore crowds out front are yelling nasty chants back and forth. Of course, they're all too far removed in distance to be heard or seen by anyone in or around Courtroom 6780. "Na-na-na-na, Na-na-na-na, Hey, Hey, goodbye," the Bush people chanted towards the Gore side. The small band of Gore partisans vainly tried to drown out the word "goodbye" by shouting "D-U-I" at key moments in the GOP chant. . . . The Gore people shouted: "Bought and paid for!" at the Bush camp—and the Bush crowd loudly responded: "No we're not!" That one was a reference to the Democratic jokes about many in the GOP crowd being paid operatives flown into Florida just to create a presence in the street . . . "because there are no Republicans that actually live in Broward County."

Making an Effort. Most of the "celebrity" observers took the second or third GOP chairs at the table, leaving the task of actually reviewing each ballot to one of the GOP lawyers in the first seat. One exception was Governor [Frank] Keating (R-Okla.), who dutifully took the main chair and leaned in for a close look at each ballot. He was a gentleman through- out the proceedings, making an effort to keep the atmosphere civil. During one of the breaks, Keating told me that the Board members appeared "to be three good people trying to make the best of a very bad process." . . .

Getting Snippy. "No clear voter intent. No vote," says my mother. The ballot was then passed to Judge Rosenberg, who removed his thick eyeglasses and slowly studied the ballot with a large magnifying glass. After about a minute, Rosenberg pro- nounced that he can see "some dimpling" and "marks around #2 [the Bush ballot spot] . . . It's a Bush vote." The ballot was then handed to Judge Lee, who quickly said, "I don't see any marks. This is a 'no vote.'" Rosenberg tries to appeal this decision, ask- ing Lee if he'd like to use the magnifying glass to examine the ballot again. "If I have to use a magnifying glass just to see some- thing, then there is obviously no clear voter intent demonstrated on the ballot," Lee [snaps] back. . . .

The End. "The last ballot," announced Judge Lee as he held up the final ballot

295

just before midnight on Saturday night. This prompted a loud round of applause from the audience. "It's a Gore vote," my mother loudly announced and smiled. Rosenberg disagreed, but Lee agreed it [was] a Gore vote. . . The three board members—using a single pad of about fifty official ballots (each previously stamped "Void")—autographed ballots for a few minutes as the accountants verified the final vote tally and County Attorney Ed Dion prepared the certification papers. . . . After a few minutes, the Board then signed the official papers and the Broward recount was history. A county attorney flew the papers to Tallahassee the next morning. . . . And, if you're wondering, Judge Rosenberg kept the large magnifying glass (but says he'd give it to the Smithsonian if they want it).

Some Final Words. Okay, so the South Florida ballots are being driven up to Tallahassee right now for the upcoming court hearing. Presumably—in true South Florida tradition—they tied one of those fuzzy things to the truck antenna and will make the slow-speed drive with the left turn signal blinking throughout the many hours it takes to get to the state capital. The long drive to Tallahassee is being covered live on TV from overhead helicopter shots. . . .

I agree with Governor Keating. I think the Broward Canvassing Board consisted of three honorable, hard-working people who each tried to do their best under very difficult circumstances. Each applied somewhat different personal standards when reviewing the ballots (note: one of the GOP objections) but collectively did what they thought was correct.

"Let's Roll"

Attack on America

Lisa Jefferson

Three of the four planes hijacked by terrorists on September 11, 2001, found their targets; a fourth plane crashed into a Pennsylvania field, killing all on board. One of the passengers on United Flight 93 was Todd Beamer, who with other passengers fought with the hijackers to keep them from carrying out their mission. Before taking action against the hijackers, Beamer used an air phone to alert ground officials of the hijacking. Taking over his call was Lisa Jefferson, a GTE operator at a customer care center near Chicago. Beamer calmly told Ms. Jefferson what was happening and said that he and other passengers were going to jump the hijackers in an attempt to save the plane. He then asked Jefferson to call his wife Lisa and to pray with him. Lisa Jefferson spoke to Dateline NBC's *Stone Phillips about her experience.*

Lisa Beamer always knew how much her husband loved his family— Lisa Jefferson was about to find out. . . . It was about 8:45 a.m., Central time, when the air phone operator at station 15 got an urgent call.

Jefferson: "And she told me that she had a real hijacking situation on her line. . . . She told me it was United Flight 93. She appeared to be traumatized. So I told her I would take over the call."

"When I took over the call there was a gentleman on the phone, very calm, soft-spoken. I introduced myself to him as Mrs. Jefferson. 'I understand this plane is being hijacked, could you please give me detailed information as to what's going on?'"

Phillips: "Those were your first words?"

Jefferson: "Yes. He told me that there were three people that had taken over the plane, two with knives and one with a bomb strapped around his waist with a red belt. . . ."

Phillips: "Did you tell him about the other hijackings of the other planes?"

Jefferson: "No, no, I didn't."

Phillips: "Do you think he was aware of that?"

Jefferson: "Not at that time. He was not. That's why he asked me what did they want, was it money or ransom. He was confused, that's why he asked me. I didn't tell him because I didn't want him to get upset, excited, or lose control, and I still felt that they had hope."

Jefferson: "I asked his name. He told me, 'Todd Beamer'. . . . At that point his voice went up a little bit. . . . 'We're going down. . . . We're going north. At this point I don't know where we're going. I don't know, I really don't know. Oh, Jesus, please help us.'"

". . . And then he told me, he said, 'In case I don't make it through this, would you please do me a favor and call my wife and my family and let them know how much I love them'. . . . So we talked."

Phillips: "Did he tell you her name?"

Jefferson: "Well, what happened after that—the plane had taken another dive down. It was flying a little bit erratic and he made another outburst, you could tell in his voice that he was very nervous but he was calm. And he just made a holler, 'Oh, God.' Then he said, 'Lisa.'. . . And I told him, "Oh, that's my name too, Todd.' So then he asked me, if he didn't make it would I just keep that promise and phone his wife. . . ."

". . . And I promised him I would do that. When the plane was flying erratic he thought he had lost conversation with me. And he was hollering in the phone, 'Lisa, Lisa.' And I said, 'I'm still here, Todd. I'm

still here. I'm not going anywhere, I'll be here as long as you will.'"

". . . He just wanted me to stay on the phone."

Stone: "Do you know whether he tried calling Lisa Beamer, his wife?"

Jefferson: "No, I'm not aware of that. . . . He had hope that he would be able to land the plane safely. He did not want to really call her and give her any bad news if he didn't have to."

But other passengers talking on the phone had learned of the planes being flown into buildings. Todd and the others reached a critical decision and now he needed all the strength he could muster.

Jefferson: "He wanted me to recite the Lord's Prayer with him. And he did. He recited the Lord's Prayer from start to finish."

. . . "All I knew is if he didn't make it, he was definitely going to the right place. From that point, he said, he's going to have to go out on faith because they're talking about jumping the guy with the bomb."

Phillips: "Is that the word he used, 'jumping?'"

Jefferson: "Yes. After that he had a sigh in his voice, he took a deep breath. He was still holding the phone but he was not talking to me; he was talking to someone else. And I can tell that he had turned away from the phone to talk to someone else. And he said, 'You ready? OK. Let's roll.'"

Moments later, screams, commotion.

Jefferson: "Then it went silent. . . . About 10 minutes later, we had heard that the plane had crashed in Pittsburgh and I knew that was his plane. It was United Flight 93."

". . . I had just lost a friend."

Phillips: "In a very short time, you learned a lot about Todd Beamer."

Jefferson: "Yes. I did."

Phillips: "What did you learn about yourself?"

Jefferson: "Well, I didn't think I was as brave as I was. I felt like I was just doing my job, actually. Which I was. I was just doing my job."

297

The Challenges of Power

Credits

❦ Pre-Columbian Era to 1783
A "New World," A New Nation

Illustrations

3: Museum of Northern Arizona **6:** Library of Congress **9:** Library of Congress **14:** Library of Congress **22:** New York State Museum **26:** Colonial Williamsburg Foundation **33:** Shelburne Museum **35:** Rhode Island Historical Society

Readings

3: Irving Rouse and José Juan Arrom, "The Taínos: Principal Inhabitants of Columbus' Indies," in *Circa 1492: Art in the Age of Exploration*, ed. Jay A. Levenson (New Haven, Conn.: Yale University Press, 1991), 509-13. Reprinted by permission of the National Gallery of Art. **4:** Bernal Díaz del Castillo, *The Discovery and Conquest of Mexico*, trans. A. P. Maudslay (New York: Farrar, Straus & Giroux, 1956 [first published in 1632 as *The True History of the Conquest of New Spain*]), 208, 215-21. Copyright 1956 by Farrar, Straus & Cudahy, renewed 1984 by Farrar, Straus & Giroux, Inc. Reprinted by permission of Farrar, Straus & Giroux, Inc. **6:** Fray Bernardino de Sahagún, *Florentine Codex: General History of New Spain*, trans. Arthur J. O. Anderson and Charles E. Dibble (Santa Fe, N.Mex. and Salt Lake City: School of American Research and University of Utah, 1975), Book 12:17-20, 26, 47-8, 83. Reprinted by permission of the University of Utah Press. **7:** Benjamin Franklin, *Writings* (New York: The Library of America, 1987), 970. **8:** Olaudah Equiano, *The Interesting Narrative of the Life of Olaudah Equiano or Gustavus Vassa, the African*, in *The Classic Slave Narratives*, ed. Henry Louis Gates, Jr. (New York: New American Library, 1987), 25, 32-4, 36-8. **10:** Gottlieb Mittelberger, *Journey to Pennsylvania*,

ed. and trans. Oscar Handlin and John Clive (Cambridge, Mass.: Harvard University, 1960), 11-21. Copyright 1960 by the President and Fellows of Harvard College. Reprinted by permission of the Belknap Press of Harvard University Press. **13:** David J. Rothman and Sheila M. Rothman, eds., *Sources of the American Social Tradition* (New York: Basic Books, 1975), 1:7. **14:** Wilcomb E. Washburn, ed., *The Indian and the White Man* (New York: Doubleday & Co., 1964), 17-8. **15:** Susan M. Kingsbury, ed., *The Records of the Virginia Company of London* (Washington, D.C.: Library of Congress, 1935), 4:58-60. **16:** Mary White Rowlandson, *A Narrative of the Captivity and Removes of Mrs. Mary Rowlandson* (Fairfield, Wash.: Ye Galleon Press, 1974 [first published in 1682 as *The Sovereignty and Goodness of God*]), 3-9, 39, 43-4, 79-80, 104-6, 120-2. **18:** Robert Calef, *More Wonders of the Invisible World*, in *Narratives of the Witchcraft Cases, 1648-1706*, ed. George Lincoln Burr (New York: Barnes & Noble, 1968), 297-9, 358, 374-5. **21:** James E. Seaver, *A Narrative of the Life of Mrs. Mary Jemison* (New York: Corinth Books, 1961), 40-7, 50-3, 57. **22:** *Indian Treaties Printed by Benjamin Franklin, 1736-1762* (Philadelphia: The Historical Society of Pennsylvania, 1938), 78. **23:** David Perry, "Life of Captain David Perry," *The Magazine of History with Notes and Queries*, vol. 35, no. 137 (1928):9-10, 23. **25:** John P. Brown, *Old Frontiers: The Story of the Cherokee Indians from Earliest Times to the Date of Their Removal to the West, 1838* (Kingsport, Tenn.: Southern Publishers, 1938), 9-10. **26:** Henry Steele Commager and Richard B. Morris, eds., *The Spirit of 'Seventy-Six* (New York: Bobbs-Merrill Co., 1958), 1:4-6. **27:** Ann Hulton, *The Letters of a Loyalist Lady* (New York: Arno Press, 1971), 69-72. **28:** Commager and Morris, *The Spirit of 'Seventy-Six*, 1:124-5. **30:** Ibid., 1:297-8. **31:** Herbert Aptheker, ed., *A Documentary History of*

the Negro People in the United States (New York: The Citadel Press, 1951), 1:9-10. **32:** Commager and Morris, *The Spirit of 'Seventy-Six,* 1:642-4. **34:** Ibid., 2:1146-7. **35:** Herman Mann, *The Female Review: Life of Deborah Sampson* (New York: Arno Press, 1972 [first published in 1792]), 247-8. **36:** Commager and Morris, *The Spirit of 'Seventy-Six,* 2:1230-2. **37:** John C. Dann, ed., *The Revolution Remembered: Eyewitness Accounts of the War for Independence* (Chicago: University of Chicago Press, 1980), 240-5.

❧ 1783-1865
Nationalism and Sectionalism

Illustrations
42: National Portrait Gallery, Smithsonian Institution **47:** The Granger Collection **49:** The Hermitage—Home of Andrew Jackson **56:** Sophia Smith Collection, Smith College **60:** The Mabel Brady Garran Collection, Yale University Art Gallery **67:** Maryland Historical Society, Baltimore **69:** Library of Congress **78:** California Section, California State Library **80:** Special Collections Division, University of Washington Libraries, negative number: NA 1511 **85:** Library of Congress **89:** American Red Cross **90:** Library of Congress **98:** Library of Congress

Readings
41: J. Hector St. John de Crèvecoeur, *Letters from an American Farmer,* in *The American Reader: Words that Moved a Nation,* ed. Diane Ravitch (New York: Harper-Collins, 1990), 32-4. **42:** George McKenna, ed., *American Populism* (New York: G. P. Putnam's Sons, 1974), 69-70. **43:** Robert Beebe David, *Finn Burnett: Frontiersman* (Spokane, Wash.: Arthur H. Clark Co., 1937), 307-13. Reprinted by permission of the Arthur H. Clark Company. **45:** James A. Henretta et al., *America's History* (Chicago: Dorsey Press, 1987), 1:230. **46:** "A Contemporary Account of the Battle of New Orleans," *The Louisiana Historical Quarterly,* vol. 9, no. 1 (January 1926):11-5. **49:** Margaret B. Smith to Jonathan B. H. Smith, March 1-5, 1829. Margaret B. Smith Family Correspondence. Manuscript Division, Library of Congress, Washington, D.C. **50:** Gary E. Moulton, ed., *The Papers of Chief John Ross* (Norman, Okla.: University of Oklahoma Press, 1985), 427-8, 440-4. **52:** Peter Nabokov, ed., *Native American Testimony: A Chronicle of Indian-White Relations from Prophecy to the Present* (New York: Penguin Books, 1991), 121-3. **53:** Catherine E. Beecher, *The True Remedy for the Wrongs of Woman,* in *Early American Women: A Documentary History, 1600-1900,* ed. Nancy Wolloch (Belmont, Calif.: Wadsworth Publishing Co., 1992), 233-5. **54:** James Williams, *Life and Adventures of James Williams, a Fugitive Slave* (San Francisco: R & E Research Associates, 1969 [first published in 1874]), 9-12. **55:** William Still, *The Underground Railroad* (Chicago: Johnson Publishing Co., 1970 [first published in 1871]), 305-6. **57:** Elizabeth Cady Stanton, Susan B. Anthony, and Matilda Joslyn Gage, eds., *History of Woman Suffrage* (Rochester, N.Y.: Susan B. Anthony, 1881), 1:165-6. **59:** Lucy Larcom, *A New England Girlhood* (Gloucester, Mass.: Peter Smith, 1973 [first published in 1889]), 153-6, 175-83, 196-200, 226-9. **61:** Thomas Man, "Picture of a Factory Village," in *The New England Mill Village, 1790-1860,* ed. Gary Kulik, Roger Parks, and Theodore Z. Penn (Cambridge, Mass.: MIT Press, 1982), 337. **62:** Wolloch, *Early American Women,* 251-2. **63:** Edith Abbott, *Historical Aspects of the Immigration Problem* (New York: Arno Press, 1969), 37; Alan Conway, ed., *The Welsh in America: Letters from the Immigrants* (Minneapolis: University of Minnesota Press, 1961), 167. **64:** American Social History Project, *Who Built America? Working People and the Nation's Economy, Politics, Culture, and Society* (New York: Pantheon Books, 1989), 1:359. **65:** Edwin A. Davis, ed., *Plantation Life in the Florida Parishes of Louisiana, 1836-1848, as Reflected in the Diary of Bennet H. Barrow* (New York: Columbia University Press, 1943), 126-36, 406-10, 427-37. **66:** U. B. Phillips and J. D. Glunt,

eds., *Florida Plantation Records from the Papers of George Noble Jones* (St. Louis: Missouri Historical Society, 1927), 110-2, 123-4, 150-3. Reprinted by permission of the Missouri Historical Society. **68:** "Testimony of Angelina Grimké Weld," *American Slavery As It Is: Testimony of a Thousand Witnesses,* in *Early American Women,* ed. Wolloch, 305-11. **71:** Jacob Stroyer, *My Life in the South,* in *Sources of the American Social Tradition,* ed. Rothman and Rothman, 1:124-6. **73:** Harriet Jacobs, *Incidents in the Life of a Slave Girl,* in *The Classic Slave Narratives,* ed. Gates, 441-2. **74:** Caroline S. Kirkland [pseud.], *A New Home, Who'll Follow?,* in *Sources of the American Social Tradition,* ed. Rothman and Rothman, 1:143-7. **76:** Paul M. Angle, ed., *The American Reader: From Columbus to Today* (New York: Rand McNally and Co., 1958), 248-50. **77:** Diary of Catherine Haun, Huntington Library, San Marino, California (MSS HM 538). Reprinted by permission of The Huntington Library, San Marino, California. **79:** W. C. Vanderwerth, ed., *Indian Oratory: Famous Speeches by Noted Indian Chieftains* (Norman, Okla.: University of Oklahoma Press, 1971), 117-22. **82:** Charles E. Stevens, *Anthony Burns: A History,* in *The American Reader,* ed. Angle, 289-91. **83:** Angle, *The American Reader,* 299-301. **84:** Henry Steele Commager, ed., *The Blue and the Gray: The Story of the Civil War as Told by Participants* (New York: The Fairfax Press, 1982), 1:39-40. **86:** Ibid., 1:61. **87:** Carol Berkin et al., *American Voices: A History of the United States* (Glenview, Ill.: Scott, Foresman & Co., 1992), 252-3. **88:** Katharine M. Jones, ed., *Heroines of Dixie: Spring of High Hopes* (St. Simons Island, Ga.: Mockingbird Books, Inc., 1990), 115-25. **90:** Commager, *The Blue and the Gray,* 1:225-7. **91:** Otto Eisenschiml and Ralph Newman, eds., *The American Iliad: The Epic Story of the Civil War as Narrated by Eyewitnesses and Contemporaries* (Indianapolis: Bobbs-Merrill, 1947), 597. **92:** Thomas Wentworth Higginson, *Army Life in a Black Regiment* (New York: W. W. Norton & Co., 1984 [first published in 1869]), 59-61. **93:** Eisenschiml and Newman, *The American Iliad,* 440-2. **94:** Commager, *The Blue and the Gray,* 1:662-8. **95:** Ibid., 1:1073-4. **96:** Eisenschiml and Newman, *The American Iliad,* 493-4. **97:** Commager, *The Blue and the Gray,* 1:714-9. **98:** American Social History Project, *Who Built America?,* 1:454. **99:** Sam R. Watkins, *"Co. Aytch": A Side Show of the Big Show* (New York: Macmillan Publishing Co., 1962 [first published circa 1882]), 19-20, 46-8. **100:** Elizabeth Keckley, *Behind the Scenes: Thirty Years a Slave and Four Years in the White House* (New York: Oxford University Press, 1988 [first published in 1868]), 103, 105, 121-2. **101:** Commager, *The Blue and the Gray,* 2:958-9. **102:** Ibid., 2:691-2. **104:** Ibid., 2:1138-41. **105:** Ibid., 2:1102-4.

❦ *1865-1919*
Industrializing America

Illustrations

119: The Newberry Library (Chicago, Illinois) **120:** Library of Congress **126:** Montana Historical Society, Helena **128:** Library of Congress **132:** Culver Pictures, Inc. **143:** Collection of Henry Ford Museum and Greenfield Village **146:** Frederic Remington Art Museum, Ogdensburg, New York **153:** Library of Congress (left); New York Public Library (right) **162:** National Archives **163:** Culver Pictures, Inc.

Readings

111: Margarita Spalding Gerry, ed., *Through Five Administrations: Reminiscences of Colonel William H. Crook,* in *The American Reader,* ed. Angle, 353-7. **113:** Arney Robinson Childs, ed., *The Private Journal of William Henry Ravenel, 1859-1887* (Columbia, S.C.: University of South Carolina Press, 1947), 238-40. **114:** Walter L. Fleming, ed., *Documentary History of Reconstruction* (Gloucester, Mass.: Peter Smith, 1960 [first published in 1906]), 1:359-60. **115:** Aptheker, *A Documentary History of the Negro People,* 2:574-6. **116:** Stanton, Anthony, and Gage, eds., *History of Woman Suffrage,* 2:336-7. **118:** Leslie H. Fishel, Jr., and Benjamin Quarles, *The Black American: A Documentary History*

301

(Glenview, Ill.: Scott, Foresman & Co., 1970), 284-8. **120:** James H. Cook, *Fifty Years on the Old Frontier,* in *The American Reader,* ed. Angle, 358-62. **121:** B. A. Botkin and Alvin F. Harlow, eds., *A Treasury of Railroad Folklore,* in *The American Reader,* ed. Angle, 357-8. **122:** Thomas B. Marquis, *Custer on the Little Bighorn* (Algonac, Mich.: Reference Publications, Inc., 1986), 80-4, 86-92, 96. Reprinted by permission of Reference Publications, Inc. **125:** David R. Wrone and Russell S. Nelson, Jr., eds., *Who's the Savage?* (Malabar, Fla.: Robert E. Krieger Publishing Co., 1982), 138-9. **127:** William L. Riordan, ed., *Plunkitt of Tammany Hall: A Series of Very Plain Talks on Very Practical Politics* (New York: A. A. Knopf, 1948), 3-8. **128:** William Elsey Connelley, *A Standard History of Kansas and Kansans* (Chicago: Lewis Publishing Co., 1918), 2:1167. **129:** Norman Pollack, ed., *The Populist Mind* (Indianapolis: Bobbs-Merrill, 1967), 394-6. **130:** May 9, 1894, *Congressional Record,* 53rd Cong., 2nd sess., 4512, in *The Populist Spirit,* ed. George B. Tindall (New York: Harper & Row, 1966), 160-3. **132:** Henry Steele Commager and Allan Nevins, eds., *The Heritage of America* (Boston: Little, Brown & Co., 1941), 919-22. **133:** Hamilton Holt, ed., *The Life Stories of Undistinguished Americans as Told by Themselves* (New York: Routledge, Chapman & Hall, 1990), 178-85. **136:** Lucy Parsons, ed., *Mass Violence in America: Famous Speeches of the Eight Chicago Anarchists* (New York: Arno Press, 1969), 25-7. **137:** Charles H. Grosvenor, *William McKinley: His Life and Work* (Washington, D.C.: The Continental Assembly, 1901), 124-5. **138:** Leon Litwack, *The American Labor Movement* (Englewood Cliffs, N.J.: Prentice-Hall, Inc., 1962), 18-20. **139:** Edward M. Steel, ed., *The Speeches and Writings of Mother Jones* (Pittsburgh: University of Pittsburgh Press, 1988), 272-4. **140:** Philip S. Foner, ed., *Fellow Workers and Friends: I.W.W. Free Speech Fights as Told by Participants* (Westport, Conn.: Greenwood Press, 1981), 24-7. **142:** Carl Resek, ed., *The Progressives* (Indianapolis: The Bobbs-Merrill Co., 1967), 219-21. **144:** Archie W. Shiels, *The Purchase of Alaska* (College, Alaska: University of Alaska Press, 1967), 134-6. **145:** Richard Harding Davis, *The Cuban and Porto Rican Campaigns,* in *The American Reader,* ed. Angle, 442-4. **147:** Willard B. Gatewood, Jr., ed., *"Smoked Yankees" and the Struggle for Empire: Letters From Negro Soldiers, 1898-1902* (Fayetteville, Ark.: University of Arkansas Press, 1987), 92-4, 96-7. **148:** Albert Edwards, *Panama: The Canal, the Country, and the People,* in *The American Reader,* ed. Angle, 454-7. **150:** Resek, *The Progressives,* 158-61, 171-2. **151:** William Allen White, *The Old Order Changeth,* in *The Progressive Movement 1900-1915,* ed. Richard Hofstadter (Englewood Cliffs, N.J.: Prentice Hall, Inc., 1963), 104-6, 133-6. **153:** John Spargo, *The Bitter Cry of Children,* in *The Progressive Movement 1900-1915,* ed. Hofstadter, 39-43. **155:** Milton Meltzer, ed., *In Their Own Words: History of the American Negro, 1865-1916* (New York: Thomas Y. Crowell Co., 1965), 156-61. **157:** Doris Stevens, *Jailed for Freedom* (New York: Boni and Liveright, 1920), 188-91. **158:** Philip S. Foner, ed., *The Voice of Black America: Major Speeches by Negroes in the United States, 1797-1971* (New York: Simon and Schuster, 1972), 725-9. **159:** Thomas A. Bailey, ed., *The American Spirit: United States History as Seen by Contemporaries* (Boston: D.C. Heath & Co., 1967), 714. **160:** William Matthews and Dixon Wecter, *Our Soldiers Speak 1775-1918* (Boston: Little, Brown and Co., 1943), 302-4. **161:** Ibid., 335-6. **162:** Kempler F. Cowling, ed., *Dear Folks at Home* (Boston: Houghton Mifflin Co., 1919), 16. **163:** Adele Comandini, ed., *I Saw Them Die: The Diary and Recollections of Shirley Millard* (New York: Harcourt Brace & Co., 1936), 18-9, 108-10. Reprinted by permission of Harcourt Brace & Co.

❦ *1919-1945*
Democracy and Adversity

Illustrations
169: Library of Congress **172:** Library of Congress **173:** Library of Congress **182:**

Library of Congress **186:** UPI/Bettmann **193:** Library of Congress **195:** Library of Congress **200:** Copyright 1944 Bill Mauldin. Reprinted by permission. **204:** AP/Wide World Photos **209:** Marine Corps Photo/National Archives **212:** Library of Congress

Readings
167: Robert P. Weeks, ed., *Commonwealth vs. Sacco and Vanzetti* (Englewood Cliffs, N.J.: Prentice-Hall, Inc., 1958), 220-3.
168: Hiram Evans, "The Klan: Defender of Americanism," in *Sources of the American Social Tradition,* ed. Rothman and Rothman, 2:416-8. **170:** Randall K. Burkett, *Black Redemption: Churchmen Speak for the Garvey Movement* (Philadelphia: Temple University Press, 1978), 47-9. **171:** John Kobler, *Ardent Spirits: The Rise and Fall of Prohibition* (New York: Putnam and Sons, 1973), 306-8. Copyright 1973 by John Kobler. Reprinted by permission of the William Morris Agency, Inc., on behalf of the author. **173:** Robert S. Lynd and Helen Merrell Lynd, *Middletown* (New York: Harcourt Brace & Co., 1929, 1956), 269-70. Reprinted by permission of the publisher. **174:** Ibid., 253-9. Reprinted by permission of the publisher. **175:** Preston W. Slosson, *The Great Crusade and After, 1914-1928* (New York: The Macmillan Co., 1930, 1958), 151-7. Reprinted by permission of Macmillan Publishing Company. **176:** Margaret Sanger, *Woman and the New Race,* in *The American Reader,* ed. Ravitch, 249-52. **178:** Jervis Anderson, *This Was Harlem: A Cultural Portrait 1900-1950* (New York: Farrar, Straus & Giroux, 1982), 155-7. **179:** Jonathan Norton Leonard, *Three Years Down* (New York: J. B. Lippincott Co., 1944), 80-2. Reprinted by permission. **180:** E. W. Bakke, *The Unemployed Worker* (New Haven, Conn.: Yale University Press, 1940), 167-75. Reprinted by permission of Yale University Press. **182:** Ann Rivington, "We Lived on Relief," *Scribner's Magazine,* vol. 95 (1934): 282-5. Reprinted by permission of Charles Scribner's Sons, an imprint of Macmillan Publishing Company. **183:** Robert S. McElvaine, ed., *Down & Out in the Great Depression: Letters From the "For-*

gotten Man" (Chapel Hill, N.C.: University of North Carolina Press, 1983), 118-9.
185: Clarence Norris and Sybil D. Washington, *The Last of the Scottsboro Boys: An Autobiography* (New York: Putnam and Sons, 1979), 17-24. Reprinted by permission of The Putnam Publishing Group.
187: Studs Terkel, *Hard Times: An Oral History of the Great Depression* (New York: Pantheon Books, 1986), 130-3. Copyright 1970 by Studs Terkel. Reprinted by permission of Pantheon Books, a division of Random House, Inc. **188:** Ann Banks, ed., *First Person America* (New York: Knopf, 1980), 67-8. **190:** Stephen W. Sears, ed., *Eyewitness to World War II: The Best of American Heritage* (Boston: Houghton Mifflin Co., 1991), 17-27. Reprinted by permission of *American Heritage* Magazine, a division of Forbes, Inc. **191:** Roy Hoopes, *Americans Remember the Home Front: An Oral Narrative* (New York: Hawthorn Books, 1977), 6-7. Reprinted by permission of The Berkley Publishing Group. **192:** John Tateishi, ed., *And Justice For All: A Oral History of the Japanese American Detention Camps* (New York: Random House, 1984), 6-7, 11-5. Reprinted by permission of Random House, Inc. **194:** Hoopes, *Americans Remember the Home Front,* 314-5. Reprinted by permission of The Berkley Publishing Group. **195:** Mark Jonathan Harris, Franklin D. Mitchell, and Steven J. Schechter, *The Homefront: America During World War II* (New York: Putnam Publishing Group, 1984), 121-2. Reprinted by permission of the Putnam Publishing Group.
196: Brendan Gill, "Young Man Behind Plexiglas," *The New Yorker Book of War Pieces* (New York: Schocken Books, 1988), 286-7. Copyright 1944, 1972 The New Yorker Magazine, Inc. Reprinted by permission. All rights reserved. **197:** Mina Curtiss, ed., *Letters Home,* in *The American Reader,* ed. Angle, 597-9. **198:** David Nichols, ed., *Ernie's War: The Best of Ernie Pyle's World War II Dispatches* (New York: Simon and Schuster, 1986), 214. Reprinted by permission of the Scripps Howard Foundation. **199:** Ibid., 277-80. Reprinted by permission of the Scripps Howard Foundation. **201:** Studs Terkel, *"The Good War": An Oral History of World War II* (New York:

Ballantine Books, 1984), 261-5, 267. Copyright 1984 by Studs Terkel. Reprinted by permission of Pantheon Books, a division of Random House, Inc. **203:** Yaffa Eliach and Brana Gurewitsch, eds., *The Liberators, Eyewitness Accounts of the Liberation of the Concentration Camps: Oral History Testimonies From the Archives of the Center for Holocaust Studies* (Brooklyn, N.Y.: Center for Holocaust Studies, Documentation, and Research, 1981), 16-8. Interview conducted by Sarah Jacobs on June 7, 1981. Reprinted by permission of A Living Memorial to the Holocaust - Museum of Jewish Heritage, New York. **205:** Sears, *Eyewitness to World War II*, 295-7. Reprinted by permission of *American Heritage* Magazine, a division of Forbes, Inc. **206:** Terkel, *"The Good War"*, 444-8. Reprinted by permission of Pantheon Books, a division of Random House, Inc. **208:** Grace Tully, *FDR, My Boss* (New York: Charles Scribner's Sons, 1949), 361-5. Reprinted by permission of Charles Scribner's Sons, an imprint of Macmillan Publishing Company. **209:** Terkel, *"The Good War"*, 57-60. Reprinted by permission of Pantheon Books, a division of Random House, Inc. **210:** Ibid., 507, 509-16. Reprinted by permission of Pantheon Books, a division of Random House, Inc. **212:** Ibid., 176, 178-80. Reprinted by permission of Pantheon Books, a division of Random House, Inc. **213:** Ibid., 538-41. Reprinted by permission of Pantheon Books, a division of Random House, Inc.

🐦 1945-2001
The Challenges of Power

Illustrations
217: *Minneapolis Star Tribune* **227:** UPI/Bettmann **230:** UPI/Bettmann **233:** UPI/Bettmann **245:** AP/Wide World Photos **249:** Library of Congress **253:** AP/Wide World Photos **260:** AP/Wide World Photos **263:** Los Angeles Times **267:** Close Up Foundation **269:** Jane Roe Women's Center **275:** Close Up Foundation **285:** Courtesy Rhonda Cornum **291:** Corbis **295:** AFP Photo/Rhona Wise

Readings
217: Franklin M. Davis, Jr., *Come as a Conqueror: The United States Army's Occupation of Germany, 1945-1949* (New York: Macmillan, 1967), 218-21, 229-30. Copyright 1968 by Franklin M. Davis, Jr. Reprinted by permission of Macmillan Publishing Company. **219:** James Brady, *The Coldest War* (New York: Crown Publishers, Inc., 1990), 145-50, 153. Reprinted by permission of Crown Publishers, Inc. **220:** Martin Russ, *The Last Parallel: A Marine's War Journal* (New York: Rinehart & Co., 1957), 293-4. Copyright 1957, 1985 by Martin Russ. Reprinted by permission of Henry Holt and Company, Inc. **221:** Eric Bentley, *Thirty Years of Treason: Excerpts From Hearings Before the House Committee on Un-American Activities* (New York: Viking Press, 1971), 161-5. Reprinted by permission of the author. This book is now out of print. In print is a play based on the book, *Are You Now or Have You Ever Been*, which is published in *Rallying Cries* (Northwestern University Press). **222:** Ibid., 154-8. **223:** Elaine Tyler May, *Homeward Bound: American Families in the Cold War Era* (New York: Basic Books, 1988), 179-81. **224:** Studs Terkel, *Race: How Blacks and Whites Think and Feel about the American Obsession* (New York: The New Press, 1992), 20-1, 26. Reprinted by permission of The New Press. **225:** Henry Hampton and Steve Frayer, *Voices of Freedom: An Oral History of the Civil Rights Movement from the 1950s Through the 1980s* (New York: Bantam Books, 1990), 22-3. Copyright 1990 by Blackside, Inc. Reprinted by permission of Bantam Books, a division of Bantam Doubleday Dell Publishing Group, Inc. **226:** Close Up Foundation, *Perspectives: Readings on Contemporary American Government* (Alexandria, Va.: Close Up Foundation, 1993), 24-5. **228:** Elizabeth Sutherland, ed., *Letters from Mississippi* (New York: McGraw-Hill Book Co., Inc., 1965), 192-4. Reprinted by permission of McGraw-Hill, Inc. **229:** Fannie Lou Hamer, Julius Lester, and Maria Varela, *To Praise Our Bridges*, in *Mississippi Writers: Reflections*

of *Childhood and Youth,* ed. Dorothy Abbott (Jackson, Miss.: University Press of Mississippi, 1986), 2:321, 324-7. Reprinted by permission of Julius Lester. **231:** Hampton and Frayer, *Voices of Freedom,* 663-4. Reprinted by permission of Bantam Books, a division of Bantam Doubleday Dell Publishing Group, Inc. **232:** Sheyann Webb and Rachel West Nelson, *Selma, Lord, Selma: Girlhood Memories of the Civil-Rights Days as Told to Frank Sikora* (Tuscaloosa, Ala.: The University of Alabama Press, 1980), 92-7, 139. Reprinted by permission of The University of Alabama Press. **234:** Hampton and Frayer, *Voices of Freedom,* 252-5. Reprinted by permission of Bantam Books, a division of Bantam Doubleday Dell Publishing Group, Inc. **235:** Terkel, *Race,* 51-4. Reprinted by permission of The New Press. **237:** Hampton and Frayer, *Voices of Freedom,* 588-91, 596, 618-9. Reprinted by permission of Bantam Books, a division of Bantam Doubleday Dell Publishing Group, Inc. **239:** Karen Schwarz, *What You Can Do for Your Country: An Oral History of the Peace Corps* (New York: William Morrow & Co., Inc., 1991), 37, 42-3, 45-6. Reprinted by permission of William Morrow & Co. **240:** Polly Greenberg, *The Devil Has Slippery Shoes: A Biased Biography of the Child Development Group of Mississippi (CDGM), A Story of Maximum Feasible Poor Parent Participation* (Washington, D.C.: Youth Policy Institute, 1990 [first published in 1969]), 243-4. Reprinted by permission of the Youth Policy Institute. **241:** Ellen Cantarow with Susan Gushee O'Malley and Sharon Hartman Strom, *Moving the Mountain: Women Working For Social Change* (Old Westbury, N.Y.: The Feminist Press, 1980), 134-5, 138-9, 141-5. Copyright 1980 by Ellen Cantarow. Reprinted by permission of The Feminist Press at the City University of New York. All rights reserved. **243:** Mary Crow Dog and Richard Erdoes, *Lakota Woman* (New York: HarperCollins Publishers, 1992), 74-6, 79-82, 84-91. Copyright 1990 by Mary Crow Dog and Richard Erdoes. Reprinted by permission of Grove/Atlantic, Inc. **246:** Robin Morgan, ed., *Sisterhood is Powerful: An Anthology of Writings from the Women's Liberation Move-

ment* (New York: Random House, 1970), xiii-xvi, xxviii-xxx, xxxv-xxxvi. All attempts possible were made to reach Robin Morgan, but were unsuccessful. **247:** Jerry L. Avorn, *Up Against the Ivy Wall* (New York: Atheneum Press, 1970), 25-7. **250:** Kim Willenson, *The Bad War: An Oral History of the Vietnam War* (New York: NAL Penguin, Inc., 1987), 107-8, 147-9. Reprinted by permission of Dutton Signet, a division of Penguin Books USA Inc. **252:** Laura Palmer, *Shrapnel in the Heart: Letters and Remembrances from the Vietnam Veterans Memorial* (New York: Vintage Books, 1987), 16-7. **253:** Philip Caputo, *A Rumor of War* (New York: Holt, Rinehart, & Winston, 1977), xii-xiv. Reprinted by permission of Henry Holt and Company. **254:** Robert Mason, *Chickenhawk: A Shattering Personal Account of the Helicopter War in Vietnam* (New York: Penguin Books, 1983), 184-7. Reprinted by permission of Viking Penguin, a division of Penguin Books USA Inc. **255:** Palmer, *Shrapnel in the Heart,* 125-6. **256:** Eugene B. McDaniel and James L. Johns, *Scars and Stripes: The True Story of One Man's Courage in Facing Death as a Vietnam POW* (New York: J.B. Lippincott, 1975), 36-40, 46, 56-7, 98-9. Reprinted by permission. **258:** Wallace Terry, *Bloods: An Oral History of the Vietnam War by Black Veterans* (New York: Ballantine Books, 1989), 236-8, 240-4, 247-50, 253-5, 257. Copyright 1984 by Wallace Terry. Reprinted by permission. **259:** Ibid., 167. Reprinted by permission of Ballantine Books, a division of Random House, Inc. **260:** Willenson, *The Bad War,* 185-7. Reprinted by permission of Dutton Signet, a division of Penguin Books USA Inc. **263:** Ron Kovic, *Born on the Fourth of July* (New York: Pocket Books, 1976), 176-80. Reprinted by permission of McGraw-Hill, Inc. **264:** Jann Jansen, *Paper Bridges: From Vietnam With Love* (New York: Signet Books, 1991), 161-3, 165. Reprinted by permission of Penguin Books USA Inc. **265:** Ibid., 242-3. Reprinted by permission of Penguin Books USA Inc. **266:** Palmer, *Shrapnel in the Heart,* 215-8. **267:** Ibid., 27. **269:** Close Up Foundation, *Perspectives: Readings on Contemporary American Government* (Alexandria, Va.: Close Up

Foundation, 1993), 32-3. **270:** Lois Marie Gibbs with Murray Levine, *Love Canal: My Story* (Albany, N.Y.: State University of New York Press, 1982), 1, 9-10, 12-3, 15-9, 28. Reprinted by permission of Lois Marie Gibbs. **272:** Tony Ulasewicz with Stuart A. McKeever, *The President's Private Eye: The Journey of Detective Tony Ulasewicz from the N.Y.P.D. to the Nixon White House* (Westport, Conn.: MACSAM Publishing Co., Inc., 1990), 5, 265-6, 268-70. Reprinted by permission of MACSAM Publishing Co., Inc. **274:** Bill Adler, comp. and ed., *Kids' Letters to President Carter* (New York: Grosset & Dunlap, Publishers, 1978), 80, 92, 108, 111. Copyright 1978 by Bill Adler Books Inc. Reprinted by permission of Grosset & Dunlap, Inc. **276:** Tim Wells, *444 Days: The Hostages Remember* (New York: Harcourt Brace Jovanovich, 1985), 412-5, 437-8, 443-4. Reprinted by permission of Harcourt Brace & Co. **277:** Robert L. Maddox, *Preacher at the White House* (Nashville: Broadman Press, 1984), 62-3. Reprinted by permission. All rights reserved. **279:** Studs Terkel, *The Great Divide: Second Thoughts on the American Dream* (New York: Pantheon Books, 1988), 185-9. Reprinted by permission of Pantheon Books, a division of Random House, Inc. **280:** Ibid., 360, 362-3. Reprinted by permission of Pantheon Books, a division of Random House, Inc. **281:** Al Santoli, *New Americans: An Oral History—Immigrants and Refugees in the U.S. Today* (New York: Viking Penguin, Inc., 1988), 57-9, 63-4, 68-79, 74-5, 83-4. Reprinted by permission of Viking Penguin, a division of Penguin Books USA Inc. **282:** Terkel, *The Great Divide*, 244-8. Reprinted by permission of Pantheon Books, a division of Random House, Inc. **284:** Rhonda Cornum and Peter Copeland, *She Went to War: The Rhonda Cornum Story* (Novato, Calif.: Presidio Press, 1992), 37-9, 193-4, 197-8. Reprinted by permission of Presidio Press, 505 B San Marin Drive, Novato, CA 94945. **286:** Scott O'Grady with Jeff Coplon, *Return with Honor* (New York: HarperPaperbacks, 1995), 36, 38, 78-9, 181-2. **287:** William M. Adler, *Mollie's Job: A Story of Life and Work on the Global Assembly Line* (New York: Scribner, 2000), 15-6, 305-6, 308-9, 312-3. **289:** Copyright 2000 by Dawn Averitt; reprinted with permission. **291:** Grand Jury Testimony of Monica Lewinsky, Part 8, August 20, 1998. http://www.washingtonpost.com/wpsrv/politics/special/clinton/stories/mltest082098_8.htm. **293:** Harry Oakes, Jr., "Please Don't Forget," http://www.k9sardog.com. Reprinted by permission of Harry Oakes, Jr. All rights reserved. **294:** Ron Gunzberger, "Home for the Holidays: or How the Florida Recount Became a Family Happening," *The Politics1 Report*, http://www.Politics1.com. Reprinted by permission of Ron Gunzberger. All rights reserved. **296:** Reprinted by permission of NBC News. Excerpted from "The Connection of a Lifetime" on MSNBC Web site, http://www.msnbc.com/news/632324.asp. All rights reserved.